GREEK MYTHS

THAT INSPIRED

FINAL FANTASY VII

M. J. GALLAGHER

Original cover art and interior illustrations by
CAEL LYONS

Edited by
KIRA RAVENS

KICKSTARTER

My deepest gratitude to the following **ULTIMA BACKERS**

Tabitha Potter

Terri White

Ryan Scesny

Rain Misoa and N. T. Embeast

IvyLash

Linda Blomqvist

Carlo Pizzo

Yasmin Estrella

Meghan Thomas

ChibiSepphy

Kazeem Omisore

James G. Kralik

Pan-Chan

Alyssa Rae

Dan Gebhart

Brooke

Marija

Vasileios Kotsidis

Katherine Preston

This book is dedicated to Kazushige Nojima,

whose storytelling and personal love of mythology

are the reason it even exists...

You might say he is my muse.

ALSO BY M. J. GALLAGHER

Norse Myths That Inspired Final Fantasy VII

The Nibelheim Incident

COMING SOON

Final Fantasy VII and the Trojan War

Mythos: Final Fantasy XVI

For more information, visit the author's website at

www.mjgallagherbooks.com

CONTENTS

Preface   xi

PART ONE:
INTRODUCTION

I   Ancient Greeks and Their Beliefs   3

II   Mythology in Final Fantasy   21

III   A Recap of the Compilation   34

PART TWO:
THE SHAPING OF THE WORLD

IV   Gaia and the Calamity from the Skies   65

V   Ancient Waters   87

VI   The Afterlife Streams   109

PART THREE:
DIVINE INSPIRATION

VII	The Maiden	137
VIII	The Resurrected	159
IX	The Goddess	186

PART FOUR:
MYTHICAL BESTIARY

X	Which Titan is Titan?	209
XI	(Dis)Integration	226
XII	Flames of Rebirth	241

PART FIVE:
AN AGE OF HEROES
PERSEUS & THESEUS

XIII	Clash of the Weapons	261
XIV	Theseus' Paradox	277
XV	The Labyrinth	299

PART SIX:
AN AGE OF HEROES
HERACLES & OTHERS

XVI	The Labours of Vincent Valentine	319
XVII	Redemption	343
XVIII	Endgame Katabases	363

PART SEVEN:
MINOR MYTHS AND MYSTERIES

XIX	Hunters, Gods, Kings, and Thieves	385
XX	Miscellaneous Myths	423
XXI	Remaking Destiny	445

| Glossary | 473 |
| Bibliography | 497 |

PREFACE

Final Fantasy VII has played a huge role in my life for 25 years now, with its compilation, remake project, and associated media reinvigorating my love for the game over and over again. It profoundly enriched my formative years; it helped shape my personal philosophies in ways no other form of entertainment has even come close to; it motivated me to begin my quest as a writer in my mid-teens, unlocking paths I could never have imagined.

Greek Myths That Inspired Final Fantasy VII is (to date) the culmination of this passion of mine.

I've had an interest in mythology on some level ever since I was a kid. Learning about the ancient Greek pantheon or hearing old Viking tales of Thor and Loki's misadventures stirred something inside me that lay simmering deep beneath the surface well into adulthood.

It was not until my first professional writing job, however, that this simmer intensified to a ferocious boil. Based initially in New Zealand and eventually back in my native Scotland, I had the privilege of exploring Australia, North America, and Europe. I scripted cultural and historical tours for a diverse range of regions, which introduced me to myth and folklore on a global scale. After that, I was hooked.

One of the most beautiful realisations for me as I studied more and more was how many of these legendary stories, characters, and monsters are hidden in plain sight in the *Final Fantasy* games. I'd always been aware of the mythical origins of figures like Odin and Hades, or creatures such as griffins and the phoenix, but when the inspiration behind Midgar (Norse), Ifrit (Islamic), or Gaea's Cliff (Greek), for example, became clearer, I discovered there was an abundance of detail that had gone into the games that I had simply never appreciated before.

I'd separately been writing *Final Fantasy* novels and original fiction for a number of years and had produced *The Nibelheim Incident* (2018) and *SeeD: The Beginning* (2019, co-authored with Micah Rodney) in association with KupoCon. By then, however, the allure of the mythological angle was too strong to ignore.

Six months after the release of *Final Fantasy VII Remake*, I published *Norse Myths That Inspired Final Fantasy VII* (2020). Now that we've had sufficient time to digest *Remake* and its extended media – including *Episode INTERmission* and the supplementary novella, *Traces of Two Pasts* – I'm satisfied some of the more abstract and controversial elements can be properly addressed in this book.

Greek mythology was always going to be my next venture. It just seemed like the obvious step, based on my own knowledge and the research I had conducted up until that point. My initial plan was to put together a volume around the same length as *Norse Myths That Inspired Final Fantasy VII*. However, the more I familiarised myself with classical lore, the further down the rabbit hole I went. As it turned out, the respective titles are not quite the same length ... not even close.

In fact, my intention to encapsulate as many Greek tales as possible developed to the extent that I've had to split the book in two. Work on its companion, *Final Fantasy VII and the Trojan War*, is well underway – and it is there that I will explore in depth the ten-year siege at Troy, the struggles of Odysseus on his voyage home, and more.

I pitched this project in September 2021 to prospective backers in a crowdfunding campaign hosted by Kickstarter. The book took twelve minutes to reach the target funding goal. For that, each and every person who made a financial pledge has my eternal gratitude. It would also be remiss of me not to acknowledge the fantastic advice and support I received from the incredible AJ Hateley, who has enjoyed repeated success with her own gaming merchandise brand, Gametee, Ltd. AJ's contribution has been invaluable.

I would also like to thank several others, starting with my editor Kira, the hero who agreed to go through it all again. Kira did a phenomenal job on *Norse Myths That Inspired Final Fantasy VII* and there is no one else I would rather have gone on this journey with. Her wealth of knowledge, professionalism, keen eye for catching all those silly mistakes, and tolerance for my working style is everything I could ask for in a project partner. I owe her much.

Cael Lyons, whose cover art and interior illustrations have blown me away from day one. Cael is an artist I have been eager to collaborate with for a long time, and it has been a joy to experience him bring my vague briefs to life. His wonderful interpretations have produced images that capture the very essence of what this book is about.

Dan Hume, whose own Greek mythology articles on *FinalFantasyForums.net* have been a tremendous source of inspiration. Dan's kind-heartedness and willingness to lend me his expertise when it was needed most is truly appreciated. I hope I can return the favour someday.

My dear friend, fellow mythologist, and podcast co-conspirator Schrodingersbabyseal, who was among the first to welcome and promote my little niche corner of the *Final Fantasy VII* fanbase. I dedicate the Narcissus mini-chapter to you and your extraordinary capacity for love and inclusivity – because you brought many of the parallels to my attention, not because you share Narcissus' infamous traits.

Fellow content creators such as Sleepezi, Vyzzuvazzadth, Maximilian Dood, Philip Hartshorn, and the Creasman brothers of the FFWeekly podcast, who have helped to refine my own understanding of the *Compilation's* complexities, as well as Cae Lumis, Shademp, Turquoise Hammer, and all the great folks at the Shinra Archaeology Department for their spectacular efforts in making those hard-to-get guidebook details accessible.

My Patreon backers, especially the Zen Reaction, Amanda Lopez, Jonathon Myhre, Alex Hancock, Bryant Peek, Gary Mountain, and Arron Landregan, for your exceptionally generous financial support. You guys are the best!

Alex Maine and KupoCon, for giving me a platform to bring my writing to a new audience, and to all the amazing people I've met through the community.

And to my fiancée, Aimée, who sacrificed more than anyone else for a whole year longer than promised. You are my rock; the crystal that lights my way.

This book is a detailed examination of my comparisons between classical mythology and the

Compilation of Final Fantasy VII. Much of it is speculative but thoroughly considered, with source citations wherever necessary. I do not claim to have uncovered the secret meanings hidden throughout the saga by Messrs Nojima, Kitase, Nomura, Sakaguchi, and others. However, it is my ambition to shine a new and colourful light on this beloved game series, to entertain you, and to help you see *Final Fantasy VII* in a way you may never have done before.

Greek Myths That Inspired Final Fantasy VII has been my first foray into the realm of crowdfunding – a remarkable learning experience. I set out to produce a piece of work that I could be proud of and one that might be as well-received as *Norse Myths That Inspired Final Fantasy VII*. I hope what you find within the following chapters surpasses those expectations ...

M. J. GALLAGHER
Glasgow, Scotland
(August 2023)

"It's all Greek to me."

– Bugenhagen, *Final Fantasy VII*

PART ONE

INTRODUCTION

CHAPTER I

ANCIENT GREEKS
AND THEIR BELIEFS

A ncient Greek myths in one form or another have been a staple of the *Final Fantasy* series for over three decades. However, before any comparisons can be made between these celebrated legends and the *Compilation of Final Fantasy VII*, it would be best to present an overview of what they entailed, how they developed, and the extent to which they have influenced entire cultures for almost 3,000 years.

It is generally agreed by scholars that ancient Greece was the cradle of Western civilisation. There are few countries or regions that can claim to have had a greater historical impact on the world. The philosophies, politics, art, and science of antiquity are not alien to modern society, despite the gulf in time between them.

The same is true of the Greek myths. Its gods are not omnipotent cosmic beings, but rather they share man's likeness, impulsivity, and flaws. The heroes once lived in well-known cities or slayed terrible monsters at sites that can still be visited today. Elements of these tales are found in works as varied as Shakespeare's *A Midsummer Night's Dream*, Dante's *Divine Comedy*, Disney's *The Little Mermaid*, or *The Chronicles of Narnia* by C. S. Lewis.

Ancient Greek mythology refers to the cultural stories or religious beliefs that existed in the lands and islands around the Mediterranean's Aegean and Ionian Seas, encompassing what is now Greece (or the Hellenic Republic, to use its official name) and the west coast of Turkey. It is the most extensive, rich, and dramatic cycle in European history – if not the world's – and additionally offers a detailed insight into the early Greeks' understanding of nature and the universe.

The tales and their contents are sometimes described as classical mythology or Greco-Roman mythology as a way of collectively identifying it with Roman traditions and literature, which adopted an abundance of Greek narratives for its native gods[1]. For example, the exploits of the Hellenes' chief deity, Zeus, were transferred to the Roman Jupiter (also called Jove), the lustful practices of beautiful Aphrodite were attributed to Venus, and the cleverness inspired by Athena was equated with Minerva[2].

The myths as they are known in their present form were first preserved through the composition of Homer, a figure estimated to have lived around 700 years before Jesus Christ[3]. His earliest poem, the *Iliad*, is an epic work comprised of 24 books that recount an episode of the Trojan War[4], but they are interspersed with references and anecdotes regarding the gods. Research has proven beyond reasonable doubt that Homer drew on a long history of oral tradition to compile this masterpiece.

The splendour and complexity of the *Iliad* and its sister poem, the *Odyssey*, almost single-handedly demonstrate that the culture of Greece was sophisticated. Following the collapse of the Mycenaean civilisation[5], the region entered its Dark Ages, and it was only towards the end of this era (in the 8th century BC) that writing systems were re-established[6]. The political and cultural landscape shifted enormously in the Archaic (circa 750 BC – 500 BC) and Classical (circa 500 BC – 323 BC) periods that succeeded it.

Ancient Greece itself – known by its inhabitants, the Hellenes, as Hellas – did not exist as a centrally governed territory before the 4th century BC, when it was conquered by Philip II of Macedon, father of Alexander the Great[7]. For almost 500 years prior to that, Hellas had been a collection of independent city-states or *poleis* (sing. *polis*) ruled by various means (such as democratically elected bodies or oligarchies)[8]. While the *poleis* should not be confused with the kingdoms or countries that feature in the myths, many of the recognisable locations do occupy the same geographical space. Athens, Sparta, Thebes, Argos, Troy, and Corinth are some that will be mentioned later in the book.

In these wondrous cities of stone and bronze, one would find palaces for nobles and wealthy merchants, temples to the gods, auditoriums for music and theatre, schools, libraries, gymnasia, public bathhouses, and much more, with harbours that were a constant hive of activity. Greece is bound to the east by the Aegean Sea and to the west by the Ionian Sea, and within its territory are more than 200 islands[9]. In antiquity, the coastal *poleis* in particular enjoyed rich trade from across the Mediterranean and beyond, benefitting from the associated prosperity. This, in turn, helped to bolster their military strength against the threat of invasion.

The countryside surrounding the cities was typically divided into communities known as *demoi* (sing. *deme*), whose loyalty was to the *polis*, not to an affluent family or landowner as they had historically been. Men of the peasant class would hunt or fish, while the fields and homes were tended by women, and it was not uncommon for poorer households to own cattle or fowl to produce their own food.

Whether a person toiled with hard labour day after day or their every need was met by maids and servants, all were expected by society to observe the same customs and moral obligations. Of these, perhaps the most definitively Greek was the concept of *xenia*, or 'guest-friendship'. *Xenia* was the practice of providing hospitality to foreigners or strangers, one which promoted safety for travellers and encouraged the building of relationships[10]. It was sacred to Zeus, king of the gods, and to disregard or break the laws of *xenia* was to anger him.

The gods were present in everyday life in ancient Greece. For example, if an animal was butchered for a meal, parts of its body would be burned as an offering to them; before wine was drunk, a small amount was ritually poured on the floor in libation; and performers of music or poetry were honoured as being divinely inspired. The gods personified love, war, rainfall, trade, childbirth, home, earthquakes, the Sun, death, merriment, fire, the seasons, athletic games, and everything in between. While men did not necessarily grovel before them, they were to be regularly venerated and appeased, lest one risk harm or ill luck at the whim of a spiteful deity.

There was no centralised 'religion' in antiquity, though, at least not in the modern sense of the word, nor was there literature that might equate, for instance, to the Hebrew Bible or the Islamic Qur'an. Temples and shrines to the twelve primary gods – the Olympians – could be found throughout Hellas, but the prominence of any particular divinity differed from region to region, based on local beliefs, history, trade, natural features, and other influences[11].

If an individual wanted to worship a god or ask something of them, they were expected to use certain prayers or rituals, as directed by a priest or priestess of that god's cult. Every Olympian had a major cult centre; some had multiple, such as Apollo, the God of Prophecy, Music, Archery, Healing, and more. The most iconic of Apollo's cults was based in Delphi, a site that was considered by the ancient Greeks to be the centre of the world. Delphi was the seat of the Pythia, a high priestess and oracle who was consulted on major decisions throughout antiquity for the prophetic wisdom she could channel.

Two other important cults were those of Demeter and Dionysus, Goddess of the Harvest and God of the Vine, respectively. As agricultural deities, Demeter and Dionysus were mankind's best friends, and the wine sacred to the latter – who was known by the Romans as Bacchus – is commonly referenced in the *Final Fantasy* series[12].

The great festival of Demeter developed around the town of Eleusis, and worshipping there was special to the Hellenes. Each year, clandestine ceremonies called the Eleusinian Mysteries were held in the temple to enlighten initiates about an eternal afterlife, symbolised by Demeter's daughter Persephone, whose annual return from the underworld heralded springtime and the sowing of crops[13].

Similarly, in what may originally have been a harvest festival to honour grapes being brought to the winepress, the celebrations surrounding Dionysus evolved into something much more. His cults mirrored Demeter's in that their rites were generally based on the seasonal life-death-rebirth theme frequently associated with agriculture and fertility, though it is Dionysus himself who is killed and resurrected in the stories.

By the Classical period, his festival – called the Dionysia – was one of the largest and most important in Athens. A core part of it was theatrical performances, and it was from these plays and poetry recitals that drama was born. The Greek tragedies and comedies, as the dramas became known, often recounted or reinvented tales that would help shape classical mythology. Some of the more famous plays included events from the Trojan War, the tragic cycle of King Oedipus[14], or alternative versions of the hero Heracles' struggles.

While the oldest Greek literature is attributed to Homer and contains many references to the gods and their domains, it is the writings of Hesiod – a farmer thought to have lived sometime between 750 and 650 BC – that present the most comprehensive creation myth. The *Theogony* (*Theogonía*, '*Birth of the Gods*') is a large-scale poem that describes how the world was made, how Zeus and the Olympians came to rule, and just how the genealogies of the great and lesser deities were formed. A second poem by Hesiod, *Works and Days* (*Érga kaì Hēmérai*), meanwhile relates to agricultural practices and common customs but also includes the tale of mankind's origins.

In the beginning, there was Chaos: a void where neither time nor space yet existed. From this nothingness sprang the primordial beings Nyx (Night) and Erebus (Darkness), followed by the more tangible Gaia, Mother Earth herself.

Gaia subsequently birthed and coupled with the heavens, Uranus, and from their union came the second order of gods: twelve children of vast power called the Titans, the embodiments of ocean currents, memory, justice, and prophecy, among other things.

Uranus gradually began to mistreat Gaia, so she conspired with the youngest of the Titans, Kronos, to take revenge on his father. Kronos claimed authority over all and sired a new generation of gods, one of whom was Zeus. Leading his five siblings in revolt against the Titans, Zeus established a base for them on Mount Olympus, the highest of Greece's peaks. They became known thereafter as the Olympians.

Having prevailed in the war for supremacy, Zeus, God of Thunder, assumed his position at the head of the pantheon, then apportioned responsibilities to the 'deathless ones', as they are called by Hesiod. Zeus' sister-wife, Hera, was designated the Goddess of Marriage and Childbirth, while their sisters Demeter and Hestia took ownership of harvests and the hearth, respectively[15].

Like many Indo-European cultures, the Hellenes believed in a cosmology that consisted of the heavens, the mortal realm, and a netherworld[16]. Zeus governed the sky and bright Olympus, where most of the gods dwelled in splendid palaces; his brother Poseidon controlled the seas, whose waters could be as temperamental as the divinity himself; and their brother Hades – after whom the summon in *Final Fantasy VII* is named – relinquished his role as an

Olympian to become Lord of the Underworld, a dark and gloomy place as far below the earth as the earth is below the heavens. The earth itself – still personified as Gaia – was common to all three, encircled by the world river, Oceanus.

Through both his marriage to Hera and his countless acts of infidelity, Zeus fathered more gods who would be welcomed into the Olympian pantheon in due course. These included Ares (whose domain was war), Hephaestus (greatest of all smiths), Athena (known for both strategy and handicraft), Apollo (famed for healing, music, and prophecy), Artemis (the divine huntress, and twin sister of Apollo), Hermes (a trickster and messenger of the gods), and Dionysus (a later addition that replaced Hestia). The twelfth Olympian was Aphrodite, Goddess of Love and Beauty, who was instead a child of Uranus. Between them, they shaped the world as it was perceived by the ancient Greeks.

Immortals of all orders and generations propagated over time, resulting in a wide variety of beings. These ranged from the monstrous, one-eyed Cyclopes and deep-water spirits like the Oceanids or Nereids to deities responsible for metaphysical concepts such as dreams (Morpheus[17]) and doom (Moros), or to the Fates (Moirai), three sisters whose purpose was to ensure that all lived out the destiny allotted to them, not unlike the Whispers of *Final Fantasy VII Remake*.

In this mystical age, the rivers, lakes, mountains, caves, forests, and grasslands were home to a plethora of fabulous entities. Most locations were associated with a minor deity or one of the many races of nymphs, female nature spirits usually depicted as attractive maidens. Hybrid creatures such as the half-human, half-horse centaurs or the goat-legged satyrs roamed the hills and woodlands, and danger existed in the form of fearsome beasts that might one day be vanquished by a hero. The Minotaur (defeated by Theseus), the Chimera (defeated by Bellerophon), and the Hydra (defeated by Heracles) are just three examples of the latter that will be referenced in the book.

As life expanded and evolved, a desire arose among the gods for mortal playthings; for souls that could populate the halls of the underworld, also named Hades after its ruler. Zeus asked his friend Prometheus, a young Titan who had sided with the Olympians in the war, to mould mankind from clay[18]. So enamoured by humans was Prometheus that he defied the Skyfather and gave man the gift of fire. This was not simply a means to kindle flames, however. It was the divine spark, the fire of creativity and free thought; the fire that would allow mankind to one day challenge the gods.

According to Hesiod's *Works and Days*, there have been Five Ages of Man: the Golden Age, Silver Age, Bronze Age, Heroic Age, and the current Iron Age. The early generations were imperfect for different reasons, and some were met by Zeus' wrath, for he detested their impiety and condemned Prometheus for his betrayal. Nevertheless, the deathless ones walked among the mortals and interfered with their affairs, and it was from their copulating that the race of demigods emerged.

The Heroic Age was the era in which the adventures and deeds of these incredible characters occurred, set in Greece's distant past. Their epic tales were primarily told by the playwrights of Athens and often debuted at the Dionysia, although some were only thoroughly recounted by later Hellenic or Roman authors.

Common tropes of the demigod myths include the hero coming to terms with their identity, battling one or more terrible monsters, or assisting their divine family in some way. Among the best known figures are Heracles (a son of Zeus whose twelve labours resulted in him ridding the world of many fiends), Perseus (a son of Zeus who killed the snake-haired Medusa), Theseus (a son of Poseidon who escaped the Labyrinth), Bellerophon (a son of Poseidon who rode the winged horse, Pegasus), Orpheus (a son of Apollo who descended into the underworld by playing music), and Achilles (a son of Thetis who was the Greeks' champion during the Trojan War).

The Hellenes believed the demigods and their descendants had long since departed the mortal world and the Olympians had retreated to heaven to preside from there. The nymphs and fabled creatures that had once populated the lands had been driven from their homes by human civilisation, just as endangered animal groups lose their habitats to deforestation or pollution in the modern day.

Unlike the warriors' feast tables at Valhalla in Viking tradition or the utopian reed fields of Aaru for the ancient Egyptians, there was no place among the gods for Greeks who led distinguished lives. Instead, all souls were thought to journey to Hades upon death, and their eventual destination in the afterlife was determined by their earthly actions[19]. Although the specifics vary from source to source, a general understanding is that righteous individuals were judged and sent to paradisical Elysium (also called the Elysian fields), criminals were sent to the cavernous depths of Tartarus, and the rest remained as ghostly shades in the grey meadows of Asphodel.

Many of the ancient Greek myths that predate antiquity most likely include some form of symbolism or parable with respect to the social laws or common behaviours of that time. The same cannot typically be said of the literary works produced in later centuries, whose main function was to inform or entertain. Nevertheless, they do contain recurring themes of divine punishment, particularly in relation to hubris (a person's excessive pride in comparison to or defiance of the gods), blood crimes (the purposeful or accidental killing of one's relative was the worst of all sins), disregarding the principles of *xenia*, or oath breaking.

The stories themselves are a plethora of wondrous events and memorable characters. However, the Greek myth cycle is extremely large and complex, accounting for more than 1,000 years of contributions. It is not always consistent, coherent, or chronologically sound, and it is normal to identify references in the *Final Fantasy* series that appear in one source but not in others. The contrasting versions of the Phoenix summon's aesthetics across the games are a prime example of this.

Later authors in the Hellenistic and Greco-Roman periods, such as Apollodorus (*Bibliotheca*) and Ovid (*Metamorphoses*), retold the known myths at great length and gathered them in compendiums. While these are an invaluable resource, many of the details contradict the works of Homer or Hesiod, for instance. Scholars must also consider any possible agenda the writer may have had for adding, altering, or omitting elements of a tale, as in the case of the *Aeneid*.

This epic poem was composed in the 1st century BC by Virgil, a Latin poet who wished to help solidify the glory of Rome by connecting its founding to the legendary heroes of the Trojan War. As such, there are episodes relating to the ten-year conflict at Troy that can only be found in the *Aeneid*[20]. However, the story focuses on Aeneas, a son of Venus (Aphrodite) who fought against the Greeks[21], meaning his perspective is markedly different from the main characters of the *Iliad* and the *Odyssey*.

Belief in the polytheistic pantheon endured across the Roman Empire until Christianity rose to prominence, the latter being decreed the official religion by Emperor Constantine in the early 4th century AD. Tolerance of the old 'pagan' cults and practices declined in the decades that followed, and worship was banned throughout the empire by 382 AD. Despite this, small pagan communities persisted in remote areas of Greece as late as the 9th century.

Widespread passion for Greco-Roman literature and philosophies was reignited during the Renaissance period in 15th and 16th century Europe, and it had a profound impact on Western culture. Included in this was a revival of academic and artistic interest in the myths, none more so than the works of Homer and Virgil. The gods' names are still spoken around the world every single day, for they are honoured in the planets of our solar system: Mercury (Hermes), Venus (Aphrodite), Mars (Ares), Jupiter (Zeus), Saturn (Kronos), Uranus (known to the Romans as Caelus), Neptune (Poseidon), and Pluto (the Greeks' later name for Hades)[22].

Ancient Greek mythology continues to inspire and influence modern art and entertainment, either directly in the myriad translations available today or indirectly through the writings of Shakespeare, Dante, et al. Tales of the gods and heroes have been brought to new audiences through cinema for well over 100 years, with notable titles such as *Jason and the Argonauts* (1963), *Clash of the Titans* (1981), *Hercules* (1997)[23], and *Troy* (2004). Beloved comic book characters like Wonder Woman and the Sandman (both DC Comics) owe their origins to Greek lore[24], while Rick Riordan's *Percy Jackson & the Olympians* is one of the best-selling novel series in history.

Videogames have also been incorporating elements of these legends since the 1980s, and the *Final Fantasy* franchise is no different. However, *Final Fantasy VII* is unique in comparison to its predecessors with respect to how global religion and mythology were adapted and implemented, including that of ancient Greece. This masterpiece of storytelling and design set the benchmark for decades to come, as will be discussed in the next chapter.

1. This occurred during the Hellenistic period that followed the death of Alexander the Great in 323 BC and ended with the emergence of the Roman Empire in 31 BC.

2. The relevance of Venus and Minerva in *Final Fantasy VII* is addressed in chapter IX.

3. Entire fields of study are dedicated to what is known as the Homeric Question or – as is perhaps more accurate – a collection of questions and concerns. For example, was Homer a real person? Were the *Iliad* and/or the *Odyssey* composed by a single poet or multiple? When, where, and under which circumstances were the poems produced? To what degree are they historically accurate? For the purposes of this book, it will be assumed that Homer was the author of the works.

4. The story of the Trojan War and its aftermath is so extensive and its influence on certain titles in the *Compilation of Final Fantasy VII* is so significant that it will be separately examined in a companion book, *Final Fantasy VII and the Trojan War*.

5. The Mycenaeans were the first distinctly Greek civilisation, rising to prominence during the Late Bronze Age (approximately 1750 BC to 1050 BC).

6. 'Alphabet' in English is derived from the ancient Greek '*alphabētos*', which was named after its first two letters, alpha (α) and beta (β). The *Compilation of Final Fantasy VII* uses Greek letters when formally presenting dates. For example, the Shinra Company discovers mako in [μ] – εγλ 1959, which means year 1959 of the '*mu*' era. The

letters are μ (*mu*), ε (*epsilon*), γ (*gamma*), and λ (*lambda*).

7. Alexander the Great (also known as Alexander III of Macedon) is considered to be one of history's greatest military commanders. He extended the Greek Empire as far as India and ruled between the ages of 20 and 33, when he died. Alexander's expansionism had a direct impact on the Roman Empire later adopting, developing, and spreading Hellenic culture. His potential connection to *Final Fantasy VII* is explored in chapter XX.

8. '*Polis*' literally means 'city' in Greek, but the term in antiquity more broadly referred to its citizenry and the jurisdiction of its governing body.

9. The Greek islands significantly range in size and historical importance. Among the most famous are Crete, Rhodes, Corfu, Ithaca, and Lesbos.

10. *Xenia* shares an etymological root with xenophobia, which is the fear of foreigners or strangers.

11. One example is that Athena, the Goddess of Craft and Warfare, was closely associated with Athens. According to one myth, the city is named after her because she proved to the people that the gift of an olive tree was more valuable to them than a saltwater spring provided by Poseidon, God of the Seas.

12. Since *Final Fantasy II*, Bacchus' Wine has been a recurring item that can typically be used to cast the Berserk status on party members. This relates to the intoxicated frenzies Dionysus' devout followers were sometimes associated with.

13. The connection between the Eleusinian Mysteries and Aerith will be discussed in chapter VII.

14. The tale of Oedipus does not feature heavily in this book, but a summarised account and its allusions in *Crisis Core* can be found in chapter XIX.

15. Although the importance of the hearth or fireplace may not translate well into modern culture, the concept of it was vital to the ancient Greeks. To them, the hearth represented home, warmth, comfort, safety, light, and social interaction, among many other things.

16. Every culture in history has an *axis mundi* within its mythology, which in the context of Greek lore is the heavens and the earth being connected by Mount Olympus. In a typical three-dimensional model, an *axis mundi* is the cosmic axis to which the worlds, realms, spiritual planes, etc. are joined or around which they revolve. Another common motif and *axis mundi* in Indo-European civilisations are world trees, such as Yggdrasill of Norse mythology.

17. The Morpheus characters of Neil Gaiman's *The Sandman* and the Wachowskis' *The Matrix*, respectively, both derive from the Greco-Roman deity associated with sleep and dreams. First named in Ovid's *Metamorphoses* (1st century AD), Morpheus appears in dreams in human form.

18. This version of the myth appears in *Bibliotheca*, a compendium work written in the 1st or 2nd century AD and traditionally attributed to Apollodorus.

19. The concept of separating those who had lived good lives from those who had lived wicked lives became popular in the Classical period and is first mentioned in Greek literature by Plato, a philosopher of the 5th century BC. Prior to this, such as in Homer's *Odyssey*, all souls gathered in the same place, although Hesiod's *Works and Days* does mention that heroes may be permitted to enter Elysium.

20. One example of details found exclusively in the *Aeneid* is the role of the Greek warrior Sinon, who convinced the Trojans to take the wooden horse into their city.

21. Like most Latin retellings of the ancient Greek myths, the *Aeneid* uses the Roman names for the gods.

22. The Greeks named the five planets visible to the naked eye after the gods, and this was subsequently adopted by the Romans. The same naming convention was eventually utilised in the 18th and 19th centuries when Uranus and Neptune were discovered. Pluto was identified in 1930 but was reclassified as a dwarf planet in 2006. Many of the respective planets' moons also relate to deities in Greco-Roman mythology. While the

name Earth is itself derived from Germanic language (possibly with regards to Jörd, the mother of Thor in Norse lore), words such as 'terrain' or 'terrestrial' refer to the Roman goddess Terra, typically conflated with the Greek Gaia. *Final Fantasy IX* fans may recognise the important connection between the worlds Gaia and Terra.

23. Hercules was the Roman name for Heracles.
24. Wonder Woman, also known as Princess Diana of Themyscira, is one of the Amazons, a mythical race of female warriors. She first appeared in comics in 1941.

CHAPTER II

MYTHOLOGY IN FINAL FANTASY

Since its conception, the *Final Fantasy* series has incorporated a wealth of global mythology into its storytelling. Franchise regulars such as the fiery jinn Ifrit, the sword-wielding Gilgamesh, the legendary blade Excalibur, or worlds like Terra and Gaia all stem from ancient lore. Every title has featured elements to varying degrees, ranging from the basic namedrops and vague references of the early games all the way to the plot intricacies and unabashed mythical influences of *Final Fantasy XVI*. The initial inspiration for it all, however, may have simpler roots.

The original *Final Fantasy*, released in 1987 on the Nintendo Entertainment System (NES, also known as the

Famicom), was the brainchild of videogame developer Hironobu Sakaguchi. Sakaguchi-san joined Square in the mid-1980s, which was at the time the computer software division of the Denyūsha Electric Company. Himself a fan of the *Dungeons & Dragons* tabletop games in addition to role-playing videogames (RPGs) such as *Ultima* and *Wizardry*, Sakaguchi-san produced his first RPG for Square in 1984, a PC text adventure called *The Death Trap*. He was subsequently part of the teams responsible for acclaimed releases on the NES such as *Rad Racer*, *King's Knight*, and *3D World Runner*, as well as many more that failed to satisfy the consumer market.

Sakaguchi-san was motivated by the idea of adapting the *Dungeons & Dragons* style of turn-based combat and character class (which would eventually become known in *Final Fantasy* as the 'job system') into an immersive, story-driven RPG that could be played on the NES. He repeatedly pitched the concept to his seniors at Square, but they did not believe the venture to be financially viable. It was only after the runaway success of *Dragon Quest* in 1986 – later released in the West as *Dragon Warrior* – that the company began to listen.

Development on *Final Fantasy* commenced soon after. As writer and director of the project, Sakaguchi-san borrowed heavily from a plethora of existing content in other games. Examples include the battle systems, random encounters, an overworld, party members, non-linear quests, coin, experience points, weapon upgrades, and even plot elements themselves. The inspirational titles *Ultima*, *Wizardry*, and *Dragon Quest* shared the common trait of sourcing the basis of their stories and bestiaries from medieval fantasy, most notably celebrated works such as J. R. R. Tolkien's *The Lord of the Rings* or the legends of King Arthur.

Sakaguchi-san, however, did not want his game to be bound by the preconceived shackles of this genre, following the path of *Ultima* in particular by expanding on the definition of 'fantasy'. The world of *Final Fantasy* would afford players the familiar medieval setting but feature aspects of science fiction as well, such as robots, airships, and time travel. Having established the environment, characters, enemies, story themes, and major plot points, Sakaguchi-san employed the services of Kenji Terada as the scenario writer to help him weave it all together.

A significant factor in their eventual success was their addition of a far greater variety of mythical creatures than had previously been presented in RPGs, tapping directly into the existing popularity of *Dungeons & Dragons*. Since the mid-1970s, the tabletop games had amassed a considerable bestiary, which contained fabled monsters from every corner of the planet. Included in this were Lich (added in 1975), Tiamat (also 1975), Marilith (1977), and Kraken (1983) – figures that would become *Final Fantasy's* initial Four Fiends[1].

From a mythological standpoint, the Fiend of Earth (Lich) was based on an undead sorcerer likely derived from the Slavic tales of Koschei; the Fiend of Water (Kraken) was based on the Nordic sea monster that would drag ships to their doom; the Fiend of Wind (Tiamat) was based on the Babylonian goddess who eventually adopted an antagonistic serpentine form; and the Fiend of Fire (Marilith) – who was originally called Karys, a localised translation of Kali – was based on a Hindu goddess associated with power and change.

It is unclear how vast the extent of Sakaguchi-san and his team's knowledge of global mythology was at that time, but it is worth noting that there are hints their work was sourced primarily from *Dungeons & Dragons* rather than the old legends themselves. For instance, concept artist Yoshitaka Amano's illustration of the chimera opponents in *Final Fantasy* depicts wings and the heads of a lion, a goat, and a fire-breathing dragon. This is inaccurate when compared to the Chimera of Greek lore, as detailed in chapter XX, but matches its counterpart in the 1977 edition of the *Monster Manual* bestiary[2].

Perhaps the most telling example, however, is the use of Bahamut in *Final Fantasy* as the King of Dragons. Despite his renowned draconic features in *Dungeons & Dragons*, Bahamut's name comes from the cosmic fish of early Islamic beliefs, said to carry the bull Kujata (another creature to appear in later titles) and the world on its back[3].

Nevertheless, there are several allusions to ancient Greek mythology in *Final Fantasy*. As well as the chimeras, players can encounter minotaurs, medusas, and hydras, or equip armour such as the Aegis Shield and accessories like the Zeus Gauntlet. This would become a recurring trait of the series.

Having enjoyed financial and critical success with *Final Fantasy,* Sakaguchi-san soon began work on *Final Fantasy II,* a game set in an entirely different universe to what had previously been created. This indirect sequel – co-written again with Terada-san and released in 1988 – focused more centrally on Biblical references than wider myths, while its final dungeon was based on Pandemonium, John Milton's description of Hell in his epic poem *Paradise Lost* (1667).

It was not until the production of *Final Fantasy III* (1990) that the writers opted to somewhat expand on the real-life mythologies implemented in the story, accepting their influence where appropriate. A prime example of this is that the game saw the introduction of summoned beasts. Among them were Odin, chief of the Old Norse pantheon[4]; Shiva, derived from the Hindu God of Destruction; and Titan, a humanoid giant whose name relates to the second generation of ancient Greek deities[5].

By his own admission, Sakaguchi-san did not put much emphasis on character development or backstories in the first three titles. That changed during the writing of *Final Fantasy IV* (1991), having learned from the experience of respected manga editor Kazuhiko Torishima. Introducing a more complex and dramatic storyline meant the histories of characters, locations, and events carried greater weight. This required Sakaguchi-san to have a deeper comprehension of the lore present in the game, classical or otherwise, so that it could blend seamlessly with his own ideas. The result was one of the most beloved RPGs ever made.

Gradually evolving from its *Dungeons & Dragons*-inspired origins, the real-life mythology that appears in *Final Fantasy IV* and its successors began to draw more and more from the old legends. One example of this would be Arachne, the game's half-human, half-spider enemy in the webbed area of the Passage of the Eidolons, adapted from the tale of Athena and the gifted weaver[6]. Another is the beautiful but deadly Siren in *Final Fantasy V* (1992), the boss of the Ship Graveyard, who is named after the mermaid-like creatures that lure sailors to their death[7]. A third might be the River Lethe of *Final Fantasy VI* (1994) that Terra and her fellow Returners raft down, which could be a reference to the girl's amnesia: Lethe is both the Goddess of Oblivion and her affiliated river in the ancient Greek underworld, whose waters cause forgetfulness when consumed[8].

Final Fantasy V also welcomed to the development team Yoshinori Kitase and Tetsuya Nomura, two men who would go on to have an enormous impact on the future of the franchise. Both were instrumental in the design of the series' fifth and sixth instalments, not to mention their contributions to the scenarios themselves.

What is interesting about this time period is that Sakaguchi-san also lists Yasumi Matsuno, creator of the

Ogre Battle games (initially released in 1993), as a source of inspiration. Where it could be argued that Sakaguchi-san focused more on the fantasy side of global myths derived from *Dungeons & Dragons*, Matsuno-san heavily incorporated unaltered real-world lore into his work. The latter joined Square in 1995, subsequently writing and directing the critically acclaimed *Final Fantasy Tactics*[9].

Sakaguchi-san was the lead producer on this game, simultaneously overseeing the development of *Final Fantasy VII*, both of which released in 1997. With Matsuno-san at the helm of one project and Kitase-san directing the other, it is not difficult to envision how concepts may have overlapped. After Sakaguchi-san's proposed detective story, set in a grim and murky New York City, was abandoned[10], *Final Fantasy VII* became a melting pot of plot and character ideas. Kitase-san and Nomura-san overhauled the foundations but opted to keep the contemporary setting rather than use a traditional medieval fantasy one[11].

They were later joined by Kazushige Nojima, a scenario writer employed by Square in 1995, who was at the same time directing *Bahamut Lagoon* (1996) with support from Sakaguchi-san. Nojima-san had earned renown for his previous work on *Herakuresu no Eikō* (*Glory of Heracles*), a videogame RPG series based on ancient Greek mythology (although not exclusively – despite its name – on the hero Heracles).

Nojima-san's personal interest in Greek lore stemmed from his childhood, following his introduction to it via the movie *Jason and the Argonauts* (1963)[12]. He was hired as a writer by Japanese game developers Data East in the late 1980s, with one of his earliest productions being *Herakuresu no Eikō II: Titan no Metsubō* (*Glory of Heracles II: Titan's Downfall*, 1989). Nojima-san would go on to script two more sequels during his employment with Data East[13].

Across these games, a plethora of Greek gods, heroes, monsters, and locations are encountered. It is evident Nojima-san had studied the subject matter in tremendous detail, drawing inspiration from stories as far-ranging as the Titanomachy (see chapter X), the Trojan War (see chapter IX), and the destruction of Atlantis (see chapter V).

Through his career, Nojima-san's fascination with mythology flourished, and in *Final Fantasy VII* he saw an opportunity to further express that. Beyond his love for the legends of ancient Greece, he was intrigued by those of other regions, none more so than the tales of Viking deities such as Odin. Nojima-san implemented the cosmology of Yggdrasill (the world tree of the Norsemen) in his vision for *Final Fantasy VII*, with Midgar and Nibelheim (two locations around which the entire plot is centred) being named after Midgard and Niflheim, respectively the realm of mankind and the primordial world of mist[14].

However, when Sakaguchi-san, Kitase-san, and Nomura-san entrusted much of the game's burgeoning premise, narrative, and character relationships to Nojima-san, it was likely inevitable that his familiarity with classical lore would find its way deep into *Final Fantasy VII's* mythos as well. The true extent of this will be examined in coming chapters.

Final Fantasy VII was a critical and commercial success, winning a multitude of awards, and the strength of its storytelling remains hugely praised to this day. It was not until 2002, though, after a restructuring at Square, that work on the *Compilation of Final Fantasy VII* commenced. It began with the feature-length movie *Advent Children* (initially only conceived as a 20-minute short film) but quickly evolved to also include the mobile-exclusive game *Before Crisis* (2004), the first entry in the metaseries to be released.

The same year, Hironobu Sakaguchi resigned from Square Enix (as the company was by then known, following its merger with Enix) and was not credited as a contributor to these spin-off titles. Nojima-san, Kitase-san, and Nomura-san, however, each resumed lead roles on the projects[15], although it was another colleague that reintroduced the influence of ancient Greek mythology to the *Compilation*.

Hiroki Chiba had worked alongside the three men as an event planner on *Final Fantasy VII* (1997), *Final Fantasy VIII* (as event director, 1998), and *Final Fantasy X* (2001), but was now tasked with scripting the scenario for *Dirge of Cerberus* (2006). *Dirge of Cerberus* was the first shooter-style game in the *Final Fantasy* series and is the only title in the *Compilation of Final Fantasy VII* not to be written or supervised by Nojima-san[16], albeit he is listed at the top of the special thanks credits.

The very name of *Dirge of Cerberus* itself contains reference to the multi-headed hound that guards the gates of the underworld in Greek myth[17]. This is no mere coincidence: As will be detailed in chapters XVI and XVII, Chiba-san's story pays homage to the Labours of Heracles, and, by extension, Nojima-san's work on *Herakuresu no Eikō*.

When Nojima-san reprised his position as scenario writer on that franchise's last entry, *Herakuresu no Eikō: Tamashii no Shōmei* (*Glory of Heracles: Proof of the Soul*, 2008)[18], production was already underway on *Crisis Core*, a new *Compilation* title designed for the PlayStation Portable (PSP) and released in Japan in 2007[19]. As before, he integrated elements from various tales of antiquity into *Herakuresu no Eikō: Tamashii no Shōmei*, such as the Trojan War and the Battle of Thermopylae[20].

It is probable that Nojima-san's involvement led to the projects influencing one another to some degree, and in *Crisis Core* he would author a story inspired by arguably the most famous myth of all. The tapestry of intertwining threads between *Crisis Core* and the Greeks' siege at Troy is so intricate that it requires its own book to fully unravel: *Final Fantasy VII and the Trojan War*[21].

Meanwhile, the remaining chapters of *this* book will explore the broader parallels between the *Compilation* and classical mythology – including those exclusive to *Final Fantasy VII Remake* (2020) and its associated media –, providing a comprehensive study of both deliberate and seemingly unintentional allusions. They will explain why the Cetra are so closely affiliated with water, who the summon Titan is really based on, the reason Cloud's novelty weapon is the Nail Bat, which legendary creature the *Highwind* airship represents, the significance of the Happy Turtle jingles in *Episode INTERmission*, and much, much more.

From concept to masterpiece, the legacy of Sakaguchi-san and his successors is a wonder for mythologists to unravel ...

1. The Four Fiends are elemental demons and main bosses in the original *Final Fantasy*, responsible for disrupting the balance of the world by syphoning energy from the Crystals. They have featured in various guises in several titles since.
2. The *Monster Manual* series is the primary collection of bestiaries for the *Dungeons & Dragons* franchise.
3. An explanation of Bahamut and Kujata's unusual connection to Greek mythology in *Final Fantasy VII* can be found in chapter V.
4. Odin's role in the *Compilation* is fully detailed in *Norse Myths That Inspired Final Fantasy VII*.
5. Chapter X of this book is dedicated to Titan in *Final Fantasy VII*.
6. Further reference to this story can be found in chapter IX.
7. Sirens first featured in Homer's *Odyssey*, but no physical description is provided in the poem. Depictions of them

as mermaids date back to the 3rd century BC, though they have alternatively been compared to birds.

8. The connection between Lethe and *Final Fantasy VII's* Lifestream is discussed in chapter VI.

9. Several plot threads in *Final Fantasy Tactics* are analogous to historic events in medieval Europe, such as the Wars of the Roses or the Crusades.

10. According to Tetsuya Nomura, Sakaguchi-san's initial plan was that *Final Fantasy VII's* main protagonists would be pursued by the hot-blooded Detective Joe after they blew up power plants in the City of Mako. The metropolis was the basis for Midgar, the detective element evolved over time to become the Turks and Vincent Valentine, and Joe is immortalised as the famous chocobo jockey.

11. Tetsuya Nomura is officially credited in the development of *Final Fantasy VII* under character design, monster design, battle visual director, and original story (along with Hironobu Sakaguchi).

12. This fact was personally confirmed by Kazushige Nojima during a short exchange on social media in August 2022.

13. The subsequent titles were *Herakuresu no Eikō III: Kamigami no Chinmoku* (*Glory of Heracles III: Silence of the Gods*, 1992) and *Herakuresu no Eikō IV: Kamigami kara no Okurimono* (*Glory of Heracles IV: Gift from the Gods*, 1994).

14. A full exploration of these comparisons can also be found in *Norse Myths That Inspired Final Fantasy VII*.

15. Despite his prominent creative position in the *Compilation of Final Fantasy VII*, Kazushige Nojima has not been an employee of Square Enix since 2003. Instead, he is contracted to produce scripts through his own freelance company, Stellavista Ltd. '*Stellavista*' is Latin for 'Stargazer', which is a name *Final Fantasy VII Remake* fans may be familiar with: Stargazer Heights is the apartment block where Tifa lives.

16. An arguable exception to this is the short story *Hoshi o Meguru Otome*, commonly translated by fans as *The Maiden Who Travels the Planet*, which was authored by

Benny Matsuyama of Studio BentStuff and was contained within the *Final Fantasy VII Ultimania Omega*.

17. Cerberus is typically depicted with three heads, though not always. His earliest appearance in ancient Greek literature is Hesiod's *Theogony*, where he is described as having 50 heads.

18. The game was published by Nintendo and released internationally in 2010 as *Glory of Heracles*.

19. Both *Before Crisis* and *Crisis Core* were directed by Hajime Tabata, who would later take the lead on *Final Fantasy XV* (2016).

20. In an interview with RPGamer in 2010, Nojima-san revealed that he had used both Thermopylae and the fall of Troy as inspiration, but he had rearranged the specifics to such an extent that players might not even recognise them. The stories had also recently featured in Zack Snyder's Spartan blockbuster *300* (2006) and Wolfgang Petersen's war epic *Troy* (2004), respectively.

21. *Final Fantasy VII and the Trojan War* is due for release in 2024.

CHAPTER III

A RECAP OF
THE COMPILATION

The story of *Final Fantasy VII* (1997) is set in a world known simply as the Planet, later called Gaia in various sources. It is a world of industrialisation and scientific advancement, where the comforts of electrical energy have eased differences between cultures. Magic exists but is no longer commonplace, restricted mainly to the military or those learned in the mystic use of materia crystals.

For half a century, the influence of regional governments across Gaia has gradually waned, each bowing in turn to the will of the Shinra Electric Power Company. The corporation had previously discovered and monopolised mako as an energy source, draining the world of its natural riches through vast facilities called reactors.

There are those who know the truth, however: Mako is another name for the Lifestream, the very life force of the Planet. The Lifestream is the ethereal sea in which spirit energy – similar to a collection of souls – gathers, following the cosmic cycle of birth, life, death, and rebirth. Over countless millennia, spirit energy has carried the memories and experiences of everyone and everything that has ever lived, but its consumption by the mako reactors has been eradicating that shared knowledge forever.

The greedy heads of the Shinra Corporation have lined their pockets at the expense of Gaia's finite resources, and the general populace has turned a blind eye to the company's devastating impact on the environment so that they may lead easier lives. Now, from their skyscraping headquarters at the pinnacle of Midgar, a tiered metropolis divided into an upper- and lower-city, the organisation dictates political, economic, and military matters around the world. However, slowly killing the Planet is far from Shinra, Inc.'s sole crime.

2,000 years ago, a meteorite bearing an extraterrestrial being crashed into Gaia, causing a wound on her surface so great that vast swells of Lifestream have been trying to heal it ever since. The alien was malevolent in nature, capable of weaving horrific illusions and infecting the ancient Cetran civilisation with its virus. To their dismay, the people found the monstrosity to be immortal and imprisoned it within the rock at a terrible cost to their race.

The Cetra dwindled in number, their inherent propensity for magic was diluted, and their history passed into legend. The Calamity from the Skies was forgotten.

When scientists of the Shinra Corporation unearthed the body of a female approximately 30 years before the events of *Final Fantasy VII*, they determined she had been Cetran. Given the ancient race's magical talents – the secret of which lay in their interactions with the Planet –, it was hypothesised that Shinra could make mako extraction more efficient by utilising the body for their own purposes. The President ordered the female's genetic material to be used to synthetically reproduce a Cetra. The endeavour was codenamed the 'Ancients Project'; the being was called 'Jenova'.

The ethically ambiguous venture yielded little success to begin with. It was only when a specific branch of the operation, dubbed 'Project Jenova S', injected the entity's cells directly into an unborn foetus that the intended results were obtained. The child, Sephiroth, was a perfect genetic match to Jenova, and it was soon discovered that exposing the boy to mako unlocked superhuman abilities within him, valuable for a wide range of military applications. This was the origin of SOLDIER, the Shinra Corporation's elite army.

Despite the later discovery that Jenova was, in fact, not Cetran but an extraterrestrial, the company continued to create SOLDIERs using the being's cells in conjunction with mako. Sephiroth eventually rose to fame as the Planet's most gifted swordsman and Shinra's most lethal weapon. He was hailed a hero of the Wutai War, his strength unparalleled.

However, five years prior to *Final Fantasy VII*, Sephiroth was sent on an assignment to the remote mountain town of Nibelheim. It was here that he learned the secrets of his birth, and, in a maddened state, he thereafter burned the town to the ground. Amid Sephiroth's attempt to reclaim the body of his 'mother', though, he was defeated by a member of his team. The details were classified by Shinra and the incident was covered up.

Final Fantasy VII's opening is set in Midgar. The main protagonist is a young man named Cloud Strife, a SOLDIER-turned-mercenary who has recently been recruited to assist the environmental terrorist organisation Avalanche[1]. The group is led by Barret Wallace, and their mission is to detonate a bomb inside one of the city's mako reactors in an attempt to slow the demise of the Planet. Their successful destruction of the facility sets in motion a chain of events that brings them to the forefront of Shinra, Inc.'s attention.

Cloud was introduced to Avalanche by Tifa Lockhart, a girl with whom he had grown up in Nibelheim. Both had been caught up in the tragedy five years earlier, when Sephiroth killed his mother (Claudia) and her father (Brian), respectively[2]. Cloud has suffered amnesia since then but, like Tifa, he blames Shinra for the atrocities of the silver-haired SOLDIER.

Avalanche continues to target Shinra, Inc. power plants, but an ambush sees the party split. Cloud meets a local flower girl, Aerith Gainsborough, who is later revealed to be the last surviving Cetra and in possession of the mysterious White Materia. A former research specimen of the company, she has been monitored for years by its infamous operatives, the Turks. During Shinra's devastating retaliation against Avalanche, Aerith is captured.

Cloud, Tifa, and Barret infiltrate the corporation's headquarters to rescue her. They discover that the remains of Jenova are now located there and that the antagonistic scientist Professor Hojo hopes to breed Aerith with a long-lived feline named Nanaki (known by his specimen categorisation, Red XIII)[3].

While the heroes are in the tower, President Shinra is murdered by Sephiroth, and control of the company passes to his son Rufus. Avalanche subsequently escapes Midgar and sets off in pursuit of Sephiroth, who has stolen the body of Jenova, and whom Cloud believes to be the real threat to the Planet.

During their journey, it comes to the party's attention that Sephiroth is seeking the Black Materia, a means of summoning the ultimate destructive magic, Meteor. They additionally recruit Yuffie Kisaragi (a rebellious ninja from Wutai), Cait Sith (a mechanical anthropomorphic cat with a questionable agenda), Vincent Valentine (a former Turk who witnessed Project Jenova), and Cid Highwind (a legendary ex-Shinra pilot) in their bid to stop Sephiroth.

The group eventually tracks him to the Temple of the Ancients, where they learn of his plan to wound the Planet as Jenova did 2,000 years ago. Sephiroth intends to absorb the gathered Lifestream himself and become a god[4]. Cloud begins to show signs of a mental breakdown as well as susceptibility to mind control by his adversary. Having secured the Black Materia, he hands it over to Sephiroth to the dismay of his comrades.

As the last Cetra, Aerith is convinced she alone can halt Sephiroth's catastrophic objective and disappears after him. They find her deep in prayer at the Forgotten Capital, a ruined city once home to a Cetran civilisation. However, while Cloud battles to maintain self-control, Sephiroth descends and pierces her heart with his blade. As Aerith dies in her friend's arms, her White Materia bounces away into the lagoon below. His very essence aflame with grief and hatred, Cloud vows to avenge the flower girl, his mother, and the people of Nibelheim.

Making their way into the permafrost region, the party reaches the Northern Crater, the location at which Jenova's meteorite struck Gaia two millennia ago. They discover that the figure they have been chasing this whole time is not Sephiroth himself but the shapeshifting Jenova specimen, which he has been manipulating from afar. At the heart of the crater, encased in crystal, is the real Sephiroth. His body has been regenerating here since his death at Nibelheim, but his consciousness has travelled the Lifestream, syphoning its knowledge and wisdom. As such, he has become dangerously powerful.

It is here that Cloud learns he is not a former SOLDIER; he is a failed experiment of Professor Hojo's, and Tifa has been too afraid to challenge his false narrative. The Jenova cells in his body are what granted Sephiroth power over the young man, luring him to this place. Psychologically vulnerable, Cloud surrenders the Black Materia a second time, allowing the real Sephiroth to summon Meteor. The crater collapses, and Cloud is swallowed by the Lifestream. The others escape aboard President Rufus' *Highwind* airship[5], but the strain causes Tifa to pass out.

She wakes from her coma a week later to the news that Meteor now looms in the sky, and that Sephiroth has created a vast shield of energy around himself. Shinra, Inc. has scheduled a live execution of Avalanche to make them scapegoats for the impending apocalypse. However, the event is interrupted by an attack on the city of Junon by the Sapphire Weapon, one of the biomechanical monsters released by the Planet to defend itself. In the chaos, the rebel group steals the *Highwind* and sets off in search of Cloud.

They find him in the southern village of Mideel, suffering the effects of mako poisoning, and apparently locked in a vegetative state[6]. Tifa remains behind to care for him, but a nearby eruption of the Lifestream tears the ground apart and engulfs the pair.

During the experience, Tifa is able to connect with Cloud's mind and explore his recollections. They establish that Cloud was never in SOLDIER, but he did accompany Sephiroth and his friend Zack to Nibelheim in his capacity as a regular infantryman. Driven by pure anger at what Sephiroth did to his mother, Cloud managed to wound and kill his hero but was seriously injured himself in the process. He was thereafter exposed to mako and Jenova cells by Professor Hojo, but Zack broke them out after years of confinement. The fugitives made it as far as the outskirts of Midgar before Zack was gunned down by the Shinra Army.

In his weakened mental state, Cloud's character became a cocktail of information blended by the mimicry abilities of Jenova's cells, comprising of his real self, Zack's memories, and Tifa's projection of her childhood friend. Having unravelled the mystery, Cloud and Tifa emerge once more from the Lifestream. The young swordsman embraces his true identity and resolves to end the threat of Meteor.

When the Shinra Corporation's attempt to blow up the asteroid is unsuccessful, the heroes turn to Nanaki's adoptive grandfather, Bugenhagen, for advice. Well-versed in Cetran lore, he suspects that Sephiroth killed Aerith because she was trying to cast the ultimate protective magic, Holy – something that could only be accomplished by a Cetra equipped with the White Materia. Returning to the Forgotten Capital, they confirm Bugenhagen's theory but realise Sephiroth is blocking Holy from challenging Meteor.

Meanwhile, Shinra, Inc. prepares to shatter the shield around the Northern Crater by firing concentrated mako from the Sister Ray cannon. As the cannon begins drawing energy from the reactors around Midgar, the Diamond Weapon – another biomechanical colossus sent by the Planet – rises from the sea and bombards the metropolis, demolishing the office of President Rufus with him inside. The Sister Ray responds by blowing a hole through both the Weapon and Sephiroth's shield, thus neutralising his defence.

However, with the company's hierarchy in disarray, Professor Hojo commandeers the cannon to provide his biological son Sephiroth – birthed by Doctor Lucrecia, his colleague in Project Jenova – with additional mako. Cloud and his comrades parachute into Midgar and defeat Hojo, later assisting with the evacuation of the upper-city's citizens.

With Meteor on its final approach, the group descends into the Northern Crater to confront their nemesis. After a lengthy battle, they are victorious, but the release of Holy is too late, and the gargantuan asteroid begins to push through its magical barrier. Their efforts have been in vain, but, just as all seems lost, the Lifestream breaches the Planet's surface and converges on Midgar to obliterate Meteor itself. Somewhere in that great ethereal sea, Aerith smiles.

The story of *Final Fantasy VII* is continued in the feature film *Advent Children* (2005). Two years have passed since Meteorfall, and a strange plague afflicts much of the population. It is dubbed 'Geostigma', an autoimmune-like condition that arises when the body tries to reject foreign genetic material but overcompensates, causing sufferers to weaken and secrete a black substance. What is not known to the public is that the foreign material is diluted Jenova cells that were distributed across Gaia when the Lifestream came to assist Holy.

Cloud, himself stricken by Geostigma and haunted by his past, operates a delivery service with Tifa, despite being increasingly reclusive. One day he is attacked by a trio of silver-haired men who bear an unusual resemblance to Sephiroth. Cloud thereafter responds to a request from the Turks – who have been aiding Midgar's refugees – and is astonished to learn Rufus Shinra survived the Diamond Weapon's attack. Rufus reveals that the leader of the mysterious men is Kadaj, and they are searching for the remains of Jenova.

Cloud is later forced to rescue a group of children who have been kidnapped by Kadaj and his quasi-brothers, Loz and Yazoo. He discovers that the three are manifestations of Sephiroth's will, and their unification with Jenova's cells would mean the return of the legendary SOLDIER.

Challenging these Remnants[7], the heroes of *Final Fantasy VII* gather in Edge, a city constructed on the periphery of Midgar. Kadaj manages to seize Jenova's remains from Rufus and is subsequently successful in his goal of becoming a vessel for Sephiroth to access the material world. Strengthened by the memories of Aerith and

Zack, Cloud battles his arch adversary once more, barely overcoming the swordsman and suffering near-mortal wounds.

Sephiroth is again banished to the Lifestream, and a spring of healing water appears at the church where Aerith previously tended her flowers. Cloud is able to use the pool to cure the citizens – and himself – of their Geostigma and reflects on the importance of his old friendships.

An extended edition of the movie, *Advent Children Complete*, was published in 2009 and supplemented by two novels, both authored by Kazushige Nojima. These are *On the Way to a Smile* (2009) and *The Kids Are Alright: A Turks Side Story* (2011)[8]. They document the activities of the heroes, Turks, Kadaj, and several new characters between Meteorfall and the return of Sephiroth, focusing primarily on the aftermath of *Final Fantasy VII* and the rise of Geostigma. The books do not add much in terms of mythos, but they offer a fascinating snapshot of the personal lives of the characters and help contextualise plot elements from *Advent Children* and later *Final Fantasy VII Remake*[9].

The *Final Fantasy VII Ultimania Omega* (2005) additionally included a novella by Studio BentStuff's Benny Matsuyama called *Hoshi o Meguru Otome*, commonly translated by fans as *The Maiden Who Travels the Planet*. Its canonicity is debatable, but it provides insight into Aerith's actions within the Lifestream following her death, culminating in the destruction of Meteor.

Similarly, and also in 2005, Square Enix commissioned the animation studio Madhouse to produce a short film which simultaneously recounts the Nibelheim incident and the Turks' pursuit of Zack and Cloud after their escape from Hojo's laboratory. The resulting anime, *Last Order*, is not considered canon to the *Compilation* but is generally mentioned in the same breath as other titles.

The backstory of the original *Final Fantasy VII* is further explored in the games *Before Crisis* (2004) and *Crisis Core* (2007), respectively beginning six and seven years prior to *Final Fantasy VII's* opening. The former follows the Turks in their ongoing conflict with a militant branch of Avalanche that pre-dates their *Final Fantasy VII* namesake. Led by an enigmatic warrior, Elfe, and an unpredictable scientist, Fuhito, the organisation's purpose is to save the life of the Planet by ending the Shinra Corporation's tyranny and greed.

After an assassination attempt on President Shinra and an unsuccessful bombing of a Midgar mako reactor, the Turks are charged with uncovering the Avalanche base. It is concluded that the group has a high-ranking mole in Shinra, Inc., and the duty of identifying them falls to Chief Verdot[10].

The Turks face a series of setbacks that allow company secrets to fall into the hands of Fuhito and for Avalanche's leaders to repeatedly elude capture, costing the lives of military personnel. The President holds Verdot directly accountable for this but finds himself blackmailed when the chief discovers the informant controlling Avalanche to be none other than Rufus Shinra.

The Turks are eventually alerted to another terrorist attack on the under-construction mako reactor at Mount Corel. Everything comes to a head when Rufus is caught red-handed, Elfe is established to be the daughter of Verdot who was thought dead, and Fuhito declares himself the leader of a new extremist faction of Avalanche. The scientist then makes off with a collapsed Elfe, leaving Verdot to denounce his affiliation with Shinra, Inc. in a bid to rescue his daughter, and the Turks barely escape before the facility explodes.

Little is heard of Avalanche in the years that follow, but a kill order is placed on the former chief. When the organisation does resurface, they are hunting for a way to activate the broken Zirconiade Materia inside Elfe, the source of her strength[11]. Fuhito plans to summon Zirconiade, the world-burning monster, from its interdimensional domain, causing a mass extinction event that would assist the Planet to recover from imminent demise.

Verdot informs the Turks of Fuhito's actions, but their contact has the operatives branded enemies of Shinra. Despite this, the Turks remain loyal to both parties and continue to battle Avalanche in Midgar. It becomes apparent that the only way to preserve Elfe's life is to go through with the summoning, albeit incomplete. Allowing

Fuhito to perform the ritual, they proceed into Zirconiade's realm, eventually defeating both creature and scientist.

Surviving the encounter against all odds, the Turks take Verdot and Elfe into hiding, as they know they cannot return to Shinra, Inc. Only a handful of them remain with the company, and their silence over the Rufus affair is rewarded. Their new roles lead them directly into *Final Fantasy VII*.

Crisis Core, meanwhile, tells the tale of Zack Fair, a young man with aspirations of becoming a SOLDIER First Class. He idolises Sephiroth and other battle-hardened warriors such as the former's companions, Genesis and Angeal. Zack plays a role in bringing the Wutai War to a close but becomes embroiled in the mysterious disappearance of Genesis, Angeal, and a significant number of other SOLDIERs.

Genesis is discovered to be in league with Doctor Hollander, a man who was involved in the Ancients Project decades earlier. The red-haired SOLDIER has unique biological properties that permit him to copy his attributes onto his subordinates[12], forming an army of cohorts. Sephiroth hypothesises that Genesis' motives relate to his strange degradation – a genetic flaw that has been hindering his ability to heal – and that he is aggressively seeking a solution. When Zack gets the chance to confront Angeal about the hostilities, his old mentor calls them all monsters, revealing that he too has mutations.

The teenage swordsman later meets and becomes romantic with Aerith but is sent on assignment to Modeoheim alongside an infantryman called Cloud. Here, Zack learns that Genesis and Angeal were imperfect specimens born of Project Jenova, failures where Sephiroth was a success. In their desperation, the two separately attack the young SOLDIER, and he is forced to duel them. Genesis ends their fight by throwing himself into a chasm, while Angeal is ultimately slain by his student.

Zack thereafter struggles to come to terms with what has happened and questions his worth as a SOLDIER. When sightings of Genesis and concurrent malfunctions at a regional mako reactor are reported, Zack and Sephiroth are sent to its site, Nibelheim. Sephiroth consequently discovers the truth of his origins as part of Project Jenova and loses his sanity, engulfing the town in an inferno. Zack realises his comrade is beyond saving and clashes with him but is heavily wounded, maintaining consciousness just long enough to see Cloud topple the legendary hero in his stead.

When he awakes four years later, Zack finds he has been kept alive in a secret laboratory at Nibelheim's Shinra Manor. He smashes out of his containment chamber and, taking the incapacitated Cloud with him, flees the area. They are labelled fugitives of the Shinra Corporation and hunted by the Turks and the military alike, not to mention Genesis, who believes Cloud's exposure to Jenova cells may be the key to preventing his own degradation.

Wishing to put an end to this once and for all, Zack journeys to Banora, the hometown of Genesis and Angeal, to confront the rogue warrior. Bested in battle, Genesis does not die and join with the Lifestream as expected. Instead, he is cured of his deteriorating condition and subsequently judged by the Planet to have an important role to play in future events. As Zack sets out for Midgar to see Aerith again, a Shinra helicopter arrives, and a pair of special SOLDIERs carry Genesis off[13]. Ashamed of his actions, Genesis later rejects the SOLDIERs' request to aid their cause and seals himself in a cavern[14].

On the outskirts of Midgar, the military finally catches up with the fugitives. Concealing Cloud behind some rocks, Zack meets hundreds of infantrymen head on. He fights long and valiantly, but, as the bullets riddle his body, he falls and is left to bleed out. With his final breaths, he passes his sword to Cloud and declares the boy to be his living legacy.

The game was rereleased in December 2022 as *Crisis Core Reunion*, a full HD remaster of the 2007 title. According to Tetsuya Nomura, it functions as a prequel to both *Final Fantasy VII* and *Final Fantasy VII Remake*, where the continuity of the *Compilation* seemingly diverges.

Chronologically, the last entry in the *Compilation of Final Fantasy VII* is *Dirge of Cerberus* (2006)[15]. The primary protagonist of this story is Vincent Valentine, who has sought seclusion in the year since the events of *Advent Children*.

Vincent is present in the town of Kalm during a festival to celebrate the recent re-establishment of the Worldwide Network, Gaia's equivalent of the internet. A sudden explosion alerts him to a coordinated military operation by an unknown army, whose intention it is to abduct large sections of the crowd. Battling his way through the streets, Vincent rendezvouses with Reeve Tuesti, the man controlling Cait Sith, and who is now commissioner of the World Regenesis Organisation (WRO).

Reeve identifies the combatants as belonging to Deepground SOLDIER, a clandestine branch of the Shinra Army that was based in the facilities below Midgar. They are commanded by an elite force known as the Tsviets, and the reconnection of the Worldwide Network was the catalyst for their emergence. En route to Edge, the pair witness a broadcast by the leader of the Tsviets, Weiss the Immaculate, who promises to purge the impure denizens of the Planet.

As Vincent gathers information about Deepground, he learns the SOLDIERs are targeting individuals who have never suffered from Geostigma. They also have a curious interest in an old research thesis of Doctor Lucrecia which theorised the relationship between Chaos and Omega. Chaos is a lifeform housed within Vincent's indestructible body; it is controlled by the Protomateria, an ancient orb whose sole function it is to restrain the beast.

Vincent journeys to Nibelheim in the hope of uncovering more about Lucrecia[16], the woman he loves, and to find out exactly what Omega is. The entity is discovered to be Gaia's final defence mechanism, a Weapon designed to assemble and transport the Lifestream to the cosmos in the event of a catastrophe. Deepground is attempting to trick the Planet through genocide into artificially awakening Omega. While in Nibelheim, the Tsviets rob Vincent of the Protomateria.

In a last-ditch effort to stop the annihilation, Vincent and the heroes of *Final Fantasy VII* converge on Midgar to engage the Deepground battalions. The WRO army fights on the surface, allowing Vincent to descend into the secret facilities below. Without the Protomateria, he struggles to contain Chaos, realising that the beast's role is to be a harbinger of death, the one whose purpose is to end all life so that Omega will rise.

However, the dark energy that permeates Chaos is the same as that of Nero the Sable, a member of the Tsviets and Weiss' younger brother. This grants Vincent an edge when the two face off. He follows Nero into the throne room at the heart of Deepground, where the dead body of Weiss awaits. Nero reveals that Omega will soon awaken in Weiss, just as Chaos did in Vincent, but is horrified when his brother suddenly stabs him. The mind controlling Weiss' actions, however, is not his own: It is Professor Hojo's.

Hojo explains that he uploaded his consciousness onto the Worldwide Network before his death three years prior. When the network was recently restored, he overthrew the real Weiss' mind in cyberspace, then hatched a plan to gain control of Omega. Only untainted Lifestream would suffice to trick the Planet, only Deepground had the resources to commit such a large-scale purge, and only Weiss had a body strong enough to withstand Omega. The final piece of the puzzle was acquiring the Protomateria.

The duo clash, and Vincent utilises his close proximity to the Protomateria to summon the strength of Chaos while maintaining his own form. Just as Hojo prepares to deal a devasting blow, Nero materialises from the darkness to cast the scientist's mind from his brother's body. He merges with the real Weiss and together the siblings invoke Omega, causing the Weapon to surge upward over Midgar, extracting the Lifestream as it ascends. In a desperate final attempt to prevent an apocalypse, Vincent assumes the form of Chaos and destroys Omega's physical being.

A short time later, Vincent visits the grotto where Lucrecia confined herself in crystal and makes peace with his past. The essence of both Chaos and Omega have now returned to the Planet. Meanwhile, somewhere below Midgar, the seal on Genesis' magical stasis is broken. He lifts the lifeless figure of Weiss and flies off into the night, asserting that they still have much work to do.

As an extension to the main title, the online multiplayer mode of *Dirge of Cerberus* was a direct prequel to the game, set prior to Meteorfall and recounting how the Tsviets seized control of Deepground. It was released exclusively in Japan in 2006, but the servers were only operational for nine months.

In this mode, the Deepground facility is ruled by the Restrictors, a special unit of cloaked SOLDIERs who control their subordinates through microchip implants. The player's character, having secretly had their restriction chip deactivated, becomes embroiled in a conspiracy to aid the Tsviets. It costs them their life, however, as Weiss uses the player to distract one of the Restrictors while he overpowers them.

Weiss' eventual victory over all Restrictors causes a fatal virus to be released into his bloodstream, and it is when neuro-connected to the Worldwide Network in search of an antidote that his mind is supplanted by Professor Hojo's. Knowing that Weiss' body will soon die, Hojo tricks Nero into leading Deepground SOLDIER's mass murder of civilians and the hunt for the Protomateria, promising it to be the secret of rebirth[17].

To date, the *Compilation of Final Fantasy VII* has no definitive ending, but the survival of the Planet has long been confirmed. In the epilogue of the original game, reproduced in the prologue of *Advent Children*, Nanaki and two young cubs from his brood climb the bluffs overlooking Midgar, observing how nature has reclaimed the metropolis. Set 500 years after the events of Meteorfall, it is a glimmer of hope that the damage caused by the Shinra Electric Power Company and their mako reactors is not irreversible. That said, it has been suggested in the *Ultimanias* that the fate of humans is not so favourable, with mankind facing extinction.

In 2015, Square Enix announced that a new project was underway which would see *Final Fantasy VII* remade for modern platforms, confirmed in 2022 to be a trilogy. Yoshinori Kitasi, Tetsuya Nomura, Kazushige Nojima, and many more of the original development staff would be at its helm, collaborating to reimagine the beauty and intricacies of the beloved 1997 title.

Over time, associated games and media were also revealed. In addition to *Crisis Core Reunion, The First Soldier* (2021) was a battle royale mobile game where prospective SOLDIER candidates fought to the death in a virtual combat arena[18], while *Ever Crisis* (2023) has been designed to recreate each entry of the *Compilation* in episodic chunks as well as deliver fresh tales.

The first instalment of the central trilogy, *Final Fantasy VII Remake* (2020), itself recounts the Midgar scenario of its original counterpart. Although the primary story beats remain intact for the majority of the game, the plot has been expanded to delve deeper into the characters and environments of the metropolis, all the while implementing details from the *Compilation* and building upon the world and mythos of Gaia. That is not to say, however, that new mysteries have not been introduced.

As in *Final Fantasy VII*, Cloud, portraying himself as an ex-SOLDIER, assists Avalanche in bombing one of Midgar's mako reactors. The team escapes through the devastated streets of the upper-city's Sector 8, but Cloud is overcome by a moment of psychological trauma and hallucinates

Sephiroth in the flames of Nibelheim. This is the first of several instances in *Remake* where Sephiroth appears in or speaks to the young man's subconscious[19], attempting to guide his actions.

Elsewhere in Sector 8, Cloud encounters the flower peddler Aerith. The girl's behaviour implies she is familiar with him, but she is being harassed by black-cloaked spectres – later called Whispers[20] –, who only become visible to Cloud when Aerith touches his arm. Pursued by Shinra security officers, the swordsman leaps onto a train bound for the Slums, regrouping with Barret and the others.

In the days that follow, the Whispers engage directly with Cloud, Aerith, and members of Avalanche to ensure that the events of *Remake* progress as they do in *Final Fantasy VII*[21]. Despite displaying benevolence at times, such as saving the flower girl from falling through a balustrade, their agenda does not necessarily align with the heroes', for they aggressively prevent Cloud, Barret, and Tifa halting the collapse of the Sector 7 Plate.

While in Aerith's presence, Cloud begins to glimpse brief visions of the future, and becomes suspicious when she remarks on things she should not yet be aware of. This is further emphasised when a version of her with memories from the near future converses with Cloud via the Lifestream, even though the real Aerith has been captured and imprisoned at Shinra Headquarters[22].

Cloud, Barret, and Tifa rescue their friend from Professor Hojo's laboratory, and she uses her access to future memories to calm Red XIII when he breaks from his own confinement. Now endowed with this shared knowledge, the beast articulates that the Whispers are arbiters of fate, whose function it is to enforce the Planet's chosen destiny: They intervene when someone is close to altering that destiny, deliberately or otherwise.

As the group attempts to flee the Shinra Building, they encounter a physical manifestation of Sephiroth outside the Jenova specimen's tank. This Sephiroth is revealed to be a robed figure that has been transformed by the illusionary powers of Jenova, though he is able to kill President Shinra and to stab Barret through the chest. The Whispers act frantically to save Barret's life, for this was not the death ordained for him. Meanwhile, another robed man leaps from the tower with Jenova in his arms.

The party steals vehicles from the lobby of Shinra Headquarters and they race along the Midgar Expressway, ultimately evading the company's security forces. Sephiroth is waiting for them at the end of the highway, but this variant is different to any that has so far appeared to Cloud or the others. Speaking to the group, he asserts that if the Planet was to die, so would humanity, and invites them to defy destiny to avert this.

Sephiroth opens a portal to the Singularity – a place beyond the construct of time – and encourages Cloud to follow him. Through their memories of the future, Aerith and Red XIII know that failing to stop Sephiroth will result in Meteor destroying the Planet, but continuing on destiny's predetermined course will cause the decline or extinction of humanity, as suggested in the epilogue of *Final Fantasy VII*. Aerith believes Sephiroth is the greatest threat to Gaia and proposes that the solution to their dilemma is to change fate itself.

Entering the Singularity, the party is challenged by a Whisper Harbinger, an entity comprised of countless arbiters and connected to all the threads of time and space that can shape the Planet's destiny. They are successful in defeating the colossal being, only to realise it had been guarding the essence of Sephiroth, imprisoned there after the events of *Advent Children*.

Using his powerful will, Sephiroth has been exerting his influence on Cloud – the nucleus of his existence[23] – from the Singularity, where time is not linear, so chronology is flexible. Freed of his shackles, however, Sephiroth is now able to access the Lifestream to restore the strength he lost at the climax of *Final Fantasy VII* (as described in *On the Way to a Smile*)[24].

The group battles the so-called One-Winged Angel after he absorbs the Whispers. The fight ends with Cloud dealing a concentrated blow to his arch enemy, though the consequence is implied to be the eradication of the arbiters of fate. Sephiroth draws Cloud into a vision of the Planet seven seconds before its demise, advising the young man that he has the capacity to change the outcome.

Back in the real world, the party resolves to distance themselves from Midgar and settle the score with Sephiroth. Aerith senses that something is different, however: Destiny has indeed been altered by their actions in the Singularity. It would seem the abolition of the Whispers has not only affected the future but also the past, for Zack has now survived the Shinra Army's onslaught and returned to the city.

The story of *Final Fantasy VII Remake* will continue in *Final Fantasy VII Rebirth*, scheduled for release in 2024.

To accompany the launch of the game's PlayStation 5 edition, *Final Fantasy VII Remake Intergrade* (2021), two extra chapters of downloadable content (DLC) were made available, titled *Episode INTERmission*. These follow the teenage ninja Yuffie Kisaragi as she seeks to infiltrate a Shinra research facility in Midgar and steal the rumoured ultimate materia. The events of the DLC are concurrent with *Remake* and culminate in Yuffie and her countryman, Sonon Kusakabe, coming face to face with Deepground SOLDIERs and Nero the Sable[25].

Scenario writer Kazushige Nojima has also authored additional works to further develop the lore of the remake project and the *Compilation*. The first of these is a short novella presented in the *Final Fantasy VII Remake: World Preview* (2020) artbook, titled *Picturing the Past*. Narrated by a former Shinra infantryman[26], the tale features the tests conducted on Aerith while she was a child captive at Shinra Headquarters and explains how the locations in her clairvoyant paintings were surveyed by the President as potential mako hotspots.

In 2021, Square Enix published Nojima-san's third *Final Fantasy VII* novel, *Traces of Two Pasts*. The book is split into three distinct sections and recounts the childhoods of Tifa and Aerith, respectively. "Traces of Tifa" explores her life in Nibelheim, her martial arts training under Master Zangan, the difficulties she endured upon arriving in Midgar, and her introduction to Avalanche. "Traces of Aerith", meanwhile, includes how she and Ifalna, her biological mother, escaped from Professor Hojo's laboratory, her youth in the care of her adoptive mother, Elmyra, and the dynamics of the Turks' surveillance of her. The third part is simply an alternative format of *Picturing the Past*.

It is evident that there is an abundance of stories yet to be told in the *Final Fantasy VII* saga, building upon the wealth of material that already exists in the *Compilation*. As will be discussed throughout this book, reference to ancient Greek legends can be found in almost every title, and *Remake* is no exception. Just how, and to what extent, future instalments of this new trilogy and its associated media will draw from the same mythological inspirations as its predecessors, however, only time will tell ...

---

1. Avalanche is written as AVALANCHE in *Final Fantasy VII*. This is also true for the Planet's biomechanical monsters, WEAPON.

2. Claudia Strife and Brian Lockhart's names were officially confirmed in the *Final Fantasy VII Remake Ultimania*, despite never being used in any of the released titles. According to Tetsuya Nomura, the names have existed for the development staff since the mid-1990s, although his original illustration for Cloud's mother identifies her as 'Claudia Strauss, aged 33'.

3. Nanaki's design contains both feline and canine elements, so his species type is ambiguous. Promotional artwork for *Advent Children* paired him with the robotic cat, Cait Sith, on the basis that they shared feline features, while he is described in *Before Crisis* as being like a mountain lion and in *Traces of Two Pasts* as leonine (lion-like). Conversely, in the novel *The Kids Are Alright*, Evan perceives Nanaki to be a dog or wolf. This is continued in *Remake* with Barret calling him a "rat-dog".

4. A function of the Lifestream is to heal substantial wounds inflicted on the surface of the Planet. If such a disastrous event occurs, the great flow of energy will be redirected to that site. The geological damage caused by Jenova's meteorite was so significant that the Planet continues to draw the Lifestream there even 2,000 years later.

5. The Shinra Army has been pursuing Sephiroth for the murder of President Shinra and tracks him to the Northern Crater. However, the primary objective of Rufus, Hojo, and other members of the Executive is to locate the Promised Land, a legendary place from Cetran lore they believe to be rich in mako.

6. Mako poisoning is alternatively known as mako addiction. It occurs when a person is exposed to excess mako, and their mind collapses due to the overabundance of memories, experiences, and information contained within the spirit energy.

7. Kadaj, Loz, and Yazoo are collectively known as the Remnants of Sephiroth. This is because they represent individual aspects of his character rather than the man as a whole. As revealed in *On the Way to a Smile*, after the events of *Final Fantasy VII*, Sephiroth lost the strength

to project his own image and attributes onto the material world. His goal is to find and use the Jenova cells as a conduit for this.

8. The years of release for the novels are the Japanese dates. It was almost a decade before they were officially translated into English by Yen Press.

9. Examples of this include how Denzel comes to live with Cloud and Tifa (*On the Way to a Smile*), why Kyrie is a thief and a con artist in the Midgar Slums (*The Kids Are Alright*), and what the true relationship is between Leslie and Don Corneo (*The Kids Are Alright*).

10. Verdot is the English localisation of the Japanese name *Verudo* in *On the Way to a Smile*, although Veld has been presented as an alternative in other official media.

11. The materia had been fused with Elfe – whose real name is Felicia – by Professor Hojo, following a historic incident in which she was believed to have perished.

12. A summarised explanation of this ability is provided in the footnotes of chapter VIII.

13. The special SOLDIERs are, in fact, Weiss and Nero, and their cause is to overthrow the Restrictors.

14. Genesis' actions in Deepground are revealed in the *Crisis Core Ultimania*.

15. The exact point at which *Final Fantasy VII Remake* fits into the *Compilation's* chronology is debatable as it seems to simultaneously be a retelling of *Final Fantasy VII* and a sequel to *Advent Children*.

16. Part of this journey was covered in the mobile-exclusive game *Dirge of Cerberus Lost Episode* (2006).

17. This detail is taken from the single player mode of *Dirge of Cerberus*, but it is easier to understand in the context of the multiplayer mode.

18. The servers for *The First Soldier* were shut off in January 2023 after four seasons of the mobile game.

19. In *Final Fantasy VII*, Sephiroth is only mentioned a handful of times during the Midgar scenario and is not shown on screen at all until later in the game. His presence in *Remake* immediately establishes a change.

20. The Whispers have different names across the various localisations of *Remake*. In Japanese, they are Feelers (*Fīrā*); in French, they are Weavers (*Fileurs*, lit. 'Spinners'); and in German, they are the Fates (*Moiren*, derived from the ancient Greek Moirai).

21. Two such examples are the Whispers injuring Jessie so that Cloud must take her place on the mission to bomb Mako Reactor 5, then halting Cloud from killing Reno at Aerith's church.

22. The mechanics of this scene between Cloud and Aerith are explained by co-director Motomu Toriyama in the *Final Fantasy VII Remake Material Ultimania Plus*.

23. *On the Way to a Smile* describes how Sephiroth discarded his unnecessary memories into the Lifestream after Cloud killed him at Nibelheim, but this later affects his sense of identity and ability to materialise as himself in the physical world. To ensure his spiritual essence never fades from existence, he binds it to Cloud's hatred of him. In this way, as long as Cloud feels anger in his heart towards Sephiroth, he will never simply be a memory.

24. This summary is based on details contained in *Remake's Ultimania*, *Material Ultimania*, and *Material Ultimania Plus*.

25. Nero's brother, Weiss, also features in *Remake Intergrade* as a superboss in the virtual combat simulator.

26. The narrator's name is not provided in *Picturing the Past* but is revealed in the "Traces of Aerith" section of *Traces of Two Pasts* to be Lonny (as localised in the English edition).

PART TWO

THE SHAPING
OF THE WORLD

CHAPTER IV

GAIA AND THE CALAMITY
FROM THE SKIES

T he tales of the ancient Greek gods, heroes, monsters, villains, and everyone in between are among the most complex and best recorded myth cycles in the world. This treasure trove is undoubtedly a gift to historians and mythologists – and to mankind in general –, but it is not without its contradictions.

Countless stories have survived centuries of oral retellings, the rise and fall of dynasties and traditions, misinterpretations and poetic licence, and the deliberate addition or omission of details to appease audiences or entire cultures. It is therefore common for multiple variations of the same legend to exist, and these contrast one another just as often as they corroborate.

A perfect example of such competing tales are the many Greek creation myths. The Orphic religion of the 5th century BC described the eternal embodiment of time[1], Chronos[2], producing Aether (in this context: the space above the world) and Chaos (the space below), as well as an egg. From this egg comes Phanes (also called Protogonus), the primordial, hermaphroditic deity of new life and creator of the cosmos.

The great poet Homer, thought to have been born around the 8th century BC, proposed a different set of events. In the *Iliad*[3], there is a suggestion that the first gods are birthed by Tethys, a divine mother figure, and fathered by Oceanus, the vast river that encircles the world.

Perhaps the most popular of the creation myths, however, is the one found in Hesiod's *Theogony*[4]. It explains how metaphysical concepts, physical entities, and natural phenomena alike were personified, helping the Greeks to make sense of the world around them.

In the beginning, there is only Chaos, the yawning void of nothingness. From Chaos springs Nyx (Night) and Erebus (Darkness), who soon couple to produce Hemera (Day) and Aether (also spelled Ether, the bright upper-sky)[5]. Eros, the primeval god of love and sexual desire, comes forth from this emptiness, too, although he is better known nowadays by his Roman name: Cupid[6].

Tangible figures also materialise from Chaos: Gaia (alternatively spelled Gaea, Earth) and Tartarus (the cavernous depths beneath the earth). Gaia then bears Uranus (Sky), Pontus (Sea), and the Ourea (Mountains) of her own accord[7].

Where Gaia embodies the land and nature, Uranus symbolises the blue firmament and starry heavens that cover every inch of her. In this way, they reflect the millennia-old belief in a Mother Earth and Father Sky. Such primordial deities have appeared in religions and cultural tales around the world, ranging from Ki and An (ancient Sumerian) to Prithvi Mata and Dyaus Pita (Vedic Hinduism) to Papatūanuku and Ranginui (Māori).

Gaia was considered the ancestral mother of all life, and her Roman equivalent was Terra, from whom stem words such as 'terrestrial' (typically defined as 'on or relating to Earth or the land'). Fans of *Final Fantasy IX* may already be familiar with this connection, for Gaia and Terra are the names of the two worlds central to the plot. However, when it comes to *Final Fantasy VII*, it is the specific story of Gaia, Uranus (whom the Romans called Caelus), and their offspring that is of greatest interest.

To mirror the patriarchal societies of antiquity, rule of the cosmos is originally assigned to Uranus. His shifting clouds and dynamic rains soon meet the wide-bosomed peaks and fertile valleys of Gaia, causing her to fall pregnant. According to Hesiod, the first fruits of their union are twelve immense children, six males and six females[8].

These siblings and many of their descendants are collectively known as the Titans ('Straining Ones'), though this is a masculine term, so it is more proper to refer to the females as Titanides or Titanesses. Some play crucial roles in Greek mythology; others are little more than a name in the genealogy of the gods. For the purposes of this book, there is no need to remember the titles or functions of the Titans, as the relevant ones will be reintroduced in due course. The recurring summoned being Titan of the *Final Fantasy* series derives his own name from this race, but his roots are separately explored in chapter X.

Satisfied with the greatness of their initial brood but yearning to further populate the world, Gaia and Uranus produce two more sets of triplets. The first of these are the Cyclopes ('Orb-Eyed'), who are rebellious one-eyed giants[9]. They are followed by the Hecatoncheires ('Hundred-Handed Ones'), terrible and immeasurably robust brutes, each with fifty heads and a hundred arms[10].

Gaia loves her children, as is her maternal nature, but Uranus is disgusted by the Cyclopes and the Hecatoncheires. Against Gaia's will, he drives them all deep into the earth, burying them in her womb and causing her tremendous agony. What affection she has for Uranus turns to hatred, and she begins to devise her revenge.

Gaia visits Mount Othrys and carves a great sickle from the rock. The heavens, she knows, are immortal but not invulnerable. One by one, Gaia asks each of the Titans to assist her in deposing Uranus, but they all reject her plea –

all except Kronos (alternatively Romanised as Cronus), her youngest and strongest son, for he loathes his father[11].

At the instruction of Gaia, Kronos takes the sickle and conceals himself in a cleft on Mount Othrys. Uranus descends that evening and prepares to force himself upon his consort, but Kronos leaps from his hiding place, still wielding the enormous blade. With an almighty swing of the sickle, he severs Uranus' genitals from his body and hurls the mutilated package out over the sea.

Blood pours from Father Sky's groin, and where it pools on the soil, new life emerges. Among these chthonic beings are the Erinyes (Furies), whose vengeance will come to be feared by all, and the Gigantes (Giants), a race that is powerful and aggressive. The tale of the Gigantes' eventual conflict with the gods, the Gigantomachy, is featured in chapter X.

With his father incapacitated, Kronos again raises the sickle and slices open Gaia's side to release the Cyclopes and Hecatoncheires. Immediately upon their liberation from subterranean confinement, however, the young Titan exiles them to Tartarus, the dark caverns as far below the earth as the earth is below the heavens[12].

Hesiod contends in the *Theogony* that Uranus then retreats to the sky, never to lie with Gaia again. Other versions of the myth claim that Kronos imprisons him deep within Tartarus. Either way, Kronos – later known to the

Romans as Saturn – assumes absolute sovereignty over the cosmos.

Watching as his brothers and sisters pair off to nurture the various branches of the Titans' family tree, Kronos chooses Rhea (youngest of the Titanesses) as his partner. Uranus curses the usurper, foretelling that Kronos will be dethroned by one of his children, just as Father Sky himself has been. When Rhea gives birth to their first baby, a girl called Hestia, the new king of the Titans swallows the infant whole in defiance of such a fate.

Each year thereafter, Kronos consumes the children that Rhea bears him: Demeter, Hera, Hades, and Poseidon. Rhea is anguished by this and, when she falls pregnant for a sixth time, she seeks counsel from Gaia, her mother.

Heeding the advice she receives, Rhea tricks Kronos by wrapping a large stone in swaddling blankets and giving that to him instead of her newborn son, Zeus. Kronos gulps down the rock without a second thought, oblivious that Rhea has smuggled the baby to the island of Crete.

Zeus grows to manhood in secret. When he is old enough, he returns to Mount Othrys, home of the Titans. Some say Zeus slashes Kronos' stomach open to free his siblings; many more say he gives his father an emetic, causing him to vomit up the stone and his other five children[13].

Now backed by his brothers, Hades and Poseidon, and his sisters, Hestia, Demeter, and Hera, Zeus declares war on

Kronos and any individual intent on preventing him from seizing control of the cosmos. The ten-year conflict that ensues is known as the Titanomachy and will be discussed in coming chapters.

The mythos of *Final Fantasy VII* does not itself boast a story of creation, but the entity analogous to Mother Earth is an important character in the saga. Throughout the *Compilation*, the world is most commonly referred to as 'the Planet'[14]. The term is regularly used in the general sense, but there are also several occasions when the Planet is alluded to as a sentient being, often with a degree of agency.

Examples of this include the phenomenon of hearing the cries of the Planet (as demonstrated by Bugenhagen when the player first visits Cosmo Canyon), the Cetra communicating with or being summoned by the Planet (as described by Ifalna in her video testimonial at Icicle Inn), or the subplot in *Final Fantasy VII Remake* where the Whispers act to maintain the Planet's desired future (see chapter XXI). Furthermore, *Remake* employs 'it' and 'her' as interchangeable pronouns for the Planet, with the latter spoken by Sephiroth and quoted from the Cetran scriptures.

The religious belief in or academic field that researches Gaia's cognisance is presented in the *Compilation* through the Study of Planetary Life, called 'planetology' in *Remake*. Avalanche as an organisation was founded on these principles, with the player being introduced to them early in the story of *Final Fantasy VII* via dialogue with Barret, then more extensively through Bugenhagen's exhibition.

Avalanche in general promotes environmentalism, but the militant actions of some regional splinter cells (such as Barret's) could be defined as eco-terrorism[15]. In the real world, public concern over environmental issues became heightened during the 1970s, resulting in popular theories such as the Gaia Hypothesis[16], which adopted the name of Mother Earth from classical mythology. It is likely that Hironobu Sakaguchi borrowed the term for his 2001 movie *Final Fantasy: The Spirits Within*, where Earth's 'Gaia' is a spiritual force that represents its ecosystem[17].

Prior to the dual worlds of Gaia and Terra in *Final Fantasy IX* (2000), however, the only game in the series to feature a name for its setting was *Final Fantasy IV* (1991), which simply called it Earth. In 2004, as part of Square Enix's promotional campaign for *Advent Children*, an official pamphlet was released that identified *Final Fantasy VII's* planet as "the world of Gaia"[18].

The canonicity of this is yet to be confirmed, but it is important to note that the name does not appear in isolation. Gaea's Cliff is a location in the original title, where 'Gaea', as mentioned before, is an alternative Romanisation of 'Gaia' from ancient Greek, specifically relating to the personified Mother Earth.

The only other instances of the name in the *Compilation* can be found in *Crisis Core*. One is 'Gaia's Wrath', which is a non-elemental magic attack used by two opponents; the other is the Gaea Malboro, presumably a monster variant based on the malboros that can be fought on Gaea's Cliff in *Final Fantasy VII*[19].

It is not the frozen precipices themselves that add weight to the canonicity of 'Gaia', however, but rather the site's broader context in the Planet's history. While the *Compilation* is without its own creation myth, details of antiquity can be obtained if the player knows where to look. The ruins of the Forgotten Capital or the wall murals in the Temple of the Ancients are just two examples from the original game. A third, significantly more elaborate, illustration might be the footage of Professor Gast's interviews with Ifalna.

2,000 years before the events of *Final Fantasy VII*, a meteorite struck Gaia in an area called the Knowlespole. The wound caused to the Planet was so severe that it was unable to properly heal itself, so it called on the Cetra for help.

Thousands of Cetra gathered at the Knowlespole and were eventually approached by an extraterrestrial entity as it emerged from the Northern Crater (the impact site). Using its mimicry abilities, the being took the form of loved ones, some of whom were dead family members, to weave illusions from its victims' past. It befriended the Cetra at first, deceiving them, and then infected them with a virus which turned them into monsters[20].

Gaia perceived this 'Calamity from the Skies' to be a tremendous threat to the natural balance of life. As long as the alien continued to contaminate its surroundings, the

Planet could never fully recover. Efforts were undertaken to destroy the fiend, but these were in vain, for it was discovered to be immortal.

As the conflict wore on and the Cetran populace diminished, Gaia produced several biomechanical goliaths deep within the earth to defend herself. Before they were released upon the world, however, a small number of surviving Cetra defeated and imprisoned the Calamity inside the Northern Crater, whose circumference is Gaea's Cliff.

Although the specifics of both tales are different, parallels can certainly be drawn between the ancient Greek succession myth (as recorded by Hesiod) and *Final Fantasy VII's* history regarding the arrival of the Calamity from the Skies. Chapter III establishes that the extraterrestrial in question is better known as Jenova, the name later given to it by scientists of the Shinra Corporation. In the Japanese version of *Final Fantasy VII*, Ifalna reveals that the Cetran epithet for the lifeform was '*sora kara kita yakusai*'. This can be translated as 'Crisis from the Sky', 'Heaven's Dark Harbinger', or 'Calamity from the Skies'. All three names appear in official Western translations of the *Compilation*, though the latter is the most common pseudonym for Jenova. In *Remake*, however, Red XIII refers to Jenova as 'the cataclysm that came from the stars'.

The importance of this is that Uranus in classical lore literally translates as 'Sky', with '*ouranos*' remaining the word for 'sky' in the modern Greek language. That said, he embodies much more than simply the firmament above the world: Uranus is the personification of the heavens, the atmosphere, the starry expanse, and the celestial bodies therein.

In Hesiod's *Theogony*, Gaia is the mother and consort of Uranus; while there may be a distinction between their cosmological generations, they are both categorised as primordial beings. Their relationship is initially one of love and productivity, with Uranus covering every inch of Gaia in a passionate embrace each day. It is only when the Cyclopes and Hecatoncheires are forced back into Gaia's womb that the dynamic shifts, spawning a hatred in Mother Earth towards Uranus for his cruelty.

Similar comparisons can be seen between the Planet and Jenova in *Final Fantasy VII*. Although the alien is a highly evolved organism capable of enduring interstellar travel, its age is indeterminate. Gaia, of course, is a planetary mass. It is therefore likely that Gaia and Jenova are two of the oldest entities presented in the *Compilation*.

The Planet and the Calamity do not share any direct affection, but this element could be reflected in how Jenova first befriends the Cetra, the stewards of Gaia. It is through shapeshifting and the ability to conjure illusions of loved ones that Jenova is said to deceive and win the trust of the tribes at the Knowlespole, just as Uranus is described in some sources as having the capacity to change his form as easily as the clouds.

According to *Final Fantasy VII's Ultimania* guidebooks, Jenova is an extremely intelligent but instinctual lifeform, riding the meteorite from deep space. As such, it cannot be held accountable for causing the primary wound to the Planet's surface in the same way that Uranus is responsible for Gaia's agony when he thrusts the Cyclopes and Hecatoncheires back into the earth. In the *Theogony*, however, Uranus is described as the first to commit evil deeds and act in shameful ways. Similarly, it could be argued that Jenova is the first being – from a plot perspective, at least – to harm the Planet and be perceived as a threat.

Like Gaia of Greek mythology, the Planet thereafter seeks the aid of her children – a term occasionally used in a metaphorical sense during the *Compilation* in reference to the world's inhabitants – in order to end the tyranny of the Calamity from the Skies. However, neither Kronos nor the surviving Cetra are able to kill their immortal adversaries, instead sealing them in a geological prison: the Titan buries Uranus in the darkness of Tartarus (some claim), while the Cetra confine Jenova to a cliff at the Northern Crater. The latter may also be a vague allusion to the cleft on Mount Othrys where Kronos hid before castrating his father.

What makes the connection even more intriguing is that the vast caverns below the meteorite's impact site, later called the Northern Cave, descend into the depths of the Planet and are the final dungeon of *Final Fantasy VII*. As will be discussed in more detail in chapter XVIII, comparisons can additionally be made between the

Northern Cave and Tartarus, the realm far beneath Gaia in Hellenic cosmology.

During the player's navigation of these caverns, they will probably encounter an ahriman (mistranslated as 'allemagne') or malboro, both of which are recurring enemies in the *Final Fantasy* series. Ahrimans are best identified as having a single eye like the Cyclopes, while malboros have countless tentacles and eyeballs, which may be an allusion in this context to the hundred hands and fifty heads of the Hecantoncheires. As it happens, Kronos also trapped his grotesque siblings in Tartarus once he had defeated Uranus.

Another peculiar similarity that exists as part of the Planet's history is the creation of Weapon. Ifalna's testimonial is unambiguous that these biomechanical colossi were never released and remain in slumber somewhere within Gaia. In fact, they only erupt from the Northern Crater during *Final Fantasy VII* when Cloud gifts Sephiroth the Black Materia[21].

In the original Japanese version of the game, there were just three Weapons: Sapphire, Diamond, and Ultima (localised in English as 'Ultimate'). The international edition, however, also included Emerald and Ruby Weapon – not to mention a spectacular cutscene of their emergence –, which were missing from the Japanese launch due to development time constraints.

The significance of the finalised sequence is the sudden release of five immensely powerful beings from the belly of the crater, which could be analogous to how Zeus freed his five siblings from Kronos' stomach. The younger gods' liberation, of course, occurred on Mount Othrys, the same location where Uranus came to lie with Gaia and where he was castrated, which, as has been speculated, already reflects the impact site of Jenova's meteor.

It should also be highlighted that in the majority of the myth's variations, Kronos vomits up Hestia, Demeter, Hera, Poseidon, and Hades after Zeus has given him an emetic, just as the Sapphire, Diamond, Emerald, Ruby, and Ultima Weapon are activated when Cloud gives Sephiroth the Black Materia. Intriguingly, one might interpret Cloud Strife's name to mean 'storm cloud', thus loosely associating him with Zeus, the God of Thunder and Lightning.

Most links between Gaia or Uranus and the Planet or Jenova relate to the early history in *Final Fantasy VII's* narrative. There are also a few more abstract comparisons, though, that can be found in the story's recent past or present.

After excavating the body of the Calamity approximately 30 years prior to the game's opening, scientists from the Shinra Corporation misidentify it as a Cetran female. The Jenova Project is thereafter initiated to use the entity's genetic material as a means to artificially produce humans with abilities equal to the Cetra. As the years progress,

Jenova's cells are utilised in a multitude of immoral experiments involving all types of people and creatures.

Of the children born from the project, Sephiroth is the greatest success. He becomes the prototype for Shinra's elite army, SOLDIER, and is eventually hailed as a war hero. However, when he learns the truth of his origins, Sephiroth loses his mind. He burns down the town of Nibelheim and breaks into the top-secret chamber at the local reactor, where the Jenova specimen is being preserved. Having claimed the head of his 'mother', the silver-haired villain is thrown into the facility's mako rivers by Cloud.

Sephiroth's body is carried by the Lifestream to the Northern Crater, where it begins to regenerate amid the abundance of spirit energy. Five years later, while Cloud and the others are at Shinra Headquarters in Midgar, Sephiroth triggers the Reunion drive[22], causing the Jenova specimen to burst from its containment and begin its journey to the crater.

Throughout the *Compilation of Final Fantasy VII*, Jenova is typically referenced using the pronouns 'she' and 'her'. There are two principal reasons for this: Jenova was discovered in the form of a mummified Cetran female, an appearance the extraterrestrial retained until its escape from Shinra HQ; and Sephiroth's research at Shinra Manor confirmed he was an infant born of the Jenova Project, having been told in his youth that his mother's name was Jenova. Despite gaining knowledge of the entity's true nature from the Lifestream, Sephiroth and his Remnants,

Kadaj, Loz, and Yazoo, continue to speak of Jenova as 'Mother' in *Advent Children*[23].

However, the alien's gender – or whether it even has a gender – is never fully verified. When discussing the Calamity in her video testimonials with Professor Gast, Ifalna repeatedly uses the gender-neutral term 'it' in the Western localisations for *Final Fantasy VII's* PC release, which most accurately replicates the original Japanese script. By extension, Jenova cannot be defined as female, thus reducing any conflicting evidence regarding the comparison with the Sky Father, Uranus.

Hesiod's version of the creation myth clearly distinguishes Uranus' paternal role in the births of many ancient figures and races. He mates with Gaia to produce the Titans, Cyclopes, and Hecatoncheires. When Uranus is castrated, however, the blood that gushes from his wound also gives life to distinct beings, including the Erinyes and Gigantes.

A common attribute of many hideous monsters encountered across the *Compilation of Final Fantasy VII* is that their mutations are caused by an injection of Jenova cells. Examples of this from the original game include Sample: HO512, Lost Number, and Heretic Hojo (mistranslated as 'Helletic Hojo')[24], whose transformation is shown in real time. As such, just as Uranus' blood brings forth new lifeforms, so do Jenova's cells, with the Erinyes and Gigantes in particular sharing the hostile and merciless features of the fiends in *Final Fantasy VII*.

Another point of interest is the method by which Sephiroth assumes authority over his 'mother'. While it was debated among fans for several years who – Sephiroth or Jenova – was in command of the other's actions, developer comments in the *Final Fantasy VII Ultimania Omega* (2005) verify that Sephiroth is the one in control.

When he is tossed into the mako rivers by Cloud at the Mount Nibel reactor, Sephiroth's consciousness does not diffuse into the Lifestream as it should. He instead absorbs an immense amount of knowledge, strengthening his will. This occurs after he has beheaded the Jenova specimen.

It could be argued that Sephiroth's authority is established upon the removal of his mother's head, just as Kronos' authority is established upon the castration of his father. The parallel further deepens when certain details are included: For instance, Kronos slices Uranus' genitals off using a giant sickle, while Sephiroth decapitates Jenova with his enormous katana, the Masamune.

A last curious similarity between Gaia of Greek mythology and the Planet in *Final Fantasy VII* is their respective characterisations. Mother Earth is typically depicted as warm and nurturing – a maternal figure profoundly connected to all. This is true of Gaia and how she cherishes her children, such as the Titans, Cyclopes, and Hecatoncheires, or how her body is home to terrestrial life. *Final Fantasy VII's* Planet, meanwhile, governs the Lifestream and distribution of spirit energy, and her loving grace and providence is described in the scriptures of the

Cetra – the Ancients who were born of her and who shaped her flesh.

There is another side to Mother Earth, however: a temperamental side. She has fire at her core and can be vengeful or reactionary when she chooses, especially to prevent harm befalling her offspring. In classical lore, for example, Gaia orchestrates the castration of Uranus as retribution for burying the Cyclopes and Hecatoncheires inside her; she gives birth to the monstrous Typhon in a bid to eradicate Zeus and the Olympians when they overthrow the Titans (see chapter XI); and she sends a gargantuan scorpion to slay the hunter Orion when he boasts that he can kill any living thing (see chapter XIX).

This is reflected in *Final Fantasy VII*, too, albeit the Planet's actions seem to be more akin to self-preservation. For instance, she unleashes the Weapons as a defensive measure when she is in imminent danger, and they consequently target the human cities of Junon and Midgar. While less obvious, Sephiroth also learns from the books in the basement library of Shinra Manor that the Planet sacrificed the Cetra during her attempts to heal the wound caused by Jenova's meteorite, presumably to reinforce the Lifestream.

It is clear in the myths that Gaia represents an older, more permanent order of immortals whose will cannot be challenged, even by Zeus. Conversely, *Final Fantasy VII* initially portrays the Planet as a weakened and dying character, although she has considerably greater influence in the saga overall. Gaia is a force to be revered, capable of determining and imposing her own destiny, as seen in *Remake*.

The relationship between the Planet and Jenova plays a significant part in the *Compilation*, and Sephiroth's role in that dynamic has already become a major plot point in the *Final Fantasy VII* remake project. While Gaia withdraws as a primary figure in ancient Greek mythology once the Olympian pantheon has been established, her presence is unquestionably felt in subsequent tales: Her contribution to the creation of humanity, her gift of prophecy, and her support of the Giants will all be addressed in later chapters.

1. Orphism was a Hellenic belief system based on doctrine credited to the legendary poet-hero Orpheus (see chapter VIII).
2. Despite their similar names and the common amalgamation of their features (popularised during the Renaissance), Chronos the God of Time and Kronos the Titan are typically considered by scholars to be two separate entities. The former lends his name to other popular titles developed by Square, *Chrono Trigger* (1995) and *Chrono Cross* (1999).
3. The *Iliad* is an epic poem attributed to Homer, set during the Trojan War.
4. Hesiod's *Theogony* is a poem, thought to have been composed in the 8th century BC, which details the origin of the world and the genealogy of the gods and other immortals.
5. Aether (or Ether) was considered by ancient and medieval science to be the fifth element, the matter that filled the universe beyond Earth's atmosphere. In the *Final Fantasy* series, it is generally a substance with

mystical properties, used for replenishing a character's Magic Points (MP). The Aether of *Final Fantasy XIV* and *Final Fantasy XVI*, however, plays a large role in the world of Eorzea and realm of Valisthea, respectively, being a source of both magic and vitality.

6. Eros was redefined in later myths as a son of Aphrodite, Goddess of Love and Beauty.

7. This is known as parthenogenesis and naturally occurs in many plant and animal species.

8. The male Titans were Oceanus (the world river), Coeus (who represented inquisitiveness and intelligence), Hyperion (father of the Sun, Moon, and the dawn), Iapetus (whose son Prometheus shaped mankind), Crius (a relatively unattested figure), and Kronos (the youngest and most ambitious of them all). The Titanides, meanwhile, were Theia (representing sight and shining objects), Themis (Goddess of Law, Justice, and Custom), Mnemosyne (Goddess of Memory and mother of the Muses), Phoebe (who had the gift of prophecy), Tethys (mother of the river gods and 3,000 water nymphs), and Rhea (youngest of the six and associated with the earth).

9. The Cyclopes' names were Brontes (Thunder), Steropes (Lightning), and Arges (Brightness).

10. The Hecatoncheires' names were Cottus (Furious), Briareus (Vigorous), and Gyges (Long-Limbed).

11. Most of the names that appear in this chapter – and the book in general – are their Latin spellings. Kronos, however, is the Romanised version of the ancient Greek variant. 'Kronos' is more regularly found in popular media than 'Cronus', hence its inclusion here.

12. The distance between Gaia and Tartarus is said to be so great that it would take a falling anvil nine days and nights to cross it.

13. An emetic is a substance that causes an individual to vomit involuntarily. What becomes of the large stone will be discussed in chapter XXI.

14. It should be noted that Western localisations of all *Compilation* entries do not capitalise 'planet', with the lone exception of the original *Final Fantasy VII*, which is

the title that most often personifies Gaia. For the purposes of identifying the Planet as both a location and a character, the same capitalisation has been utilised in this book.

15. While it is not made clear in localised scripts of *Final Fantasy VII*, Avalanche was not established by Barret, but rather the organisation originated at Cosmo Canyon. This is further explored in *Before Crisis*. At least three separate factions of Avalanche are involved in *Final Fantasy VII Remake*, with in-game content explaining that there are regional cells. Prior to the events of *Remake*, Barret's group is excommunicated by Avalanche HQ for their relative extremism. Members of Avalanche HQ's Midgar branch feature in *Episode INTERmission*.

16. Conceived by James Lovelock, the Gaia Hypothesis is a scientific theory that proposes Earth is a superorganism which has a synergistic relationship with its inhabitants to maintain its complex ecosystem.

17. As an additional nod to Greek mythology in *The Spirits Within*, Earth's Gaia is fired upon and damaged by the Zeus Cannon, a space-borne weapon attached to an Olympic-class Assault Space Station. Zeus, the chief of the Olympians who hurls thunderbolts at the earth, is one of the figures in classical lore that Gaia most opposes.

18. Square Enix representatives distributed the pamphlets at the Electronic Entertainment Expo (E3) in 2004. This has since been corroborated multiple times across multiple official mediums, most recently with the Platinum trophy for the PlayStation 4 port of *Final Fantasy VII*, which is titled 'Gaia's Guardian'. However, the name Gaia does not appear in *Final Fantasy VII Remake* nor its extended media.

19. *Crisis Core* does indeed include both spellings of the name.

20. Kazushige Nojima's novel *The Kids Are Alright* contradicts the original script, whereby Professor Hojo's understanding of the virus was that it made the Cetra become paranoid and turn against each other. However,

85

it is explicit in the *Crisis Core Complete Guide* that Jenova's virus literally caused the Cetra to mutate.

21. The post-game content of *Before Crisis* introduced the Jade Weapon, whose release is triggered by the summoning of Zirconiade in the months preceding *Final Fantasy VII*. Meanwhile, *Dirge of Cerberus'* plot involves the Omega Weapon, the Lifestream's failsafe mechanism.

22. The Reunion drive is the instinctive desire of all Jenova cells to reunify as a single entity. This primarily affects weak-minded individuals who have been exposed to such cells.

23. Jenova's name is suspected to be a conflation of 'Jehovah' (a form of the Hebrew name of the God of Israel used in some versions of the Bible, alternatively Latinised as 'Yahweh') and the Latin word for 'new', '*novus*'. '*Nova*' is the feminine nominative singular of '*novus*', which reflects Professor Gast identifying Jenova as a female when he named the faux-Cetra. It has been theorised that 'Jenova' could be interpreted to mean 'New God'.

24. These monsters' respective exposure to Jenova cells was later confirmed in the companion *Ultimanias*.

CHAPTER V

ANCIENT WATERS

A common feature in the stories of ancient Greek gods and heroes is water. More accurately: the importance of seas, rivers, and springs. For example, the Homeric creation myth (not to be confused with Hesiod's *Theogony*) proposes that all life originated from Oceanus and Tethys; one of the most prominent Hellenic deities is Poseidon, Lord of the Seas; navigation of the underworld is often described in terms of crossing rivers such as the Styx; and the epic of Jason and his ship, *Argo*, recounts his voyage to capture the Golden Fleece; while Homer's *Iliad* and *Odyssey*, respectively, detail how the Greeks sailed to Troy, and Odysseus later sailed home.

It is unsurprising that classical lore is so heavily inspired by water. Greece – or the Hellenic Republic, as it is officially known – boasts more than 200 islands, distributed throughout the Aegean and Ionian Seas in the easternmost realm of the Mediterranean. Many of the larger islands, such as Crete and Rhodes, historically enjoyed their own sovereignty, independent of the kingdoms and city states on the mainland, and myriad tales of conflict or travel between them exist.

The theme of water features in the *Compilation of Final Fantasy VII* through Aerith and the Cetra. As in Greek mythology, it relates to both the physical and spiritual world, with allusions to its wider role in the story often occurring in unexpected ways. The connection between the Cetra and water is not hidden, nor is it explicit or obvious.

As mentioned in the previous chapter, Hesiod's *Theogony* lists Pontus, a son of Gaia, as the primordial sea god. Other sources provide a female counterpart for Pontus[1], Thalassa, who is said to have spawned all the species of fish. Neither of these entities play a noteworthy role in any creation myth, but they do appear in ancient Greek art and later Roman mosaics. Of particular interest is that both Pontus and Thalassa have been depicted with red crab claws for horns, and are regularly accompanied by sea serpents.

According to the *Theogony*, nature starts to get a bit more fascinating after the births of the Titan siblings Oceanus and Tethys. Oceanus is the great river that encircles the world (which was perceived to be flat by many Hellenes). He is responsible for currents and is the source of all fresh and salt water. His influence permeates every spring, every river, every wave; life simply could not prosper without Oceanus.

The significance of this was not lost on the people of antiquity. In the *Iliad*, Homer indicates that Oceanus and Tethys are the primordial father and mother[2], rather than Uranus and Gaia. Hesiod, meanwhile, makes them the parents of all rivers and the deities that control them, as well as the 3,000 Oceanides (sing. Oceanid), who are divine female beings that serve a wide variety of functions[3].

Both Homer and Hesiod are clear in their descriptions of Oceanus: He is a flowing river, located at the edge of the world. In the *Theogony*, it is Tartarus (the cavernous depths beneath the earth) that lies beyond Oceanus; in the *Odyssey*, it is the ashen shores that lead to Hades, the underworld. The *Iliad*, on the other hand, notes that the Elysian fields (also called Elysium) can be found to the west[4].

Like Pontus and Thalassa, Oceanus and Tethys are also portrayed in ancient art and pottery. It is typical that Oceanus is represented with bull horns or the actual head of a bull, an animal that is also closely associated with Poseidon. In some Roman mosaics, however, Oceanus is shown with a serpent's tail on his lower body and red crab claws for horns, which instead compares to Pontus and Thalassa.

During Hesiod's story of creation, Oceanus refuses to take part in the Titanomachy, a ten-year conflict that arises after Zeus liberates his brothers and sisters from Kronos' stomach and declares war on the Titans. The purpose of the war is to determine which generation of gods can claim rule of the cosmos: Kronos and the Titans, or Zeus and the Olympians, named so because they establish their home on Mount Olympus, the tallest mountain in Greece. The Titanomachy is violent and terrible, with seismic disturbances so destructive that the whole world is reshaped.

In the end, thanks to the help of the Cyclopes, Hecatoncheires, Gigantes, and even Titans such as Prometheus (Forethought), the Olympians are victorious. Zeus declares himself the chief of the pantheon, and in time he brings order to the universe. Reigning with authority over his family and all immortals, he makes sacred laws, enforces oaths, judges quarrels, and takes whatever and whomever he wants.

The Cloud Gatherer's first act is to punish those who opposed him, but no sentence is passed against Oceanus. Some scholars have theorised that Zeus knows better than to make an enemy of lifegiving water, while others have pointed to Hesiod's writings, where Oceanus sends his daughter Styx (an important river that flows into the underworld) and her children[5], including Nike (Victory) and Kratos (Strength)[6], to fight for the Olympians.

This is not to suggest, however, that Zeus allows Oceanus to retain sovereignty of the seas and rivers. After the Titanomachy, Zeus and his brothers, Hades and Poseidon, draw lots to determine which domain each of the three will govern. Zeus becomes Lord of the Heavens, Hades becomes Lord of the Underworld, and Poseidon becomes Lord of the Seas. It is decided that the earth and its inhabitants will fall under common rule.

Known as Neptune to the Romans, Poseidon has the power to tame the wildest waters or churn up great typhoons. He can be restless and cruel at times, demanding and ambitious, but he is not characteristically hateful. The Hellenes worshipped Poseidon at temples throughout Greece, believing him to be responsible for earthquakes – hence his moniker of 'Earth-Shaker' – and the merciless tidal waves that often accompanied them. These could be particularly devastating to the coastal regions and islands.

Poseidon was generally envisioned to be a muscular, bearded figure, wielding a three-pronged trident, and riding through the sea in a chariot pulled by horses or hippocampi (sing. hippocampus, mythical creatures that are part-equine, part-aquatic). His strong association with horses and bulls was derived from pre-Hellenic cultures[7], with a prime example perhaps being the Minoan veneration of the latter, eventually inspiring the tale of the Cretan Bull and the birth of the Minotaur (see chapter XV)[8].

Although Poseidon is often found on Mount Olympus or in water sources across ancient Greece, his golden palace is at the bottom of the Aegean Sea, described as a beautiful abode crafted from coral and pearls. In Plato's writings[9], however, Poseidon's domain is the allegorical island of Atlantis, located somewhere in the Atlantic Ocean.

Like his brother Zeus, the Lord of the Seas fathers many important children. His wife is Amphitrite, a sea nymph and either a daughter or granddaughter of Oceanus and Tethys (depending on the source), who bears Poseidon a son: Triton. Triton is the messenger god of the seas and is generally depicted as a merman (with a fishtail rather than legs), bearing a conch shell that he blows like a trumpet.

Poseidon does not always remain faithful to his wife, though. By various nymphs and mortals, he is father to heroic figures and beasts such as Theseus, Bellerophon, and Pegasus, all of whom feature in later chapters[10].

Given his command of oceans and rivers, it is unsurprising that Poseidon also participates in Greek mythology's version of the Great Flood[11]. According to the *Bibliotheca*[12], Zeus determines that humanity has become wretched and has abandoned *xenia*, the sacred principals of hospitality[13]. With the help of Poseidon, he drowns the world, and the only survivors are Deucalion and Pyrrha, who had hidden in a giant chest. When the flood recedes, Deucalion and Pyrrha follow an oracle's instruction to throw rocks over their shoulders, which Gaia then transforms into a new race of humans.

It is unclear what connection, if any, the Great Flood has to the tragedy of Atlantis, itself a pseudo-myth created as a metaphor for the hubris of nations. Plato describes Atlantis in his works *Timaeus* and *Critias* as being an island that was as large as a continent, rich in natural resources, with a strong naval force. Mountains were said to trace the shoreline and encompass a vast plain that was oblong in shape. Around Atlantis' city were moats and ringed walls, with canals and tunnels carved through the cliffs to serve as passages for its boats.

Poseidon held dominion over the island, and his son Atlas became its king[14]. Following a terrible earthquake and flood, Atlantis sank into the ocean in a single night, having lost favour with the gods. The existence of the isle and its treasures has since been the subject of much debate among scholars, inspiring an immense range of literature and art over the centuries.

The *Compilation of Final Fantasy VII* is not without its own lost civilisations, and there are far more parallels with the water-based myths than one might presume. As detailed in chapter IV, at the time of Jenova's arrival on the Planet 2,000 years before the events of the main saga, the world was primarily populated by a race of nomadic magic users called the Cetra[15].

The player is briefly introduced to their history in *Final Fantasy VII* through Sephiroth, who reviews countless tomes in the basement library at Shinra Manor during Cloud's recollection of the Nibelheim tragedy. Sephiroth explains that the Cetra's purpose was to migrate across Gaia, nurturing the earth. When their harsh journeys were eventually complete, they would find peace and happiness in their Promised Land; for the Cetra, this meant their spirit energy would return to the Planet and join the Lifestream.

However, when disaster struck Gaia 2,000 years ago, the Cetran tribes were brought to the brink of extinction by Jenova. The ancestors of modern humans survived because they hid and ignored the pleas of the Planet. All that remains of the Cetran civilisations in the original *Final Fantasy VII* are two unique locations: the Temple of the Ancients and the Forgotten City.

The latter, also known as the Forgotten Capital, is the abandoned ruins of a millennia-old municipality. It lies within a deep valley, bound on all sides by rugged mountains. The city itself encircles a colossal tower of bleached and petrified coral branches, while its environment contains the remnants of what might once have been a vibrant reef. The *Ultimania Omega* additionally states that its foundations originally lay beneath the sea. As if to exemplify this, the area is named the Coral Valley[16].

In fact, the entirety of the Forgotten City and its surrounding region is crammed with water references and motifs. The crumbling buildings of the former capital are shaped like conch shells; some of their interiors are decorated with seashells and starfish; a sacred spring resides by the library where the entrance to the underwater palace is found[17]; the staircase to this secret palace is typically blocked by a clownfish nestled in the tentacles of an anemone[18]; and the Key to the Ancients – used by Bugenhagen to activate an archaic waterfall projector[19] –

requires a submarine to acquire it from the bottom of the ocean. The importance of it all is that it establishes a strong connection between water and the ancient Cetran civilisation who lived here. With this identified, specific allusions to Greek mythology can be proposed.

There are two monster types fought in the Coral Valley area that are worthy of mention: malldancer and acrophies. Malldancers are relatively basic in that their battle design resembles a golden seahorse. As it happens, when the player first emerges from the Sleeping Forest into the Coral Valley, every random encounter the party faces will include at least two malldancers. In the broader context of the region, this may be a vague reference to the hippocampi that pull Poseidon's chariot.

The same field location (at the northern entrance to the Sleeping Forest) also has a treasure chest containing a Water Ring accessory, which any character can equip to absorb Water-elemental damage in battle. This counterbalances the increase in Water-elemental attacks by local opponents, such as the powerful 'Aqualung' magic cast by the area's boss, Jenova LIFE.

Meanwhile, the acrophies are somewhat more peculiar by design. They are creatures whose left half is a giant red crab and whose right half is a fanged snake, with the two joined by a body of coral. This is intriguing because the crab claws and serpent were traditionally symbolic of Oceanus, Pontus, and Thalassa when the primordial sea deities were presented on mosaics[20]. To reinforce the link, an acrophies' strongest attack is 'Huge Tidal Wave', and a Water Ring can be stolen from it in battle.

As is highlighted earlier in the chapter, both Oceanus and Poseidon are also closely associated with bulls or bull imagery. While there are no bovine monsters to be fought around the Coral Valley in *Final Fantasy VII*, it may not be a coincidence that the adjacent Sleeping Forest – an area through which the player must pass to initially reach the valley – is where the Kujata Materia is obtained.

Kujata – mistranslated as 'Kjata' in the initial English localisation of *Final Fantasy VII* – is a summoned creature based on the gargantuan bull of early Islamic cosmology. According to its creation story, Kujata stands in the cosmic sea on the back of a fish too large to comprehend. He breathes twice per day, and because his nose is below the water, this causes the ebb and flow of Earth's tides, which also happens to be the responsibility of Oceanus in classical mythology. The summoning of Kujata in *Final Fantasy VII* triggers a magical attack called 'Tetra-Disaster', the last part of which has the bull sending shockwaves through the land. This, in turn, reflects Poseidon's epithet of 'Earth-Shaker'.

In isolation, these comparisons may seem relatively abstract, but similar allusions can additionally be found at the Temple of the Ancients. Rather than include all of them here, however, chapter XV is dedicated to exploring the parallels between the temple and the Labyrinth that features in the legend of the hero Theseus and the Minotaur, whose births both also involve Poseidon.

Several weapons can be acquired for various player characters within the Temple of the Ancients. It could be speculated that Cloud's Nail Bat and Aerith's Princess Guard relate to the tale of the Labyrinth (as explained in chapter XV), but the inspiration behind the respective weapons for Cid and Cait Sith is perhaps less ambiguous.

Cid Highwind is the closest protagonist *Final Fantasy VII's* system has to a dragoon, and he typically uses spears in battle. Almost immediately upon entering the temple's interior, the player can pick up the Trident for Cid[21], and its three-pronged head matches the description of Poseidon's iconic polearm.

Meanwhile, Cait Sith's weapon of choice in *Final Fantasy VII* is a megaphone, through which he shouts commands to the giant animatronic moogle he rides around on. At the Temple of the Ancients, the player can find the Trumpet Shell for the robotic feline[22], with artwork contained in the *Ultimania Omega* verifying its design to be a conch shell. In the Greek myths, Triton uses a conch shell as a trumpet to herald the coming of his father or to deliver messages. It is unlikely, therefore, that the symbols of *both* Poseidon and Triton have been included at this location by fortuity.

If this assumption is true, it could be contended that Cid's association with the Trident is also not a coincidence. When the player first encounters Cid in Rocket Town, he is a world-famous pilot employed by the Shinra Corporation. During an attempt by President Rufus and Palmer to repossess his airplane, the *Tiny Bronco*, Cid, Cloud, and the other party members escape on the craft, although it is shot down and crash lands in the sea shortly after.

The *Tiny Bronco* then becomes a mode of transportation and can travel in shallow coastal waters or along rivers on the overworld map. In the game, its acquisition is necessary to progress the plot because it unlocks access to both the Temple of the Ancients and Bone Village, the gateway to the Coral Valley.

A bronco was historically a wild or half-tamed horse, with the word being popularised by cowboys in the United States[23]. Given that Poseidon in Greek mythology is overlord of the seas, rivers, and horses – which are believed to pull his chariot through the waves –, Cid's ownership of both the *Tiny Bronco* and the Trident creates a surprising connection[24].

Another curious addition to the Temple of the Ancients is the presence of the Bahamut Materia, dropped by the Red Dragon boss upon its defeat in the mural room. This chamber is of the utmost importance because it contains the puzzle device used to shrink the temple and transform it into the Black Materia. Along its walls are paintings depicting an older Cetran civilisation invoking the ultimate destructive magic, Meteor.

Bahamut has been a recurring draconic figure since the original *Final Fantasy* (1987) and is obtainable as a summoned being in every title between *Final Fantasy III* and *Final Fantasy VII*. As referenced in chapter II,

Bahamut's position as the Dragon King is borrowed from *Dungeons & Dragons* rather than genuine archaic sources. However, in early Islamic cosmology, Bahamut is the cosmic fish upon whom Kujata stands, further strengthening the correlation between the Cetra and water in quite an unexpected way[25].

It should also be noted that *Final Fantasy VII's* lead scenario writer, Kazushige Nojima, simultaneously worked as director on *Bahamut Lagoon* (1996), itself scripted by Motomu Toriyama. Toriyama-san was an event designer for *Final Fantasy VII* and was responsible for many of the scenes involving Cloud and Aerith, the two mandatory playable characters during the Temple of the Ancients section of the game. It is improbable that both Toriyama-san and Nojima-san were oblivious to the origins of Bahamut's name[26], nor is it likely that Kujata's debut in the *Final Fantasy* series occurred in *Final Fantasy VII* by chance, based on its mythological affiliation with Bahamut[27].

Prior to joining Square in 1995, Kazushige Nojima's last project for videogame developers Data East was to write and direct *Heracles no Eikō IV: Kamigami kara no Okurimono* (translated as *Glory of Heracles IV: Gift from the Gods*). Like its predecessors, the title incorporated a huge amount of ancient Greek stories and figures.

The main protagonist of the game is a boy who lived in the city of Atlantis thousands of years ago. Atlantis is shown during a flashback to be a nation that valued knowledge and wisdom above all else, striving to build a shining future for all. When the city is attacked, the souls of its citizens go into a deep sleep for millennia, surviving its ruin.

With the tale of Atlantis still fresh in Nojima-san's mind, it may also have been a source of inspiration for the Forgotten Capital in *Final Fantasy VII*. Where Atlantis is described by Plato as sinking into the sea in a single night, the Forgotten City is brimming with imagery of the seabed; and where Atlantis lies on an oblong plain surrounded by mountains and ringed with moats, the Forgotten City can be found in an elongated valley (best viewed from the overworld map), encircling a tower of coral, and boasting a range of water channels[28].

Both Atlantis and the Forgotten Capital are struck by catastrophe. Plato references violent earthquakes and floods, while it can be presumed that the desolation of the Cetran civilisation is attributed to Jenova and the meteorite[29]. By extension, the Temple of the Ancients meets a similar fate: Like Atlantis, it is situated on a large, mountainous island, and it disappears into a great cavity when Cait Sith solves the internal puzzles to shrink the structure.

There is also a comparison to be made between the demise of the Atlanteans and the Cetra. It is reported in Plato's *Critias* that all Atlanteans perished when their island was submerged. Conversely, the Cetra's war against Jenova did leave a small number of survivors. However, across the *Compilation of Final Fantasy VII*, Aerith is repeatedly

100

identified as the last of the Cetran race. Her death at the Water Altar and subsequent burial in the sacred spring represents the extinction of the Cetra, paralleling the extinction of the Atlanteans who sank into the sea.

In the mythos of *Final Fantasy VII*, though, the history of humans is quite the opposite. Sephiroth is very clear during his monologue at the Shinra Manor basement that humans endured and prospered because they hid from the disasters faced by the Planet. This may be a possible allusion to the Great Flood story, where Deucalion and Pyrrha are not drowned by Zeus' stormy deluge and Poseidon bursting the riverbanks because they conceal themselves in a wooden chest. After they emerge, the pair becomes responsible for repopulating the human race, although they do so via the divine power of Gaia rather than more traditional methods.

In terms of connections between water and the Cetra, those can be further refined by considering Aerith in isolation. Aerith lives at the Gainsborough residence – the history of which is provided in Kazushige Nojima's novel *Traces of Two Pasts* –, located in Midgar's Sector 5 Slums. The house is unique in *Final Fantasy VII* because it is the only place in the Slums where running water can be seen (except for the sewers).

This unique feature is elaborated on in *Final Fantasy VII Remake*, with the river that flows past the Gainsborough home expanding by the time it reaches the Underdeveloped Land beyond the town, where the children of the Leaf House orphanage like to play. In an interview with the Square Enix

North American team in 2020, *Remake's* co-director Motomu Toriyama stated that the river brings nutrients from the Lifestream to both the residence's garden and the Sector 5 church, allowing flowers to grow in abundance.

Toriyama-san's explanation for this is peculiar because it reflects Oceanus' role in mythology. Homer and Hesiod agree that Oceanus is the great river that borders the physical world and the afterlife, a trait similar to the ethereal existence of *Final Fantasy VII's* Lifestream[30]. Meanwhile, in his *Theogony*, Hesiod references how the currents produced by Oceanus and the actions of his countless daughters help life to prosper. A particular function of these Oceanides is that they keep watch over youths, which might extend to the Leaf House orphans in *Remake*.

One of the most prominent links between Aerith and water in the *Compilation of Final Fantasy VII* is her 'Great Gospel'. 'Great Gospel' is Aerith's final Limit Break in the original game[31], where her prayers are answered by a downpour of healing rain[32]. It also features in *Advent Children*, with the rain curing the citizens of Edge of their Geostigma afflictions.

In the latter example, however, a cleansing spring additionally bursts from beneath the Sector 5 church during Cloud and Kadaj's fight there, when Kadaj misses his target and blasts the ground with magic. It is in the pool created by the spring that Cloud eventually wakes after his battle with Sephiroth, having teetered on the brink of passing into the Lifestream himself.

The importance of this detail is that neither Poseidon nor Oceanus are affiliated with healing water, but both are connected to springs. There is a selection of Greek myths where Poseidon strikes the ground with his trident to draw forth lifegiving water, while several Oceanides are considered to be the personification of springs and water sources[33].

Despite his influence on elements of the *Final Fantasy* series, Poseidon is never mentioned by name in any of the mainline titles. The closest he comes to it is by means of a statue in *Final Fantasy IX's* Alexandria Castle which depicts Neptune. Curiously, though, a running theme has developed in the games whereby Poseidon's brother Hades is regularly associated with the seabed. The mythology connecting Hades, the underworld, and the Lifestream will be explored in the next chapter.

1. One such source is Apollonius of Rhodes, a 3rd century BC author best known for the *Argonautica*, an epic poem about Jason's quest for the Golden Fleece.
2. The Homeric creation myth is believed to have been influenced by its Babylonian counterpart. The latter describes how the union of the primordial freshwater god (Apsu) and saltwater goddess (Tiamat) brought into existence the first generation of deities.
3. The Oceanides were responsible for many different things, both in water and on land. Some were nameless nymphs of springs, others played significant roles in mythology, such as Metis, mother of the goddess Athena. Although the number of Oceanides is specified to be

3,000, this is generally interpreted to mean 'innumerable'.

4. Elysium, also later called the Fortunate Isles or the Isles of the Blessed by Hesiod, was an afterlife location separate to the gloomy realm of Hades. It was said to be reserved for heroes and distinguished individuals whose spirits were worthy of an easy and happy eternity. A more neutral location for non-heroic souls is the Asphodel meadows.

5. The Styx is one of the five infernal rivers of Hades, often personified as an Oceanid by the same name. In many accounts, to cross the Styx is to pass into the afterlife, ferried by the boatman Charon. The other rivers are the Acheron (Woe), Cocytus (Lamentation), Lethe (Forgetfulness), and Phlegethon (Flaming).

6. Kratos is the name of the main character in Sony Computer Entertainment's *God of War* series. According to developers, however, he was not intentionally based on Kratos of Greek lore, and the similarities between the two are a "happy mistake".

7. Poseidon was the chief deity of the Mycenaean culture that preceded the Greek Dark Ages, embodying traits later attributed to Zeus and Hades.

8. The Minoans were the first advanced civilisation in Europe, dating back to around 3500 BC. In an original Minoan version of the Minotaur story, it is possible Poseidon himself was the white bull that Pasiphae slept with, rather than it being a gift from the sea god. This would further equate Poseidon with Oceanus, who was often depicted in art as having the horns or head of a bull.

9. Plato was a Greek philosopher born in Athens in the 5th century BC. Along with his teacher, Socrates, and his famed student Aristotle, he is widely considered to be one of the most influential thinkers in history.

10. Poseidon was also the father of several monsters, giants, and Cyclopes. Well-known examples include Orion, the huntsman who could walk on waves, Chrysaor, who sprang from Medusa's neck when Perseus beheaded her,

and Polyphemus, the man-eating Cyclops encountered by Odysseus.

11. Flood myths are commonplace in cultures all around the world. These typically relate to civilisations being destroyed by a god or various deities, often as an act of divine retribution. Similar tales can be found in the beliefs of ancient Mesopotamia, Hinduism, or Native Americans, for instance. Perhaps the most recognisable alternative in the West is the story of Noah's Ark.

12. The *Bibliotheca* is a compendium of Greek legends dating to the 1st or 2nd century AD. Its authorship was historically attributed to Apollodorus of Athens, but this is disputed. For ease, the book will assume this to be true.

13. To the Hellenes, hospitality was a very important part of life. Heavily associated with Zeus, *xenia* (guest-friendship) was the sacred connection between guest and host, and those who broke its laws would be punished by the gods. Another example of a tale involving Zeus, *xenia*, and a flood can be found in Ovid's fable of Baucis and Philemon.

14. Atlas, son of Poseidon, is not to be confused with the Titan Atlas, son of Iapetus and brother of Prometheus, who was condemned by Zeus after the Titanomachy to bear the weight of the sky. Some say it is the latter Atlas who lent his name to the Atlantic Ocean.

15. Unlike modern humans, the Cetra had an inherent propensity to wield magic by directly accessing and channelling the power of the Planet.

16. Coral Valley is the literal translation from Japanese, although the earliest localisations of *Final Fantasy VII* named it 'Corral Valley'. More recent ports have dubbed it 'Corel Valley', which is also inaccurate. Corel is the hometown of Barret Wallace, separate to the Coral Valley.

17. The 'World Guide' section of the *Ultimania Omega* verifies that the spiked, conch-like structure in the shaded grove is, in fact, a library. The glowing orbs inside the building are said to be thoughtforms left behind by the Cetra who lived there, perhaps documenting their

culture in the way books might. Along with the airships shown in the presentation at Shinra HQ's Visual Entertainment Hall in *Final Fantasy VII Remake,* this would indicate the Cetra were not a primitive civilisation.

18. In nature, clownfish and anemones are typically found in shallow reefs and lagoons, and their existence is so interdependent that the former are sometimes called anemonefish.

19. As a beautiful precursor to this book, when Cloud asks Bugenhagen if he can read the Ancients' glyphs etched around the crystal projection device, the old man replies in the PC edition of *Final Fantasy VII,* "It's all Greek to me!"

20. It is also possible that the acrophies relates to the myth of Heracles and the Lernaean Hydra, a serpentine monster that dwelled in a lake. During Heracles' battle with the Hydra, a giant crab emerges from the deep. Heracles eventually kills both, with the crab being raised into the heavens as the constellation Cancer.

21. The Trident can later be purchased in Junon after the player gains control of the *Highwind.* As discussed in chapter XIII, the party's escape from Junon also has mythological links to Poseidon.

22. Like the Trident, the Trumpet Shell can be acquired in Junon.

23. This is reflected in Cid's Southern US accent in both *Advent Children* and *Dirge of Cerberus.*

24. The connection between the *Tiny Bronco* and Poseidon is not unique: As will be discussed in chapter XIII, there is also a link between the *Highwind* and Pegasus, a child of Poseidon. Furthermore, chapter VI of *Norse Myths That Inspired Final Fantasy VII* explores the parallels between the Gold Saucer and the Cosmic Tree, Yggdrasill. One could argue that the eight-wheeled *Buggy,* a gift from Dio (whose name translates as 'God' in Italian), is a reference to Odin's eight-legged steed, Sleipnir.

25. The enemy intel entry for Bahamut in *Final Fantasy VII Remake* also calls him a king of dragons and advises that

he was historically worshipped by the Cetra in times of war. Such lore did not previously exist in the *Compilation*.

26. Perhaps in tribute to Nojima-san and Toriyama-san's work on *Bahamut Lagoon*, *Final Fantasy VII* was the first game in the series to introduce multiple versions of Bahamut, additionally making Neo Bahamut and Bahamut ZERO obtainable to summon in battle. Bahamut SIN (alternatively called Bahamut Tremor, *Advent Children*), Bahamut Fury (*Crisis Core*), and Whisper Bahamut (*Remake*) have since appeared in the *Compilation*. The variants are referred to by Professor Hojo as 'Bahamut strains'.

27. Interestingly, it is widely accepted by scholars that Bahamut (cosmic fish) and Kujata (cosmic bull) derive from the same allegorical root as Behemoth (primeval bull) and Leviathan (primeval fish) in the Hebrew Bible. Behemoth and Leviathan, of course, are also recurring monsters in the *Final Fantasy* series.

28. The moat at the entrance to the city, the pool beneath the Water Altar, and the source of the waterfall when Bugenhagen uses the Key to the Ancients are just three examples.

29. The presentation at the Visual Entertainment Hall in *Remake* is deliberately ambiguous in its statement that the meteor impact 2,000 years ago is what ended the Cetran civilisation.

30. In Marlene's monologue at the opening of *Advent Children*, the Lifestream is defined as the river of life that circles the Planet. The connection between Oceanus and Aerith joining the Lifestream will be discussed in coming chapters.

31. Limit Breaks are unique attacks or abilities that become available to the characters when their emotions are heightened or when a damage gauge is filled in battle, for instance (the specifics vary from title to title).

32. There is a fun, indirect allusion to this elsewhere in *Final Fantasy VII*. The game contains novelty weapons for

107

each playable character, with Aerith's being an umbrella, thus maintaining the theme of rain.

33. It is worth noting that *Advent Children* introduces the concept of Aerith also being able to communicate or sense things via water. This is continued in *Crisis Core*, where she senses Zack's imminent death through the rain. The respective endings of *Final Fantasy VII Remake* and *Episode INTERmission* additionally contain scenes where the rain makes Aerith feel uneasy about changes the party's actions may have caused. However, there is no apparent suggestion that this was inspired by classical mythology.

CHAPTER VI

THE AFTERLIFE STREAMS

*F*inal Fantasy VII has long been praised for its beautiful, intricate storytelling and its handling of complex issues such as environmentalism, capitalism, and terrorism. It inherently addresses the impact of these, both on a personal level for the characters (such as their motivations to join Avalanche) and on a global scale. In-game dialogue between Cloud and Barret introduces the player almost immediately to the narrative that the Planet is dying due to humanity's consumption of mako energy, and the shadow of death perpetually lingers from then on.

The theme of life and death in *Final Fantasy VII* is neither vaguely defined nor restricted to a one-size-fits-all approach. The game intimately explores the ways in which the passing of a loved one can affect individuals differently, and how grief can destroy a person if left unchecked. As such, a more polished description of the theme in *Final Fantasy VII* is perhaps 'loss', specifically the loss experienced by those left behind.

The afterlife in the *Compilation* is represented by the Lifestream, a vast, flowing sea of souls whose currents simultaneously exist in the material and spiritual worlds. Mako is the Shinra Corporation's euphemistic name for these great streams, distracting the public from the truth behind their modern conveniences.

The Lifestream was first conceptualised by Hironobu Sakaguchi, creator of the *Final Fantasy* franchise and producer of its seventh instalment. Sakaguchi-san drafted the game's initial scenario, focusing on its setting, the City of Mako (which would later become Midgar), and the function of spirit energy. According to Tetsuya Nomura and Yoshinori Kitase[1], who also heavily contributed to early versions of the story, Sakaguchi-san had prepared a detailed premise for how life cycled through the Planet and the wider universe.

The idea itself was rooted in the grief the producer had been suffering since his own mother passed away during the development of *Final Fantasy III*[2]. He wanted to encourage players to consider what happens after death, ensuring this question was at the heart of *Final Fantasy VII* (and subsequently doing the same with his animated film, *Final Fantasy: The Spirits Within*). While Sakaguchi-san did not script the death of Aerith – which remains to this day one of the most iconic moments in videogame history –, it should be noted that there is an unusually high number of main characters in *Final Fantasy VII* who have lost mothers or female loved ones[3].

When Kazushige Nojima joined *Final Fantasy VII's* staff as a scenario writer, Kitase-san and Nomura-san entrusted him with further development of the Lifestream's concept. A degree of inspiration for the cycle of spirit energy can likely be found in the principles of reincarnation[4], often associated with Eastern religions such as Buddhism or Hinduism, or through the Monad of Gnosticism (also called the One or the Absolute), proclaimed to be an infinite wellspring of knowledge and spiritual energy.

Another possible influence is Mount Hōrai of Japanese literature, itself derived from older Shintō and Buddhist beliefs. In the book *Kwaidan: Stories and Studies of Strange Things*, authored in 1904 by Lafcadio Hearn, Hōrai's atmosphere is made up of countless souls, and inhaling these will allow one to absorb their ancient knowledge and understanding. Although Hearn's interpretation is distinct from earlier utopian perceptions of Mount Hōrai in Japanese folklore, where there was no sorrow and food was plentiful, the similarities to the Lifestream and the use of materia are unquestionable[5].

However, as highlighted in the previous chapter, Nojima-san had worked on the *Heracles no Eikō* series in the years that preceded *Final Fantasy VII*. It is not unreasonable to presume that he would have drawn on his passion for and expertise in classical mythology to some extent when

111

sculpting the finer details of the Planet's afterlife. As it happens, there is substantial evidence to support this.

The oldest Hellenic accounts of the afterlife can be found in Homer and Hesiod's poems, where the underworld of Hades is portrayed as a dark and dank place, with emphasis on a main river or rivers. The writers' depictions are not contradictory as such, although certain features may be alluded to in one of the works but not in others.

In Hesiod's *Theogony*, when Zeus and the Olympians eventually overthrow the Titans, many are imprisoned in the subterranean abyss of Tartarus. The Skyfather then apportions domains and responsibilities to the gods, and to his brother Hades he gives rule of the underworld.

Hades establishes his kingdom in the bleak, cavernous roots of the earth that exist above Tartarus. This realm, too, comes to be known as Hades, thought to mean 'Unseen', hinting at its spiritual nature. In time, he takes a queen to join him in his halls: Persephone, who will be discussed further in the next chapter.

The *Theogony* also dedicates multiple lines to describing the river Styx, on whose icy waters the immortals swear binding oaths. Styx is said to be the eldest daughter of the Titan Oceanus, the great stream that encircles Gaia and provides her with currents. One tenth of Oceanus' waters is allocated to Styx, branching off beneath the earth to cascade into the underworld.

While Homer's *Iliad* does not offer much on the geography of Hades, the *Odyssey* contains an entire section in which Odysseus sails there to obtain guidance from the ghost of the prophet Tiresias. According to Homer, the shores of Hades lie at the edge of the world, beyond the stream of Oceanus, which must be crossed to reach them. There is no sunlight there; everything is shrouded in darkness.

The importance of Oceanus and Styx in the *Odyssey* and *Theogony*, respectively, is to identify the boundary between the living world and the afterlife. In both instances, this partition between life and death is presented as flowing water. Homer also makes reference to other rivers in Hades, namely Cocytus (the river of lamentation), Phlegathon (the river of flames), and Acheron (the river of sorrow). Along with Lethe (the river of forgetfulness), which is mentioned in later sources, these waterways perform integral roles in the functioning of the underworld.

As a border between life and death, Styx became synonymous with Charon, the ferryman, whose job it is to transport recently deceased spirits from the shores at Hades' entrance across to its gloomy halls[6]. Many Hellenic poets and playwrights, though, claimed it is the Acheron that flows past the underworld's gates, not the Styx.

It was proposed that the further someone travels along the Styx, the deeper into Hades (and ultimately Tartarus) they will get and the more severe their infernal punishment will be. However, the principle of separating those who have lived righteous lives from those who have lived wickedly was not popularised until the Classical period. Writers of the Archaic period did not differentiate between the groups[7].

In the *Odyssey*, for example, Homer lists the spectres of Greek kings and warriors, noble ladies, untested youths, the elderly, and women who died in childbirth as all dwelling in the meadow of Asphodel. This plain is not to be thought of as flowery or fertile, though; rather it is dusty and grey like ash.

Ordinary Hellenes believed that when the time came, their souls would be met and escorted to the gates of the netherworld by Thanatos (whom the Romans called Mors), the iron-hearted personification of death[8]. Distinguished individuals such as demigods, heroes, or royalty would instead be collected by Hermes, the divine messenger of Olympus, who occupied several roles. Psychopomps – beings that guide the dead into the afterlife – are commonplace in global mythology and Hermes is the psychopomp-in-chief of classical lore.

In post-Archaic literature, the eventual destination of a person's spirit in the afterlife is based on their earthly actions, as determined by the three judges of the underworld[9]. Those who live heroic, exceptional, or virtuous lives are granted access to Elysium (also called the Elysian fields), a verdant paradise which is often analogous to the Isles of the Blessed. Here, there is no toil or strain, only joy. Criminals and oath breakers, meanwhile, are condemned by the judges to Tartarus.

The majority of souls, though, whose lives have been unremarkable, find themselves in Asphodel. Contrary to Homer's depiction, the meadows are not typically barren in works by subsequent authors. Many sources highlight that the deceased have to drink from the river Lethe before they can enter Asphodel's fields. In doing so, the waters of forgetfulness strip them of their memories and thus their identity. What remains of the spirit is a ghostly shadow of whom the individual had once been, an entity known as a 'shade' (*skiā*).

The Latin poet Virgil expanded on this concept in the *Aeneid*, in which the Trojan hero Aeneas descends into the underworld to speak with his father in Elysium. Aeneas learns that those who wish to be reincarnated must take a long draught of oblivion from the Lethe, returning to the mortal world in a new form with no recollection of their past life.

Lethe was named after a daughter of Eris, Goddess of Strife, and identified with forgetfulness and amnesia. In the Orphic mysteries[10], her counterpart was a daughter of Gaia and mother of the Muses: Mnemosyne, a Titaness whose domain was memory and remembrance. Initiates of Orphism were taught to drink from the pool of Mnemosyne (occasionally said to be a river) rather than Lethe, granting them unfathomable knowledge.

There is a significant number of parallels to be found between the afterlife realm of Hades in Greek mythology and the functionality of the Lifestream in the *Compilation of Final Fantasy VII*. The narrative of the original game is unambiguous from the opening scenes, where mako is described as the lifeblood of the Planet, a finite resource whose consumption will lead to catastrophic consequences. It is not until the party arrives at Cosmo Canyon and is treated to the virtual display at Bugenhagen's planetarium, however, that the unsettling truth regarding the exact nature of mako is revealed.

Marlene's simplified monologue during *Advent Children's* introduction summarises the Lifestream as the river of life that circles the world, giving life to the Planet and its inhabitants. It is the ethereal sea in which spirit energy – a term that can be equated to souls – gathers, following the cosmic cycle of birth, life, death, and rebirth. Over countless millennia, spirit energy has carried the memories and experiences of everyone and everything that has ever lived: the accumulated knowledge and wisdom of Gaia's history.

It is a beautiful concept that suggests death is not the end but merely a redistribution of energy. Bugenhagen explains in *Final Fantasy VII* that all organic beings are allotted strands of spirit energy from the Lifestream when they are brought into the world[11]. At death, the body decomposes[12], and that same spirit energy re-joins the Lifestream, now imprinted with the deceased's consciousness and essence.

The souls that return to the Planet merge with the great river and roam with its currents. Their memories and knowledge continue to exist on some level, but their individuality is normally lost, much like a drop of ink slowly dissolving in a glass of water. In time, the spirit energy will be redeployed to other living things. This process is not only true for the Planet but for the universe itself, as elaborated on in *Dirge of Cerberus*.

There are instances, however, where the dead can retain their identity and form in the Lifestream. In fact, the struggle between Aerith and Sephiroth centres around this crucial plot point. Kazushige Nojima's novel *On the Way to a Smile* includes two trilogies of mini-chapters that address it, respectively titled "Lifestream: White" and "Lifestream: Black".

The Black episodes explore the challenges faced by Sephiroth after his defeat by Cloud at *Final Fantasy VII's* climax, and his ambition to rematerialise on the surface. Specifically, the villain's consciousness cannot assume a definitive shape because he has already cast away the memories of his life, which he deemed to be worthless. The act of forfeiting pieces of his identity bears a striking similarity to the process of reincarnation in Virgil's *Aeneid*, where one must drink from the waters of oblivion before they can be reborn.

Aerith, meanwhile, utilises her abilities as a Cetra in the White chapters to seek out the lingering spirits of other Ancients who have not yet dispersed into the sea of souls. She hopes they may assist her in easing the anger and despair of those who have died of Geostigma, guiding their essences to merge with the Lifestream[13]. In doing so, she has undertaken the role of a psychopomp, similar to Hermes.

A more extensive explanation of how Aerith's spirit perceives its presence and interaction with others in the Lifestream is contained in *Hoshi o Meguru Otome*, a short story authored by Benny Matsuyama of Studio BentStuff and commonly translated by fans as *The Maiden Who Travels the Planet*[14]. Two recurring themes in the tale are the afterlife's portrayal using water analogies, and how the consciousnesses of the deceased are able to manifest around Aerith.

Although she is by no means the only character to die in *Final Fantasy VII*, the transition from life to death is emphasised most fully by Aerith's passing. As detailed in the previous chapter, water symbolism features heavily during this scenario: The flower girl is murdered at the Water Altar beneath the Forgotten Capital; the Holy Materia drops into the lagoon below; and she is laid to rest in a sacred spring, where her departure from the physical world is visually represented by her body sinking to its depths.

Hoshi o Meguru Otome expands on this by recounting it all from Aerith's perspective. When her body reaches the bottom of the pool, she feels herself continuing downward to a lower level, eventually arriving at a sea of energy comprised of millions of streams. As such, there is a consistent use of water imagery between life and death, likening the transition to the topography of the classical underworld.

The second key element of the novella is the numerous encounters Aerith has with individuals who perished during *Final Fantasy VII*. In order of appearance, these are Avalanche members Jessie, Biggs, and Wedge, Barret's friend Dyne, President Shinra, Aerith's first boyfriend Zack, and Professor Hojo.

Each of the figures exists in the same realm, so there is no obvious distinction between the afterlife destinations of the righteous (such as Aerith), the wicked (Hojo and the President), heroes (Zack), or murderers (Dyne). This mirrors the Homeric version of the underworld, where all spirits come to the plain of Asphodel, irrespective of their earthly deeds.

Final Fantasy VII itself also supports this premise. The Promised Land of the Cetra is attested in the game to be the location to which the Ancients travelled once the hardships of their life were at an end. Although the Shinra Company interprets this to be somewhere on the world map, it is later verified that the Cetra considered the Lifestream to be their Promised Land, and the supreme happiness they could attain was eternal rest. While this may evoke comparisons to Elysium of Greek mythology, there is no evidence to suggest the Promised Land was a special or isolated region of the Lifestream, albeit reference is made in the Cetran scriptures quoted in *Final Fantasy VII Remake* to a "paradise".

Hoshi o Meguru Otome also describes the spectral profiles of the characters that Aerith engages with. She can

119

initially only perceive other consciousnesses as indistinguishable shapes because their memories of themselves have dissolved into the Lifestream, even though their cores still remain.

However, when she begins to grow concerned about Cloud, Barret, and Tifa, Aerith's thoughts spark a reaction nearby. A shadow rises from the mako, its features becoming more defined as it converses with the flower girl. The gradual reconstruction of its memories allows the apparition to resume the appearance it had in life: that of Jessie.

Characters such as Zack, though, whose sense of self is much stronger, are quicker to form and remember Aerith. Subsequent meetings also indicate that artificial body parts or weapons (such as Dyne's gun-arm) can be projected, and that a spirit's clearest features are a reflection of how they identify themselves. For example, Aerith recognises President Shinra by the clarity of his expensive suit, not by his face.

These traits are remarkably similar to those of the *skiā*, or shades, in Homer's *Odyssey*. Odysseus visits Asphodel during the epic poem, and a crowd of spectres is drawn to him when he puts sheep's blood in a trough. However, the ghosts – including his own mother and the hero Achilles – do not realise who he is until they drink this sacrificial offering, the catalyst that triggers their self-awareness.

The reinvigorated shades thereafter ask about loved ones or express individual personalities, such as Achilles' pride in hearing of his son Neoptolemus' achievements, or Ajax's refusal to forgive Odysseus for winning Achilles' armour at his expense. This is also the case in *Hoshi o Meguru Otome*, in which the phantoms encountered are depicted with a range of emotions and desires, and some like Zack and Hojo even recall their history with Aerith[15].

It should be noted that while the Lifestream serves as a spiritual domain for those who have died, it is additionally part of the material world, typically in liquid state[16]. This is the form in which it is extracted and processed (as mako) by the Shinra Corporation, or can occasionally breach the surface of the Planet at spots called mako fountains. During *Final Fantasy VII*, Cloud falls into the jade green currents of the Lifestream twice – first at the Northern Crater, then again at Mideel – and although he does not drown, the overabundance of spirit energy has a devastating impact on his mind, resulting in a condition known as mako poisoning.

The mechanics of the Lifestream itself do differ from the netherworld of Greek mythology, where the souls do not dwell in the rivers that cascade through Hades but rather in the meadows of Asphodel, the groves of Elysium, or the dark abyss of Tartarus. Nevertheless, it is difficult to ignore the parallels between the imagery of *Final Fantasy VII's* afterlife and the characteristics of its Hellenic counterpart.

For spirit energy to return to the Planet in the *Compilation*, it must separate from its corporeal body and descend to the Lifestream, where it will gradually merge with the great river as it weaves across Gaia. This loosely corresponds to the journey into the underworld, whereby the soul of the deceased is taken to the subterranean banks of the Styx (or Acheron) and can only reach its final destination by being ferried across the river by Charon.

The Styx, in this context, is the boundary between the material and spiritual realms, an attribute shared by Oceanus in the *Odyssey*. Despite being located almost exclusively in the afterlife depths of Hades, the Styx is a tangible entity, just like the Lifestream, which is described by Rufus in *Advent Children* as flowing between the edge of life and death. Oceanus, meanwhile, is the primordial river that encircles the world and produces the currents that rove to every corner of it; this echoes the simplistic definition of the Lifestream given by Marlene in the movie's opening. As mako, of course, it is an everyday natural resource that directly affects the physical plane, akin to oil or coal.

Perhaps the most important comparison to be made between the Lifestream and the Greek underworld is how the afterlife is closely associated with the loss of memory and identity. The concept of the dead conceding their individuality to preserve the lifecycle of the Planet and universe is not dissimilar to the purpose of the river Lethe in mythology[17].

As previously mentioned, many sources attest that the deceased cannot be admitted to the meadows of Asphodel unless they drink from the waters of forgetfulness. The consequent eradication of any sorrow or anger a soul may feel towards their death is analogous to Aerith assisting the victims of Geostigma to join the Lifestream in *On the Way to a Smile*. Furthermore, Virgil's partnering of the Lethe with reincarnation in the *Aeneid* profoundly resembles the cycle of spirit energy in *Final Fantasy VII* in general.

By contrast, the waters of Mnemosyne grant the consumer vast quantities of knowledge. This, too, mirrors the properties of the Lifestream, specifically its effects on living beings. Mako poisoning occurs when a person's brain is flooded by an overwhelming amount of spirit energy, causing the mind to lose itself in a sea of information and fragmented memories. Cloud is very seriously afflicted by this toxicosis after he falls into the Lifestream at the Northern Crater and requires Tifa's help to reassemble his true recollections and identity[18].

It is also worth highlighting that Sephiroth's goal in *Final Fantasy VII* is to absorb the Lifestream and acquire its boundless energy and knowledge, thus becoming godlike. He means to do so by smashing Meteor into the Planet, then positioning himself at the centre of the impact zone, where an immeasurable magnitude of spirit energy will be redirected to heal the wound. In this way, the resurrected Sephiroth's actions may relate to the Orphic mysteries, which teach that eternal salvation from the cycle of life and death is awarded to those who drink from the river Mnemosyne.

In addition to the parallels between the Lifestream and the chthonic waterways of Hades, the latter likely also contributed to the design of a location in *Final Fantasy VII* that is deeply linked to death and the underworld. The origins of Nibelheim are explored in *Norse Myths That Inspired Final Fantasy VII*, where evidence is presented to illustrate it is derived from Niflheim, the primordial realm of icy mist in which the afterlife halls of Hel are later established. Similar to Hades, Hel is the name of the bleak netherworld as well as the deity that governs it.

The first mako reactor was constructed by Shinra, Inc. on Mount Nibel, and both the facility and Nibelheim itself play a critical role in the *Compilation*. The town is home to Cloud and Tifa and was, before this, the birthplace of Sephiroth as part of the Jenova Project, the revelations of which are an eventual catalyst for the war hero burning the village to the ground and murdering its denizens.

What might not be immediately apparent with regards to the portrayals of Nibelheim's environment across the *Compilation* are its subtle connections to the Styx. For instance, in *Dirge of Cerberus*, Vincent infiltrates the caves beneath Shinra Manor – whose own crypts and shackled skeletons create further imagery of death – via an extensive sewer system. These subterranean watercourses also appear in an extra mission of the game's international edition, titled "Stygian Sewers", where 'Stygian' is the adjective form of 'Styx'[19].

The significance of water in Nibelheim is reintroduced in the novel *Traces of Two Pasts*, which features a waterfall lagoon as Tifa's favourite picnic spot and the fast-flowing Gunnthra River in the foothills of Mount Nibel. The latter is where Tifa initially meets her martial arts instructor, Master Zangan, and on its banks she commits to training as his disciple. In Norse mythology, Gunnthra is one of the Élivágar, a group of icy rivers that snake through Niflheim and are associated with swearing oaths[20]. As such, Tifa vowing to study under Zangan by the edge of the Gunnthra reflects the function of Styx in Greek lore.

According to Hesiod's *Theogony*, Styx (the goddess who embodies the infernal river) was honoured by Zeus for her support of the Olympians during the Titanomachy (see chapter X for details of this conflict). Any pledge sworn in her name is binding and cannot be broken, lest the oath breaker suffers severe punishment.

It is unlikely to be a coincidence, then, that the most important promise between any two characters in *Final Fantasy VII* is made at the water tower in Nibelheim's town square. When the teenage Cloud informs his crush, Tifa, that he is leaving home to join SOLDIER, she convinces him to swear that he will come save her if she is ever in trouble. Cloud fulfilling this vow when she is gravely injured by Sephiroth at the Mount Nibel reactor is key to Tifa later being able to help her childhood friend unravel the mystery of his identity. It is also worth noting that the incident at

Nibelheim is what ultimately leads to Cloud losing his memories in the first place[21].

Final Fantasy VII's application of water as a major theme for depicting its afterlife seemingly extends to the summoned being whose name was inspired by the ancient Greek warden of the dead. That said, Hades in the game and the grim immortal from classical lore are somewhat different.

The Hades of mythology governs from his palace at the heart of the underworld, ruling over every soul that resides within its halls. His primary focus is to maintain the laws of life and death, ensuring none of his subjects ever escape his realm. Entering the gates of the afterlife is easy but getting back out again is a tricky task, even for heroes. The god can be cold and harsh, but he is not unfair, nor is he needlessly cruel.

For example, when Orpheus comes to plead for the return of his beloved wife, Eurydice, Hades is charmed by the bard's beautiful music, and agrees to free Eurydice if certain conditions are met (see chapter XVIII). When Heracles asks to borrow Cerberus, Hades' many-headed hound[22], the King of the Dead grants the strongman permission if he can subdue the beast. There is also plenty of literary evidence to show he is respectful and affectionate towards Persephone, his queen (albeit he did initially abduct her).

Over time, the Hellenes came to adopt euphemisms for Hades because they were afraid to speak his name aloud. The most common in use by the Classical period was Plouton (the 'Wealthy One'), which was eventually Latinised as Pluto and conflated with the Roman god Dīs Pater (or his gloomier predecessor, Orcus).

Hades has been a recurring figure in the *Final Fantasy* series since *Final Fantasy VII*, enjoying a variety of designs and roles[23]. These incarnations have ranged from the robed, skeletal druid who can be invoked by Cloud and his comrades to the legendary synthesist of *Final Fantasy IX's* Memoria or the influential Ascian in *Final Fantasy XIV*.

While there are undoubtedly links to be made between the respective versions of *Final Fantasy's* Hades and the theme of death, deep water is a more prevalent thread that connects them. For instance, Hades in the 2006 re-release of *Final Fantasy V* is battled in the Sealed Temple, a bonus post-game dungeon located underwater, while a secret battle with Hades in *Final Fantasy IX* is triggered by examining rocks on the seabed of the Ocean area in Memoria[24], among other later examples.

In *Final Fantasy VII*, the Hades Materia can be obtained aboard the sunken Shinra Gelnika aircraft (alternatively translated as 'Guernica')[25]. It is revealed by Reno and Rude that the plane was shot out of the sky by a Weapon, one of the colossal biomechanical monsters produced by the Planet. Now situated at the bottom of the sea, the Gelnika is only accessible by submarine, and visiting it often attracts the Emerald Weapon to the player's position[26].

It is here that the franchise trend of affiliating Hades with water was initially established. A possible explanation is that it alludes to the importance of rivers in the Greek underworld, while another is that the seafloor is as close as it gets geographically to the nether realms[27].

Final Fantasy VII's Hades is aesthetically dissimilar to how he is generally depicted in Hellenic and Roman art. Rather than an imposing bearded deity on his throne, the summon is a skeleton wearing a heavy cowl, preparing a pot of bubbling potion through sorcery. Hades' attack, 'Black Cauldron', deals non-elemental damage to all opponents in battle as well as inflicting a range of status ailments via the malevolent fumes of his concoction.

The character model shares a number of traits with the Grim Reaper, a psychopomp and embodiment of death that has been popularised in European folklore. The Reaper is therefore more closely equated to Thanatos of Greek lore than Hades, which is supported in classical works: Thanatos is described in places as being garbed in a black robe and enveloping men in a dark cloud when he comes to claim their spirit[28]. The latter detail might be represented in the gases of the summon's cauldron.

Despite being named after the King of the Dead, Hades' alignment in *Final Fantasy VII* is not Death[29], but the status effects he casts, such as Poison, Sleep, and Paralyzed, can perhaps be compared to a person's demise through sickness. This was amended for his summoning in *Before Crisis*, in which his attack can additionally cause Instant Death for enemies.

The underworld and its ruler are so complexly entwined with ancient Greek beliefs and religious cults that the content of this chapter only peels back the top layer on its myriad myths and intricacies. As such, the book will return time and again to Hades the god and Hades the afterlife realm, starting with an analysis of Aerith and Persephone, Queen of the Dead.

1. Nomura-san and Kitase-san's comments were made in an interview with Japanese magazine *Gamaga* in 2007.
2. Sakaguchi-san stated this in an interview with *PlayStation Underground* in 1997.
3. In *Final Fantasy VII*, the mothers of Cloud, Tifa, Aerith, Red XIII, and Marlene are all deceased; Sephiroth believes his mother died in childbirth; Barret mourns his wife; and Vincent laments the loss of Lucrecia. The *Compilation* continues the trend, with *On the Way to a Smile* confirming the mothers of Yuffie and Rufus passed away in their youths, and Reeve and Denzel's mothers die during the course of the book; Genesis murders his adoptive parents, and Angeal's mother commits suicide in *Crisis Core*; *Before Crisis* reveals Verdot's wife, who is also Elfe's mother, died years earlier; and *The Kids Are Alright* tells the story of Evan's search for his mother, only for him to discover she has died at the Great Glacier; while Kyrie's parents were killed by gangsters when she was a child.

4. Reincarnation is the belief that the soul or spiritual essence of a living being can depart its body at death, then begin a new life within a different physical form.

5. Materia is *Final Fantasy VII's* in-game mechanic for magic use in battle. However, these crystal orbs also enjoy their own lore within the *Compilation*. It is said that the knowledge and wisdom of the Cetra is stored within materia, which is itself a condensed form of spirit energy. The Cetra, who preceded modern humans, were capable of supernatural feats. By engaging with materia, the wielder may freely access the powers of the Cetra, using it to interact with the Planet and conduct magic.

6. Charon expects to be paid for this service, which is why most ancient Greeks were buried with a coin in or on their mouth. Any individual who had not been given the appropriate funerary rites was doomed to wander the riverbanks aimlessly for a hundred years.

7. An exception to this is that Hesiod's *Works and Days* mentions demigods and heroes may be welcomed at the Isles of the Blessed, located at the western edge of the world. This eternal paradise was distinct from Hades.

8. Thanatos and his connections to *Final Fantasy VII* are examined more thoroughly in chapter XVII.

9. The names of the three judges are Minos, Rhadamanthus, and Aeacus.

10. Orphism was a set of religious beliefs associated with Dionysus, God of the Vine; Persephone, Queen of the Underworld; and Orpheus, a mythical poet and son of Apollo. Its mysteries (secret rituals and hymns) centred around death and resurrection, specifically through tales of entering and returning from Hades.

11. The exact point at which spirit energy is allocated is unclear, whether it be at seeding, fertilisation, or birth. This reflects the real world, where similar questions have important religious, ethical, and philosophical consequences.

12. According to the *Ultimanias*, beings with high concentrations of mako in their bodies (such as monsters or SOLDIERs) might instead dissipate entirely into spirit

energy shortly after death. Zack is a prime example of this at the conclusion of *Crisis Core*. The lore has also been put to practical use in *Final Fantasy VII Remake*, where biological enemies fade into spirit energy when killed in battle.

13. As explained in *On the Way to a Smile* and the *Final Fantasy VII 10th Anniversary Ultimania*, the increasing volume of these angry souls begins to corrupt the Lifestream, causing a divergence in the regular current. This corruption is not to be conflated with Geostigma itself, which is the body's autoimmune reaction to the presence of foreign genetic material (Jenova cells). The Jenova cells were distributed around the world as a side-effect of the Lifestream breaching the Planet's surface to destroy Meteor.

14. While this novella appears in the *Final Fantasy VII Ultimania Omega* and was officially licensed by Square Enix, its canonicity with respect to the rest of the *Compilation* is disputed by many. Aside from a few key details, its story is compatible with the other titles.

15. There are a few unique examples in *Final Fantasy VII* of characters not following the universal system of spirit energy joining the Lifestream. For instance, the NPCs that provide tutorials early in the game perish when the Sector 7 Plate collapses, but their ghosts can later be found in Junon to offer support to the player. The figures encountered in the Temple of the Ancients, meanwhile, are manifestations of Cetran spirits that have remained on the physical plane to protect the temple.

16. Materia and mako stones are two examples of spirit energy in solid state, while fumes and gases can be seen around reactor facilities or natural fountains.

17. As highlighted in chapter II, a river by the name of Lethe also features in *Final Fantasy VI*. Among the main characters that must raft down its rapids is Terra Branford, who is suffering from memory loss.

18. Cloud also experienced mako poisoning prior to the events of *Final Fantasy VII*, caused by Hojo's experimentation on him at Nibelheim. In his weakened

mental state, Cloud's personality became a cocktail of information blended by the mimicry abilities of Jenova's cells, comprised of his real self, Zack's memories, and Tifa's projection of her childhood friend. It is this version of the protagonist that the player is presented with when the game begins.

19. The specific use of 'Stygian' regards anything of or relating to the Styx, while the generic adjective 'stygian' refers to something that is unpleasantly dark, gloomy, or foreboding. In isolation, the latter would be appropriate for the mission. However, as is discussed at length in chapters XVI and XVII, *Dirge of Cerberus* is heavily influenced by Greek mythology, and other mission titles include "Zephyr Heathlands", "Cyclopean Causeway", and "Deep Labyrinth". Zephyrus is the divine personification of the West Wind; the Cyclopes are one-eyed giants who helped the Olympians defeat the Titans (see chapter X); and the Labyrinth is where the hero Theseus confronts the Minotaur (see chapter XV).

20. For example, in *Helgakviða Hundingsbana II* (an Old Norse poem), it is mentioned that the character Dagr swore an oath on the river Leipt, another of the Élivágar.

21. At the Mount Nibel Mako Reactor, before defeating Sephiroth, Cloud is impaled by the legendary swordsman's Masamune. Professor Hojo confines Cloud to a mako recovery unit and conducts experiments on him as part of Project Sephiroth Copy, but he suffers from severe mako poisoning and is branded a failure.

22. Cerberus is most commonly represented as a three-headed canine, but there are many other versions. His earliest mention is in Hesiod's *Theogony*, for example, where he is described as having 50 heads.

23. Hades was retrospectively added to *Final Fantasy V* as a necromancer-type enemy in the Game Boy Advance edition of the game (2006).

24. The group of Alexandrian soldiers led by Steiner in *Final Fantasy IX* are the Knights of Pluto, meaning Hades' Classical alias is also referenced. The same can technically be said for *Final Fantasy VII* because the

dwarf-planet Pluto features in the animation of Safer Sephiroth's 'Super Nova' attack.

25. Heaven's Cloud is a weapon that can be picked up for Cloud Strife in the sunken Gelnika. The sword's name in Japanese is *Ame-no-Murakomo*, which translates more literally as the 'Gathering Clouds of Heaven'. In Japanese legend, the blade was wielded by a storm god, Susanoo. 'Cloud Gatherer' was one of Zeus' common epithets in ancient Greek mythology, creating an interesting proximity link to the Hades Materia, not to mention the underwater realm of their brother, Poseidon.

26. The Emerald Weapon is one of *Final Fantasy VII's* superbosses and an unplanned encounter with it will likely result in a game over.

27. The hadal zone is the deepest region of an ocean, derived from the concept of Hades as an underworld.

28. Thanatos is also mentioned by name in *Final Fantasy VII Remake* during the battle with Jenova Dreamweaver, who uses the defensive move 'Thanatos Denied'.

29. The element of Death is instead attributed to the summon Odin, who is based on the chief of the Norse pantheon and a death god in his own right. Hades has no elemental alignment, but materia combinations can add the status effects inflicted by 'Black Cauldron' to a player character's offensive or defensive capabilities.

PART THREE

DIVINE
INSPIRATION

CHAPTER VII

THE MAIDEN

ncient Greek mythology was written and recorded throughout the Hellenic and Roman worlds for more than a thousand years, spanning from Homer's *Iliad* to the eventual rise in Christianity in the 4th century AD. Many narratives and concepts found in the stories are distinct to Classical Greece, originating in the Athenian festival plays or the philosophical dialogues of Plato, for instance.

Like most cultures, however, elements of the Hellenes' religious beliefs can be traced back to earlier civilisations such as the Mycenaeans or, in certain cases, to Mesopotamia in the Near East[1]. One example of this might be how historic evidence indicates Poseidon, not Zeus, was the chief deity of the Bronze Age Greeks: He was venerated as the god responsible for cleansing, life-giving water[2].

Two other prominent figures thought to derive from the Mycenaean period are the goddesses Demeter and Persephone, known to the Romans as Ceres and Proserpina. Demeter – who is listed as a sister of Zeus and one of the twelve Olympians in Hesiod's *Theogony* – was an agricultural deity, specifically associated with the reaping and threshing of corn and other grains. Farming was of critical importance for feeding the local settlements (and later whole *poleis* or *demoi*[3]), so it is unsurprising that the Goddess of the Harvest would be highly revered.

Festivals dedicated to Demeter and Persephone, her daughter by Zeus[4], were held across Greece each year during harvest time (around September), but the largest and most famous of the celebrations took place in the small town of Eleusis (also called Elefsina), located northwest of Athens[5]. Worship of the goddesses was conducted in secretive ceremonies at the temple there, with participants being sworn never to reveal what was done, said, and shown. These rituals came to be known as the Eleusinian Mysteries (not to be confused with the Dionysian or Orphic Mysteries, which will be addressed in the next chapter).

Given their clandestine nature, many details surrounding the Mysteries have remained obscure. Their purpose was significantly more complex than the primitive agrarian thanksgivings from which they had evolved: They offered enlightenment to initiates and returning practitioners on how to achieve happiness in this world and passage to a blessed afterlife.

The latter element relates to the tale of Persephone's abduction, itself an allegory about seasonal change[6]. The divine mother and daughter were two aspects of the annual agricultural cycle: Persephone represented the coming of spring and the sowing of seeds, while Demeter represented the end of summer and the reaping of grain, as well as its cultivation beforehand. However, the people of antiquity required a way to explain Persephone's absence in the months of winter, when the soil is firm and no crops can grow.

The answer is found in the *Homeric Hymn to Demeter*[7], an early poem that is the original written source of this myth, believed to have been dramatically re-enacted during the Eleusinian Mysteries. According to the hymn, Gaia produces the narcissus flower (more commonly known as the daffodil) to entice Persephone while she is out in the fields with friends one day[8]. As the girl bends to pluck the narcissus, most beautiful of all the blooms in the meadow, the ground around her splits open and Hades rides out in his chariot. The King of the Dead seizes Persephone and carries her to his gloomy palace at the heart of the underworld, where he makes her his queen.

When Demeter realises her daughter is missing, she abandons her duties to search every corner of the earth, but to no avail. The Goddess of the Harvest eventually learns that Zeus had permitted Hades to take Persephone as his wife, so, driven by anger and despair, she retaliates by allowing the world's crops to fail. The land loses its fertility without Demeter's nurture, causing widespread famine, and the desperate pleas of mankind prompt Zeus to demand that Hades frees Persephone from his custody.

Hades loves his queen and is saddened by the prospect of losing her, but he recognises he cannot disobey his brother. Instead, he gives Persephone some pomegranate seeds to eat before she journeys back to the surface, knowing that once she has tasted the food of the underworld, she is obliged to revisit his kingdom.

Hermes brings Persephone to Eleusis, where Demeter has arranged for a temple to be built in their honour. Appeased by her daughter's release, Demeter relinquishes her wrath, and heeds the call of Olympus to rejuvenate the earth so that crops may grow again. It is decreed that each winter, Persephone must re-join Hades and rule the dead by his side[9], but the warmth and blossoming flowers of springtime will herald her rise again, to be with her mother and the immortals[10].

Despite her worship as a goddess of vegetation and fertility, Persephone's involvement in other myths almost exclusively relates to the underworld. Examples include her persuading Hades to let Orpheus' wife return to the legendary bard because she is so moved by his music (see chapter XVIII) or being tricked by the cunning Sisyphus into consenting to his rise from the dead. There is even a fable similar to her abduction in which she fosters the infant Adonis to manhood below the earth at the request of

Aphrodite, only to fall in love with him, forcing Zeus to order Adonis to split his time between the two goddesses.

Persephone is regularly referred to in the stories as the dread queen, simply because people feared death. As with her husband, there was a degree of taboo around speaking her name aloud, so the Hellenes applied alternative euphemisms. Of the dozens known from the Eleusinian Mysteries and other local cults, she was most often called Cora (or Kore), which means 'Maiden'.

The world of *Final Fantasy VII* does not have an equivalent of the Mysteries – with the arguable exception of the Study of Planetary Life[11] – but it does contain an ancient race whose lives concerned the cultivation of the land and its close ties to spirit energy and the afterlife. As examined in chapters IV and V, the Cetra were nomads who could converse with the Planet, following her guidance to migrate and settle the fields and hillsides. Their hard labours supported the flow of the Lifestream, which would enrich the land in an agricultural sense[12].

Aerith Gainsborough is the last surviving Cetra at the time of *Final Fantasy VII*, with details of her past revealed during the original game, *Compilation* titles such as *Before Crisis* and *Crisis Core*, and the supplementary prose works by Kazushige Nojima and Benny Matsuyama. She is born at Icicle Inn to Professor Gast, a former Shinra scientist, and Ifalna, a Cetran woman residing in the shadow of the Northern Crater, where her ancestors kept vigil over the imprisoned Calamity from the Skies.

Shortly after Aerith's birth, Professor Hojo tracks down Gast, murdering his former mentor to claim his wife and daughter as research specimens. Aerith is raised in a laboratory at Shinra Headquarters, where daily experiments are conducted on Ifalna. During this period, Aerith learns about spirit energy from her mother, and together they create an impressive collage of associated wall art in their living quarters. However, according to the short story *Picturing the Past*, when the girl is seven years of age, she exhibits supernatural abilities by visualising landscapes around the world that may be rich in mako. The company scientists begin to test Aerith, while Hojo pushes Ifalna's endurance far beyond the boundaries of ethics.

This development is the catalyst for the captives' planned escape, as portrayed in Nojima-san's novel *Traces of Two Pasts*. Mother and daughter are smuggled out of the Shinra Building by a staff member named Faz, but Ifalna decides against rendezvousing with her liberators and instead heads for the church in Midgar's Sector 5 Slums. However, the experiments exact their toll on Ifalna, who collapses at the nearby train station but remains conscious long enough to entrust Aerith's safety to Elmyra, a local resident[13].

At home with Elmyra, the child senses her mother has returned to the Planet (meaning her soul joined the Lifestream when she died). Aerith continues to communicate with Ifalna on a spiritual level, but this proves more and more challenging as she grows older. She also detects the death of Elmyra's husband, Clay Gainsborough, despite him perishing in Wutai amid the war[14].

During her teens, Aerith attempts to run away from home on at least two occasions: once in *Before Crisis* and once in *Traces of Two Pasts*. In the former instance, she is pursued to the church by Avalanche operatives and urged by the group's leader, Elfe, to guide them to the Promised Land[15]. Avalanche's plan is thwarted by the player's Turk character.

Chronologically, the example in *Traces of Two Pasts* takes place earlier and is Aerith's first time visiting the church. The man who freed Aerith and Ifalna from Hojo's laboratory, Faz, escorts her there and tries to force her to come live with him. She is saved by Elmyra, while Faz is shot from the shadows by an unseen Turk.

The building is thereafter a regular haunt for Aerith, who is enchanted by the scented flowers that naturally bloom in its nave. It is at this exact spot that she initially meets Zack[16], the SOLDIER who becomes her first love and who encourages her to sell the florae, so that Midgar can be filled with their beauty. Many years later, while tending the patch at the chapel, Aerith also senses Zack's fatal injuries from afar.

The mysterious girl appears in the iconic opening sequence to *Final Fantasy VII*, carrying a basket of flowers onto a street in Sector 8 of Midgar's Plate. It is in this guise that she engages Cloud after he and Avalanche have blown up Mako Reactor 1, offering the player the opportunity to buy a bloom from her[17]. Cloud's acquisition is mandatory in *Remake's* corresponding scene, with Aerith remarking that the species of yellow flower she gives him symbolises loved ones being reunited[18].

The pair cross paths again at the Sector 5 church days later, where Cloud helps Aerith evade capture by Reno of the Turks[19]. The sequence of events that follows brings them to the Sector 7 Slums while the Turks are preparing to cause an entire district of the Plate above to come crashing down. Aerith is apprehended by Tseng during her rescue of Barret's daughter, Marlene, and agrees to return to Shinra Headquarters on the condition that the young girl is taken to Elmyra's house. Although this occurs off-screen in *Final Fantasy VII*, Aerith's search for Marlene at Seventh Heaven is playable in *Remake*, with Tseng confronting them at the bar while they are talking about flowers.

Cloud, Barret, and Tifa subsequently infiltrate the Shinra Building to retrieve their friend from the clutches of Professor Hojo. Things do not go according to plan, but they manage to escape when the Jenova specimen breaks from its confinement and – in the form of Sephiroth – murders President Shinra. The party thereafter sets off in hunt of the legendary SOLDIER, culminating in Aerith's attempt to activate the Holy Materia at the Forgotten Capital, where she is killed.

Desperate to avenge her death, Cloud leads the group across the snow fields to the north, eventually arriving at Icicle Inn. It is here that the player is able to watch the old videotape interviews between Gast and Ifalna, whose relationship ultimately resulted in Aerith's birth. Meanwhile, the flower girl's story progresses in the novella *Hoshi o Meguru Otome*, as discussed in the previous chapter.

Aerith is only featured on screen three more times in *Final Fantasy VII*: in the waterfall display at the Forgotten Capital, when Bugenhagen places the Key to the Ancients in the music box; as a fleeting apparition at the church, should the player regain access to the Sector 5 Slums; and in the closing seconds of the finale, which alludes to her actions within the Lifestream (as well as being a callback to the game's opening movie)[20]. In *Advent Children*, Aerith first interacts with Cloud from the afterlife by joining their minds in a flowery meadow, then momentarily appears to him in the church one last time at the climax of the film.

It is worth highlighting that the chapel is not the only location in Midgar where flowers are known to bloom: The tiered, butterfly-filled gardens around Elmyra's house are also abundant in floral colours. *Final Fantasy VII Remake* additionally introduces a vegetable patch beside the entrance of the grand home, with the produce in the kitchen suggesting it is eaten by Aerith and Elmyra.

Interestingly, *Traces of Two Pasts* confirms the flowers at the house and the church grew there long before Aerith arrived. Moreover, Motomu Toriyama, *Remake's* co-director, disclosed in an interview that the cause is the nutrients brought by the mako-rich river that meanders through the Gainsborough property[21]. Toriyama-san advised the same stream also runs beneath the church, although he did indicate that Aerith being a Cetra is a contributing factor to the flowers' continued prosperity[22].

When it comes to drawing parallels between Aerith and the ancient Greek myths surrounding Persephone, the two major themes are their associations with nurturing plants and with the afterlife. These themes demonstrate an array of similarities and connections, some of which may be obvious, some of which may not.

The *Homeric Hymn to Demeter* explains that the blossoming of flowers each spring signals Persephone's imminent ascension from the underworld, which, in turn, permits seeds to germinate, fruit and vegetables to develop, and so on. In *Final Fantasy VII*, as a survivor of the Cetra, Aerith is deeply linked to the cultivation of nature, initially in an environment where greenery is sparse due to mako being sucked from the earth. Flowers are so rare in Midgar that they have effectively become synonymous with the girl. Like Persephone, Aerith is not responsible for the creation of the world's flora but rather for the care and nourishment of it.

Comparisons can also be made between their respective mothers, Demeter and Ifalna. While the *Compilation* does not present a great deal of information about Ifalna, she is knowledgeable in the history and traditions of the Cetra (as revealed in her testimonials to Professor Gast), and proficient in their supernatural gifts (maintaining her communication with Aerith after she dies). The Cetra, of course, assisted the Planet by farming and settling the land, which is the divine domain of Demeter, Goddess of the Harvest, in Hellenic lore.

Intriguingly, prior to her capture by Shinra, Inc., Ifalna's home was Icicle Inn in the permafrost region, where the soil is infertile and the ice never melts[23]. This can be likened to the Eleusinian Mysteries teaching that winter is the result of Demeter withering the land as she mourns the loss of her daughter every year, albeit only for the months Persephone spends in the underworld.

Elements of the nurturing, protective mother-daughter relationship Demeter has with Persephone can be glimpsed between Ifalna and Aerith throughout the *Compilation*, although it is much more expanded upon in *Traces of Two Pasts*. For instance, Aerith learns about the workings of nature from her mother, which is best evidenced during *Remake* in the wall art of the duo's quarters at the Shinra Building.

The artwork is a huge collage of organic life, from plants and animals to monsters and magic, depicting the cyclical flow of the Lifestream and even figures from the Cetra's distant past. The latter are separated into two distinct groups: farmhands gathering wheat from a field, and priests and priestesses performing a ritual[24]. This seems to be a direct allusion to the Eleusinian Mysteries, which related specifically to the harvesting of crops, and whose secret ceremonies were conducted by hierophants (priests and priestesses of the Mysteries).

Furthermore, in this context, the changing seasons and annual return of Persephone are reflected in the Lifestream's cycle of birth, life, death, and rebirth. It is also unlikely to be a coincidence that the wall art's two most recurring images are flowers and butterflies. Flowers are symbolic of Persephone's life-giving attributes in springtime, while the ancient Greek word for 'butterfly' is Latinised as *'psyche'*, which can alternatively refer to a person's 'soul', especially with regards to it being detached from the body at death[25]. In this way, Persephone's connection to the afterlife is accounted for[26].

It should also be mentioned that the artwork was produced in the same time period as when Aerith's Cetran abilities manifested[27]. While in a trance, the young girl visualises and illustrates landscapes that are rich in life and vegetation, subsequently perceived by Shinra's scientists to be mako hotspots. This provides yet another parallel to Persephone's association in mythology with the revitalisation of nature.

In various sources across the *Compilation*, Aerith intimates that her capacity to communicate with Ifalna's spirit diminishes as she gets older. When the party is imprisoned in Hojo's laboratory during *Final Fantasy VII,* she tells Cloud and Tifa that she now struggles to discern the voices of the Planet, but they are clearest at the church in the Sector 5 Slums. This may be a factor in how she was able to sense Zack's injuries concurrent to his death scene at the end of *Crisis Core*[28].

Traces of Two Pasts reveals that Ifalna and Aerith were bound for the church to gain sanctuary when the former collapsed and passed away. According to *Final Fantasy VII Remake's Material Ultimania*, the building itself was initially erected during Midgar's construction as a place to commemorate workers who had lost their lives, and for locals to receive spiritual healing. The flowers that soon began to sprout in its nave were considered a miracle.

This creates a deeper link between the church, the flowers, and the afterlife. Aerith's own affiliation with the chapel is so profound that she appears there (either alive or as an apparition) in every main entry of the *Compilation* she features in[29]. In particular, her fleeting spectral presence at the church late in *Final Fantasy VII* and again in *Advent Children* might loosely correspond to Persephone being escorted directly to the temple precinct at Eleusis when she is released from Hades.

There is a possible supplement to this hinted at in *Final Fantasy VII Remake*. The *Homeric Hymn to Demeter* notes that the flowers of springtime herald Persephone's ascension each year, meaning they also signify her return to Demeter. In *Remake*, the yellow flowers represent loved ones being reunited, which is doubly relevant in *Traces of Two Pasts*, when the young Aerith feels her mother's spirit among the blooms of Elmyra's garden.

The book describes the property as having copious amounts of plants and flowers when the girl is first taken there, but it is very well maintained by the time the player's Turk character stumbles upon the estate in *Before Crisis*, around a decade later. The extent of this is best expressed in *Remake* itself, with a plethora of flower species and a vegetable patch on show, which correlates with Persephone being a goddess of growth. Akin to the wall art at Shinra Headquarters, the abundance of butterflies in the garden may also symbolise the souls of the Lifestream.

The topography surrounding the Gainsborough home is of specific interest when compared to the myth of Persephone's abduction. The *Homeric Hymn to Demeter* is relatively vague in terms of illustrating the spot where Hades rode from the earth to grab the maiden: It happened in a flowery meadow known as the Plain of Nysa.

Ovid's *Fasti*, however, paints a much more vivid picture: Within a shady valley is a place drenched in the spray of a waterfall, where all the colours of nature can be found in the flora that grows there. This bears a remarkable likeness to the terraced land around Elmyra's house. Additionally, Persephone (or Proserpina, as Ovid calls her) and her friends pick a variety of flowers to fill their woven wicker baskets (including lilies). This not only mirrors Aerith herself but also the scene in *Remake* in which Cloud helps her collect a selection of blooms for the Leaf House.

As for the similarities between Aerith and the kidnapping of Persephone, these are not limited to the garden's landscape, for the Cetran girl has experienced more than her fair share of abductions. Two such examples are Hojo's apprehension of Ifalna and the infant Aerith from Icicle Inn, and Tseng detaining her in exchange for Marlene's safety. Reno (in *Final Fantasy VII*), Avalanche (in *Before Crisis*), and Faz (in *Traces of Two Pasts*) have also each tried to seize her from the Sector 5 church.

Moreover, there are patterns to be uncovered in the cycle of captivity and freedom that Aerith goes through, all of which are analogous to Greek mythology. The first is that since she became a teenager, the attempts to abduct Aerith have been in the presence of flowers: Reno, Faz, and Avalanche's efforts occur in the nave of the church, while Tseng secures her at Seventh Heaven in *Remake*, immediately after she and Marlene discuss the yellow flower behind the bar. These may each be an allusion to Persephone being plucked from the meadow.

Persephone's captor, of course, is Hades, King of the Dead, which might establish a further connection. Aerith is twice imprisoned at Shinra Headquarters (by Hojo and Tseng, respectively) and twice freed (by Faz and Cloud). As it happens, all four occasions are aligned with death: Hojo murders Professor Gast; Ifalna dies during their escape to the Slums; countless civilians perish in the collapse of the Sector 7 Plate; and President Shinra is slain by Sephiroth.

Aerith losing her own life is perhaps a less subtle nod to Persephone being taken to the underworld, where she eventually comes to rule over the souls of the dead alongside

Hades. The flower girl does not share this role in the mythos of *Final Fantasy VII*, but her preserved consciousness in the Lifestream allows her to assist other spirits and to affect the flow of energy within the great river, as explained in chapter VI. In this way, Aerith has a substantial degree of influence in the afterlife, just as Persephone does.

While Aerith's murder and Persephone's kidnapping are not to be confused in terms of how they come to be in the respective realms of the dead, the former may support the earlier proposal that the permafrost region references the earth withering as Demeter mourns her daughter's departure. Specifically, the entire section that follows Aerith's death takes place in the frozen wastelands, from the snow fields north of the Forgotten Capital to the precipices of Gaea's Cliff.

In a similar vein, where the Eleusinian Mysteries associated seasonal change with the cycle of birth, life, death, and rebirth, it is not likely to be a coincidence that the videotapes concerning the newborn Aerith should become accessible so soon after the flower girl is killed, nor that they are hidden in *Final Fantasy VII's* only winter town. A related observation, albeit abstract, is that this exact segment of the game is bookended by two battles against Jenova: Jenova LIFE at the water alter and Jenova DEATH at the Whirlwind Maze. As such, encounters with the extraterrestrial fiend seem to touch on the same lifecycle[30].

Classical depictions of Persephone typically interpret her to be a young goddess with a sheaf of grain rather than flowers, but she has a distinct attachment to various flora. There are dozens of Greek myths that recount tragic romances, a number of which end in a mortal male being transformed into a flower, or a new species blooming from his spilled blood. The tales of Narcissus, Hyacinthus, Crocus, and Adonis are all such instances[31].

Curiously, the *Homeric Hymn to Demeter* and Ovid's *Fasti* explicitly list the narcissus, hyacinth, and crocus flowers (among others) as being picked by the maiden and her friends before she is snatched away by Hades. Adonis, meanwhile, whom Persephone loved and fostered, died in the arms of Aphrodite, and from the mixture of his blood and her tears sprang the red anemone.

Despite Persephone being wed to Hades against her will, many of the stories that involve the pair present a relationship of respect and affection. Aerith does not have a husband, by consent or otherwise, but there is evidence in both *Hoshi o Meguru Otome* and *Advent Children* that she spends some time in the Lifestream with Zack, her first boyfriend. During the ending to *Advent Children Complete*, yellow flowers are shown to be blossoming at the site where Zack was shot dead. This could be a vague allusion to the tragic romances in which new flowers symbolise the demise of mortal men, two of whom (Adonis and Narcissus) have a direct link to Persephone.

To conclude, Aerith's name is frequently spoken aloud by the other characters of the *Compilation*, unlike the epithets used by the cult worshippers of Persephone (including Cora). That is not to say there are no parallels, though. The flower girl's name in Japanese romaji is '*Earisu*'[32], which is a deliberate derivation of 'Earth', just as *Final Fantasy VI* has Terra as a leading lady[33]. The purpose behind this was to emphasise Aerith's connection to the Planet as a Cetra, but it also corresponds to Persephone, herself a goddess of agriculture. *Traces of Two Pasts* further introduces a period during Aerith's youth where she had to use an alias to avoid unwanted questions from the people of Sector 5[34].

Incidentally, the euphemistic name most commonly applied to Persephone was Cora or Kore: 'Maiden'. The Japanese word for 'maiden' or a young, innocent female in general is '*otome*', which forms part of the title for Benny Matsuyama's novella, *Hoshi o Meguru Otome*. Therefore, just as Persephone is the 'Maiden' of Greek mythology, who descends to the underworld each year, Aerith is the 'Maiden' of *Final Fantasy VII*, who travels the Planet and its afterlife rivers.

1. The Mycenaeans were an early Greek civilisation that existed during the Late Bronze Age (approximately 1750 BC to 1050 BC). Ancient Mesopotamia occupied what is now Iraq, Kuwait, and parts of Iran, Syria, and Turkey. It included distinguished empires such as Sumer, Assyria, and Babylon over the span of approximately 5,000 years.

2. Poseidon's association with water during the Mycenaean era evolved into him being a sea god by the time of Homer, while Zeus inherited the crucial role of revitalising water provider via the rain from his storm clouds.

3. *Poleis* were ancient Greek city-states, and *demoi* were the rural communities within the *poleis'* jurisdictions.

4. Most accounts name Zeus as Persephone's father. In the later Orphic myths, however, she was the daughter of Zeus and his own mother, the Titaness Rhea.

5. The festival lasted for nine days in and around Athens, a region known as Attica. It was only on the last night that initiates who had travelled to Eleusis would enter the Telesterion – the temple sanctuary – to take part in the great ceremony.

6. Comparative mythology has shown that stories similar to the abduction of Persephone predate Hellenic literature by millennia, with renowned historian Samuel Noah Kramer suggesting traces of them can even be found in the ancient Sumerian legend of Ereshkigal and the dragon Kur.

7. The Homeric Hymns are a collection of 33 anonymous songs that predate the Classical period and celebrate individual gods. They are called so because they make use of the same poetic techniques as Homer's work, not because they were composed by him.

8. A separate connection between Aerith and Narcissus (the figure after whom the flower is named) in the context of *Final Fantasy VII* is proposed in chapter XIX.

9. The *Homeric Hymn to Demeter* advises that Persephone is required to spend a third of the year (four months) in the underworld, while later Roman writers such as Ovid and Hyginus extended this to six months.

155

10. According to the hymn, the goddess Hecate (often associated with witchcraft) takes Persephone's place in the months when the latter is absent from the underworld.

11. The Study of Planetary Life is known simply as planetology in *Final Fantasy VII Remake*. It concerns the research of spirit energy and the Lifestream, based on the principle that the Planet is a living organism.

12. The town of Banora with its dumbapple plantation is an example of bountiful farming in soil enriched by the Lifestream. This is explained in the *Crisis Core Ultimania*. However, Banora itself is not affiliated with the Cetra.

13. *Traces of Two Pasts* follows *Final Fantasy VII Remake's* continuity. In the original game, Ifalna dies at the Sector 7 Slums station.

14. Clay's name is confirmed in *Traces of Two Pasts*.

15. This branch of Avalanche is a large military organisation and the antagonist of *Before Crisis*. It preceded the smaller regional cells, one of which is eventually led by Barret Wallace in Midgar and features heavily in *Final Fantasy VII* and *Remake*.

16. During *Crisis Core*, Zack falls from Midgar's upper-city and smashes through the roof of the church, landing on the flower bed. The same thing happens with Cloud in *Final Fantasy VII*.

17. Depending on the player's dialogue choices, Cloud may not purchase a flower or may not even get the option.

18. In the English localisation of *Remake*, Aerith says lovers used to exchange these yellow flowers when they were reunited. However, this deviates from the Japanese script and other localisations, which imply friends or family are also included in the tradition. The particular species of flower is not confirmed in *Remake* or its extended media, but it most closely resembles a lily, specifically a Golden Stargazer.

19. In *Final Fantasy VII*, Reno orders the troopers accompanying him to attack Cloud and Aerith. Subsequent *Compilation* entries have retconned the

156

Turks' relationship with the girl to one of surveillance and protection. Reno does come for Aerith at the church in *Remake*, but it is later implied by his partner, Rude, that their agenda is to ensure she is clear of Sector 7 (for the imminent collapse of the Plate).

20. Contrary to popular belief, the visuals of Aerith's face illuminated by the glow of mako (which respectively appear in the opening and ending movies of *Final Fantasy VII*) do not truly match. She has her eyes open in the former, while her eyes are closed, then slowly open in the latter. It may be worth noting that the opening to *Remake* mirrors the ending to *Final Fantasy VII*.

21. Toriyama-san's comments were made during an interview with Square Enix's North American team in 2020. They contradict a line in *Crisis Core*, where Aerith tells Zack she planted the flowers at the house herself.

22. The Leaf House orphanage in Sector 5 (*Remake* only) also has a lot of greenery around it, but it is unclear if this is due to Aerith's care or its proximity to the energy-rich waters.

23. The permafrost is a consequence of the Planet redirecting spirit energy to the Northern Crater to heal the wound caused by Jenova's meteorite.

24. Illustrations contained within the *Final Fantasy VII Remake Material Ultimania* show specific character designs that were produced for the Cetra, one of which is listed as 'Ancient Priestess'.

25. There is also a female character in Greek mythology called Psyche, whose tale revolves around being the mortal lover of Eros, the God of Love. Psyche has to descend into the underworld during the story.

26. Curiously, the wall art includes Pegasus, one of the most recognisable creatures in Greek lore. There is no direct link between the winged horse and Persephone, but a reason for its presence is proposed in chapter XIII. There also appears to be a phoenix, now a universal symbol of rebirth; this is explored in depth in chapter XII.

27. There is a consistency issue with regards to how and when the wall art was created. *Remake's* co-director,

Motomu Toriyama, has stated Ifalna and Aerith produced it together (which would explain the differences in style, quality, and height), while Kazushige Nojima wrote in *Picturing the Past* that Aerith is solely responsible for the art, painting it herself over the course of a week after her 'awakening' as a Cetra.

28. Another contributing factor to this is the rain falling through the church's ceiling. As described in chapter V, water can act as a vessel for spiritual communication.

29. Aerith is not present at the church in *Hoshi o Meguru Otome*, *On the Way to a* Smile, or *Picturing the Past*, though these are supplementary works. In the epilogue of *Episode INTERmission*, her absence is so unusual that it is portrayed as ominous.

30. The player faces a manifestation of Jenova in President Shinra's office during *Final Fantasy VII Remake*. This encounter takes place earlier than in the original game, where Jenova BIRTH is fought aboard the cargo ship en route to Costa del Sol. *Remake's* monster is called Jenova Pulse (Jenova Dreamweaver in the English localisation), whereby 'Pulse' alludes to the heartbeat of an unborn child.

31. Each of these stories can be found in Ovid's *Metamorphoses*.

32. Japanese phonetics do not typically use the 'th' sound, which led to the infamous transliteration of Aerith's name in the original localisation of *Final Fantasy VII*, 'Aeris'.

33. Terra is named after the personification of Mother Earth in Roman mythology, cognate with Gaia in ancient Greek.

34. The name Aerith chose was Ronna and she pretended to be a distant relative of Elmyra.

CHAPTER VIII

THE RESURRECTED

The Eleusinian Mysteries, as discussed in the previous chapter, were among the most famous religious ceremonies of ancient Greece, particularly with respect to agriculture and the afterlife. They were not the only rites of this kind, however, and Demeter and Persephone were not the only divinities associated with the harvesting of crops.

From at least the 7th century BC – but possibly as early as the Mycenaean era –, Dionysus was widely worshipped as the God of the Vine. Like Demeter, he was one of the twelve Olympians, albeit a later entry to the pantheon at the expense of Hestia[1]. Where Demeter oversaw the reaping of grains for bread, cereal, and the stockpiling of seeds, Dionysus was responsible for the cultivation of grapes and the making of wine. He was described in some sources as having rich locks of hair and wearing purple robes, presumably to match the colour of his produce.

Dionysus (whom the Romans called Bacchus) was known as both a god of merriment and of madness, reflecting the dual aspects of alcohol. He could inspire confidence and liberty[2], or he could promote wild behaviour and violence. In the myths, devout female followers of Dionysus, called maenads ('raving ones') or Bacchantes, were said to rove towns and countryside alike in frenzied intoxication, energised by the ecstasy of the freedoms their deity bestowed upon them. Such frenzies regularly resulted in bloodshed or even death. This is why, since *Final Fantasy II*, Bacchus' Wine has been a recurring item that will typically cast the Berserk status on party members.

The cult of Dionysus believed in expressing oneself, free from the shackles of society's oppression. This included lowering the barriers of class and gender divide, exploring sexuality, or denouncing civilised life and returning to nature. The tales of Dionysus generally involve a retinue of mythical creatures from the forests and hillsides, such as centaurs (half-human, half-horse) and satyrs (humanoid nature spirits with the ears and tail of a horse[3]), which represent mankind's primitive side. The god himself is often responsible for the metamorphosis of his followers into hybrid beings, symbolising their transition back to the wild. So extensive is his entourage of inebriated revellers that it gets its own name: the Thiasus.

By the 5th century BC, Dionysus had two relatively distinct sets of cult rituals: the Dionysian Mysteries and the Orphic Mysteries, each with their individual practices and associated myths. The major cult centres could be found in Attica, a region comprising of Athens and its surrounding lands. The Dionysian Mysteries were by far the elder, with reference to certain stories appearing in Hesiod's *Theogony* and a trio of dedicated Homeric Hymns. They likely started as thanksgiving festivities to celebrate the harvested grapes being taken to the winepress, while the role of seasonal change and the vines' annual death and rebirth was gradually incorporated[4].

There are only snippets of the original myth cycle captured in Hesiod and the hymns, with Homer outright ignoring Dionysus' place in Olympus. The earliest sources for many of the known tales are the dramatic compositions of the Classical period, which were comprehensively collected and recounted in Apollodorus' *Bibliotheca* as well as in the works of later Greek and Roman authors.

Dionysus is most commonly portrayed as the son of Zeus and Semele, a princess from the city-state of Thebes. Hera, the jealous Queen of Heaven, learns of her husband's promiscuity and suggests to the pregnant Semele that she asks to see Zeus in his true form. The Skyfather swears an oath on the river Styx to grant whatever Semele wishes for, and he is bound by his promise, even if it means her inevitable death.

As Semele perishes under the intensity of Zeus' dazzling and burning glory, he plucks the unborn child from her womb and sews the baby inside his own thigh. When the nine months' term is complete, the immortal infant Dionysus emerges. This is how he acquires the epithet of 'Twice-Born'.

To protect him from Hera's wrath, Zeus leaves the boy to be raised by the nymphs of Mount Nysa[5], who keep him safely hidden in a cave. In the valleys around Nysa, the beautiful, effeminate youth discovers the grapevine and teaches himself the art of winemaking, which he thereafter shares with others wherever he visits.

When Dionysus has grown to manhood, he travels far and wide, often mistreated and enduring many hardships because he is not believed to be a god. He is also depicted in later Hellenic writings as a warrior, leading his Thiasus in campaigns to India and Northern Africa[6].

A number of the myths tell of how Dionysus offers wrongdoers a chance to repent, delivering divine punishment when they do not. These consequences range from turning a pirate crew into dolphins to having the ruler of Thebes ripped apart by his own mother while she is in a Bacchic frenzy.

During his wanderings, Dionysus longs to meet Semele, and eventually descends into the underworld to reclaim her soul. He defies the power of Hades and leads his mother up to Olympus, where he makes her an immortal[7]. Dionysus' journey to the kingdom of the dead and subsequent ascension into heaven prove to the people of Greece that he is indeed a god. The Dionysian Mysteries are thought to have featured this tale in their representation of death and rebirth.

Dionysus' suffering at the hands of those he encountered can be equated to Demeter's grief as she searched for Persephone (see chapter VII), and it was this misery that those oppressed by society (such as women, peasants, or slaves) found most relatable. He was a god that characterised both joy and sorrow, and he was present in the daily lives of the Hellenes in a way that the other Olympians – with the exception of Demeter – were not.

Separate to this myth cycle were the Orphic Mysteries, based on a series of hymns believed to have been composed by the legendary bard Orpheus[8]. Literary evidence confirms that Orphism was prominent by at least the 5th century BC, but its religious practices are likely to significantly predate that[9].

The Orphic Hymns, of which 87 have survived, were not written down until the late 3rd or early 2nd centuries BC. They contain details of a genealogy for the ancient Greek gods that rearranges Hesiod's *Theogony* in some parts and entirely revises it in others[10], complementing what few fragments of older sources have ever been discovered.

Orphism is considered to have evolved from a branch of the Dionysian Mysteries, and its rituals also placed much emphasis on the journey into and return from the underworld. Its most revered deities were Dionysus himself and Persephone, who, in these reformed stories, is his original mother.

According to the prevalent myth, Dionysus' first incarnation is an infant called Zagreus, born to Zeus and Persephone[11]. Zeus loves the boy and names him heir to the throne of Olympus, which enrages his wife, Hera. Driven by hatred, Hera directs the Titans to murder Zagreus and consume his body, but Athena saves his heart, and Zeus obliterates the brutes with his thunderbolts.

Mankind rises from the ashes of the Titans, their corporeal flesh and blood forever tainted by sin. The divine soul of Zagreus, however, is reborn as Dionysus when Semele falls pregnant to Zeus. In this way, he is blessed with two mothers, so the epithet of 'Twice-Born' can also be applied to the Orphic myths. An alternative version of the tale is that Dionysus is born after Athena buries Zagreus' heart in Zeus' thigh, thus integrating the Dionysian and Orphic variants.

The death and resurrection of Dionysus was the foundation of the Orphic Mysteries: It created the distinction between the mortal body and the immortal soul, offering hope of a beautiful and eternal afterlife to initiates (as discussed in chapter VI). Unlike Persephone, he was not worshipped with a degree of apprehension, simply because he did not represent the underworld; instead, he personified life that conquers death.

Nevertheless, Dionysus remained the suffering god, just as a pruned vine shrivels and becomes gnarled in winter. Over time, though, his role in society changed from a deity who gave humanity freedom through drunken ecstasy and inhibition to one who granted freedom through divine influence and artistic expression, a domain previously occupied by the Muses[12].

Before the Classical period of ancient Greece, literature was relatively inaccessible because only a fraction of the Hellenic population could read. Even when formal education became widespread, it was primarily limited to males and non-slaves. Everyone else relied on stories and cultural beliefs being passed down orally, but these could also be enjoyed through performances of poetry, choral songs, and dialogues.

By the 5th century BC, the religious festivals of Dionysus had developed into one of the most openly celebrated events across Greece, chiefly due to participation being non-discriminatory. While the Mysteries were practiced in dedicated temples and sanctuary precincts, general veneration of the Twice-Born took place in the theatres of Athens and beyond. The plays performed there were sacred; to attend them was an act of worship.

Of the myriad festivals that honoured Dionysus, the largest and best known was the annual Dionysia. The main events (called the Greater Dionysia) were held in Athens around springtime, consisting of processions, sacrifices, and a swathe of competitions. Playwrights, poets, singers, actors, and other creators and performers were considered to be servants of Dionysus, and they vied for the most prestigious prizes each year.

Poems would be recited by professional actors or bards, while theatrical productions would dramatise them, typically including musical elements. Thought to be the earliest form of drama, the Greek tragedies originated from the Dionysia[13], where re-enactments of Dionysus' joyful resurrection were accompanied by the sorrow of the deeds done to him.

Over time, the works centred more and more on various gods and heroes from mythology, drawing inspiration from a range of sources. For example, the *Iliad* and the *Odyssey* were used to script supplementary episodes from the Trojan War, such as in Euripides' *Trōiades* ('*Trojan Women*')[14]. The only fully surviving plays of this kind come from Athens, composed by Aeschylus and the aforementioned duo, each of whom were illustrious winners of the Dionysia competitions. Of the scores of dramas known to have been written during the Classical period, all but 32 are incomplete.

While the *Compilation of Final Fantasy VII* as a whole does not incorporate much poetry, *LOVELESS* is an epic that boasts a major role in *Crisis Core*. In the game's modern era, *LOVELESS* is normally regarded as a stage production, but the ancient roots of the literary masterpiece are the subject of study and debate. Of particular interest is how deeply associated it is with the main antagonist, Genesis

Rhapsodos, who has become synonymous with the poem's verses.

Genesis is introduced in *Crisis Core* as a rogue SOLDIER First Class who has abandoned his duties in the Wutai War to lead a mass exodus of his subordinates. He is a close friend of Zack's mentor, Angeal, as well as the legendary swordsman Sephiroth, and is one of the few people in the world capable of matching the latter in a duel. Like Angeal and Sephiroth, Genesis has fan clubs with members all over the Planet. Two individual organisations are encountered by Zack during *Crisis Core*, although they can be amalgamated later in the game, depending on the player's actions.

Shortly after Genesis' disappearance in Wutai, it is discovered that he can copy his attributes onto other people and has been exploiting this to build a following from the SOLDIER renegades. He is able to do so because he is a product of Project Jenova G (Project Gillian), and the specifics of his birth yielded some unusual qualities[15].

According to the *Crisis Core Ultimania* and the *Complete Guide*, Gillian is a Shinra scientist who consents to being injected with Jenova cells. Genesis thereafter has her genes (and thus diluted Jenova DNA) mapped onto him when he is still in the womb. While the infant is deemed a failure of the Ancients Project[16], he is monitored as a youth and gradually begins to exhibit the assets required to join the superhuman combatants of SOLDIER.

Genesis is adopted in his early childhood by wealthy landowners in the remote town of Banora, famed for its apple trees that bear fruit at random times throughout the year. The secret behind their abundance is that the regional soil is extremely rich and fertile, thanks to the Lifestream currents in that corner of the world flowing very near to the surface.

The apples themselves are formally known as Banora Whites but are also affectionately called 'dumbapples' on account of their inconsistent ripening. When he is a boy, Genesis invents an award-winning juice made from the Banora Whites[17], which subsequently becomes the town's largest export. Advertisements for the beverage can be found all over Midgar in *Final Fantasy VII Remake*.

Genesis is regularly seen with a dumbapple in his possession during the second half of *Crisis Core*[18], and he is obsessed with the epic poem *LOVELESS*, often quoting lines or reciting entire stanzas when he appears in the game. His fixation on the legend is a decisive aspect of his character. The original plot of *LOVELESS* relates to three friends who have been separated by war. The men had sworn an oath together that they would seek 'the Gift of the Goddess', the true nature of which remains a mystery.

Across the *Compilation*, the theatre production of *LOVELESS* is alternatively referred to as a play (*Final Fantasy VII*), a stage drama (*Crisis Core*), or a musical (*Remake*), though the focus of the story is said to change from year to year[19]. The ancient poem's fifth and final act has been lost, so the fate of the friends and whether they attain the gift is open to interpretation. Genesis composes his own ending and creates a space in the Banora Underground for him to receive the Gift of the Goddess[20], specifically via a statue of the Goddess and an enormous orb of red materia[21].

During his youth, Genesis stumbles upon the extensive cave network beneath Banora, the site of a former mako mine owned by the Shinra Company. Construction of the mine had unexpectedly ceased many years earlier, with Banora itself erected above the caverns to conceal their existence. The *Crisis Core Complete Guide* hints at the reason for this being the unearthing of a Weapon, parts of which the player can view while Zack navigates the Depths of Judgement area of the Banora Underground[22].

Soon after the mass SOLDIER desertion, Genesis establishes his army's base at Banora, utilising its subterranean passages for their activities and the experimentation on the copies[23]. The motivation for his insurgence is that he has been suffering from a rare type of degradation since a sparring accident with Sephiroth and is convinced he must aggressively force the key to his recovery from Shinra.

Genesis eventually concludes that Jenova cells alone can halt his deteriorating state, so he dispatches his legions all around the Planet in search of the extraterrestrial specimen's storage. The copies have not only inherited a degree of his strength and abilities during the transplant process, but his aspirations, too. However, while most of them retain their human form, some mutate and take on monstrous features, growing wild and fierce.

Zack battles against the Genesis copies many times and in many locations throughout *Crisis Core*, but he engages the real Genesis in direct combat on only two occasions: once at the mako excavation site near Modeoheim and once in the Banora Underground. During the former exchange, Genesis' degradation is accelerating, and he hurls himself into the dark chasm of the mine when he is defeated by the young SOLDIER, resurfacing several months later.

By the climax of the game, Genesis' body has substantially decayed, and he has run out of options on how to reverse the decline. He believes his salvation is the Gift of the Goddess mentioned in *LOVELESS*, and to receive it, he must re-enact the epic by duelling Zack[24]. Genesis lures the hero into the depths of the Banora Underground so he can 'perform' with the Goddess statue as his audience, then absorbs the power of the Lifestream from the giant materia.

The vast quantity of spirit energy channelling into Genesis cures his degradation and restores his vitality, but it comes at the cost of his strength. He loses to Zack a second time and finds himself in a spiritual plane, confronted by Minerva, an entity whose actions reflect the will of the Lifestream[25].

The *Crisis Core Complete Guide* explains that in these final moments Genesis has reached the point where he is no longer afraid of dying, but he is determined to regain his SOLDIER honour. So resolute is this desire that the Lifestream accepts he yet has a role to fulfil on behalf of the Planet, allowing him to return to the mortal world.

Genesis is thereafter transported to Deepground by Weiss and Nero, but he refuses to participate in their plan to seize control of the facility. He seals himself in a watery cocoon beneath Midgar's Slums, only to reawaken after the events of *Dirge of Cerberus*.

There is no better place to start when comparing Genesis and Dionysus than their respective synonymy with dumbapples and grapes. To the ancient Greeks, Dionysus was the God of the Vine, so the cultivation and harvesting of grapes was sacred to him. Genesis, meanwhile, was raised in Banora, the sole region on the Planet where dumbapples grow. This is an important feature of *Crisis Core's* plot, for his continued presence in the town is repeatedly indicated: After his re-emergence post-Modeoheim, he is always in the possession of a ripe Banora White. The significance of the apples is also highlighted very early in the game when Angeal gives Zack an anecdote about them en route to Fort Tamblin[26].

As for why grapes were not incorporated instead, there is evidence to suggest multiple religious and mythological influences are at play here, as explored in *Norse Myths That Inspired Final Fantasy VII*[27]. The rogue SOLDIER's name has understandably led to associations with the *Book of Genesis*, the first volume in the Hebrew Bible and Old

Testament of the Christian Bible. The volume covers the creation story of Judaism and how humanity lost its innocence when Eve tasted the forbidden fruit, generally identified in modern times as an apple.

The fruit of the dumbapples themselves is soft and white, but the outer flesh is a unique shade of bluish-purple. These colours are more reflective of traditional red or purple grape varieties than they are of apples[28]. The Banora White trees that surround the town are also unusual in shape: Rather than growing upright, many of their trunks arc back down towards the ground, with the fruit hanging from vine-like branches.

In the myths, Dionysus is fostered as a youth by the nymphs of Nysa, and in the valleys there he discovers the art of winemaking, which he popularises around the world. Genesis has a similar history in *Crisis Core*: Labelled a failure of the Jenova Project, he is adopted by the wealthy landowners of the Banora plantation and takes advantage of his access to the fruit to invent an award-winning apple juice at a young age, turning it into a major export[29].

The writers of antiquity were relatively inconsistent in their descriptions of Dionysus, although his rich, flowing locks and purple robes are mentioned in one of the earliest sources[30], the *Homeric Hymn (7) to Dionysus*[31]. Genesis himself wears a leather trenchcoat that is deep red in colour, first appearing in it during the hidden epilogue of *Dirge of Cerberus*.

172

Like Dionysus, Genesis is well-travelled: The antagonist has scenes on four separate continents during *Crisis Core*[32], mostly carrying his signature dumbapple and quoting stanzas regarding the mysteries of *LOVELESS*. This parallels the Twice-Born, who is said to have brought the secrets of vine cultivation to people wherever he went, as well as teaching them his divine Mysteries.

Authors and poets from the Hellenistic and Roman eras further embellished Dionysus' character by including military campaigns in the wanderings of his Thiasus, which is comprised in part by men and women the god has liberated from society's restraints and transformed into hybrid creatures. This is analogous to the copies of the Genesis Army, primarily individuals who have abandoned their life with SOLDIER and Shinra to follow the ideals of their leader, himself an accomplished warrior. It could be contended that Genesis offers an escape from the authoritarian corporate and militaristic regime, just as Dionysus offers freedom to the oppressed.

Through the genetic traits of the diluted Jenova cells in Genesis' body, the copies have also literally undergone metamorphosis as part of their new identity. The combatants of the Genesis Army are typically depicted as being violent or frenzied, not unlike the satyrs and maenads of the Thiasus, becoming less human and increasingly ferocious as the game progresses. On a more abstract level, this can be extended to the autonomous Shinra weapons, which are repetitively sent haywire during the Genesis Army's attacks.

There are also specific examples of Genesis' words and actions inspiring madness in others. By revealing to Angeal and Sephiroth that they were born of the Jenova Project, both descend into despair and brutality in their own ways: Angeal deserts SOLDIER and eventually mutates into the diabolic Penance, while Sephiroth's research at the Shinra Manor basement is the catalyst for his annihilation of Nibelheim. This resembles the tales of Dionysus and how he inflicted devastation upon those who had persecuted him by sending the offenders or those around them into Bacchic deliriums[33].

In addition to his innumerable copies, Genesis is also revered and followed by his fan clubs. It is perhaps no coincidence that where Sephiroth and Angeal have single organisations admiring them in the game[34] – the Silver Elite and Keepers of Honor, respectively –, Genesis has two: Red Leather and the Study Group. Their existence and optional amalgamation may be a reference to the distinct cults of Dionysus – practitioners of the Dionysian Mysteries and practitioners of the Orphic Mysteries –, whose myths and rituals were later merged by the Romans in their festivals for Bacchus[35].

A key factor in the beliefs of these cults was that through the hardships he faced, Dionysus was a suffering god, and by his rescue of Semele from the underworld or his rebirth from the soul of Zagreus, he was also a god who conquered death. The plot of *Crisis Core* centres around Genesis' battle to find a cure for his degradation. Through his own actions or otherwise, he loses his SOLDIER honour, is spurned by his closest friends, kills his parents over their perceived betrayal[36], and yet, for the longest time, he keeps failing to discover a way to prevent the continuous decay of his body. Then, when he finally succeeds, it is at the cost of his life, and only by Minerva's grace is he returned to the physical realm. In this way, Genesis, too, has suffered and conquered death.

The Banora Underground integrates symbolism relevant to the stories of Dionysus and the broader theme of death and resurrection. As described in chapter XVIII, there are several correlations between this endgame dungeon and the depths of Hades in ancient Greek mythology. It is therefore appropriate that the purging of Genesis' degradation to end his anguish should occur here, just as the cycle of the Dionysian Mysteries concludes with Dionysus overcoming death by reclaiming his mother's spirit from the underworld and ascending to Olympus.

The element of resurrection in the Orphic Mysteries comes from the earlier incarnation of the god, the infant Zagreus, being consumed by the Titans, only to have his heart salvaged by Athena so that Dionysus may be born from it. While the allusion is a bit more vague, this version of the myth might also be reflected in the Banora Underground.

The giant red materia set in the subterranean cavern by Genesis seems to act as a conduit for him to absorb the

Lifestream and heal his degradation. When he then finds himself in a spiritual plane following his defeat by Zack, the orb held by the nearby Goddess statue is glowing like the materia had been. As the brilliant glare intensifies, Minerva appears before Genesis in place of the figurine, with her expression representative of the Lifestream's decision to send him back from the afterlife.

The next chapter will explore the nature of Minerva in detail, but the critical component here is that she shares her name with the Roman Goddess of Wisdom, Strategy, and the Arts, who is conflated with the Greek Athena. As such, the red materia's association with Minerva and it being the instrument for Genesis' salvation could indeed mirror Athena saving Zagreus' heart so that Dionysus can be reborn from it.

These climactic scenes are not the only instances in *Crisis Core* in which Genesis is suggested to have been killed and resurrected. After Zack's mission to Banora ends with the town being obliterated by the Shinra Air Force's bombs, the company officially declares that Genesis has died, but he and his army lay siege to Midgar months later. Similarly, Genesis throws himself into the abyss of the mako excavation site and is presumed to have perished, then eventually presents himself to Zack and Sephiroth at the Mount Nibel reactor.

As an extension to this, the *Crisis Core Ultimania* explains that Genesis is voluntarily sealed in a water-based prison soon after he is retrieved from Banora by

176

Deepground. He remains in stasis until after *Dirge of Cerberus*, when he emerges to fulfil his duty as a protector of the Planet. This could be a metaphor for his final resurrection, visually represented by Genesis ascending into the heavens with the body of Weiss in his arms.

In addition to creating parallels between the revival aspects of Genesis and Dionysus, *Crisis Core* also establishes that the former's fan clubs both hold annual memorial events in the hope that their beloved hero will return from the dead[37]. If this was not already an unambiguous reference to the Mysteries of Dionysus' dual cults, then the English localisation of Red Leather's variant, the Genesis Resurrection Fest, and the club's email encouraging members to strengthen their faith in his resurrection may alleviate any uncertainty.

Intriguingly, it is not only the manners of Dionysus and Genesis' 'rebirth' that are analogous, but so too are the uniqueness of their respective births and how these form an integral part of each figure. While there is no direct comparison to be made with regards to being born twice, it could be said that both of them have two mothers.

As previously mentioned, a prominent Orphic belief was that Dionysus was initially born of Zeus and Persephone, then of Zeus and Semele when the soul of Zagreus was placed inside her womb. Genesis, meanwhile, was a product of Project Jenova G and injected with Gillian's cells while he was a foetus. In this way, it might be contended that both

Gillian and Genesis' unnamed birth mother share a maternal claim over him[38].

Perhaps the most substantial influence that the God of the Vine had on the development of Genesis Rhapsodos' character, however, are the hymns, poetry, and theatre associated with the cults and festivals of Dionysus. The antagonist's degrading body is ultimately the motivation for his actions in *Crisis Core*, but it is his obsession with *LOVELESS* that inspires him in general, so much so that his recitals of lines and verses from the epic are what he is best identified with.

Poems that were spoken aloud in ancient Greece – as part of the Dionysia festivals or elsewhere – were called rhapsodies, and an actor or bard who performed them was a rhapsode (*rhapsōidos*). It is from this term that Genesis' surname is derived. 'Genesis' itself is also an ancient Greek word, meaning 'creation', 'beginning', or 'origin', which most likely relates to him being the first surviving child of the Jenova Project.

Although the surname Rhapsodos does not feature in the Japanese edition of game, it is revealed in the *Crisis Core Ultimania* that having a character who quoted poetry fitted better than other early ideas such as Genesis being a pianist or flute player[39]. The latter may have been more akin to Orpheus, the legendary musician to whom composition of the Orphic Hymns is ascribed.

The existence of *LOVELESS* had already been established in *Final Fantasy VII* – albeit as a trivial inclusion – and advertisements for its stage production can be seen in *Before Crisis* (Midgar) and *Dirge of Cerberus* (Edge). As such, director Hajime Tabata proposed it should be expanded upon in *Crisis Core* as part of Genesis' story rather than something entirely new being created for it.

LOVELESS' popularity as a classic drama is repeatedly alluded to in the game, yet the *Compilation* is unclear in its English localisations about how the theatrical versions are categorised. As it happens, the Greek tragedies performed in theatres during the Dionysia were as much musicals as they were dramatic re-enactments, with large quantities of their narratives or dialogues sung. Unfortunately, the vast majority of poems and plays composed for the Dionysia are either lost or incomplete. The same is true for *LOVELESS*, whose fifth and final act is unknown except for a single phrase: *"Even if the morrow is barren of promises, nothing shall forestall my return."*

Like the Greek tragedies and Orphic Hymns in the real world, the poem and its origins have been the subject of academic research for many years. During *Crisis Core*, Zack can engage with and receive mail from the Study Group, a Genesis fan club that doubles as an organisation devoted to interpreting the mysteries of *LOVELESS*. The greatest of these – both for the Study Group and for Genesis personally – is what the Gift of the Goddess represents.

LOVELESS' fabled divinity was first introduced in *Crisis Core*, although she is not wholly without precedent, as will be discussed in the next chapter. With her infinitely mysterious gift – described in the poem to be the bringer of life –, the three friends in the ancient epic hope she will guide them to everlasting bliss.

According to an email from the Study Group, the common interpretation is that the gift is a source of immortality. This may be a direct reference to the Orphic Mysteries, which taught that deliverance from the cycle of life and death is awarded to those who drink from the river Mnemosyne in the underworld (as explained in chapter VI).

The same correspondence mentions a theory that it is the Planet who will become immortal, not any one individual, suggesting this could mean either "all-consuming destruction" or "all-healing salvation" for humanity[40]. These opposing outcomes also reflect Dionysus and the dual nature of alcohol: The bringer of merriment or the bringer of madness.

The Study Group goes on to advise that the most prevalent hypothesis among scholars regarding the Gift of the Goddess, however, equates it to the Banora Whites. This is likely due to their ripening and reaping throughout the year, made possible because their trees grow in soil enriched by the Lifestream. As is extensively reviewed in chapters VI and VII, the Lifestream embodies the cycle of spirit energy, including the redistribution of souls.

Assuming the latter theory to be true, the dumbapples of Banora, which have already been compared to the grapes of Dionysus, symbolise both rebirth and immortality, just as the God of the Vine did in the Dionysian and Orphic Mysteries. Furthermore, the fertilisation of the land around Banora may itself be the gift, in which case the Goddess of *LOVELESS* could be analogous to Demeter, the suffering deity with whom Dionysus shared responsibility for the annual harvest in ancient Greece.

The true identity of the Goddess has been a source of debate and speculation among fans since the release of *Crisis Core*. As with the significance of her gift, there are competing proposals in respect of this. The leading contenders will be examined more thoroughly in the next chapter, supported by evidence from across Greco-Roman mythology.

1. By the Classical period, competing beliefs and schools of thought alternatively included either Dionysus or Hestia, Goddess of the Hearth, in their depictions of the Olympians.
2. The word 'liberty' itself actually derives from Liber (or Liber Pater, 'Free Father'), a native Roman god who was conflated with Dionysus.
3. Satyrs are normally portrayed nowadays as having the horns and legs of a goat, but this was a later amendment in Hellenic tradition. Up to and including the Classical period, they had horse-like features and were known for their sexual deviancy. The original goat-men were called pans, after the nature god Pan.

4. Some scholars have argued over the centuries that the Dionysian Mysteries were simply an extension of the Eleusinian Mysteries (themselves discussed in the previous chapter), with Dionysus being conflated with Iacchus, a minor Eleusinian deity. Given the secretive manner of both cults, there is currently no way to verify this to any significant degree of certainty.

5. The myths are ambiguous in whether Mount Nysa is connected to the Plain of Nysa mentioned in the *Homeric Hymn to Demeter*, where Persephone was abducted by Hades.

6. The stories regarding Dionysus' exploits in India and Northern Africa seem to be analogous to Alexander the Great's military conquests, which occurred many centuries after the Dionysian and Orphic Mysteries were established.

7. When she is raised to heaven, Semele becomes known as Thyone, a goddess also associated with Bacchic frenzy.

8. The tale of Orpheus' own descent into the underworld is found in chapter XVIII.

9. It is thought by many that the renowned Greek philosopher Pythagoras, who lived in the 6th century BC and is famed for his political, religious, mathematical, and scientific teachings, contributed to early Orphism or was at least an initiate of it.

10. These works are typically referred to as the Orphic theogonies, all of which have been lost. The best attestations that remain are direct quotes on the Derveni papyrus.

11. Zagreus' role outside Orphic traditions is unclear, with scarce mention of him. He seems to be affiliated with the underworld, while the playwright Aeschylus may have even suggested Zagreus is a son of Hades.

12. The Muses are nine goddesses said to inspire art, literature, and science, and are responsible for the sparks of creativity one might experience. According to Hesiod's *Theogony*, their mother was Mnemosyne, whose waters of remembrance were a critical part of the eternal happiness promoted by the Orphic Mysteries (see

chapter VI). Orpheus himself is generally attested to be a daughter of Calliope, one of the Muses.

13. Greek dramas are typically subcategorised as tragedies, comedies, or satyrs (a combination of both, not to be confused with satire).

14. Details from Euripides' *Trōiades* can be found in chapter IX.

15. Genesis copies are individuals – mainly SOLDIERs – who have been injected with Genesis' cells. These unique cells contain some of Jenova's mimicry abilities, causing the recipient to replicate Genesis' appearance, strength, and characteristics.

16. The purpose of the Ancients Project was to produce a child comparable to a Cetra.

17. According to a trophy Zack finds in the Banora Underground, Genesis won first prize in the processed foods category of the National Agricultural Awards.

18. Genesis does not begin to carry dumbapples around with him until after his alleged death at Modeoheim.

19. For example, in the first year of *Crisis Core's* timeline, a member of the Study Group reveals that the production of *LOVELESS* is centred on the romance between one of the three friends and a woman from the opposing nation. However, a digital pamphlet distributed by Square Enix in 2021 noted that the ending of the musical *Loveless* (as it is written in *Remake*) is different to the regular production, which may be an allusion to how *Crisis Core's* finale is altered during the events of *Remake*.

20. The lines of Genesis' personal fifth act can be seen amid the glowing octagonal crest and symbols of Zack's 'Apocalypse' Limit Break.

21. This part of the Banora Underground is called the Light of Doom. It is where Zack and Genesis' final battle takes place. The *Crisis Core Complete Guide* confirms the giant red sphere is similar to the Huge Materia of *Final Fantasy VII*.

22. The aesthetics of the colossus closely resemble the Emerald Weapon of *Final Fantasy VII*, but the *Complete Guide* simply lists it as unidentified. It should be noted

that Emerald Weapon is clearly shown emerging from the Northern Crater in the original game.

23. The equipment needed to produce Genesis copies was stolen from Shinra Headquarters by Doctor Hollander, the scientist originally responsible for Project Gillian and now collaborating with Genesis to cure his degradation.

24. Genesis likens the three friends of *LOVELESS* to himself, Sephiroth, and Angeal. Sephiroth and Angeal are dead by the end of *Crisis Core*, but they are both represented by Zack, who carries the former's cells following Hojo's experiments on him at Nibelheim, and the latter's spirit, embodying the honour of a SOLDIER.

25. Minerva will be discussed in detail in the next chapter.

26. The anecdote relates to his childhood in Banora and how he would steal the fruit from local farms. However, Angeal's honour prohibited him from picking dumbapples on one wealthy man's estate because his son (Genesis) was a friend.

27. *Norse Myths That Inspired Final Fantasy VII* proposes several connections between Genesis' degradation and the role of the apples of rejuvenation in Viking lore.

28. There are, however, numerous types of purple-skinned apples in the real-world, such as the Black Diamonds of Tibet.

29. The age at which Genesis won his award is not confirmed in *Crisis Core* or its associated media. However, a newspaper clipping in the Banora Underground quotes the boy as saying it would be his dream to serve an apple to the hero Sephiroth. The *Crisis Core Complete Guide* notes that Sephiroth joined the Wutai War when he was less than ten years old, so Genesis must have been at least that age, as his birth preceded Sephiroth's.

30. It should be noted that this description can also be applied to the hero Odysseus, as depicted by Homer in the *Odyssey*.

31. Dionysus has three separate songs dedicated to him, identified as Hymn 1, Hymn 7, and Hymn 26.

32. Zack and Genesis share scenes in Banora (located on the same archipelago as Mideel, according to the *Crisis Core*

Ultimania), Midgar, Modeoheim, and Gongaga. The Genesis copies are also fought outside Fort Tamblin in Wutai.

33. The Dionysian myths regarding what becomes of characters such as Lycurgus of Thrace and Pentheus of Thebes are among the most gruesome in all classical lore.

34. 'Silver Elite' and 'Keepers of Honor' are the English localisation names for the Sephiroth and Angeal fan clubs. The original Japanese names can respectively be translated as the 'Premium Fan Club' and 'The Forest Society'. During the events of *Crisis Core*, Cissnei – one of the Turks – also establishes a fan club for Zack.

35. These wine-fuelled frenzies, orgies, and the free mixing of classes and genders were gradually restricted or outlawed by the Roman state.

36. The *Crisis Core Ultimania* explains that Genesis' parents agreed to provide surveillance for the Shinra Company as he grew older as part of the adoption. Despite their genuine love for him, Genesis considers this an act of betrayal and murders them for it. Zack and Tseng find the graves during their mission to Banora.

37. Zack receives an email from the Study Group as he is escaping Nibelheim, while a notification from the Red Leather club arrives once he reaches Gongaga. This implies the festivities are held at different times of the year, just like the Lesser Dionysia (around the winter solstice) and the Greater Dionysia (around the spring equinox).

38. It is also possible to toss Jenova into the parental mix here, although Genesis is never implied to view Jenova as his mother in the way that Sephiroth does.

39. Associating Genesis with music was initially intended to be an allusion to Gackt, the Japanese singer, musician, and actor on whom the character's look is based.

40. The perceived mortality of the Planet is a very important plot component of *Final Fantasy VII*, with the player being introduced to Avalanche's plight to prevent Gaia's demise in the game's opening scenes.

CHAPTER IX

THE GODDESS

Despite the wealth of influence that classical mythology has had on the *Compilation of Final Fantasy VII,* via the scenario writing of Kazushige Nojima or otherwise, there are very few examples of deities or characters in it being referenced by name. This book examines the inclusion of Gaia (Mother Earth, see chapter IV), Hades (King of the Underworld, see chapter VI), and Typhon (Zeus' fiercest opponent, see chapter XI), but there are a handful more who appear in a much less prominent capacity.

For instance, the Heavy Vulcan is a weaponised prosthetic for Barret, named after the Roman God of Fire, Volcanoes, and the Forge (known as Hephaestus to the ancient Greeks)[1]; 'Pandora's Box' is a rare enemy skill that can be learned from the dragon zombie of the Northern Cave, which relates to the tale of the first woman, Pandora, inadvertently unleashing numerous evils upon the world[2]; and Felicia (the real name of Elfe) is the militant leader of the eco-terrorists Avalanche during *Before Crisis*, possibly derived from Felicitas, a Roman goddess linked to nature, prosperity, and good fortune who was worshipped by commanders in the imperial army.

There are, however, two more Roman goddesses who are directly referenced in the *Compilation*: Minerva and Venus. The former is of significance to the wider plot of *Crisis Core*, while the latter may be a subtle hint towards Cid's character arc in *Final Fantasy VII*, with potential implications regarding the mysteries of *LOVELESS*. These subjects will be explored in this chapter.

In Roman mythology, Minerva is the Goddess of Wisdom, Arts, Strategy, Healing, Civilised Society, and more and was one of the most revered deities in the empire[3]. She was conflated with Athena of Hellenic religion from around the 2nd century BC onwards, with the pair sharing countless stories and attributes. They do have a substantial difference, though: Where Minerva is not associated with violence or offensive warfare[4], Athena is traditionally less passive, playing a key role on the battlefield in the *Iliad*, for example.

Athena (also called Athene) is the favourite daughter of Zeus, and of all his mortal and divine offspring, her birth is arguably the oddest. According to Hesiod's *Theogony*, she emerges from Zeus' forehead, fully-grown, clad in splendid armour, and brandishing weapons of war[5].

Athena is thereafter welcomed as one of the twelve Olympians and beloved by most for her beauty and wisdom[6]. She is an eventual contributor to the creation of mankind, breathing life into the figures moulded from water and clay by Prometheus[7], a second-generation Titan who sides with Zeus during the Titanomachy and is the Skyfather's dearest friend until his perceived betrayal for giving humanity fire[8]. As the ages of man progress, Athena's interaction with and influence over them increases.

When the time comes for the gods to seek veneration as patron deities of the burgeoning city-states (*poleis*), Athena and Poseidon both stake a claim to the region of Attica. Striking the earth with his trident, Poseidon draws a spring of saltwater; Athena, meanwhile, plants the first olive tree[9]. The inhabitants of the country determine that the goddess' gift is far more valuable to them and so name their *polis* after her. This is the mythical origin of Athens, now the capital city of Greece.

Reflecting her prominence in Hellenic religion and her eminence among the Olympians, there are dozens of legends concerning Athena's deeds. While many of these are anecdotal or rationalise her affiliation with places, people, or things, she does commonly feature as part of grander myths, such as the Gigantomachy[10], the adventures of the heroes Perseus and Heracles, or the instigation, conflict, and aftermath of the Trojan War[11].

There are also a number of stories dedicated to Athena's wrath, which is typically directed at those who violate the sanctity of her shrines throughout ancient Greece. An infamous illustration of this is her transformation of the nymph Medusa into a monstrous Gorgon (see chapter XIII), either because Poseidon (as his Roman equivalent, Neptune) makes love to Medusa in a temple of Athena (Minerva) or because the maiden boasts she is more attractive than the goddess[12].

The punishment of hubris – a person's excessive pride in comparison to or defiance of the gods – is a recurring theme in classical mythology. Athena is a main character in one such tale[13], where she agrees to a weaving contest with a young woman named Arachne. The girl's arrogance and blasphemous portrayal of the gods in her woven art is her undoing. In retribution, Athena turns her into the first spider – or arachnid –, so that her descendants will spin majestic webs forever[14].

Despite her being a patron of warfare, literary accounts of Athena rarely depict her in active combat. Those that do primarily relate to the Trojan War, but there are other instances, such as the Gigantomachy, where she openly engages enemies. Akin to the Roman Minerva, Athena was more generally regarded as an advisor to Zeus and a defender or guardian, although many believed she was always present on the battlefield, observing both sides. Her favour was said to lie with the victors, and she was considered the protector of heroes; thus, by extension, she was also the Goddess of Heroic Endeavour.

Athena has a complex role in Homer's *Iliad* and *Odyssey* as well as the supplementary works of the Epic Cycle[15], for she is worshipped by the Greeks and Trojans alike. According to legend, Troy itself was founded when the goddess carved a wooden effigy in the image of Pallas – a childhood friend she had accidentally killed – and sent it down from heaven. It was prophesied that the city would never fall so long as the statue, called the Palladium, remained within its walls[16].

During the war, however, Athena allies herself with the Greeks, and she favours King Odysseus of Ithaca above all others, due to his intelligence and cunning. Odysseus helps steal the Palladium, and it is from his ingenuity and conception of the Trojan Horse that the Hellenes ultimately prevail. That said, some sources credit Athena with planting the idea in his mind.

In the *Odyssey*, after the sacking of Troy, Athena sends a devastating storm to destroy most of the Greek fleet as they sail home, personally hurling Zeus' thunderbolts at certain ships[17]. She at last takes pity on the stranded Odysseus and persuades the gods to intervene, orchestrating the conclusion to his ten-year return journey to Ithaca.

As with the majority of ancient Greek immortals, there are multiple facets to Athena: For example, in addition to her wisdom, guardianship, vengeance, and transformations, Zeus' daughter is one of three female Olympians who swear a sacred oath never to marry or take a lover[18]. Arguably the best known of the shrines built in Athena's honour was dedicated to this aspect of her, erected at the summit of the Acropolis, the elevated citadel that overlooks Athens. It is called the Parthenon (the Temple of the Virgin), and its inner chamber was designed specifically to accommodate a statue that was among the most impressive the city had ever seen: Athena Parthenos, the Virgin Athena[19].

The *Compilation of Final Fantasy VII* has to date featured the character Minerva in *Crisis Core* (including its remaster, *Crisis Core Reunion*) only[20]. In it, she serves two brief but distinct functions: For many players of the game, she is encountered solely in the cutscene that follows Genesis' defeat by Zack at Banora; those who strive to complete the toughest of the 300 SOLDIER side-missions, however, can also challenge her in battle.

As explained in the previous chapter, Genesis places a feminine statue in the Banora Underground to represent the Goddess in his re-enactment of *LOVELESS*. In the international edition of *Crisis Core*, the effigy itself is a robed figure with an ornate crown of sorts, holding an apple-shaped orb.

Genesis has visibly deteriorated by the time he duels with Zack and begins to channel the Lifestream in a bid to cure his degradation. Although he succeeds, he remains weakened once his colossal, metamorphosed form, Genesis Avatar, has been conquered, finding himself in a spiritual plane when Zack delivers the knock-out blow. As the rogue SOLDIER approaches the Goddess statue, he is confronted by Minerva, dressed in golden armour over a white gown, with a lavish spear in one hand and an enormous decorative shield in the other. Momentarily gazing upon Genesis, she offers him a chance for redemption by returning him to the mortal world.

Throughout *Crisis Core*, the player can take Zack on assignments around the Planet to fulfil a plethora of tasks for a variety of people or groups. These range from suppressing an insurrection by the remnants of the Wutai Army to eliminating dangerous monsters on behalf of Professor Hojo's laboratory or hunting for treasure as instructed by a young Yuffie Kisaragi.

The most difficult of these optional questlines is the Great Cavern of Wonders, a narrative concerning the Shinra Company's investigation into an unusual energy disturbance in a vast subterranean network near the Northern Crater. As Zack descends into the unexplored caves, he is accosted by more and more ferocious creatures and robotic weapons that have been sent berserk by the mysterious power. Eventually, he identifies its source to be Minerva.

Minerva – called the Reigning Deity – is *Crisis Core's* superboss, and she is fought by Zack on a battlefield that is suspiciously reminiscent of the Banora Underground's Depths of Judgement area. Unlike during her appearance to Genesis, Minerva enters the fray ready for combat, wearing a crested golden helmet to match her magnificent breastplate and greaves. She wields her spear and shield, and on her back is a gilded adornment with six wing-like appendages, which spins as she unleashes her fury on Zack.

The dual meetings with Minerva during *Crisis Core* relate to different aspects of her Roman namesake, and even more to their Hellenic counterpart. She presents herself to Genesis in the spiritual realm, where she replaces the Goddess statue and symbolises the will of the Lifestream, according to the *Crisis Core Complete Guide*. The Lifestream has already eradicated Genesis' degradation, so Minerva grants him the opportunity to regain his SOLDIER honour, which he has come to realise is the Gift of the Goddess, as clarified in the *Ultimanias*. In this way, she embodies the same patronage of heroic endeavour that Athena does.

On a more abstract level, Minerva's inherent association with the Lifestream – and thus the spirit energy that imbues all new lives – may hint at Athena being the deity attested by Apollodorus and Ovid to having breathed life into humans after Prometheus created them from clay. It is separately worth mentioning that Genesis Avatar, the hulking armoured form taken by the antagonist when he absorbs the Lifestream, sports a crested helmet akin to that worn by *Crisis Core's* Minerva and traditionally by Hellenic soldiers, whose champion was Athena.

Genesis, of course, is inspired by the Goddess of *LOVELESS* and her mysterious gift, which he interprets to be his salvation. Where Odysseus regularly prays to Athena for assistance, Genesis devotes himself to the Gift of the

Goddess. Correspondingly, Athena favours the King of Ithaca during the Trojan War, just as the ex-SOLDIER is supported by the will of the Lifestream at *Crisis Core's* conclusion.

Further parallels between Genesis and Odysseus will be explored in this book's companion title, *Final Fantasy VII and the Trojan War*. As such, it is unlikely to be a coincidence that when the former comes face to face with what may be an incarnation of the divinity, she is depicted as the spear-wielding Minerva, a derivation of Athena (by way of her conflation with the Roman Goddess of Wisdom, Healing, and Strategy).

Subtle allusions to other aspects of Athena can also be found in and around Banora. For instance, her wrath might be represented when Zack and Tseng first arrive there. The pair are on assignment to locate and confront Genesis and soon encounter the town's mechanised anti-Shinra warden: the Guard Spider. This autonomous weapon could be a reference to Arachne, who is arguably the most famous recipient of Athena's anger, as described above. As it happens, a variant of the Guard Spider that can be battled later in the game is indeed named Arachno[21].

The Goddess statue itself – placed in the Banora Underground by Genesis as part of his plan to re-enact *LOVELESS* – may additionally hold some curious links to Athena. As previously highlighted, *Crisis Core* shares many similarities with the Trojan War myth cycle, to which both Athena and the Palladium significantly contribute. The

Palladium is carved by Athena and resides in her temple at the heart of Troy. This reflects the Banora statue's direct association with Minerva at the end of *Crisis Core*, not to mention the Goddess' role in *LOVELESS*, *Final Fantasy VII's* very own epic myth.

Another of Athena's facets seems to be incorporated by the sculpture, although it has been lost to those who played the international edition of *Crisis Core* or the title's 2022 remaster, *Crisis Core Reunion*. Rather than the female clad in an off-the-shoulder robe and crown, the figurine's design in the Japanese release included a veil or headscarf, with her hands clasped in prayer around a smaller orb at her breast[22]. This was allegedly amended by developers to avoid any misunderstanding that the image related to the Virgin Mary[23].

Intriguingly, however, when Christianity rose to prominence in the 4th century AD, most of the Roman Empire was converted, and by the end of the 6th century, the Parthenon in Athens (the Temple of the Virgin) had been repurposed as a church dedicated to Mary. It could therefore be asserted that the intention of the original design for the statue in Banora's subterranean caves was to symbolise a divine virgin. If so, the word 'loveless' itself may allude to the celibacy of the Goddess or, by extension, Athena Parthenos.

Athena's warfare side, meanwhile, is much more evident during Zack's clash with Minerva in the Great Cavern of Wonders. The aesthetics of her golden armour, crested helmet, deadly spear, and ornate shield are a close comparison to how Athena is attested to emerge from Zeus' head in Greek mythology. It is also her most commonly depicted guise in classical sculpture[24].

Clues to the superboss' identity can be seen as early as the first mission in the questline. The player's reward for successfully completing the initial duty is the Aegis Armlet, a defensive accessory[25]. The art and literature of antiquity often portrayed Athena as wearing or bearing the aegis, an item that has been imagined in many different ways[26]. For instance, its description in the *Iliad* suggests it is either an animal pelt or a shield, while other sources imply it to be something closer to a leather or snakeskin sash. The aegis was thought to offer heavenly protection to the wielder, and to be 'under the aegis' was to be under the protection of the god that possessed it.

Another Great Cavern of Wonders side-mission involves the G Spartan enemies, a type of Genesis copy. These are an homage to the warriors of the ancient Greek state of Sparta, of which Athena was also the patron. Numerous Genesis copies are named after soldier or warrior classes from across history or fantasy. Besides G Spartan, there is G Hoplite (Greek armoured infantryman) and G Centurion (Roman military commander).

As for Minerva herself, the Reigning Deity's attacks in battle are of particular interest, too. To supplement her occasional spear thrusts and slashes, she conjures elemental magic spells. One of these is 'Thor's Hammer', which generates a large storm of electricity. In Old Norse mythology – the religious beliefs of the Vikings –, lightning occurs when Thor, the God of Thunder, strikes something (or someone) with his hammer, Mjöllnir. In this way, Mjöllnir equates to Zeus' thunderbolts, so Minerva's use of 'Thor's Hammer' in *Crisis Core* is analogous to Athena hurling her father's lightning in the ancient Greek tales. Her destruction of Ajax the Lesser's ship in the *Odyssey* is a perfect example of this.

Minerva's most devastating offensive by far is 'Judgement Arrow', where her armour, shield, and shoulder adornments detach and reassemble as a great mechanical bow, initially blasting Zack with intense beams of energy. The definitive blow comes when the goddess deploys her spear as the 'arrow' to fire upon Zack, thereby innovatively adapting the weapon of Athena rather than changing it[27].

It may simply be chance that Minerva's prime attack is the 'Judgement Arrow' and the clash with her takes place in a location that mirrors the Banora Underground's Depths of Judgement. It might also be coincidental that Genesis interprets Minerva to be the Goddess of *LOVELESS*, while many academics in the *Final Fantasy VII* universe are convinced the Gift of the Goddess is dumbapples. What is unlikely to have been an oversight by developers, however, is that the Trojan War – one of the greatest myth cycles the world has ever known and from which *Crisis Core* draws much inspiration – is instigated during an episode that involves Athena, an apple, and judgement.

The Judgement of Paris is briefly mentioned in Homer's *Iliad*, although it is more extensively recounted by later writers, such as Euripides in his play *Trōiades* ('*Trojan Woman*'). According to the legend, the gods, nymphs, and lesser immortals gather to celebrate the wedding of Peleus and Thetis, whose story will be told in *Final Fantasy VII and the Trojan War*. Everyone is invited to the wedding but Eris (Discordia to the Romans), the Goddess of Strife. Angered by her exclusion, Eris disrupts proceedings by tossing a golden apple into the feast hall, with the words 'To the Fairest' inscribed upon it[28].

Each believing themselves to be the most attractive deity and thus its rightful owner, the apple is claimed by Hera, Athena, and Aphrodite. Zeus is unwilling to decide between his wife, his favourite daughter, and the Goddess of Love and Beauty herself, so he passes the responsibility to Paris, a prince of Troy. After careful consideration, Paris chooses Aphrodite, leaving her fellow goddesses feeling scorned and vengeful. This judgement sets in motion a chain of events that ultimately spark the Trojan War[29], with Aphrodite on one side and Athena (and Hera) on the other.

The *Crisis Core Complete Guide* acknowledges that Minerva is often perceived to be the Goddess in *LOVELESS*, but the actual nature of her existence is something akin to a summoned being. This would explain the red colour of the giant materia globe in the Banora Underground[30], further linking Minerva and the curing of Genesis' degradation. Moreover, it creates enough ambiguity to question whether another figure is *LOVELESS'* Goddess and, if so, who it might be.

The epic's divinity is introduced in *Crisis Core*, although she is not entirely without precedent. The poem's prologue (as quoted by Genesis beneath the Goddess statue) describes her descending from the sky as war sends the world hurtling towards catastrophe, spreading her wings of light and dark afar. There is no account of the Goddess' appearance except that she wields a bow, unleashing her arrows upon those deserving of them as the end of the conflict approaches.

During *Final Fantasy VII's* cinematic opening, a billboard advertisement for the stage production of *LOVELESS* is displayed above the Sector 8 theatre, visible again when Cloud first meets Aerith. The poster contains a dark-haired woman and is accompanied by text that reads, "MY BLOODY VALENTINE"[31].

Near the climax of that game, when the player's party is aboard the *Highwind* airship, Cid speaks to Cloud about *LOVELESS*, which has been performed every summer since he was a kid. Cid recalls that he fell asleep while attending the play but was woken in time to watch the last scene, where the female lead tells her lover that she cannot understand why he is leaving. The man promises to return to her, even if she does not promise to wait. The lines stood out to Cid, although he admits to Cloud that he is only just beginning to grasp their meaning.

The exchange indicates two things: One is that the annual theatre production is a love story, which is verified in *Crisis Core* to focus on the prisoner of war character and a woman from the opposing nation who rescues him[32]; the second is that the context of Cid finally comprehending the lines relates to his newfound appreciation of Shera.

When Cid and Shera are initially encountered in Rocket Town during *Final Fantasy VII*, they are living together but are not romantically involved. Cid is verbally abusive towards her because he holds her responsible for ruining his dream of being the first person to pilot a rocket in space[33], though he relents later in the game when Shera is discovered to have been right all along. It is revealed in *Advent Children* that Cid has named his new airship after her, while *Dirge of Cerberus* confirms the pair has eventually married.

Considering the evidence, it could be proposed that Cid and Shera's relationship in *Final Fantasy VII* is itself a blossoming love story. As if to exemplify this, Cid's most powerful polearm can be obtained from an old man outside the item store adjacent to the home he cohabits with Shera: the Venus Gospel. A gospel is traditionally a book in the Christian New Testament that narrates the life and teachings of Jesus Christ, while Venus was the Romans' name for Aphrodite, the Goddess of Love. In other words, 'Venus Gospel' might be interpreted to mean 'Love Story' and can be connected to *LOVELESS* via Cid and his feelings for Shera.

Despite the possible comparisons to be made between the Banora Whites and Aphrodite's golden apple in the Judgement of Paris[34], there is little else in *Crisis Core* to suggest that the Goddess of *LOVELESS* symbolises the ancient Greek Goddess of Love. Both the epic poem and its theatre adaptation are set against the backdrop of war. This is not the domain of either Venus or Aphrodite, yet they do typically consort with their respective pantheon's God of War, Mars (Roman) or Ares (Greek). History has shown that love and war share an unusual affinity.

LOVELESS speaks of the Goddess spreading her wings, then of firing her arrow, albeit its intended target is not specified. Aphrodite herself is not associated with archery, but she does have a retinue in the myths called the Erotes[35]. This group of winged male deities personifies all aspects of love, including requited and unrequited, sexual, reproductive, marital, homoerotic, and more, and they are normally depicted with bows and arrows[36]. Arguably the most famous among them is Eros, a son of Aphrodite by Ares[37], whose arrows can inflict uncontrollable desire and lust, and which are often deployed at his mother's behest. Eros is better known nowadays by his Roman name: Cupid.

However, while she is the embodiment of love in general, Aphrodite's particular area is that of passionate and pleasurable love, closely related to sex and procreation. As such, chastity is an affront to her, so it could be said she is in direct opposition to any virgin goddess, just as she is to Athena during the Trojan War.

It might therefore be contended that the imagery used in *Crisis Core* to represent the Goddess of *LOVELESS* – in either the veiled statue of the original Japanese edition or in the poem's description of the deity – does not support her being inspired by Aphrodite or Venus. This, of course, is reflected in the ancient epic being called *LOVELESS* and not *LOVE*.

The secrets of *LOVELESS* and its missing final act will likely remain a catalyst for deep speculation and debate among fans of the *Compilation* for many years to come. Even if the morrow is barren of promises, perhaps the conclusion of the *Remake* trilogy will provide a definitive identity for the Goddess; or perhaps, as Genesis says, to ponder the mystery is the gift itself ...

1. The Heavy Vulcan can be purchased at Cosmo Canyon, whose subterranean caverns are the only location in *Final Fantasy VII* where volcanic activity is found. Alternatively, the Cosmo Candle is a sacred bonfire around which local ceremonies are held.

2. 'Pandora's Box' is a localisation of an enemy skill in the Japanese version of *Final Fantasy VII* called '*Nantaka???*', which translates as 'Something???'. Despite the common usage of the metaphor (which means to release several previously contained problems), it should be noted that Pandora opened a forbidden jar in the myth, not a box. The story concerns how Zeus punishes Prometheus for giving mankind fire, gifting both the innocent, curious Pandora and the jar of sorrows to Prometheus' brother Epimetheus. Its opening condemned humanity, not unlike Sephiroth activating

the Black Materia to summon Meteor, hence the Northern Cave link.

3. Alongside Jupiter (Zeus) and Juno (Hera), Minerva was a member of the Capitoline Triad, the divine trio at the centre of Roman public religion.

4. This was the domain of Mars, the God of War, known to the Greeks as Ares.

5. In the *Theogony*, Zeus' first wife is a wise and cunning Oceanid called Metis. When Metis falls pregnant, he swallows her whole to prevent her from giving birth. In time, Zeus develops a headache so horrific that the only way to relieve the pressure is to crack his skull open. That is when Athena, the child of Zeus and Metis, steps out.

6. As with all the children born from Zeus' infidelity, Hera holds a grudge against Athena.

7. This version of humanity's creation myth is one of many and can be found in Apollodorus' *Bibliotheca* and Ovid's *Metamorphoses*.

8. By gifting fire to mankind, Prometheus deliberately disobeys and incurs the wrath of Zeus. This is because he does not simply give them the means to kindle flames but bestows upon them the divine spark, the fire of creativity and free thought, which might one day allow mortals to challenge the gods.

9. Wine and olives were two of the most important trading commodities in ancient Attica, contributing directly to the wealth of Athens and its wider region. The tale of the city's beginnings is attested in Apollodorus' *Bibliotheca*.

10. The Gigantomachy is the war waged on heaven by the Giants and is discussed in chapter X.

11. Further information on these myths can be found in coming chapters.

12. The first version is told by the Roman poet Ovid in *Metamorphoses*. Medusa does not consent to Poseidon's approach in earlier accounts, so the punishment is even less just.

13. This myth, too, is found in Ovid's *Metamorphoses*.

14. The term 'arachnid' is derived from the ancient Greek word '*arákhnē*' ('spider') and refers to a classification of

joint-legged arthropods that includes spiders, scorpions, and other creepy crawlies.

15. The Epic Cycle is a collection of ancient Greek poems, composed in the same style as Hesiod and Homer, which relate to the Trojan War. They typically add details or whole episodes to it that are not found in the *Iliad* or the *Odyssey*.

16. Another palladium (itself called 'the carving that fell from heaven') was housed in a temple in Athens' Acropolis. It was an image sculpted from olive wood and dedicated to Athena Polias, the protectress of the city. This palladium was considered to be the holiest of all the goddess' artefacts.

17. The goddess' support turns to vengeance when Ajax the Lesser (not to be confused with the more famous Ajax the Mighty) disregards the sanctity of her temple and harms one of her priestesses.

18. The other virgin goddesses in the Olympic pantheon are Artemis and Hestia.

19. It should be noted that there was no cult associated with Athena Parthenos, nor did the Parthenon host priestesses who worshipped the statue. The celebrated sculpture was removed from the Parthenon sometime in the first half of the 1st millennium and its current whereabouts are unknown.

20. Minerva's outfit was also made available in 2022 as a downloadable costume in the mobile game *The First Soldier*.

21. As mentioned in footnote 14, spiders and scorpions are both arachnids, hence the connection between the Guard Spider and the Guard Scorpion. The latter was originally fought in *Final Fantasy VII* and appears in *Remake* as the Scorpion Sentinel.

22. While the statue itself changed for the international version of *Crisis Core*, its original design can still be viewed on the pedestal in the Banora Underground where Zack places the Goddess Materia. This is also true in *Crisis Core Reunion*.

23. In Christianity, Islam, and other religions, Mary is the mother of Jesus of Nazareth. Her epithet of 'Virgin' relates to the belief held by some religions of Jesus' Immaculate Conception.

24. The Homeric Hymns and Pindar's *Olympian Ode 7* specify that Athena's weapon of war is a spear, though the ancient texts are not explicit with regards to her helmet and shield.

25. The Aegis Armlet (alternatively called the Aegis Shield, among other things) has been a recurring defensive gear item since the original *Final Fantasy*. The armlet can be obtained during the Midgar raid in *Final Fantasy VII* and equipped as armour. Incidentally, the Minerva Band is also armour than can be acquired in *Final Fantasy VII*.

26. Athena is regularly shown to be in the possession of the aegis, but it is generally said to belong to her father, Zeus.

27. Artemis, not Athena, is the Olympian goddess best associated with the bow and arrow.

28. The golden apple came from Hera's orchard in the Garden of the Hesperides and is known throughout literature as the Apple of Discord. 'To the Fairest' is the traditional consensus for how the ancient Greek '*Tē kallistē*' should be translated into English, though it also means 'to the most beautiful'. It seems a curious coincidence that the Goddess of Strife throwing an apple bearing 'To the Fairest' shares similarities to the surnames of *Final Fantasy VII's* contrasting protagonists, Cloud Strife and Zack Fair.

29. In return for Paris declaring her the fairest of the goddesses, Aphrodite promises she will make the most beautiful woman in the world fall in love with him. This later turns out to be Helen of Sparta, who elopes to Troy with Paris. Helen's husband, King Menelaus, then raises a great Greek army to reclaim her.

30. Materia orbs in the *Compilation* are divided into various colours and categorised by their function. Summon Materia is always red, with one exception during *Advent Children* when Kadaj utilises a blue sphere (typically Support Materia) to call on Bahamut SIN.

31. Variations of the poster can be found in *Remake* and across the *Compilation* but "MY BLOODY VALENTINE" is only present on *Final Fantasy VII's* version. This was a tribute by the game's developers to the Irish alternative rock band My Bloody Valentine and their celebrated album *Loveless*, released in 1991.

32. The prisoner of war is one of the three friends featured in *LOVELESS*.

33. Shera is an engineer who worked on the Shinra No. 26 rocket that Cid was due to pilot. In the minutes preceding the rocket's launch, she was still testing a fault in one of the oxygen tanks. Unwilling to let her die, Cid aborted the launch, but it was never rescheduled. During *Final Fantasy VII*, Cloud, Cid, and Shera are aboard the Shinra No. 26 when it is sent into space to destroy Meteor. The faulty oxygen tank explodes and almost prevents Cid's escape.

34. Aphrodite is associated with golden apples in multiple myths. Another example is when she gives three of them to Melanion (also known as Hippomenes) so that he can win the heart of the huntress Atalanta.

35. The members, numbers, and roles of the Erotes differ across the sources. Among the earliest writers to mention the group by name are Pindar and Sappho in the 5th or 6th century BC, though Eros (Love) and Himeros (Desire) are attested in Hesiod's *Theogony*.

36. Love and passion can sometimes be unexpected, irrational, or counterintuitive. The ancient Greeks conceptualised such yearnings in their myths as the manipulation or mischief of the Erotes, who could influence an individual by shooting them with their enchanted arrows.

37. Hesiod instead lists Eros as one of the primordial gods born from Chaos. This makes him a sibling of Gaia (Earth), Tartarus (the subterranean depths), Nyx (Night), and Erebus (Darkness).

PART FOUR

MYTHICAL
BESTIARY

CHAPTER X

WHICH TITAN IS TITAN?

T he *Final Fantasy* series has long had several recurring features that fans associate with its titles and have come to expect with each new entry. Examples of these include curative items such as Phoenix Downs and Elixirs, or iconic creatures such as chocobos and moogles. Summoned beings have also secured a place in this category since their introduction in *Final Fantasy III*, with many distinct figures returning on a regular basis[1].

Although their appearances and specific functions can differ from game to game, summoned beings – sometimes simply called 'summons' – are powerful entities that can typically be called into battle by the player characters to assist them against opponents. *Final Fantasy VII's* variants are found inside special materia orbs and become available to a party member when the materia is equipped to their weapon or armour.

Final Fantasy VII Remake establishes a degree of lore with respect to the summons, indicating in the enemy intel biographies for Shiva, Ifrit, and Bahamut that they once existed in the physical world at the time of the Cetra or early mankind. This is supported during the virtual reality display at Shinra Headquarters' Visual Entertainment Hall[2]. What is important about such mythos is that it suggests all summoned beings in the *Compilation of Final Fantasy VII* may have lived on the Planet at one point, including Titan.

In his first few *Final Fantasy* incarnations, Titan was the archetype of a classical strongman or muscular brute, initially appearing as a summon in *Final Fantasy III* (although there is a rock golem identified as Titan in the Giant's Cave during the original *Final Fantasy*). His look and presence have consistently evoked a sense of raw force on a primitive level[3], yet the mythological roots of his name are ambiguous.

In ancient Greek lore, there is no single character called Titan; rather, the Titans (loosely meaning 'the Straining Ones') were the generation of gods that preceded the Olympians. The question then becomes: Which of these immense entities, if any, do *Final Fantasy's* summons truly embody?

As referenced in chapter IV of this book, the Titans are most commonly attested in the creation myth of Hesiod's

Theogony[4]. The initial twelve were born of the union between Gaia (Mother Earth) and Uranus (Father Sky). There were six males (Oceanus, Coeus, Hyperion, Iapetus, Crius, and Kronos) and six females (Theia, Themis, Mnemosyne, Phoebe, Tethys, and Rhea).

Many of the siblings' offspring were also considered to be Titans, such as the sons of Iapetus, who were Prometheus, Epimetheus, Atlas, and Menoetius; or the children of Hyperion and Theia, Helios (the Sun), Selene (the Moon), and Eos (Dawn). Curiously, some of these names have been explicitly or implicitly used across the *Compilation of Final Fantasy VII* as well as the *Remake* continuity, as will be highlighted in coming chapters[5].

Following the castration of his father, the youngest and most wily of the Titans, Kronos, assumes supremacy over all things. He becomes obsessed with a prophecy that says he will be deposed by one of his own children, and so swallows each of the newborn infants he sires upon Rhea, his sister-consort. Rhea, however, tricks Kronos upon the birth of their sixth child, smuggling the baby Zeus away, while her tyrannical brother consumes a blanketed stone in his place.

When Zeus returns to Mount Pelion as a young adult and frees his siblings (Poseidon, Hades, Hera, Demeter, and Hestia), they declare war on the Titans and establish a home for themselves on Mount Olympus. The ten-year conflict that arises from this comes to be known as the Titanomachy and quite literally reshapes the world.

According to Hesiod, it is Atlas and not Kronos who leads the Titan army against the Olympians. Atlas is the eldest of Iapetus' sons and an exemplary warrior, who, along with his brother Menoetius, is among the Olympians' fiercest opponents. It is generally accepted by modern scholars that Menoetius (whose name means 'Doomed Might') represents violent anger and rash actions, not to mention excessive pride.

As the war rages on without either side gaining advantage, Zeus journeys to Tartarus, the primordial caverns deep beneath the earth, where Kronos has so unwisely imprisoned the Cyclopes and Hecatoncheires. Zeus offers these respective one-eyed and hundred-handed triplets their freedom, should they fight with him against the Titans. They are quick to accept his terms.

It is the Cyclopes who craft Zeus' thunderbolts, the very weapons he would forever be associated with. He uses these to slay Menoetius and others, and when the Titan army takes to the field of battle, the Cloud Gatherer hurls his lightning at its ranks. The blasts cause the earth to crack and quake, with explosive eruptions and fiery winds driving back his enemies and setting the vast woodlands aflame.

At the climax of this seismic conflict, the *Theogony* describes how the Hecatoncheires hurl 300 boulders in quick succession onto the Titans, burying them in a mound of rock. Zeus then commands that the gods who fought against him shall be bound and cast into Tartarus. For Atlas, however, he has other plans.

212

In *Final Fantasy VII*, the Titan Materia is obtained from the core of the destroyed mako reactor near Gongaga[6]. When the player visits this remote mountainside town, they can learn from its denizens that the facility exploded three years earlier, killing many of the residents. The people of Gongaga thereafter voted to outlaw the use of mako energy and to instead live with nature. It is a sad place, epitomised by the graveyard on its periphery, while the terrain around the ruined power plant is now a wasteland, where it was once a vibrant forest.

There are loose connections to be drawn here between Titan's acquisition at the Gongaga reactor and the conclusion of the Titanomachy. For example, Hesiod specifies that Zeus bombarding the Titans with his thunderbolts causes great releases of energy, fiery eruptions, and a reshaping of the land. This is mirrored in the explosion at the mako reactor, which decimated the surrounding environment and burned much of the woodland area. By extension, several of Gongaga's townspeople lost their lives, just as Titans like Menoetius do.

Zeus banishes every male Titan who opposed him during the ten-year war to Tartarus, with the exception of Atlas (and Kronos, in some sources). While Tartarus later became known in Greek mythology as a place of torment for wicked souls, it is described in the *Theogony* as being a large, bleak prison within the underworld. This may be analogous to the presence of *Final Fantasy VII's* Titan at Gongaga, where gloominess hangs heavy in the air and death greets visitors as they pass the graveyard.

Since *Final Fantasy III*, the summoned monster has been associated with the element of Earth. This likely derives directly from classical lore, where the Titans are the children of Gaia. Furthering this connection, *Final Fantasy V* introduced a signature Earth-elemental attack for Titan called 'Gaia's Wrath', variations of which can be seen throughout the series.

As is established in chapter IV, the world of *Final Fantasy VII* is often referred to as Gaia in supplementary media and can be thought of as a character similar to Mother Earth in the Hellenic myths[7]. It could therefore be speculated that an explosion at the Gongaga reactor, whose function it was to drain the Planet of its lifeblood for the Shinra Company's profit, is the retribution – or wrath – of Gaia.

Additionally, respect for the health of the Planet is shown by the townspeople of Gongaga when they abandon their use of mako energy. To have the Titan Materia collectable from the exact location where Gaia's alleged wrath was centred – the reactor core – may not be a coincidence.

That said, *Final Fantasy VII's* version of Titan's attack, 'Anger of the Land', was initially translated into English from the Japanese '*Daichi no Ikari*'. The context of '*daichi*' here is certainly closer in meaning to 'land' or 'ground' than it is to 'Earth' or 'the world', which undermines any potential parallel. However, it should be noted that the change may have been to avoid confusion with the naming of Gaea's Cliff, the relevance of which is also discussed in chapter IV.

The summoning animation for 'Anger of the Land' begins with Titan emerging from a mound of earth when called into battle[8]. He is clad only in jewellery and a loin cloth[9], with clouded eyes and a length of white hair falling between his bulging shoulder muscles. Roaring, Titan grabs the ground with both fists, then heaves a huge wedge of the terrain upward before ultimately slamming it down on the opponent(s).

While these actions may or may not be an allusion to the earthshattering manner in which the elder gods clash with the Olympians during the Titanomachy, there are also some vague similarities to Hesiod's description of the Titans' final defeat. His poem details the Cyclopes blinding the Titans with flashes of lightning, represented in the summon's cloudy gaze; the Hecatoncheires scooping enormous rocks to smash down on their adversaries is not unlike *Final Fantasy VII's* Titan utilising the land as a weapon; and the imprisonment of the Titans in the subterranean depths of Tartarus may explain the summon's emergence from an earthen mound.

As previously mentioned, Titan in *Final Fantasy VII* does not embody the characteristics of any particular figure from the millennia-old Greek tales. However, it could be argued that he shares a few features with less classical depictions of an elder god who, in recent centuries, has come to be associated with Earth.

With the dust of war still settling in the aftermath of the Titanomachy, Zeus sentences Atlas to bear the weight of the sky for eternity. It is a masterstroke that simultaneously incapacitates his most dangerous foe and relieves himself of such a gruelling duty.

Accounts vary with regards to the exact spot where Atlas stoops to shoulder the heavens, but it is generally agreed to be somewhere at the western edge of the known world. The Atlas Mountains in North Africa are named after him, as is the Atlantic Ocean, both of which lie far to the west of Greece. The Titan's story used to be so renowned that, since the 16th century, maps of the world have been called *atlases*.

Nowadays, rather than holding up the sky, Atlas is most commonly portrayed as a muscular, semi-naked man carrying the globe on his back, hence the modern connection to Earth. While the image is inaccurate, it does serve as a reminder of his punishment for being the deity that led the Titans into every battle. This is reflected in *Final Fantasy VII's* Titan whenever he is called to fight: He is a furious strongman wearing only a loin cloth, whose elemental affiliation is Earth and whose primary attack has him lift the ground above his head.

It is also possible to identify abstract resemblances to Kronos, the self-styled king of the Titans until his dethronement by Zeus. He is the father of the earliest

Olympians, which may account for the summoned being's more aged appearance. Furthermore, 'Gaia's Wrath' in Greek mythology might refer to her plotting the castration of Uranus, a devastating deed that is carried out by Kronos[10].

The similarities between Titan and Kronos, then Titan and Atlas, are more pronounced in later *Final Fantasy* titles, particularly *Final Fantasy XIII* (2009) and *Final Fantasy XV* (2016), respectively. Titan's role as a fal'Cie in *Final Fantasy XIII* is to protect Gran Pulse's ecosystem, and he contributes to this by consuming weaker species and giving birth to new ones, which is reminiscent of Kronos swallowing and eventually regurgitating his children.

Meanwhile, when the Astral Titan is first encountered in *Final Fantasy XV*, he is literally holding up the meteorite that he prevented from striking the planet millennia ago. The meteorite, in this instance, symbolises the sky or the heavens, thus mirroring Atlas' punishment in the myths.

The relevance of this is that *Final Fantasy XIII* was co-written and directed by Motomu Toriyama, while one of its lead artists was Tetsuya Nomura. The original draft of *Final Fantasy XV's* plot was scripted by Kazushige Nojima, who is also responsible for the *Fabula Nova Crystallis* mythos that encompasses both in-game universes[11]. *Final Fantasy XV* itself was derived from Nomura-san's concept and character designs for the abandoned *Final Fantasy Versus XIII* title, and he became the initial director on the former[12]. All three men contributed to the story and scenarios of *Final Fantasy*

VII, increasing the probability that the influences behind its incarnation of Titan may not have been too different.

There is, however, another possibility. Early Greek writers such as Hesiod and Homer make very clear distinctions between the Titans and the Gigantes, a race of beings that were also said to be the spawn of Gaia and Uranus. Confusion arose among some later authors, though, who conflated the two groups[13], and this was further compounded in Renaissance art during the 15th and 16th centuries.

Applying the attributes of the Gigantes (sing. Gigas) to *Final Fantasy VII's* Titan raises some interesting, alternative parallels. As such, the question asked at the start of the chapter might conclude: Is Titan of the *Final Fantasy* series even a Titan?

According to the *Theogony*, as referenced in chapter IV, when Kronos slices off his father's genitals, new life springs forth from Gaia where his blood pools. Among the resulting creatures are the powerful, aggressive Gigantes, or 'Giants'[14]. The Giants' name has become synonymous with huge things, but in the myth they are no larger than the Olympians; the initial meaning of their name is something closer to 'Earthborn'.

Some sources say the Gigantes fight on Zeus' side during the Titanomachy, and he shows them favour when the war ends. Other sources, such as Apollodorus' *Bibliotheca* and Ovid's *Metamorphoses*, portray the Giants as fearsome brutes – occasionally said to have snakes for legs – whose purpose it is to challenge the rule of the Olympians. The conflict between the two is known as the Gigantomachy.

Apollodorus provides the fullest account of the Gigantomachy but describes the Giants being birthed by Gaia in her anger at the Titans' imprisonment in Tartarus[15]. The mighty fiends battle their way to the summit of Mount Olympus, forcing the gods to rely on the hero Heracles to aid in their defence and eventually secure their victory.

Heracles – whose exploits are further detailed in chapters XVI and XVII of this book – is responsible for slaying and injuring many Gigantes. One such foe is Ephialtes[16], whom he blinds in the right eye by shooting an arrow into it, while Apollo (the God of Archery) does the same to his left eye.

Perhaps the most famous of the Giants that Heracles overcomes, however, is Alcyoneus, whose actions previously instigated the war[17]. When the hero's poisoned arrow strikes Alcyoneus, he falls to the ground but is immediately revitalised because he draws strength from his mother, Gaia. Heracles has encountered someone similar before: Antaeus, a Gigas he wrestled to the death but could only kill by lifting him over his head, thus severing the Giant's connection to the land.

In Alcyoneus' case, though, Heracles is advised by the Goddess Athena that the Giant cannot be defeated while he remains on his native Greek soil. So, Heracles drags

Alcyoneus to Italy and buries him under Mount Vesuvius, where his continued writhing is believed to be the source of earthquakes and volcanic activity in the region. At the end of the Gigantomachy, Athena does the same with Enceladus, the most powerful Giant of all, trapping him under Mount Etna on the Italian island of Sicily.

The most compelling argument for why *Final Fantasy VII's* Titan shares more in common with the Gigantes than the Titans is that the latter – including Atlas – do not have a significant affiliation with the element of Earth in Greek mythology. On the other hand, Giants such as Alcyoneus and Antaeus channel strength directly from contact with the ground. This is reflected in the game, where the summoning of Titan inflicts Earth-elemental damage to opponents. In addition, the Titan Materia itself can be used by the player to customise weapons and armour with offensive or defensive Earth-elemental attributes[18].

Furthermore, Titan's dependence on Earth is absolute because his attacks have no effect on airborne enemies; and they can even heal opponents that are predominantly aligned to the element of Earth. This compares to the story of Heracles wrestling with Antaeus, in which the hero struggles to slay the Giant until he separates him entirely from the ground.

Besides Atlas' depictions in classical art, Titan's design could also be based on Antaeus specifically. Antaeus challenges passers-by to wrestling matches, then places the skulls of his victims in a temple dedicated to his father,

Poseidon. In ancient Greece, it was customary for wrestlers to strip down for a contest[19], which might explain why Titan is almost naked in his summoning animation[20]. As for his clouded eyes, the blinding of Ephialtes by Heracles and Apollo may have been the inspiration for that.

It is also intriguing that there are parallels between the Gigantomachy and the Titan Materia's presence at the Gongaga reactor, just as with the Titanomachy. Although earthquakes in antiquity were generally attributed to Poseidon, Apollodorus' account of the Gigantomachy (written in the 1st or 2nd century AD) places responsibility for the seismic and volcanic activity around Mount Vesuvius on Alcyoneus.

Vesuvius, of course, is historically infamous for its eruption in 79 AD, which destroyed the city of Pompeii. The deadly mountain still looms in the distance of Pompeii's remains, just as the ruined mako reactor is still clearly visible from the mountainside village of Gongaga. In both cases, the inescapable backdrop of the explosive cause of death for so many local inhabitants continues to be a solemn reminder of the tragedy that once occurred there.

It is worth highlighting that while *Final Fantasy VII* itself did not have in-game biographies or data entries for summons, Titan's aesthetics and characteristics had not deviated much since his introduction in *Final Fantasy III*. The importance of this observation is that *Final Fantasy IV's* Titan arguably has the most significant plot contribution prior to *Final Fantasy XIII's* fal'Cie[21], and his book in the Eidolon Library specifically alludes to him being a "great giant"[22], suggesting he was conceptualised as a Gigas[23].

Conversely, it cannot be ignored that actual Gigas enemies exist in the world of *Final Fantasy VII*. These lofty, purple-skinned ogres can be fought by Cloud and the others in the Whirlwind Maze of the Northern Crater[24]. In this way, as with mythology, each Gigas is connected to the Planet, Gaia, by association with the crater's perimeter, Gaea's Cliff, not to mention their magical attack 'Quake3' (or 'Quaga'), the most powerful Earth-elemental spell in the game.

The Gigas Armlet can also be stolen from them, and subsequently equipping the armour to any player character will significantly boost their own strength. This is a likely reference to the bracelets worn by these giants, who, in addition to their loin cloth and bulging muscles, bear a remarkable resemblance to Titan[25].

The attributes of the Gigas ogres seem to suggest that *Final Fantasy VII's* development team was aware of the Greek myths concerning the Giants. Perhaps, then, it is indeed right to assume the answer to the question of 'Which Titan is Titan?' is more complex than meets the eye. Interestingly, this is not an isolated case, as will be discussed in the next chapter.

1. Shiva, Ifrit, Ramuh, Titan, Odin, Bahamut, Phoenix, and Leviathan had all appeared as summoned beings in at least two titles prior to *Final Fantasy VII*.

2. Unused text contained within *Final Fantasy VII's* code verifies that a similar concept was due to be disclosed by Sephiroth during the Temple of the Ancients scenario but was cut from the final release of the game.

3. Titan's design in the series up to and including *Final Fantasy VII* was based on concept art created by Yoshitaka Amano.

4. Many historic literary works reference a poem called the *Titanomachia*, which has been lost or destroyed and whose composer is also contested. What *is* known, however, is that numerous details of the poem differ from Hesiod's account of the war.

5. In addition, Eos is the name of the world in which *Final Fantasy XV* is set. Darkness being driven back by the light of dawn is an important theme in that story.

6. Gongaga is the hometown of Zack Fair. Both the village and the ruined reactor are locations visited in *Crisis Core*, while the player's Turk character and Cait Sith attend the facility in the aftermath of the explosion during *Before Crisis*.

7. More emphasis is placed on the concept of the Planet being a character during *Crisis Core*, where Minerva is introduced as the personification of the Lifestream's will (see chapter IX). This is reaffirmed in *Final Fantasy VII Remake* through references to Cetra scriptures and the Whispers acting to maintain the Planet's preferred future.

8. A simplified version of 'Anger of the Land' also appears in *Before Crisis*.

9. The wrist and ankle bracelets worn by Titan are not to be confused with the Titan Bangle armour. *Crisis Core* and *Remake* updated it to the Titanium Bangle, albeit the name of titanium metal itself is a reference to classical mythology.

10. It is perhaps also worth mentioning the astronomy perspective regarding Titan's name: Titan is one of the

moons of Saturn, where Saturn is the Roman god equated to Kronos.

11. *Fabula Nova Crystallis Final Fantasy* is a sub-category of games within the *Final Fantasy* series that share a common mythos. *Final Fantasy XIII, Final Fantasy XV, Final Fantasy Type-0,* and their spin-off titles are the best known of this grouping.

12. Tetsuya Nomura was replaced as director during *Final Fantasy XV's* development by Hajime Tabata, who had previously directed *Before Crisis* and *Crisis Core.*

13. The conflation of Titans and Gigantes was likely caused by the works of Euripides, a 5th century BC playwright. The 1st century AD Latin author Hyginus even listed figures such as Iapetus among the Gigantes in *Fabulae.*

14. Hesiod wrote that the Giants were so aggressive that they were born with armour on their bodies and spears in their hands.

15. The *Theogony* states that it is Typhon, not the Gigantes, whom Gaia births to challenge the Olympians after the Titans have been imprisoned in Tartarus. Typhon is the focus of the next chapter.

16. Some believe this to be the same Ephialtes who, along with his brother, Otus, (collectively known as the Aloadae) confronts the gods by piling Mount Ossa and Mount Pelion upon Mount Olympus.

17. Alcyoneus is said to have stolen the sacred cattle of Helios, God of the Sun, before scaling Mount Olympus in an attempt to force himself upon Hera, Queen of Heaven and the wife of Zeus.

18. In *Final Fantasy VII's* materia system, linking special types of materia orbs to others can produce combined effects.

19. Statues of Heracles, known as the divine patron of the gymnasium, commonly display him in nude poses.

20. The only real description of the Giants' clothing comes from the *Theogony*, where Hesiod says they were born in gleaming armour and equipped with spears. This depicts them as something akin to the footsoldiers of Hellenic armies.

21. Rydia's summoning of Titan early in *Final Fantasy IV's* story knocks the heroes Cecil and Kain unconscious, and results in a landslide that prevents them from returning to their home kingdom of Baron.

22. This has been quoted from the English localisation of *Final Fantasy IV*, initially released in North America in 1991 as *Final Fantasy II*. The Eidolon Library itself is a building in the Feymarch (Land of the Summons) where the player can read about the history of eidolons (the summoned beings of the game).

23. Interestingly, Titan's appearance in the *Final Fantasy* series predates the Titans' introduction to the bestiaries of *Dungeons & Dragons* (1993). In the latter, they are explicitly classified as a race of giants, paralleling the interpretation of Hironobu Sakaguchi and his development teams.

24. The skin colour of the Gigas opponents in *Final Fantasy VII* is a possible reference to Porphyrion. According to Pindar, Porphyrion is king of the Giants and involved in the Gigantomachy. His name means 'Purple One'.

25. The same could be said – albeit to a lesser degree – of Vincent's second Limit Break transformation, Death Gigas, although it is also clearly based on Frankenstein's Monster.

CHAPTER XI

(DIS)INTEGRATION

The stories of the *Final Fantasy* franchise have been integrating global legends and monsters since its inaugural title in 1987. As was discussed in chapter II, much of the material used in the early games was borrowed from the mythos and bestiaries of *Dungeons & Dragons* rather than directly from the respective cultures to which they relate.

In the decades that followed the release of the first *Final Fantasy*, however, more and more content was created within the series which, in turn, encouraged newer entries to draw on its own universal lore. Alongside recurring summoned beings such as Ifrit, Shiva, and Bahamut came characters like the many-armed, sword-wielding Gilgamesh or the multiple incarnations of Cid and several superbosses including the Ultima and Omega Weapons[1]. *Final Fantasy*

XIV and its expansions are the pinnacle of this self-contained mythos, with whole sections of the games paying inventive and nostalgic tributes to the franchise.

Final Fantasy VII is no different in its reimagining of various elements from prior titles, and the development team elected to implement, among other things, plot and design aspects that had been influenced by *Final Fantasy VI*, also co-written and directed by Yoshinori Kitase. For instance, *Final Fantasy VII* maintained its predecessor's non-medieval fantasy setting, as well as the weight of importance it placed on the backstory between its lead protagonists (Terra Branford and Cloud Strife, respectively) and villains (Kefka and Sephiroth).

However, not all the shared concepts are quite as consequential. The playable character Cait Sith in *Final Fantasy VII*, for example, is an evolution of the esper by the same name in *Final Fantasy VI*[2], both of which are based on the fairy cats of Scottish (*Cait Sìth*) and Irish (*Cait Sídhe*) folklore. In a similar vein, the summon Typhon in *Final Fantasy VII* has mythological origins, but the brute's unusual aesthetics were plucked straight from the previous game.

Typhon (also called Typhoeus, meaning 'Hurricane') is mentioned in ancient Greek literature as early as the *Iliad*, albeit in a single reference, but the *Theogony* is the first to provide a substantial summary of the myth. According to Hesiod, when the Olympians achieve victory in the ten-year war for supremacy, the Titanomachy, Zeus casts most of the

Titans who opposed him into the depths of Tartarus, the vast chasm beneath the earth (Gaia). Disgusted by the treatment of her children, Gaia retaliates by mating with Tartarus, who is also a primordial entity born from the void of Chaos. From their union comes Typhon, the youngest and most fearsome of all among Gaia's offspring. Apollodorus has a similar account in his *Bibliotheca*, except the conception of Typhon occurs in the aftermath of the Gigantomachy, not the Titanomachy[3].

The *Theogony* describes Typhon as being extremely powerful, with a hundred draconic snake heads growing from his shoulders, each alive with fiery eyes and flicking tongues. These heads emit a cacophony of terrible sounds, ranging from speech only the gods can understand to the ferocious barking of dogs or the bellowing of a bull.

This is expanded upon quite considerably by Apollodorus, who writes that Typhon is an amalgamation of man and beast, and the largest and strongest of Gaia's children. His winged upper body is humanoid in form, rising so high that his head brushes the stars. The hundred serpents do not extend directly from Typhon's shoulders in Apollodorus' retelling, rather they are the fingers of two enormous hands, but from his waist descend great coils of vipers[4].

The sheer size and might of Typhon allow him to launch an assault on the gods by throwing red-hot rocks into the heavens, and only Zeus instantly perceiving the danger he poses to Olympus prevents the monstrosity from seizing rule of the cosmos. The two engage in cataclysmic battle, with Zeus hurling thunderbolts and Typhon belching flaming stormwinds from his horrid jaws[5]. The seas and skies boil while the ground is scorched, causing the inhabitants of Gaia and Tartarus alike to tremble under such immense force. As the land disintegrates and melts in the tremendous heat, Zeus strikes Typhon down with lightning, trapping him beneath the earth.

In Apollodorus' account, while Typhon attacks heaven, the other gods flee to Egypt and transform into animals. In this way, the Greek and Egyptian deities could be conflated, which was important because Alexandria in Egypt became the intellectual and cultural centre of the Mediterranean during the Hellenistic period.

Various other versions of the story claim Typhon is buried beneath a volcano, often specifying Mount Etna on the Italian island of Sicily, which to this day remains almost constantly active[6]. His fiery breath is said to be responsible for the smoke and ash that billow from Etna, and from him come all violent winds that do not benefit mankind, such as tempests and cyclones.

Whether Typhon's incarceration was under a volcano, within the deep gulf of Tartarus, or in any of the alternative locations presented in Greco-Roman literature, it is generally agreed that he eventually becomes the mate of the hideous Echidna ('She-Viper'), commonly attested to be half-woman, half-serpent. Between them, Typhon and

Echidna produced some of the most infamous monsters in classical mythology.

The lists of their offspring differ from writer to writer, but these are typically regarded as being incomplete rather than inconsistent. Among them are a selection of weird and wonderful fiends: Cerberus, the many-headed hound of Hades; Orthrus, a two-headed guard dog killed by Heracles; the Hydra, a formidable water serpent with regenerating heads; the Chimera, a fire-breathing hybrid later slain by Bellerophon; the Nemean Lion, a ferocious beast whose hide cannot be pierced; the Sphinx, who terrorises travellers and makes them answer riddles; and the Harpies, bird-like females who personify storm winds[7]. There are several other creatures that do not feature in this book, but the tales involving those named will be addressed in coming chapters.

Final Fantasy VII's Typhon is a summoned being that can be acquired in the Ancient Forest – located on a mountaintop between Gongaga and Cosmo Canyon – during the last third of the game[8]. His name in the original English localisation is Typoon, which could be a mistranslation of either 'Typhon' or 'Typhoon'. From an etymological viewpoint, the words mean roughly the same, for Typhon was the immortal responsible for destructive winds, while a typhoon is a tropical storm.

The summon itself is based on the Typhon character of *Final Fantasy VI* (also known as Chupon): a squat, flying villain whose body primarily consists of two repulsive, large-jawed heads joined by a torso, with a pair of stumpy arms and smoke exhausts at his shoulders. He is incoherent when he speaks but remarkably powerful, almost as if he is a parody of the legendary brute. Typhon is introduced in *Final Fantasy VI* as the partner of the mischievous octopus Ultros, carrying him onto the player party's airship and then blowing the heroes overboard at the end of their battle.

What is interesting about the duo is that Ultros' name is a localisation of the Japanese '*Orutorosu*', which is more literally translated as 'Orthros'. Orthros (Latinised as Orthrus), as mentioned above, is a two-headed canine from Greek mythology and a child of Typhon. It could therefore be contended that Ultros' tentacles might better reflect the serpent limbs or fingers of the colossal Typhon of antiquity, while the name Orthros may, instead, better suit the dual heads of *Final Fantasy's* Typhon.

To aid with the transition of *Final Fantasy VI's* 2D models to *Final Fantasy VII's* 3D models, Tetsuya Nomura made minor changes to Yoshitaka Amano's concept art previously used for Typhon. The most significant of these was that the exhaust pipes were replaced by twisted, tentacle-like appendages sprouting from behind the shoulders of the summon's primary head. While the purpose of this is unclear, it may have been a way to integrate both Ultros' and Typhon's earlier features.

By implementing the change, however, Nomura-san – deliberately or otherwise – brought Typhon's design slightly closer to the depictions of his mythical namesake, who is said in the *Theogony* to have a hundred snakes extending from his shoulders (albeit the exhausts might have been a reference to his association with volcanoes). Alternatively, from the perspective of Typhon's secondary head in *Final Fantasy VII*, these appendages could represent the coiling vipers below the waist that are described by Apollodorus and others. The storm giant's terrible jaws, as cited in *Prometheus Bound*, are also prominent in Amano-san's and Nomura-san's designs, with the secondary head of the latter's including a forked snake tongue.

It is during Typhon's summoning animation in *Final Fantasy VII*, though, that the parallels with ancient Greek literature truly emerge. When the creature is called into battle, he materialises in a tornado, cackling and roaring unintelligibly. The primary head exhales a blast of wind through his nostrils to generate another hurricane whose swirling gale lifts the opponent(s) and chunks of rock into the air[9]. Typhon's secondary head then turns the battlefield upside down, slamming the opponent(s) into the heavens (which are now beneath them) and causing the boulders to crash against the clouds.

The animation reflects several details found in the classical stories of Typhon's conflict with Zeus. Its tornadoes can easily be attributed to Typhon being the master of destructive winds, with the summon's nasal squall alluding to his Greek counterpart's stormy breath when duelling the King of the Gods. The laughing and roaring likely refer to the sounds of all kinds being emitted by Typhon's serpent limbs, while smashing the opponent(s) and earthen shards into the inverted sky might relate to the monstrosity hurling rocks at heaven.

What is especially curious about Typhon's attack in *Final Fantasy VII*, called 'Disintegration', is that it deals substantial Fire-, Ice-, Lightning-, and Earth-elemental damage to enemies, despite the materia itself being aligned to the element of Wind. The affiliation with wind is consistent with mythology and the animation for 'Disintegration', although it could be speculated that the Lightning, Fire, and Earth components also link to the fight against Zeus' thunderbolts and Typhon's eventual imprisonment below a volcano[10].

The Typhon Materia's placement in the Ancient Forest seems not to have been influenced in any significant way by Hellenic lore. Its proximity on the overworld map to Gongaga and thus the Titan Materia (as discussed in the previous chapter), however, produces an intriguing coincidence. As with the Titans, Typhon was conflated with the Gigantes by poets of the Classical period, such as Euripides and Nonnus, and was still considered a Giant as late as the 1st century AD in Hyginus' *Fabulae*. A probable explanation for this is that all were said to be children of Gaia, and many sources describe them as having serpents for legs or feet. To have both Titan and Typhon obtainable in the same geographical region (albeit accessible at separate points in the game) may reference this connection.

An even more abstract analogy exists with respect to the tale of the Greek deities escaping Olympus, transforming into animals, and seeking sanctuary in Egypt when Typhon lays siege to the heavens. In these accounts, Typhon is equated with Set, the ancient Egyptian God of Storms, Violence, and Disorder, who is often portrayed with the head of the Set animal (*Sha*, also called the Typhonic beast), thought to be an imaginary canine creature.

Set, like Typhon, is a son of the earth (Geb) and commonly an antagonist in Egyptian mythology, whose cycle heavily features the conflict between Set and his nephew Horus. In later beliefs, however, his actions are reconciled, and he becomes the protector of the sun god Ra during his nightly journey through the underworld. To the Egyptians, Set was Lord of the Red Lands, their name for the deserts that lay beyond the flood plains of the Nile River.

Set is an alternative translation of the Japanese '*Seto*', the name of Nanaki's father in *Final Fantasy VII*[11]. Similar to the Typhonic beast, Nanaki and Seto are from a species of fictional quadrupeds, incorporating attributes of both wolves and lions. The narrative of a subplot in the game is that Nanaki despises his father and believes him to be a coward, only to learn that Seto was a great warrior who sacrificed himself to protect their home, Cosmo Canyon, thus loosely paralleling the redemption arc in the Set-Horus myths[12].

Cosmo Canyon itself is a red desert landscape, which is Set's domain, although the subterranean passages traversed en route to the site of Seto's petrified body are full of volcanic activity, which is Typhon's domain. As with Gongaga and the Titan Materia, the overworld adjacency of the Ancient Forest to Cosmo Canyon may indicate there is possibly more of a link than meets the eye between Seto and the Typhon Materia.

Applying the principle that elements of the Typhon legend might be found in less obvious places across the *Compilation of Final Fantasy VII*, there is one instance that stands out above the rest. Chapters XVI and XVII of this book provide a comprehensive breakdown of how Greek mythology and the Labours of Heracles inspired *Dirge of Cerberus*. The game's plot centres around Vincent Valentine attempting to thwart Deepground's plans of artificially awakening the Omega Weapon, a colossal entity whose function it is to gather the Lifestream and transport it to another planet, where life may begin anew.

Unlike some Indo-European cultures, the Hellenes did not generally prophesise the end of the world. Hesiod wrote of the Ages of Man in his poem *Érga kaì Hēmérai* (*Works and Days*), remarking that the current race of humanity will be annihilated by Zeus at the end of the fifth era, the Iron Age. No mention is made of what becomes of the world itself.

Despite being the greatest threat the gods ever face, Typhon is not associated with any foretold doomsday. It could be argued, however, that the level of destruction he brings upon heaven and earth makes him the closest thing in Greco-Roman mythology to an apocalyptic event. A potential allusion to this might exist in *Final Fantasy VII's* Ancient Forest, where both the Typhon Materia and Cloud's Apocalypse sword can be obtained.

In *Dirge of Cerberus*, when Omega materialises above Midgar, it takes the form of a winged humanoid from the midriff up, with a trio of armoured, serpentine limbs coiling to the ground below. The Weapon's shoulders are heavily reinforced and have two wings sprouting from each side, capable of carrying it skyward. Long tendrils of pure spirit energy extend from its shoulders, too, connecting the beast to the old mako reactors of the city, syphoning whatever Lifestream remains in the power plants.

So lofty is Omega's head that it parts the clouds when it emerges, its eyes aflame with mako. The night sky is initially calm, but by the time Vincent transforms into Chaos and commences his attack on the towering creature, a storm encircles Midgar, with flashes of lightning seen in the distance[13].

Omega's appearance bears striking resemblance to Typhon's description in classical literature, with many details being lifted directly from Apollodorus' account in *Bibliotheca*. The humanoid torso, wings, and coiling lower half can be found here, as can the imagery of the monster's head brushing the heavens. Omega's glowing eyes and the lengthy strands absorbing the Lifestream meanwhile reflect Typhon's fiery gaze and the hundred draconic snakes slithering from his shoulders, as noted in Hesiod's *Theogony* and elsewhere.

What is especially interesting about the comparison between Omega and Typhon is that their similarities do not seem to be limited to aesthetics, which is consistent with *Dirge of Cerberus* drawing significant inspiration from the Greek myths. For example, Typhon is a child of Gaia and Tartarus, the primordial embodiments of earth and its subterranean depths (quite literally deep ground); Omega, on the other hand, is a Weapon produced by the Planet and born from the pure Lifestream gathered in Deepground, the vast complex beneath Midgar.

In addition, Typhon is said to be the youngest but strongest of all of Gaia's children. This is also true of Omega, who will transport all life from the Planet in the event of an apocalypse, meaning – under intended circumstances – it should be the last Weapon to be born[14]. Unlike the terrestrial Weapons encountered in *Final Fantasy VII*, Omega is built to travel the cosmos, suggesting it is inherently more powerful than its siblings.

A final parallel can perhaps be found at the climax of *Dirge of Cerberus*, where Cloud and the other heroes of the *Compilation* sever the connections between Omega and the mako reactors, allowing Vincent to enter Omega's body to overcome its driving villain, Weiss. Despite their success, Omega takes flight towards the heavens, requiring Vincent (as Chaos) to engage the ascending Weapon head-on. Their collision results in a monumental explosion in the skies above Midgar, with shockwaves visible from space. The outcome is that Omega returns to the Lifestream, which, in turn, is redistributed across the Planet[15].

This is not unlike Hesiod and Apollodorus' stories of Typhon utilising the strength bestowed upon him by Gaia to launch an assault on heaven. When the gods see Typhon soaring towards Olympus, Zeus alone challenges the great monster, just as the immortal Vincent is the only one able to defeat Omega. Zeus flies after Typhon and their battle ends in devastation, with the latter being cast down into Tartarus or trapped beneath Mount Etna (depending on the source). Omega's ascent being halted in a titanic blast may be an allusion to this, as might its violent disintegration into spirit energy, free to re-join the Lifestream within the confines of Gaia.

This chapter has proposed how the terrible patron of destructive storms in Greek mythology may have appeared in more than one capacity across the *Compilation*. As it happens, this kind of representation is not an isolated case in the franchise, nor even among the summoned beings of *Final Fantasy VII*: The next chapter will examine the many forms of Phoenix.

1. Since *Final Fantasy II*, most titles in the series have featured a character called Cid who is unconnected to any of his counterparts. A common theme (including *Final Fantasy VII's* Cid Highwind) is that these men are engineers and/or associated with airships.

2. In *Final Fantasy VI*, espers are magical beings historically in conflict with humans. Cait Sith was an esper called Stray in the game's original release on the Super Nintendo Entertainment System (SNES), but this was updated for all later editions.

3. Most myths regarding Typhon's origins are variations of Hesiod's tale. However, this is not true in the case of the *Homeric Hymn to Pythian Apollo*, where Hera is angry with Zeus and arranges for Typhon to be brought forth as a plague upon mankind.

4. Neither Apollodorus nor later authors provide a specific number of coils below Typhon's waist, but artwork and pottery from antiquity typically depict these as a handful of large serpents, or only two in one instance.

5. The playwright Aeschylus described Typhon as having horrid jaws in *Prometheus Bound*, a play written in the 5th century BC.

6. Some say the blazing forges of the smithing and artisan god Hephaestus (whom the Romans knew as Vulcan) also lie beneath Mount Etna.

7. The Harpies are among the few instances where parentage is contradictory in various sources. Only in the Latin version of the *Argonautica*, written in the 1st century AD by Valerius Flaccus and based on an earlier Greek epic by the same name, are the Harpies said to be children of Typhon.

8. The Ancient Forest can only be accessed on the overworld map by either defeating the Ultima (Ultimate) Weapon and scaling the resultant crater or by breeding a chocobo capable of crossing mountains.

9. This specific method is reminiscent of *Final Fantasy VI*, where Typhon blows the party off the *Blackjack* airship using his 'Snort' attack.

10. In *Before Crisis*, Typhon is a Comet-elemental summon.

11. It should be noted that the precipice over which Seto's petrified body stands is localised in English as Cet Wall, although the menu screen cannot be accessed from this field to confirm in-game. The detail is found in the data files of *Final Fantasy VII*.

12. One of the most famous ancient Egyptian myths concerns Set's theft of Horus' eye. This might be the inspiration behind Nanaki losing an eye while in captivity at Shinra Headquarters.

13. This occurs in the opening section of chapter 12, titled "Omega and Chaos".

14. See chapter IV for an explanation of Gaia's relationship to the Weapons.

15. Vincent tells the crystal-encased Lucrecia what becomes of Chaos and Omega during the ending of *Dirge of Cerberus*.

CHAPTER XII

FLAMES OF REBIRTH

Among the most recognisable and powerful summoned creatures across the *Final Fantasy* series is Phoenix, a spectacular avian entity based on the renowned mythological bird of the same name, itself said to be immortal. It is typically associated in the games with the element of Fire or is capable of reviving allies who have fallen in battle. More often than not, calling forth Phoenix will allow the player to utilise its offensive *and* regenerative abilities simultaneously.

Two incarnations of Phoenix can be found in the *Compilation of Final Fantasy VII*: One in the original game, the other in *Crisis Core*[1]. Although similar, they have relatively distinct features derived from multiple sources of classical literature – as do the contexts of how their respective materia are acquired.

It is generally accepted by modern scholars that the phoenix myths should be attributed to the Greeks, but there is a degree of crossover with beliefs documented in ancient Egypt. One of the earliest written references to the bird is contained in *Cheírōnos Hypothêkai* (*Precepts of Chiron*)[2], a fragmented poem thought to have been composed by Hesiod, who lived in the 7th or 8th century BC. It is alleged here that a phoenix can live almost 1,000 times longer than man.

Among the most prominent Hellenic accounts of the phoenix is that of Herodotus of Halicarnassus, one of the world's first great historians. He recorded in *Historíai* (*The Histories*)[3], dated at around 430 BC, that he learned of the creature from the Egyptians but did not consider their folklore to be true.

According to Herodotus, the phoenix was described as being the size of an eagle, with feathers of gold and red. It lived in Arabia (now the Arabian Peninsula) and only returned to Heliopolis in Egypt once every 500 years or so to bury its parent[4]. The deceased bird was supposedly carried from Arabia in an egg made from myrrh by the younger phoenix, who would inter it in the Temple of Ra[5].

Archaeological finds at Heliopolis have indicated that Herodotus' retelling of the myth likely relates to Bennu, a primordial avian deity of ancient Egypt also heavily associated with the Sun and lifegiving. Nevertheless, variations of the legend are found in several sources from antiquity, with many details changing or evolving over the centuries.

For instance, there was no definitive consensus about the phoenix's size, features, colour, or even genus. Perhaps its most famous depiction comes from Pliny the Elder, the Roman author and philosopher responsible for *Naturalis Historia* (*Natural History*), compiled in the 1st century AD. Pliny corroborated Herodotus' account of the phoenix being as large as an eagle but claimed that its plumage was entirely purple, except for the golden feathers around its neck or the blue ones on its tail[6].

These attestations are less conflicting than they seem at first glance, however, because the colourisation may be linked to the origin of the bird's name. 'Phoenix' is the Latin transliteration of the ancient Greek '*phoinīx*', which some scholars have argued shares an etymological root with Phoenicia, a civilisation that existed on the easternmost shores of the Mediterranean Sea (in what is now areas of Lebanon and Syria). It is believed to refer to a specific type of dye commonly exported by Phoenicia called Tyrian purple, whose colours can range from deep yellow to crimson or plum, suggesting 'phoenix' might loosely translate as 'the purplish-red bird'.

Despite the myriad inconsistencies, certain aspects of the phoenix were frequently captured in classical art, such as its connection to the Sun. Ancient Egyptian portrayals of Ra and Bennu had typically included a solar disc above the divinities' heads to symbolise rebirth, which stemmed from the observation that the Sun's daily cycle involves its disappearance (death) at dusk and re-emergence (resurrection) at dawn. This was eventually adopted by the phoenix motif and developed into a burning nimbus or halo around the bird's crown, with rays of brilliant sunlight shining forth.

The longevity of the phoenix's life had already been established in the works of Hesiod and Herodotus, but it was not until much later that Roman literature introduced a concept more familiar to modern pop culture: It was proposed that the phoenix renews itself at death rather than there being multiple generations[7]. The bird was reported to construct its own funerary nest using myrrh, incense, and other fragrant substances, only to be reborn by hatching from the bones or remains of its previous incarnation. In this sense, the nest was a metaphor for both the tomb and the egg.

However, the fire and rejuvenation properties found in medieval heraldry and contemporary media are primarily drawn from *Phoenix*, a 4th century AD poem by Claudian, himself a Latin writer from Alexandria, Egypt[8]. In the poem, the phoenix is attested to live in a paradise at the eastern edge of the world – where the Sun rises – and is immune to the illnesses that afflict other animals.

According to Claudian, when the bird is ready to shed its aged body, it builds a pyre for itself. Helios, God of the Sun (known to the Romans as Sol), answers the phoenix's prayer, letting his radiant warmth ignite the death throne.

The phoenix will be consumed by the flames and from the ashes will its renewed form emerge to live again. The cinders of the pyre will then be carried to the temple at Heliopolis for burial as part of the bird's sacred ritual.

Rebirth, particularly by fire, has historically been a powerful symbol, so the phoenix came to epitomise resurrection as well as an entity 'rising from the ashes' of tragedy or oppression. Since the Middle Ages, more fantastical notions have been popularised, such as the bird's demise by self-combustion, its tears having healing qualities, or its feathers being capable of reversing death. As it happens, the latter characteristic has become a regular feature of the *Final Fantasy* games.

Despite celebrated franchise artist Yoshitaka Amano producing the concept illustration of a phoenix during the development of *Final Fantasy III*[9], it was not until *Final Fantasy V* that the creature made its inaugural appearance. That said, it was the former title that introduced the iconic item which has since become synonymous with the series: the Phoenix Down (albeit by the name 'Fenix Down'[10]).

Both *Final Fantasy V* and *Final Fantasy VI* incorporated the death and rebirth lore that surrounds the magnificent bird. Specifically, the player obtains Phoenix to summon when the wind drake Hiryu sacrifices his life in *Final Fantasy V*, while Locke's deceased lover, Rachel, bonds with the Phoenix Magicite in *Final Fantasy VI* after he uses it to briefly resurrect her[11].

In *Final Fantasy VII*, Phoenix can be called into battle by equipping the Phoenix Materia[12], which itself is acquired one of two ways. Towards the end of the game, after the party has parachuted into Midgar and the Shinra Corporation has fallen, the orb becomes available for excavation at Bone Village, an archaeological site.

There is, however, an opportunity to obtain the Phoenix Materia much earlier if certain conditions are met. This occurs during the siege of Fort Condor, a natural bastion located on a mountaintop that houses a mako reactor. Sometime after the power plant was made operational, a giant condor arrived and established a nest at its crown. The Shinra Company has been attempting to remove it by force for several years, but those who live on the mountain have been hiring soldiers and weapons to defend the extraordinary creature.

Fort Condor may be optionally visited by the player at any time after the Mythril Mine scenario, offering the chance to help combat the Shinra military in a battle strategy minigame. It is revealed by a senior villager that the condor roosting atop the reactor is incubating an egg, and that condor eggs only hatch once every few years.

The siege there is one of four compulsory missions to hijack Shinra's efforts of recovering Huge Materia from mako reactors around the Planet. It takes place while Cloud is incapacitated at Mideel, with Cid temporarily promoted to party leader. Under his command, the hired soldiers and weapons of Fort Condor make a stand against the advancing army.

If the player wins the battle[13], they are presented with a cutscene that begins with the condor perched over its egg. Cracks appear across the egg's shell, generating a great sphere of light around the facility and the colossal creature, followed by an eruption of flames. The blaze engulfs the condor, and in its midst, the silhouette of a firebird can be seen. When the inferno recedes, the condor collapses and crashes down the mountainside, dead.

A gold-feathered chick simultaneously emerges from the giant egg, slowly taking flight as Cid rushes to the reactor rooftop. The newly hatched condor leaves behind a scattering of shell fragments and the Phoenix Materia, suggesting several parallels between this event and ancient myths.

Perhaps the most obvious comparison to be drawn here is the death of the adult condor immediately preceding the birth of the chick. In particular, the older bird has been consumed by flames to make way for new life, just as Claudian's poem describes the death of the phoenix. The immense sphere of fire that engulfs the bird is also of significance because it likely symbolises the Sun: According to Claudian, it is the rays of Helios that ignite the phoenix's pyre.

When the player first learns of the condor from the fort's villagers, there is no mention of its mate, despite the presence of the egg[14]. Only one adult and one chick ever appear, and they are not shown to be alive at the same time. This may be an allusion to the Roman variants of the phoenix myth, whereby there is always a single bird, born from the remnants of the earlier body.

The latter element here is not directly reflected in the condor chick hatching from an egg, but there are a few curious similarities. First of all, the eggs are only said to hatch once every few years, which could be a nod to the fabled longevity of the phoenix. It was also reported by Herodotus that sightings of the bird exclusively occurred when it departed its home and returned to Heliopolis to bury its predecessor. This, in turn, might explain why the condor chick flies from the nest immediately upon the death of its parent[15].

It is additionally worth highlighting that the colours of the condor's eggshell (inside of which the Phoenix Materia is seemingly produced) blend from gold to red to purple. These combine Herodotus and Pliny's respective descriptions of the phoenix's plumage, and, by extension, the range of hues found in traditional Phoenician dyes[16].

On a more abstract level, the potential acquisition of the Phoenix Materia at Fort Condor comes at a fitting time in the narrative of *Final Fantasy VII*. The plot is progressed by the player's party travelling to Mideel to check on Cloud's wellbeing, where an eruption of the Lifestream causes the blond hero and Tifa to plunge into the river of souls. It is in the Lifestream that Tifa connects with her childhood friend's subconscious and pieces together the fragments of his identity. Cloud is thereafter 'reborn' as his true self.

Phoenix is also one of the five summoned creatures Zack can obtain for his Digital Mind Wave reel during *Crisis Core*[17]. The player receives the materia as a reward for solving the first of the Seven Wonders, a set of sidequests that become available shortly after Zack arrives in Nibelheim.

He is part of a Shinra investigation team that has been dispatched to the town, led by Sephiroth and accompanied by Cloud. Their assignment is to determine the cause of reported malfunctions at the regional mako reactor, as well as the strange disappearance of the facility's employees.

A young boy in the town square informs Zack that there are seven mysteries around Nibelheim[18]. One of these relates to the village's water supply recently turning blood red. Zack discovers the source of the discolouration to be an orb of Phoenix Materia in the basin of the water tower. He removes it and thereafter puts it to personal use.

The tragedy that subsequently befalls Nibelheim plays out in *Crisis Core* much as it does in Cloud's recount during *Final Fantasy VII*, only with certain scenes amended or omitted. Having learned the truth of his origins as part of the Jenova Project, Sephiroth loses his mind and sets the entire town ablaze, slaughtering its denizens. Zack and Cloud try to stop their superior at the reactor, but both are gravely wounded.

Professor Hojo orders for the pair to be placed in mako recovery units at the basement laboratory of Shinra Manor. When Zack escapes his confines four years later, he finds Nibelheim has been reconstructed exactly as it was and Sephiroth's atrocities have been covered up by the Shinra Company.

As with the summon's acquisition in *Final Fantasy VII*, the broader context of the Phoenix Materia's presence in Nibelheim is analogous to Greco-Roman mythology. It is the reward for the initial Seven Wonders quest and is thus the prize most likely to be attained by the player. Given that it must be accessed prior to Sephiroth's massacre, it foreshadows events to come.

The destruction of Nibelheim is a core part of the *Compilation's* narrative because it establishes the motive for Cloud and Tifa's anti-Shinra activity and their determination to stop Sephiroth. Not only do they lose their hometown, but Sephiroth is personally responsible for the deaths of Claudia Strife and Brian Lockhart, Cloud's mother and Tifa's father, respectively[19].

The phoenix is most often associated with fire and rebirth, two motifs that can also be applied to Nibelheim. The town is utterly ravaged by Sephiroth, specifically by burning it to the ground. While the ferocity of the blaze is captured in many entries across the *Compilation of Final Fantasy VII*, *Before Crisis* alone displays the immediate aftermath of the devastation and the charred structures that remain. At the behest of President Shinra, Nibelheim is rebuilt and populated by individuals under a non-disclosure contract with the Shinra Company[20].

This reflects the imagery of the phoenix being reborn from the ashes of its previous incarnation, as both *Final Fantasy VII* and *Crisis Core* show the town to be an exact replica of the original. By extension, the theme of resurrection may also apply to Zack, who emerges from the basement of Shinra Mansion four years after being officially classified as killed in action[21].

Another, less apparent lore connection regarding the Phoenix Materia in *Crisis Core* is the discolouration of Nibelheim's water supply. While all Summon Materia in the *Compilation* is red − with the sole exception of the blue sphere used by Kadaj to invoke Bahamut Tremor during *Advent Children*[22] −, there is little evidence to suggest the orbs generally contaminate their surroundings[23]. This implies the Phoenix Materia is unique in its ability to dye the water red, which may be a reference the bird sharing etymological roots with Phoenicia.

Phoenix's designs in both *Final Fantasy VII* and *Crisis Core* are relatively similar, but the respective summoning animations do differ. In the original game, Phoenix is depicted as a large bird with a magnificent and imposing wingspan. The feathers of its wings are predominantly red and gold, but the plumage of its body is multicoloured. Those at its crest are fiery crimson, and its long, thin tail is supplemented by elegant peacock-like quills.

Crisis Core's variant of Phoenix shares most of these features, though its crown and outer wings are brightly aflame, and its tail is blue and purple[24]. It should also be pointed out that this version has an elongated beak, which resembles the ancient Egyptian artwork of Bennu, typically equated to a crane or heron. The model in *Crisis Core Reunion* reverts back to the shorter beak but retains the primary hues of red, purple, and gold.

Elements of the design have been plucked from several historical sources. For example, where Herodotus wrote that the phoenix was mainly red and gold in colour and around the size of an eagle, Pliny the Elder's account describes the bird as having a purple body, a feathered crest, and a blue tail with tufts of rose. The Roman author Lactantius, meanwhile, contested in the 3rd century AD that the phoenix was even larger than an ostrich.

In the *Final Fantasy* series and its extended media, Phoenix's combined offensive and regenerative abilities are normally referred to as the 'Flames of Rebirth'. However, while the name has been retroactively included in re-releases of older titles, it was not introduced in a new entry until *Final Fantasy XIII*. Its singular alternative, 'Rebirth Flame' – as used in *Crisis Core* –, did not appear before *Final Fantasy VIII*.

Final Fantasy VII's equivalent is 'Phoenix Flame', and the summoning animation when a player character calls the bird into battle begins with a golden droplet falling to the ground and igniting. Phoenix rises from the flames and spreads its wings wide, encircled by a great halo. Rays of brilliant light and heat burst forth, dealing significant Fire-elemental damage to all opponents, and reviving any ally that has been knocked out to full HP[25]. When the Phoenix Materia is linked with the Final Attack Materia[26], the entire party can be resurrected in battle, thus preventing a game over.

The summoning itself contains multiple mythological and literary references, with the details of Claudian's poem *Phoenix* taking a central role. The least ambiguous are the parallels between the effects of 'Phoenix Flame' and the bird's relationship with both the Sun and rebirth. These are represented in the Fire damage to enemies and bringing fallen comrades back to life, respectively. The halo and rays of light also draw heavily from historical Sun-phoenix iconography.

The bed of flames from which Phoenix emerges in the animation should be highlighted, too, particularly given its ignition by a golden droplet[27]. This may symbolise Helios answering the phoenix's prayer to light its pyre in Claudian's poem, but it could separately allude to earlier myths where the bird's funerary nest was built from myrrh and incense. The oil extracts of these substances are both flammable and gold in colour, and 'tears of incense' are explicitly identified by Dante as a food source of the phoenix in his *Divine Comedy*, an epic poem composed in the 14th century.

In *Crisis Core's* 'Rebirth Flame' summoning, the Phoenix Materia explodes in a cloud of burning feathers, which then converge to form the firebird (akin to its appearance in *Final Fantasy V*). The flaming Phoenix races skyward, pausing only to let out a tremendous shriek and combust in a fiery sphere of light and golden pinions.

Like with *Final Fantasy VII's* incarnation, the connection between the bird and the Sun is portrayed here, but *Crisis Core* also references the later phoenix myths. Following a successful summoning via the Digital Mind Wave, the player receives a Phoenix Down in their item inventory, while Zack is granted the Raise status effect.

The function of Raise is to automatically resurrect Zack if his HP is reduced to zero during combat, and its activation is indicated by a golden feather above the SOLDIER's head. If the status is spent, it can be reinstated by consuming a Phoenix Down. As previously mentioned, Phoenix Downs have been recurring items in the series since *Final Fantasy III*. They are primarily used to revive party members who have been knocked out in an enemy encounter.

The down feathers of a bird are those found on its undercoat, as opposed to pinions, which are the outer layer of feathers on its wing[28]. While the classical phoenix has always been synonymous with rejuvenation, adaptations in more recent centuries have claimed its feathers are able to bring people back from the dead.

The distinction between an item raising the fallen and bestowing invulnerability or immortality upon an ally has been embraced by *Final Fantasy's* developers, for Phoenix

Downs are certainly not capable of the latter. However, it is important to emphasise that they can only resuscitate those who have been knocked out in battle; they cannot restore life to a person who has died, such as Aerith Gainsborough, who is among the most iconic examples in videogame history of characters that are killed during the course of the story.

In one form or another, elements of the phoenix myth have been a staple of the *Final Fantasy* franchise for more than 30 years. With Phoenix's glorious return in *Crisis Core Reunion*, being anticipated to feature in a future instalment of the *Final Fantasy VII* remake project, and playing a key role in the plot of *Final Fantasy XVI*, that is unlikely to change anytime soon.

1. There is also a third instance, but it is minor: Phoenix can be fought as an opponent in *Final Fantasy VII G-Bike*, a mobile-exclusive spin-off that was available in Japan between 2014 and 2015.

2. *Cheírōnos Hypothêkai* is a poem about the wise centaur Chiron teaching the hero Achilles.

3. *Historíai* is Herodotus' invaluable record of ancient traditions, cultures, geography, politics, conflicts, and more.

4. Heliopolis was one of the oldest cities in ancient Egypt and was the centre for worship of Ra (later Ra-Atum). Helios, the Hellenic personification of the Sun, lent his name to what became the 'City of the Sun' in Greek. It was originally called *Iwnw*, 'the Pillars', and its remnants are now located in a district of Egypt's capital, Cairo.

5. Ra was the falcon-headed creator god of the ancient Egyptians and had been an important deity since the 25th century BC. While his role was extensive and varied over

time, he was best known as a solar god, which led to his conflation with Helios by the Greeks.

6. The description of purple feathers can also be found much earlier in *Exagōgē*, a 3rd century BC play by Jewish dramatist Ezekiel the Tragedian.

7. Pliny's *Naturalis Historia* and Ovid's *Metamorphoses*, also completed in the 1st century AD, were among the first pieces of literature to add these details to the phoenix myth.

8. Alexandria was founded by Alexander the Great in 331 BC and remained a Hellenic city for around 300 years before falling under Roman rule.

9. The Phoenix is a common enemy type that was cut from *Final Fantasy III* late in development, but details of it can still be found in the game's coding.

10. 'Fenix' is the Old English spelling of 'phoenix'.

11. In *Final Fantasy VI*, espers are magical beings historically in conflict with humans. Magicite is the post-mortem remains of an esper, which can be used by the player characters to learn magic or summon that same being.

12. While Phoenix is primarily summonable using the Phoenix Materia, this can also be done via the Master Summon Materia. The same is true for all summons.

13. The player can win by either completing the minigame or by losing the minigame, then defeating the CMD Grand Horn, a bipedal monster that functions as an end-of-level opponent. If Cid and the others lose to the Grand Horn, they will be ejected from Fort Condor and cannot re-enter for the rest of the game. It is worth noting that the death of the condor occurs irrespective of the battle outcome.

14. The English localisation for the original PlayStation release of the game implied there are multiple adult birds, although this was amended in later editions.

15. The parent condor's death by flame and simultaneous hatching of the egg is relatively distinct from the classical phoenix myth, but it does closely mirror the life cycle of

the phoenix in *Dungeons & Dragons*, as introduced in 1994.

16. The same colours appear on the giant egg in the background of the Fort Condor minigame of *Final Fantasy VII Remake's Episode INTERmission*. However, the phoenix parallel is absent here because both the player's and opponent's headquarters and outposts are guarded by multiple condors.

17. Digital Mind Wave (DMW) is the style of Limit Break used in *Crisis Core* and works by lining up reels like those of a slot machine. The five summons obtainable for the DMW are Ifrit, Bahamut, Bahamut Fury, Odin, and Phoenix.

18. The Seven Wonders of Nibelheim are i) the town's water turning red, ii) the changing portrait at the inn, iii) the fiendish bomb whose face looks different, iv) the laughter coming from the safe at Shinra Manor, v) the moaning coming from the mansion's basement, vi) a treasure in the flames of Nibelheim, and vii) a gift from the boy to Zack.

19. According to Tetsuya Nomura, Claudia Strife (initially Claudia Strauss) and Brian Lockhart have been the canon names of these characters since the original *Final Fantasy VII's* development. However, it was not until *Remake* and its extended media that the names were officially verified.

20. Reference to Nibelheim's reconstruction and its new inhabitants is made in a confidential Shinra report and a letter from Zangan, both found in Tifa's old bedroom during *Final Fantasy VII*. Further details are presented in the novel *The Kids Are Alright*.

21. Zack is advised in an email from Kunsel that Shinra's Department of General Affairs announced his death.

22. Bahamut Tremor is known in localised versions of *Advent Children* as Bahamut SIN, which may additionally be an allusion to the monstrous entity from *Final Fantasy X*.

23. Two caveats to this are that the Knights of the Round Materia causes the crystal pyramid encasing it to glow,

and the materia Scarlet's researchers are working on in *Remake* warps and discolours the surrounding mako during synthetic saturation.

24. A similar design with peacock-like feathers seems to appear in *Remake*, found on the wall painting in Aerith and Ifalna's old room at Shinra Headquarters.

25. HP (or Health Points) is a measure of a party member's health during battle. If their HP value reaches zero, the character is knocked out and cannot participate further until they are revived. If all party members' HP reach zero, the game is over.

26. In *Final Fantasy VII's* materia system, linking special types of materia orbs to others can produce combined effects.

27. More droplets are emitted alongside Phoenix's rays of light.

28. Phoenix Pinions are items that appear in some *Final Fantasy* titles, often with similar properties as Phoenix Downs but sometimes having direct connections to the Phoenix summon, as is the case in *Final Fantasy VIII* and *Final Fantasy IX*.

PART FIVE

AN AGE
OF HEROES

PERSEUS & THESEUS

CHAPTER XIII

CLASH OF THE WEAPONS

I t should be unsurprising that classical mythology itself contains countless inconsistencies across the various sources, primarily due to the volume of content, diversity of writers, and changing cultures and tastes from the Greek Dark Ages to the height of the Roman Empire one thousand years later. From Homer and Hesiod to the Athenian playwrights, then to Latin authors such as Ovid and Virgil, no two versions of any myth are an exact match.

The same is true of later interpretations and adaptations, ranging from Dante and Shakespeare to the relatively modern medium of filmmaking. While by no means the first movie to reproduce a tale from antiquity for cinema audiences[1], one of the earliest major releases was *Jason and the Argonauts* in 1963[2]. The film is based on the epic of the Greek hero Jason and his voyage to obtain the Golden Fleece of a divine ram, drawing heavily from Apollonius of Rhodes' 3ʳᵈ century BC masterpiece, *Argonautica*.

Unlike fellow protagonists such as Heracles and Theseus, Jason's story is not examined in this book. However, that is not to suggest his adventures have no claim over influencing *Final Fantasy VII* in some way: Kazushige Nojima, the lead scenario writer for most of the *Compilation* and *Remake*, has personally confirmed it was *Jason and the Argonauts* that initially sparked his interest in Greek mythology when he was a boy.

Nojima-san, of course, was responsible for scripting three entries in the *Herakuresu no Eikō* (*Glory of Heracles*) series during the late 1980s and early 1990s, prior to his employment with Square. This presented the perfect opportunity for the fledgling writer to create his own adaptations and put his own twist on classical tales such as the Trojan War or the destruction of Atlantis. Nevertheless, Nojima-san's characters, narratives, and themes were reasonably faithful to events in the ancient source material rather than later retellings.

The chapters of the book have so far attempted to offer compelling evidence that Nojima-san deliberately wove and continues to weave threads of Hellenic lore into the very fabric of *Final Fantasy VII*. That said, there is a curious anomaly that arises during one set piece of the original game: A scenario that does not seem to have been directly inspired by a Hellenic myth but by the cinematic revision of one.

Clash of the Titans (1981) centres around the legendary exploits of the demigod Perseus and features two of the most recognisable creatures in Greek mythology: the winged steed Pegasus and the snake-haired Medusa. However, it would be misleading to imply that the film is an accurate representation of the archaic accounts of the hero[3]. The details of Perseus' feats attested by Hesiod, Apollodorus, or Ovid, for instance, differ quite considerably, not to mention the terrible sea monster in *Clash of the Titans* is derived from medieval folklore of Northern Europe[4].

In mythology, Perseus is a son of Zeus by Danaë, a princess of the city-state of Argos[5]. When the cruel King Acrisius learns his daughter has given birth, he has mother and child placed in a wooden chest and cast out to sea. They are eventually found and saved by a fisherman from the island of Seriphos, the brother of its ruler King Polydectes.

As the years go by, Polydectes begins to desire Danaë for himself, so he removes Perseus by sending the young man on a quest to bring back the head of the Gorgon Medusa, a task presumed to be a suicide mission. Perseus is aided by two of his divine half-siblings, Athena and Hermes, who gift him the weapons and equipment he needs to slay Medusa. Among the treasures are a sword, a shield, a satchel, and Hermes' winged sandals, the latter of which allow the hero to run through the air at tremendous speed[6].

Arriving at the island where the Gorgon sisters live[7], Perseus avoids being turned to stone by Medusa's fatal stare by looking at her only in the reflection of his polished shield[8]. He is victorious with this technique and decapitates her, stuffing the head of hissing snakes into the satchel and taking flight again. Unbeknownst to the demigod, two entities are subsequently born from Medusa's severed neck, one of whom is Pegasus[9].

On his return to Seriphos, Perseus passes over the coastline of Ethiopia, where he spots a beautiful maiden chained to a sea rock, Princess Andromeda. Andromeda is the daughter of King Cepheus and Queen Cassiopeia, and she is to be sacrificed to appease the gods for her mother's hubris, boasting the girl was more attractive than all the Nereids[10]. As punishment, Poseidon has summoned the monstrous Cetus, generally described in the myths as a sea serpent or dragon with a fishlike tail.

Perseus is determined to further prove his worth as a hero, so he dives into the water and slices through the brute with the sword given to him by Athena. As his reward for rescuing Andromeda, she agrees to marry him. Perseus conveys Medusa's head back to the court of Polydectes as promised, having realised by now that the king intended to send him to his death. In revenge, he presents the gruesome trophy for Polydectes to behold, only for it to petrify the older man.

Meanwhile, in *Clash of the Titans*, when King Acrisius banishes Danaë and the baby Perseus from Argos, Zeus ends the king's life and orders Poseidon to release one of the last remaining Titans, the Kraken, to destroy the city. Many years later, in retribution for the Skyfather transforming her own son Calibos into a hideous satyr-like creature[11], the goddess Thetis mysteriously teleports Perseus to her patron city of Joppa[12].

Perseus soon discovers Joppa's princess, Andromeda, is under a curse. It is revealed that Thetis is behind this, too[13]: Andromeda had been engaged to Calibos before his metamorphosis and the enchantment is to prevent the girl from wedding anyone else. Sneaking into the royal palace, Perseus finds the princess in a deep sleep, but her spirit is being carried off each night to receive instructions from Calibos to perpetuate his mother's malevolent spell.

The hero is successful in freeing Andromeda from the curse and winning her hand in marriage, having located Pegasus and secured the stallion's services during his endeavours. Enraged by Queen Cassiopeia's declaration that her daughter is more beautiful than Thetis herself, the goddess demands Andromeda is sacrificed to the Kraken, or Joppa will be decimated.

Perseus seeks a way to defeat the sea monster and learns that, to do so, he must cut off Medusa's head and utilise her supernatural powers, so he sets out to kill the Gorgon. In Joppa, when the chosen day arrives, Andromeda is shackled to the sacrificial rock to await the Kraken, but as it approaches, Perseus swoops out of the sky on Pegasus. He lifts Medusa's head in the direction of the Titan, causing it to petrify and crumble into the water. Andromeda is unbound, and she and Perseus live happily ever after.

It may not be obvious at first, but the events in *Final Fantasy VII* comparable to *Clash of the Titans* are those that play out when Tifa regains consciousness in Junon. This follows Cloud's mental breakdown at the Northern Crater, Sephiroth's consequent acquisition of the Black Materia, the catastrophic emergence of the Planet's biomechanical guardians, Weapon, and the protagonists barely escaping aboard Shinra's *Highwind* airship.

Barret informs Tifa that Sephiroth has used the Black Materia to summon Meteor, which now looms in the sky like a fiery giant. President Rufus believes a public execution of Avalanche members will help placate the growing civil unrest in the wake of Meteor's apocalyptic threat, regardless of whether the group is responsible or not.

Tifa and Barret are escorted to a media conference where Director Scarlet is leading a television broadcast of the execution. The blonde villainess oversees Tifa being cuffed to the chair in her 'special' gas chamber, taunting her maliciously. However, as the process commences, an alarm sounds to warn citizens that the Sapphire Weapon is headed straight for Junon.

A clear parallel begins to develop in this context between Tifa and Andromeda: In the respective tales, they are the sacrificial lambs, despite neither being to blame for the threat that has arisen. The life of Andromeda is the price of Queen Cassiopeia's hubris, as decreed by Thetis during *Clash of the Titans*. Similarly, the Shinra Company makes Avalanche the scapegoat for Meteor's summoning, and Tifa is selected by Scarlet as the prisoner whose death will impact the audience most. Where Andromeda's demise is intended to appease the gods, Tifa's is to appease society.

A peculiar aspect of the Junon sequence is that it starts with Tifa in a coma. Her subconscious has been ruminating on her unwillingness to challenge the truth of Cloud's identity, because she has known since their initial reunion in Midgar that his recollection of the Nibelheim incident is inaccurate. As such, it could be argued that the psychological torment Tifa endures in her coma resembles Calibos' nightly torture of Andromeda, a character first encountered in the film while she is sleeping.

When Thetis delivers her ultimatum concerning the princess' fate, she does so by speaking through a stone statue during Andromeda and Perseus' packed wedding ceremony. This, too, is loosely reflected in *Final Fantasy VII*, when Scarlet takes centre stage at a media gathering and announces to the world that Tifa is to be executed live on television.

The designated victims are then tied up to face their doom: Andromeda is chained to Joppa's sacrificial rock to await the sea monster, while Tifa is strapped to the gas chamber chair. In both cases, it is at this moment that the scenario's marine 'titan', respectively the Kraken or the Sapphire Weapon, rises from the ocean depths[14].

The Kraken is presented in *Clash of the Titans* with a humanoid torso and long, serpentine lower half. Its body is comprised of armoured scales and fins, four clawed hands, and a hideous face. These exact features are found on the Sapphire Weapon, too, albeit it has only two arthropod-like limbs for forearms and is further protected by the large plates and spines of its exoskeleton[15]. It should additionally be noted that the Weapon's particular blue-purple colour scheme seems to have been influenced by the Fiend of Water in the original *Final Fantasy*, also called the Kraken.

The Sapphire Weapon attacks Junon by first ramming into the city's harbour, simultaneously generating a massive tidal wave, then blasting intense rays of energy from its maw. One such beam burns a hole through the ceiling of Scarlet's gas chamber, offering Tifa an escape route. However, as the colossus prepares to unleash another volley of energy upon Junon, a shell fired from the Mako Cannon blows its head from its shoulders, causing it to collapse lifelessly into the bay.

The death of the Sapphire Weapon is comparable to the Kraken's demise in *Clash of the Titans*, where the brute is accosted by Perseus and Pegasus as it approaches Andromeda's sacrificial rock. While the Weapon is killed by having its head obliterated, the Kraken is killed by the decapitated head of Medusa. As the sea monster turns to stone, though, its own head also shatters and its body crumbles into the surf.

Pegasus does not appear in *Final Fantasy VII* (nor does any other flying horse, for that matter), but he can be seen in earlier work by scenario writer Kazushige Nojima. In the initial *Herakuresu no Eikō* title (1987), the winged steed transports the protagonist, Heracles, to Olympus, although he is not controllable by the player. This changes in the subsequent games of the franchise, themselves scripted by Nojima-san, where Pegasus can be mounted by the player character on the overworld map and flown to otherwise-inaccessible locations.

The importance of this observation is that the equivalent function in the *Final Fantasy* series is performed by airships; in *Final Fantasy VII*, the role belongs to the *Highwind*. During the Junon sequence, after Tifa climbs through the cavity in the gas chamber's ceiling, she is rescued from the gigantic barrel of the Mako Cannon by the *Highwind*, which has been commandeered by her friends. In this way, the airship coming to Tifa's aid amid the attempted execution is analogous to Pegasus carrying Perseus to Andromeda to save her from sacrifice.

Interestingly, the parallels are not limited to *Final Fantasy VII*. Chapters XVI and XVII of this book explore the extent to which *Dirge of Cerberus* is infused with the myths of Heracles, as well as being sprinkled with nods to *Herakuresu no Eikō*[16]. Of specific note are the Pegasus Riders that Vincent encounters in the Midgar wastelands. These Deepground SOLDIERs are driving hoverbikes with several aesthetic likenesses to the *Highwind*, such as the slender metallic body, long nose, and twin tail fins. The Pegasus bikes especially resemble the aircraft once it has cast off its propellers and activated its jet engines, as shown prior to the party's descent into the Northern Cave.

There may also be a vague allusion to this speculated conflation in *Remake*. The key character artwork for Aerith in the original game depicts her gazing upon the *Highwind*. While her fascination is supplemented by dialogue with Cloud aboard the cargo ship between Junon and Costa del Sol, the flower girl is killed before she has a chance to ride the craft. The airship is missing from Aerith's corresponding key art for *Remake*, but it is arguably mitigated by the curious and inexplicable inclusion of a winged white horse on the wall painting in her old bedroom at Shinra Headquarters[17].

A last intriguing link between *Final Fantasy VII* and *Clash of the Titans* relates to Junon itself. Although Perseus and Andromeda's story is mainly set in Joppa, the only city that the Kraken directly attacks is Argos, where Perseus was born. This is portrayed as the creature rushing through the coastal waters to produce an enormous tidal wave. The tsunami breaches the harbour and crashes into Argos, tearing down buildings and drowning its citizens. The same imagery is used in *Final Fantasy VII* when the Sapphire Weapon lays siege to Junon.

Argos is a historical location that is frequently mentioned in Greek mythology. It is thought to have been populated for approximately 7,000 years, making it the oldest continuously inhabited site in Europe. In antiquity, Argos was a wealthy and influential *polis* (city-state) and a powerful rival of Sparta. Its ancient citadel stands atop the hill of Larisa, with much of the surrounding municipality eventually taking shape between its rocky slopes and the adjacent bay[18]. The defensive walls around the elevated stronghold have been damaged and rebuilt multiple times over the centuries, and the current incarnation dates to the Middle Ages.

Junon shares many of Argos' compositional and geographical traits and is itself a fortified coastal city constructed against the incline of a lofty promontory[19]. During *Final Fantasy VII*, the player first accesses Junon via the old fishing village at the foot of the hillside; this is the elder settlement, now known as Under Junon, which was once a bustling port. It is additionally worth highlighting that the official novel *Traces of Two Pasts* describes Junon's history as a republic with influence as far-reaching as Nibelheim, and thus comparable to a *polis*.

In the context of mythology that inspired *Final Fantasy VII*, however, the most important aspect of Argos is that its divine patron was Hera, the wife of Zeus and Goddess of Marriage and Childbirth[20]. Hera features in *Clash of the Titans* during numerous scenes set on Olympus, although she makes little fuss about Zeus commanding the Kraken to destroy Argos. Conversely, she plays a significant role in *Jason and the Argonauts* – the film that introduced Kazushige Nojima to ancient Greek myths – as the protector of its leading hero.

Jason's voyage aboard the *Argo* – named after its builder, Argus, a member of Argos' royal family – is one of the great epics in classical lore. It therefore may not be a coincidence that the sole occasion it is mandatory for Cloud and the group to cross the sea by ship in *Final Fantasy VII* comes at the conclusion of their initial visit to Junon, a city that can be connected to Argos and Hera, via its parallels to the former[21].

Another tale that involves the Queen of Heaven is how her son Hephaestus earns his place among the Twelve Olympians. When he was a newborn, Hera cast Hephaestus from Mount Olympus in her disgust at his lameness. He returns several years later, by this time a master craftsman. Hera has recently accepted the anonymous gift of an exquisite golden throne, but upon sitting on it, she becomes trapped by an enchantment. The lone individual capable of releasing Hera from the throne is Hephaestus, its creator. The God of the Forge goes on to fashion some of the most incredible weapons and artefacts in all mythology.

It could be contended that Hera's association with Junon is also represented in the specifics of Tifa's public execution. First of all, Tifa is bound to the chair in the gas chamber similar to the way in which Hera is imprisoned on the golden throne. Furthermore, she is detained there by Scarlet, Shinra's Director of Weapons Development[22], who rose to her position through innovative arms designs during the Wutai War[23], just as Hephaestus achieves prominence as the deity responsible for crafting divine weapons.

The piece of evidence that perhaps best demonstrates the likely link between Argos and Junon, however, is that Hera's Roman equivalent is Juno, who was considered to be the patron goddess of the Empire. Junon, as it happens, is Juno's name in French.

Hera is depicted throughout Greek mythology as a jealous wife, often interfering in the lives of Zeus' lovers and illegitimate children. Perseus is one of the rare few who do not suffer her wrath, possibly because he was born into the royal line of Argos. He and Andromeda ultimately go on to start a dynasty of their own, counting among their descendants other celebrated heroes and demigods such as Heracles and Theseus, who are themselves the focus of coming chapters.

1. Two of the earliest feature films inspired by classical mythology are *L'Île de Calypso* (*The Island of Calypso*, 1905), a French adaptation of Odysseus' encounter with the Cyclops Polyphemus, and *Helena* (1924), a German silent drama based on the *Iliad*. It was not until the mid-1950s that American film studios began to produce their own works, with *Ulysses* (1955, Paramount Pictures) and *Helen of Troy* (1956, Warner Bros.) among the first.
2. Although it did not initially enjoy huge box office success, *Jason and the Argonauts* was critically acclaimed upon its release and includes some of the most iconic stop-motion animation of the era.
3. The original *Clash of the Titans* features Harry Hamlin as Perseus and Lawrence Olivier as Zeus. It was remade and released in 2010, with Sam Worthington as Perseus, Liam Neeson as Zeus, and Ralph Fiennes as its villain, Hades.

4. The Kraken was generally described from the 18th century onwards as a huge octopus-like horror that could drag ships to their doom.

5. King Acrisius imprisons Danaë in a secret chamber to prevent her from falling pregnant and fulfilling a prophecy that he would be killed by his grandson. Zeus visits the chamber in the form of golden rain, causing her to conceive Perseus.

6. Hermes and his sandals are discussed in more detail in chapter XIX.

7. Medusa is one of three Gorgons attested in classical lore. Her 'sisters' were Stheno and Euryale, both of whom were immortal, while Medusa was not.

8. The correct terminology here is that Medusa could 'petrify' people, which is exactly where the Petrify, Petrification, or Stone status effects in the *Final Fantasy* series come from. Medusa's signature ability is specifically mirrored in *Final Fantasy VII* through attacks such as 'Stone Stare' by Gagighandi enemies and 'Petrif-Eye' by Gighee and Demon's Gate.

9. As referenced in chapter IX, many accounts of Medusa claim she was a beautiful nymph who was transformed into a Gorgon by Athena because Poseidon had slept with her in one of the goddess' temples. Medusa had fallen pregnant by the Lord of the Seas, but her new serpentine lower half prevented her from giving birth to Pegasus and his brother, the handsome youth Chrysaor. Pegasus' adventures with the hero Bellerophon are addressed in chapter XX. It should be noted, however, that Medusa is commonly depicted in ancient Greek art with human legs.

10. The Nereids are the water nymph daughters of the aquatic god Nereus.

11. Calibos is not based on any mythical figure but is rather an original character introduced in *Clash of the Titans*.

12. Joppa is an ancient port city situated in modern day Israel, part of a region that was ruled by the Phoenicians in antiquity. Pliny the Elder places Andromeda's sacrifice here rather than in Argos. Joppa is better known

nowadays as Jaffa, famed for its oranges and for lending its name to Jaffa Cakes.

13. In *Clash of the Titans*, Thetis appears among the Olympians. However, in mythology, she is one of the Nereids (see footnote 10) and has varying roles. Arguably the most famous tale relates to Thetis immersing her infant son Achilles in the river Styx, as recounted in *Final Fantasy VII and the Trojan War*.

14. The fullest description of Cetus is provided in Ovid's *Metamorphoses*, in which he is portrayed as a sea dragon commanded by Poseidon. The Kraken and Medusa are both referred to as Titans in the 1981 movie adaptation, hence its title. In mythology, though, neither is one.

15. The Sapphire Weapon's features are perhaps best viewed in Tetsuya Nomura's original concept art.

16. *Dirge of Cerberus* is the only entry in the *Compilation of Final Fantasy VII* that was not scripted by Kazushige Nojima. While Nojima-san is first to be acknowledged in the 'Special Thanks' section of its credits, the game was instead written by Hiroki Chiba.

17. The importance of the images in the wall art is discussed in chapter VII. Pegasus is almost universally described as white in classical literature.

18. Argos is situated on the northernmost shore of the Argolic Gulf, itself part of the Aegean Sea.

19. It is revealed in *Final Fantasy VII* that the Shinra Corporation built most of Junon during wartime. However, it is never clarified which conflict is being referenced, especially given that the Wutai War commenced only 15 years before the start of the game. The answer might instead be the international war alluded to in the "Early Material File" section of the *Ultimania Omega*, then reintroduced as a concept in *Traces of Two Pasts*.

20. Hera's affiliation with Argos is established in literature as early as Hesiod's *Theogony*.

21. The player only has to board the cargo ship once to progress the story in *Final Fantasy VII*, but it functions as an optional mode of transport between Junon and

Costa del Sol until the *Highwind* becomes available. It should be noted that the submarine is also acquired at Junon later in the game for underwater exploration.

22. Scarlet's department is alternatively known in *Final Fantasy VII Remake* as the Advanced Weaponry Division.

23. This detail is later verified during *Episode INTERmission*.

CHAPTER XIV

THESEUS' PARADOX

Theseus' Paradox, alternatively known as the Ship of Theseus, is a conundrum in classical philosophy that concerns a field of study called identity metaphysics[1]. It was first proposed by Plutarch, a Greek historian and biographer who lived between the 1st and 2nd centuries AD, and is named after the legendary founder-king of Athens.

In his most celebrated written work, *Bíoi Parállēloi* (*Parallel Lives*), Plutarch applies this philosophical problem to a ship of tremendous cultural and historic value to the Athenians: the vessel aboard which Theseus sailed to the island of Crete to confront the Minotaur (see chapter XV), then preserved in the city's harbour upon his return. Over countless generations, each of its wooden planks and timbers had rotted and been replaced, until not a single piece of the original boat remained. Plutarch then questions whether or not it could still be considered the same ship.

The principles of Theseus' Paradox can be applied to humans as well. The cells in a person's body age and are damaged over time, so they constantly replicate to produce healthier substitutes. In terms of biology, this continuous change means you quite literally become a different person, so the philosophical dilemma of identity relates to whether *you* are still *you*.

It is therefore appropriate – albeit an intriguing coincidence – that the character whose existential crisis is critical to the plot of *Final Fantasy VII* should share so many connections with the story of Theseus' life. While several of the latter's adventures are attested by authors such as Apollodorus and Ovid, the most extensive account is found in Plutarch's *Bíoi Parállēloi*.

Those who have delved deep into Greek mythology's rich tapestry of epics and anecdotes will know all too well that certain tropes or themes recur regularly throughout the cycle. Heroes achieving fame for killing a monster that has terrorised local provinces, mortals facing the wrath of a god whose love they have spurned, or a new species of flower blooming to symbolise the untimely death of a beautiful youth are all such examples.

Yet another is the tales of adolescent male protagonists – usually of dubious parentage – and their endeavours to obtain or secure a sense of identity. Perseus does not truly believe Zeus is his father until he is aided on his quest by his half-siblings Athena and Hermes (see chapter XIII); the only indication in Bellerophon's childhood that he is a son of Poseidon is his knack for taming horses (see chapter XX)[2]; and the core plot of Oedipus' tragedy is the catastrophic misunderstanding of which royal house he belongs to (see chapter XIX). One of the best-known occurrences of this archetype, however, is Theseus and his mysterious origins.

Theseus is a king who embodies everything the Athenians deemed important in a person's character: He is intelligent, noble, courageous, strong, cunning, athletic, just, and attractive, and his legendary deeds are many. The most iconic of these is his defeat of the Minotaur in the Labyrinth, as will be examined in the next chapter.

Theseus is born a prince of Troezen, a small city-state located in the Peloponnese, a region of Greece renowned in antiquity for its entrances to the underworld[3]. His mother is Princess Aethra, but he has no father, which makes the boy feel different to those around him as he grows up. By his teens, Theseus gains a reputation for his impressive strength, speed, and competitiveness, unaware that the blood in his veins is of divine heritage.

It is also common in Greek mythology that heroes and demigods have two recognised biological fathers – one human and one immortal[4]. In the case of Theseus, he is conceived by Aethra, herself a young maiden, when King Aegeus of Athens visits Troezen's royal palace, and on the same night, she has a sexual encounter with Poseidon as she bathes in a local spring[5].

Aegeus later leads the princess onto a hill overlooking the city and buries his sword and sandals beneath a great rock. He instructs Aethra to bring any son she may bear him to this spot once he is old enough, and to tell the lad the secrets of his birth if he can recover the items.

When at last Theseus' comes of age and is able to roll away the boulder, his mother's revelations begin to rouse the self-identity he has always longed for. His ambition has outgrown Troezen, and he is convinced his future lies in Athens. For years, Theseus has admired Heracles, and realises he will have to emulate the strongman's heroic feats if he wishes to stake his claim as heir to the Athenian throne. The bold prince decides to travel to Attica via the dangerous land route rather than making the voyage by sea. The challenges he faces along the way are known as the Labours of Theseus.

There are six trials in total, each loosely corresponding to an underworld opening whose vicinity is inhabited by a chthonic being[6]. In the first confrontation, he engages the brute Periphetes and acquires a giant bronze club from him, a weapon with which Theseus becomes synonymous. He thereafter slays a number of notorious beasts and bandits in the remaining labours, carving a formidable name for himself[7].

When he arrives in Athens, Theseus acts with humility towards his exploits so as not to antagonise his unsuspecting father, King Aegeus. He initially presents himself at the royal court with a degree of anonymity but later exposes his sword at a banquet, where Aegeus can see it. The old king remembers the blade he once buried at Troezen, embraces his son, and formally acknowledges him as successor to the throne[8]. In this way, Theseus' identity is fully established.

Personal growth and self-identity are key themes in *Final Fantasy VII*, too. For instance, when the player's party first leaves Midgar, Aerith agrees to accompany the others on their journey so that she might learn her place in the world as the last surviving Cetra. Red XIII, meanwhile, addresses the flawed resentment he harbours towards his father at Cosmo Canyon and is encouraged by Bugenhagen to help the group reduce the Planet's misery and become a noble warrior[9].

By far the most complex character in *Final Fantasy VII* in terms of identity, however, is the game's lead protagonist, Cloud Strife. Who Cloud thinks he is when he is introduced to the player stands in stark contrast to who he discovers himself to be when the layers of his past are peeled away. His story boasts similarities with various heroes across Greek mythology, but none are more prominent than the parallels with Theseus.

Cloud was born in the backwater town of Nibelheim, situated at the foot of a treacherous mountain range. His father is said to have died when he was very little[10], so he

281

was raised by his mother, Claudia. Tetsuya Nomura's original character illustrations suggest Claudia conceived Cloud while she was in her teens[11].

As a kid, Cloud separates himself from the other children; he feels he does not fit in with Tifa and her friends. When she falls from a cliff on Mount Nibel, Cloud is blamed for her injuries, triggering a fierce desire in him to prove he is not weak. He often gets into fights, not caring who it is against.

The years pass by and Cloud becomes inspired by Sephiroth, the celebrated war hero. He believes Tifa will notice him if he grows stronger, and by the age of 14, he is determined to depart Nibelheim for Midgar. It is his goal to join SOLDIER and follow in Sephiroth's footsteps: He wants to be known as the best.

During *Final Fantasy VII*, Cloud initially recounts his return to Nibelheim as a SOLDIER, two years after leaving. He portrays his younger self as a cocky but competent warrior who wields the giant Buster Sword. It is not until he and Tifa are in the Lifestream that Cloud's mind pieces together the true version of events: He had come home to Nibelheim a nameless infantryman, concealing his face because he was ashamed that he had not achieved his dream of enlisting in SOLDIER. Nevertheless, his contribution was crucial, as it was Cloud who picked up the Buster Sword – which belonged to his friend Zack – and used it to stab the villainous Sephiroth.

In the context of the Nibelheim tragedy's respective retellings, it could be argued that the Buster Sword symbolises identity. For much of the game, Cloud perceives himself to have played the role of Zack during the incident, the SOLDIER First Class who was sent to the town along with Sephiroth. Zack's most iconic feature is the Buster Sword, so Cloud's possession of the great blade in both the present and in his flashback reinforces the misdirection of who he really is.

Alternatively, while stranded in the Lifestream, Cloud's subconscious comes to accept the SOLDIER with the Buster Sword at Nibelheim was, in fact, Zack. The twist in the plot is that Cloud *was* present, too, which is only revealed in his moment of heroism when he wounds Sephiroth, thus associating the weapon with Cloud's true self.

A comparison can be made here to the importance of Theseus' sword. By having the strength to recover the buried blade, the young man unlocks the answers to his identity that he has been seeking his whole life. Moreover, despite having already established his courage and aptitude as a warrior by the time he arrives in Athens, it is the sword that verifies who Theseus is to King Aegeus, because the prince elected to withhold the exact nature of his lineage when he introduced himself.

There may also be a further allusion to this element of the tale in *Final Fantasy VII*: the Rune Blade acquired on Mount Nibel. The weapon is found in a treasure chest on a secluded ledge, accessible shortly after the player has reached the mountain trail from Nibelheim. This could be a loose reflection of Aegeus hiding his sword in the hills overlooking Troezen, as the Rune Blade can be equipped exclusively by Cloud, who was born in the local town.

As mentioned, however, Theseus' weapon of choice in Greek mythology is actually his bronze club, which might account for the inclusion of the Nail Bat in *Final Fantasy VII*. All playable characters in the game can obtain a novelty weapon, such as Cid brandishing a mop as a polearm or Aerith using an umbrella instead of a staff[12]. Given the similarities to Theseus that exist, it may not be a coincidence that Cloud's unique and only non-sword weapon is a contemporary club.

The connection is continued in the sidequests of *Final Fantasy VII Remake*, where Cloud is rewarded with the Nail Bat by the orphans of the Leaf House for successfully eliminating the hedgehog pie king in the Sector 5 Slums. This relates to the second half of the "Kids on Patrol" odd job; the first half requires Cloud to locate five children around Central District, each of whom is identified by a wooden Buster Sword replica they carry. A sixth boy later joins them, and strapped to his back is a crudely reinforced baseball bat. As such, when all six orphans gather outside the Leaf House, the 'club' once again becomes equated to the Buster Sword.

The respective histories of Cloud's and Theseus' childhoods are also analogous in a number of ways: Both were raised by a young, single mother[13]; neither knew their father; both felt different from their peers as they grew; and both left their homes as teenagers with the goal of earning renown as heroes.

The latter point is of particular interest because Theseus is specified by Plutarch to have been inspired by the valour and exploits of Heracles, widely considered at the time to be the strongest man in the world. Cloud, on the other hand, makes no secret of his ambition to emulate the achievements of Sephiroth, regarded as the greatest soldier of his generation.

Another peculiar link between the two protagonists concerns the Labours of Theseus. The Prince of Troezen's reputation as a warrior is founded on his six encounters with the monsters and bandits along the coastline of the Saronic Gulf, each of which takes place near entrances to the realm of Hades.

As explained in chapter VI of this book, *Final Fantasy VII's* Nibelheim also has very deep ties to the underworld with respect to both classical and Norse mythology. Not only does Cloud hail from the town but his most heroic act as a teen is to defeat the murderous Sephiroth at the Mount Nibel reactor, just as Theseus slays many of the Saronic Gulf's worst killers.

According to Nibelheim's folklore, the spirits of the dead pass through the mountain en route to the afterlife, meaning it, too, could be interpreted as an entrance to the underworld. This is important to Cloud's story because his desire to become a hero was sparked at a young age by his inability to save Tifa tumbling from a cliff. The accident, in turn, occurred when Tifa climbed Mount Nibel the day her mother passed away, following the path her spirit may have taken.

The speculative comparisons presented up until now have largely focused on content found in the original *Final Fantasy VII*. However, several more details of Cloud's childhood are offered in the official novel *Traces of Two Pasts*, released in 2021 as supplementary material to *Remake*. The additional information does not simply compliment the proposed parallels between Cloud and Theseus, but rather enhances them.

As part of its examination of the ancient Greek underworld, chapter VI also highlights the increased presence of water in Nibelheim during *Traces of Two Pasts*, albeit in the context of references to the river Styx. The water tower at the centre of town already plays an iconic role in Cloud and Tifa's backstory and the promise they make together, but the novel reveals there is a local fountainhead that is a favourite spot of Tifa's, while her initial interaction with Zangan happens when he is exercising in the fast-flowing Gunnthra River on the outskirts of Nibelheim[14].

Although the emphasis on water could merely reflect Nibelheim's association with the underworld, it might separately serve as a nod to Poseidon's contribution to Theseus' conception. Poseidon's authority over water was not limited to the seas, and he was one of Troezen's two patron deities[15], hence his appearance at the spring when Aethra goes to bathe after her intercourse with Aegeus.

There is no substantial connection between Cloud's birth and Poseidon, but there is a short anecdote about his actual father provided in *Traces of Two Pasts*. He is supposedly a handsome traveller and Claudia is put in charge of finding him suitable lodging in Nibelheim, but the young girl falls in love. It is said he is like the wind, always on the move, yet he remains in Nibelheim until Cloud is an infant. One day, he vanishes into the mountains and is presumed to have been killed, for only his belongings can be found. The nomadic nature of Cloud's father is why the boy is later accused of leading Tifa onto Mount Nibel, resulting in her accident.

This account bears some significant similarities to the myth of Aegeus and Aethra. For instance, Aegeus is journeying home to Athens when he stays overnight at the royal palace in Troezen, and it is here he is introduced to the princess, just as Cloud's parents meet during his dad's stopover in Nibelheim. While Aegeus does not linger in Troezen to learn if his union with Aethra produces a son, he does prepare for the eventuality by burying his sword and sandals on the nearby hill. This resembles the disappearance of Cloud's father, as all that is ever discovered on the mountain is his pack[16].

The Hellenes generally believed Heracles to be their greatest mythical hero, but the Athenians held Theseus in higher regard. According to legend, he ascends to the throne of Athens in the wake of Aegeus' death and for many years rules with strength, dignity, and justice, while being adored by his subjects[17]. He is even credited by some as having invented democracy.

As Theseus grows older in the tales, however, he is unable to escape his thirst for danger and adventure. He begins to let himself be led astray, often wandering a bit too far from the path of nobility. The single largest influence on him is his friend Pirithous, a son of Zeus and the mortal Dia, who shares the Skyfather's knack for controversy and womanising[18]. Pirithous, like Theseus, is also a king and a skilled warrior[19], meaning they can understand each other in ways those around them cannot.

Among the most famous stories of the pair are the Centauromachy and the Attic War[20], but it is their descent into the underworld that is of specific interest[21]. Theseus' wife, Antiope, is killed during the Attic War, so he is receptive to Pirithous' proposition that they seek out new brides. They first kidnap Helen of Sparta[22], then set out to claim Pirithous' chosen prize: Persephone, Queen of the Dead and Hades' spouse.

From a cave entrance on the southern cape of the Peloponnese[23], the bold duo wind their way down into the dark halls of the netherworld. Hades greets them at his palace, but he is all too aware of their blasphemous endeavour. Feigning hospitality, he invites the men to take a seat, trapping them on the Chair of Forgetfulness.

As punishment for the mere intention of stealing his beloved Persephone, the King of the Underworld leaves Theseus and Pirithous bound to the stone bench, neither able to speak. The chair's enchantments empty Theseus' mind, and he loses his sense of self, only to be freed when Heracles passes them by chance some time later[24]. Theseus scrambles back to the land of the living, but Pirithous is not so lucky: His soul is doomed to remain with the spirits of Hades forever.

It is curious that so many of the known myths regarding Theseus' life involve an influential friend, because so much of Cloud's identity in *Final Fantasy VII* is impacted by his relationship with Zack. It should be noted, however, that while Zack's monumental contribution to the overall saga is recognised by his lead role in *Crisis Core* (and cameos elsewhere in the *Compilation*), his inclusion in the original title came relatively late in development[25]. It was so late, in fact, that the initial Japanese release of *Final Fantasy VII* in January 1997 did not contain the optional flashback of Zack and Cloud's flight from Nibelheim[26].

Zack's existence is hinted at on a handful of occasions as the game progresses. Of these, the earliest are the comments made by Aerith and Elmyra during the sequence where the flower girl guides Cloud through Midgar's Slums: The unnamed SOLDIER is referred to when Aerith mentions her first boyfriend. Their connection is reinforced if the player visits Zack's parents in Gongaga while Aerith is in the party. She tells Cloud that Zack loved women and was a real ladies' man, so she assumed he had met someone else when he did not return to her after an assignment five years ago.

It is not until the illusion of Nibelheim burning, produced by Sephiroth at the Whirlwind Maze, that the black-haired swordsman is at last shown in person. Furthermore, his identity is only revealed when Cloud's subconscious recalls the truth of the tragic events in his hometown[27]: Zack was the SOLDIER who had accompanied Sephiroth on the mission to Nibelheim, albeit Cloud was also present in his capacity as an infantryman.

Sephiroth seriously wounds the pair at the Mount Nibel reactor before being hurled into its depths by the blond private. The heroes are subsequently transported to the basement laboratory of Shinra Mansion and secured inside mako tanks for approximately four years. During this period, they are experimented on with Jenova cells, and Cloud succumbs to severe mako poisoning[28]. Zack is eventually able to liberate them from their confines and carries his friend to freedom.

However, on a bluff overlooking Midgar, the Shinra Army catches up with the fugitives and opens fire on them. Zack charges into battle and is mercilessly gunned down. Having been left for dead, Cloud drags himself over to the fallen SOLDIER and takes up the Buster Sword, the shards of his fractured mind being reshaped by the Jenova cells in his body. He begins to assimilate Zack's memories and characteristics, which, in conjunction with Tifa's recollections of their childhood, form the basis of Cloud's reconstructed persona.

There are multiple parallels that can be drawn between Cloud and Zack's relationship with that of Theseus and Pirithous. To start with, the Greek companions are both demigods and celebrated warrior kings in their own right. Likewise, Cloud and Zack are proficient swordsmen with supernatural strength: Zack is a SOLDIER First Class, enhanced by a delicate balance of mako energy and Jenova cells; Cloud, meanwhile, was exposed to a derivative process at Shinra Manor, then inherited Zack's identity and combat abilities through the power of Jenova.

One of the most defining attributes shared by Theseus and Pirithous in their adventures together is their womanising. By their later years, the duo has established a reputation for romantic exploits. This may be reflected in the dating mechanics of *Final Fantasy VII*, where the player is presented with a variety of dialogue options throughout the game that alter the number of affection points (AP) allocated to Aerith, Tifa, Yuffie, and Barret. During Enchantment Evening at the Gold Saucer, whichever of the four characters has accumulated the highest value of AP goes on a date with Cloud[29].

In addition, Pirithous is specifically attested in the classical tales to have been a philanderer, which might account for Aerith describing Zack as a ladies' man. This is one of the few shreds of information provided about his personality in the original *Final Fantasy VII*, and it is

291

expanded upon in *Crisis Core* with Zack's flirtatious behaviour towards women[30].

Theseus and Pirithous' expedition into the Kingdom of the Dead is of greatest intrigue with regards to Cloud and Zack's fate. As mentioned earlier in the chapter, Nibelheim can be compared to the underworld, so the two being sent to the town as part of Shinra's investigation team is analogous to Theseus and Pirithous' endeavours.

On a more abstract level, the purpose of the latter's venture is for Pirithous to claim Persephone, whose similarities to Aerith are extensively explored in chapter VII. It is this exact assignment, of course, that leads to Zack and Aerith's romance in *Final Fantasy VII* coming to a premature end.

Following the catastrophic events at Nibelheim, the injured Cloud and Zack are captured and imprisoned in the mako tanks at Professor Hojo's laboratory beneath Shinra Mansion. This resembles Hades binding Theseus and Pirithous to the Chair of Forgetfulness in his subterranean palace, the effects of which restrict the men's memories and identities, just as mako toxicity inhibits Cloud's. Moreover, while Zack does manage to escape the horrors of Nibelheim, the consequence of these actions is his death[31]; this can be likened to Pirithous, who is denied rescue and is forced to linger among the souls of the deceased.

There is also another set of circumstances that parallel this particular myth, again relating to Cloud's incapacitation: When the Northern Crater collapses during Sephiroth's activation of the Black Materia, Cloud is lost to the party. He is subsequently discovered to have fallen into the Lifestream and to have washed ashore near the town of Mideel, suffering from an extreme case of mako poisoning. What is especially curious about this is that the young man is found at the local clinic, his mind broken and void of any sense of self, but he is not in one of the hospital beds; he is slumped in a wheelchair.

Cloud's mute, absent, and immobile condition, resulting from his plunge into the Lifestream, may therefore be an allusion to Theseus entering the halls of the afterlife and being confined to the Chair of Forgetfulness. Just as Theseus is trapped in that state until he is saved by Heracles during his own descent into the underworld, Cloud requires Tifa's support in the Lifestream to piece together his memories so that he might return to the realm of the living once more.

It is also worth highlighting that the subplot of Cloud's mental breakdown, debilitating mako poisoning, and the eventual reconstruction of his identity is bookended by Zack's two mandatory appearances in the game: The first is amid Sephiroth's illusion at the Whirlwind Maze, while the second is during Cloud's recollection of the true events at Nibelheim. As such, Pirithous' influence on Theseus is additionally reflected in this subplot.

The sequence in Cloud's mindscape and the revelations of his identity are among the most important and iconic

293

parts of *Final Fantasy VII*. Cloud remembers things he should have no knowledge of and cannot recall things he should; he embodies the genetic traits and superhuman abilities of a SOLDIER without ever joining Shinra's elite force; and he is both the hero and an anonymous grunt in the tragedy of Nibelheim's destruction.

For much of *Final Fantasy VII*, Cloud is simultaneously his real self and not his real self. His story arc could thus be argued to be a fusion of the mythology behind the Athenian founder-king and the philosophical conundrum of Theseus' Paradox. The underlying question remains open to interpretation: If Cloud's memories, personality, and genetic makeup have been replaced by the memories, personality, and genetic makeup of others, is he still Cloud ...?

1. A paradox is something that may initially appear contradictory, inconsistent, or absurd but may prove to be true when investigated. Conversely, it can also be something that at first seems reasonable but is later proven to be illogical or contradictory.
2. A remnant from his predecessor's worship during the Mycenaean era, Poseidon is closely associated with horses. He was believed to have fashioned the very first steed as a gift to his sister Demeter, and his sea chariot is drawn by hippocampi in some accounts – mythical creatures that are half-horse, half-fish.
3. Heracles and Orpheus are both said to descend into Hades from caverns in the Peloponnese (see chapter XVIII), while the many-headed Hydra guards an underwater entrance at Lake Lerna.

4. Bellerophon (son of both Poseidon and King Glaucus of Corinth) and Orpheus (son of Apollo and King Oeagrus of Thrace) are two more examples.

5. Depending on the author, Aethra's intercourse with Poseidon alternatively occurs on the nearby island of Sphaeria.

6. In Hellenic tradition, Theseus' path follows the coastline of the Saronic Gulf, which is said to include a string of six entrances to the underworld.

7. Theseus disposes of several murderous individuals en route to Athens: Periphetes, known for crushing travellers' skulls with his club; Sinis, who loved to bend pine trees and then release them to rip his victims in two; the Crommyonian Sow, a rampant wild pig believed to be a child of Typhon and Echidna; Sciron, who pushes people off a cliff to feed an enormous turtle in the bay below; Cercyon, a giant who challenges Theseus to a weaponless duel, during which the hero is said to invent wrestling; and Procrustes, whose specific form of murder is to stretch the bodies of lodgers on an iron bed.

8. In *Bíoi Parálleloi* (*Parallel Lives*), Plutarch compares the life of Theseus to that of Romulus, the mythical founder-king of Rome.

9. The secret truth of Nanaki's father, Seto, is that he was not a coward who abandoned his village but that he single-handedly thwarted the Gi Tribe's invasion at the cost of being turned to stone.

10. Prior to the publication of *Traces of Two Pasts*, there was only one reference to Cloud's father in the entire *Compilation of Final Fantasy VII*. It occurs in the original game if the player chooses to visit the boy's childhood home during the flashback to the Nibelheim tragedy: Cloud will tell his comrades in the present that his father passed away.

11. Nomura-san's early artwork for Claudia shows that her surname was to be Strauss and her age 33, presumably at the time of her death. Cloud is 16 when this happens, meaning he was born when Claudia herself was around 17.

12. Novelty weapons or joke weapons are a recurring feature in the *Final Fantasy* series, often having absurd appearances or being of little practical benefit. *Final Fantasy VII's* variants boost an individual character's offensive stats at the expense of materia usage, for none of the weapons have materia slots.

13. There is also a vague contrast between Claudia and Aethra: Aethra's name means 'Bright Sky', while Claudia is a feminine equivalent of 'Cloud' (the Japanese romaji of their names are *Kuraudia* and *Kuraudo*), so Claudia Strife can be interpreted as 'Storm Cloud'.

14. Zangan, whose first name is Rashard, according to *Traces of Two Pasts*, becomes Tifa's martial arts master. Their relationship is explored in the book and his teachings develop her into the powerful fighter she is by the time of *Final Fantasy VII*.

15. Troezen's other patron was Athena.

16. Although separate, this does not conflict with the Rune Blade parallel presented earlier in the chapter.

17. King Aegeus hurls himself from a cliff when he incorrectly presumes Theseus has been killed on his mission to the Labyrinth. However, his name has been immortalised by the Aegean, which the sea was called in his honour.

18. This is Pirithous' parentage according to Homer. In other accounts, he is the son of Dia and her husband, Ixion, whose own story likely inspired the design of the equine Aeon by the same name in *Final Fantasy X*: Ixion was the father of the race of centaurs.

19. Pirithous is King of the Lapiths, a tribe from Thessaly.

20. The Centauromachy relates to a battle that occurs at Pirithous' wedding between his Lapith kinsmen and his drunken centaur guests. The Attic War concerns the attack on Athens by the Amazons (a legendary group of fierce female warriors), when Theseus abducts and marries one of their own, Antiope. A varied account of the myth can be found in Shakespeare's *A Midsummer Night's Dream*.

21. Plutarch gives a very different account of Theseus and Pirithous' final adventure, so the details here are taken from Apollodorus and earlier writers such as Pindar.

22. This is the same Helen over whom the Trojan War is later fought.

23. Cape Tainaron – now known as Cape Matapan – is the southernmost point of mainland Greece.

24. Heracles journeys to the underworld as part of his twelfth and final labour, where he seeks permission to borrow Cerberus, the hellhound of Hades. Details of this story can be found in chapter XVII.

25. Lead creators on *Final Fantasy VII* such as Yoshinori Kitase (director) and Kazushige Nojima (scenario writer) have commented in multiple interviews that the resolution of the Nibelheim plot twists – including details of Zack's involvement – was completed late in development.

26. The optional flashback was first introduced in the North American edition of the game, with its equivalent, *Final Fantasy VII International*, releasing in Japan in October 1997. The sequence itself is triggered by returning to the Shinra Manor basement once Cloud's memories have been restored.

27. Unlocking this truth and uncovering Cloud's identity is Tifa's goal while their minds are connected in the Lifestream.

28. These experiments are part of Project Sephiroth Copy, as is clarified in the *Ultimania Omega*. Chapter VI of this book explains that mako poisoning occurs when a person's brain is flooded by an overwhelming volume of spirit energy, causing the mind to lose itself in a sea of information and fragmented memories.

29. A similar mechanic features in *Remake*, influencing whether Aerith, Tifa, or Barret will share an intimate scene with Cloud in the flower garden.

30. Zack's interactions with Cissnei are a prime example of this, although it can also be found in dialogue with the SOLDIER fan club members or the receptionist at Shinra Headquarters.

31. This outcome is changed after the Whispers are defeated in *Final Fantasy VII Remake*.

CHAPTER XV

THE LABYRINTH

T he Labyrinth and the Minotaur are perhaps two of the most recognisable aspects of Greek mythology. A person does not typically need to be familiar with the legend concerning them to know that one is an ancient maze and the other is a fearsome monster who is part man, part bull. Labyrinths of varying descriptions have been adopted by cultures all around the world since prehistory, while derivations of the Minotaur have featured in literature and popular media for centuries, ranging from Dante's *Divine Comedy* to Terry Gilliam's 1981 film *Time Bandits* or the *Dungeons & Dragons* role-playing game.

What might be less clear to anyone without knowledge of the classical stories is how the Minotaur came to exist, why *the* Labyrinth was built to contain him, and how the hero Theseus fits into all of it. Furthermore, fans of *Final Fantasy*

VII may be surprised to learn that this particular myth is likely to have inspired one of the game's most memorable sequences.

The tale is primarily set on Crete, a large island located in the southern waters of the Aegean Sea. Crete has been inhabited by humans for approximately 130,000 years and was once home to the Minoans, who are considered to be Europe's first advanced civilisation[1]. It is perhaps for this reason that the Hellenes believed Zeus was smuggled there as a baby and raised among its striking mountains and verdant plains (as discussed in chapter IV).

While there are numerous versions of the story, the best known are generally credited to mythographers such as Apollodorus and Ovid, or to Diodorus Siculus, a 1st century BC Greek historian. The legend begins with King Minos II[2], a great-grandson of Zeus, who rules Crete and its surrounding isles at the same time that King Aegeus – the mortal father of Theseus – rules Athens.

One day, Minos prays to Poseidon for a sign that his sovereignty is favoured by the gods. Poseidon sends a magnificent white bull from the sea in response, expecting the king to sacrifice the beast in his honour[3]. So beautiful is the creature that emerges from the waves, however, that Minos decides to offer up a bull from his own herd instead.

The Lord of the Oceans is enraged by this act of impiety. To punish Minos, he curses his wife, Queen Pasiphaë, so that she lusts after the white bull and falls pregnant to it[4].

300

Poseidon then instils madness in the animal and its rampage across Crete terrorises the island's populace[5].

In due course, Pasiphaë gives birth to a son called Asterion, usually depicted in the myths as having the body of a human and the horned head, hooves, and tail of a bull[6]. Minos commissions the famous inventor, engineer, and architect Daedalus to design and construct a dwelling for Asterion adjacent to the royal palace, where the abomination can live, while being unable to escape from it. Daedalus creates an elaborate, maze-like complex full of twisting corridors, identical rooms, hidden alcoves, false doors, and dead ends. This is what becomes known as the Labyrinth[7].

Several years later, to prevent the destruction of Athens at the hands of Minos' navy, King Aegeus agrees to annually surrender seven young men and seven maidens to Crete as compensation[8]. The 14 tributes are released one by one into the Labyrinth as prey for the dreaded Minotaur (the 'Bull of Minos'), and none ever find their way back out again. It is said the brute gores and devours all those who enter his lair.

When Theseus learns of this, he plots to shatter the arrangement by volunteering himself as a tribute in order to kill the monster. He sails to Crete and is imprisoned beneath the royal palace to await his turn as Asterion's meal. While Theseus is in the cells, he is visited by a daughter of Minos and Pasiphaë, Princess Ariadne, and they fall in love at first sight. Ariadne has convinced Daedalus to disclose the secret to surviving the Labyrinth, which she will share with the hero if he promises to take her home to Athens and marry her.

Ensuring he is selected as the initial tribute, Theseus is escorted to the Labyrinth, where he sneaks in a ball of thread gifted to him by Ariadne. He ties one end of the string to the gate as Daedalus instructed, unwinding the rest while he slowly progresses through the dark stone passageways; by doing so, he can follow the thread back to the entrance.

Theseus eventually reaches the chamber at the heart of the maze and clashes with the Minotaur. Some accounts say the Athenian prince slays the beast with a sword or even his iconic bronze club, although most claim he is unarmed and bludgeons Asterion to death with his bare fists.

Victorious in his endeavour, Theseus uses the string to retrace his steps and re-emerges from the Labyrinth to discover Ariadne has liberated the other tributes and their ship's crew. They flee the palace and set sail for Athens, leaving Crete and King Minos far behind.

During the voyage, Theseus and his newly betrothed decide to stop overnight on the island of Naxos. The hero receives a dire warning in his dreams from the god Dionysus, demanding that he abandons Ariadne or the whole company will face the Olympian's wrath[9]. Heartbroken by the ultimatum, Theseus and his entourage raise the ship's anchor while the young princess sleeps.

The above version of events on Naxos is told by Diodorus Siculus in his *Bibliotheca Historica* (*Library of History*), but it is one of many variations. These portray Theseus with widely differing degrees of admirability. For example, Ovid indicates in *Metamorphoses* that Theseus cruelly deserts Ariadne because he has no more use for her, and she is mercifully rescued and wed by Dionysus.

Plutarch, on the other hand, offers an attestation in *Life of Theseus* that the protagonist is blown out to sea and has to battle strong winds for days to return to the island, only to find his lover has died[10]. In this adaptation, Theseus is deeply overcome by grief. Homer, meanwhile, writes in the *Odyssey* that Ariadne is killed on Naxos by the goddess Artemis, acting on behalf of Dionysus.

The previous chapter of this book establishes a number of similarities between Theseus and Cloud Strife, the primary hero of *Final Fantasy VII*. The myth that is arguably most synonymous with Theseus in classical lore is his encounter with the Minotaur, so it should come as no surprise that the 1997 game also boasts its own labyrinthine dungeon: the Temple of the Ancients[11].

During the course of *Final Fantasy VII's* plot, Cloud and his companions learn that Sephiroth is in search of the Black Materia, through which he means to cast the ultimate destructive magic, Meteor. The party pursues the villain to a millennia-old pyramid, hidden in the jungle of a secluded island.

They discover Tseng of the Turks in the temple's antechamber, gravely injured from a sword wound. He informs Cloud and Aerith that Sephiroth is inside and gives them the Keystone required to enter the structure's interior[12]. Negotiating a sophisticated maze of intersecting walkways, long staircases, galleries that lead nowhere, and a clock puzzle, the player characters eventually arrive at the centre of the temple.

Within the room is a huge wall mural which depicts the priests of a historic Cetran culture using the Black Materia to summon Meteor[13]. Sephiroth briefly appears before Cloud and Aerith and reveals that he intends to inflict damage to the Planet so devasting it will threaten its very life, implying this can be achieved through Meteor.

Sephiroth's presence has a visible impact on Cloud's mental stability, making him susceptible to manipulation by his former hero. Uncertain how to proceed, Aerith asks the spirits of the temple about the glowing model at the head of the mural room. They advise that the pyramid itself is the Black Materia and it can only be reduced in size by solving the model's puzzles, which, in turn, must be completed from inside the chamber[14], resulting in the puzzle-solver being crushed. Cait Sith proposes that he should be the one to undertake this, as he is a stuffed toy cat that is being controlled from afar[15].

Once the temple has shrunk to form the Black Materia crystal, Cloud and Aerith are able to retrieve it. Sephiroth again materialises alongside them, causing Cloud to lose autonomy of his actions. The young man hands the materia over to Sephiroth, and as Aerith attempts to comfort him in his anguish, he begins punching her, then falls unconscious.

Cloud dreams he is in the Sleeping Forest with Aerith. She explains that she has to leave him to help save the Planet: Her goal is to carry out a task only a Cetra can perform (praying to Gaia to activate Holy). Try as he might, though, Cloud cannot follow her in the dream, and he is alarmed when Sephiroth descends from the treetops to warn him that the girl must be stopped. These events ultimately lead to Aerith's death at the Forgotten City.

The Temple of the Ancients in *Final Fantasy VII* draws design and aesthetic inspiration from several historic cultures in the real world. Perhaps the most instantly apparent are the Mesoamerican influences of its exterior, which resembles many of the pyramids constructed by the Maya or Aztec civilisations in what is now Central America[16].

Labyrinths also feature in Mesoamerican art and architecture and have been associated with rituals, tribal identity, and the afterlife, among other things. Prime examples of Maya complexes are the multi-level, subterranean site at Yaxchilan or the so-called 'Palace of the Underworld' at Toniná[17], itself believed to have been a shrine to the spirits of the dead. While the Temple of the Ancients is not typically connected with the afterlife in *Final Fantasy VII*, Cloud and Aerith do engage with manifestations of long-deceased Cetra there, who have remained to protect the pyramid.

In addition to this, the glyphs and paintings on the walls of the mural room are akin to those found in ancient Egypt, whereas the doorways that encircle the clock puzzle display Roman numerals above them. An inclusion of particular interest, however, is highlighted in the 'World Guide' section of the *Ultimania Omega*: The archaic pillars that can be seen in the antechamber, the mural room, and a few other locations within the temple are specified to be Corinthian columns. This architectural style is derived from the ancient Greek city-state of Corinth.

While the latter proves *Final Fantasy VII's* development team was prepared to implement designs from antiquity, there is substantial evidence to indicate their labyrinthine concept for the Temple of the Ancients sourced multiple ideas from the myth of Theseus and the Minotaur. Fascinatingly, these are not limited simply to the maze or even to the warrior prince.

The temple is situated on a prominent but unfrequented landmass to the south of Junon, itself being one of the largest islands on *Final Fantasy VII's* overworld map and occupying the same southern seas as the archipelago on which the town of Mideel resides. A dense forest sprawls across the centre of the island, while along its northeast coastline is a towering mountain range. This geography is remarkably similar to Crete with respect to its size, natural features, and position in the Aegean Sea relative to mainland Greece. Just as Theseus has to sail to Crete with the other tributes, the player must navigate coastal waters in the *Tiny Bronco* to reach the Temple of the Ancients[18].

It is also worth noting that the Cetra in the murals of the pyramid's innermost chamber are likely the oldest culture to be portrayed in the *Compilation of Final Fantasy VII*. This reflects Crete being home to the Minoans, Europe's oldest advanced civilisation.

In classical mythology, the Labyrinth is created by Daedalus to contain the Minotaur, a monstrous aberration that is too dangerous to live among the general populace. While there is no equivalent beast imprisoned within the Temple of the Ancients, it could be contended that the structure itself was designed to confine the Black Materia – magic so destructive it can endanger the life of the Planet.

This is not to suggest, however, that there are no potential references to the Minotaur. For example, the player can battle doorbull enemies in the temple, which, despite their name, have no bovine qualities except for the horns on their head[19]; Asterion is known to kill his prey by goring them, which could compare to Tseng being stabbed by Sephiroth and left to perish[20]; and Theseus beating his opponent with bare fists in most literary accounts may explain the addition of Cloud's appalling assault on Aerith[21].

Elements of the maze-like area within the Temple of the Ancients do, of course, parallel the descriptions of King Minos' Labyrinth in the Greek myths. The myriad passages, dead ends, and secret alcoves are all present, as is the inability for the player characters to depart the dungeon once they have entered (at least not until they have achieved their goal), but these are not necessarily unique to Daedalus' magnificent complex.

What might further support the notion that the pyramid's interior was inspired by the Labyrinth on Crete are some abstract allusions to the genius of Daedalus himself. He is an artisan whose handiwork is considered second only to the objects produced at Hephaestus' divine forge, and his inventions are generations ahead of his peers'. Writers like Plato and Diodorus Siculus detail the automata (mechanised statues) he builds, while others attest he is capable of fashioning devices that accurately mark the passage of time.

The Temple of the Ancients houses many supernatural components – such as the Cetran spirits or the mysterious pool that shows Cloud and Aerith a vision of the recent past[22] – but there is also an instance of a technological marvel: the clock puzzle[23]. The hour and minute hands of the clock are controlled by an entity that identifies itself as the Time Guardian, but their incremental movements imply mechanical attributes rather than magic, further corroborated by the seconds needle ticking independent of the player's commands.

It is not inconceivable that this relates to Daedalus' wondrous contraptions, which happen to be a recurring feature in the *Herakuresu no Eikō* series. Given that Kazushige Nojima scripted the scenarios for three games in that franchise prior to joining Square, it can be presumed he was familiar with the mythology surrounding Daedalus.

Cait Sith's involvement at the Temple of the Ancients is also peculiar with regards to how it might connect to the legendary inventor, whose story continues after Theseus triumphs in the Labyrinth: Following the death of his son Icarus[24], Daedalus travels to the island of Sicily and lives as a guest of King Cocalus. The king's daughters become fond of the old man and the animated toys he makes for them.

However, King Minos of Crete tracks him down and presents a riddle to Cocalus that he knows only Daedalus can solve: How can a piece of string be threaded through a Triton shell? Daedalus' solution is to tie one end of the string to an ant and lure it through the shell with honey. When Minos demands the craftsman is returned to him, Cocalus and his esteemed guest conspire to murder the Cretan royal.

What is interesting here is that Cait Sith is classified in the *Compilation* and its wider media as a stuffed cat doll brought to life by Reeve Tuesti (which rides around on a giant animatronic moogle in *Final Fantasy VII*)[25]. It could be argued that this is reflective of the mechanical toys and automata created by Daedalus in the myths. Moreover, Reeve himself is Shinra's Head of Urban Development (or Director of Urban Planning, as the title is given in *Remake*) and is therefore the company's architect-in-chief, just as Daedalus was celebrated for his architectural ingenuity, including the design of the Labyrinth.

It should also be pointed out that the player can obtain a weapon for Cait Sith while in the Temple of the Ancients: the Trumpet Shell. As highlighted in chapter V, artwork contained within the *Ultimania Omega* verifies this natural megaphone to be a conch shell[26]. Alternative to the proposal that this is a nod to the sea god Triton, the Trumpet Shell may instead allude to Daedalus solving Minos' challenge while on Sicily, because the context of Cait Sith's contribution to this part of *Final Fantasy VII's* plot is that he solves the Black Materia puzzle to shrink the pyramid[27]. Labyrinths are also commonplace in Celtic culture, from which Cait Sith's folklore roots derive.

Chapter XIV provides the mythological background to Theseus and his bronze club. By extension, Cloud's comparisons with the Athenian hero might explain why his novelty weapon in *Final Fantasy VII* is the Nail Bat. The Nail Bat's acquisition at the Temple of the Ancients lends additional weight to the speculation that this sequence is analogous to the tale of Theseus in the Labyrinth, especially the versions in which the demigod uses his club to slay the Minotaur.

Applying the same principle to the Princess Guard – a magical staff for Aerith found exclusively in the temple[28] – suggests its name may be a vague reference to Ariadne, the Princess of Crete who helps Theseus survive the maze. However, when Aerith and Ariadne's roles in their respective stories are paired in this fashion, an entirely new set of similarities emerge.

Once the pyramid itself has transformed into the Black Materia and is collected by Cloud, the blond protagonist is mentally overwhelmed by Sephiroth. In this puppet state, he hands the crystal to the villain, then ultimately loses consciousness and dreams of an exchange with Aerith in the Sleeping Forest.

There are several parallels here in relation to Theseus parting ways with Ariadne on the island of Naxos. To begin with, this portion of the myth does not occur until Theseus has successfully escaped the Labyrinth (with the aid of Ariadne), just as Cloud and Aerith do not separate until they have escaped the Temple of the Ancients.

The positions are reversed in *Final Fantasy VII*, however: Where Theseus and the tributes abandon Ariadne, Aerith is compelled to leave Cloud and their friends behind. She informs Cloud of this in a dream, telling him she must do so to save the world from Sephiroth. The circumstances mirror Theseus being visited by Dionysus in a nightmare (according to Diodorus Siculus) and instructed to depart Naxos immediately to spare the lives of the tributes and crew from the God of the Vine.

Dionysus' involvement here is particularly relevant to Cloud's interactions with Sephiroth. For instance, not only does Sephiroth invade the young man's dream once Aerith has run off towards the Forgotten Capital, his presence at the Temple of the Ancients causes Cloud to lose control. As is explored in chapter VIII, Dionysus was known as a god of both merriment and madness, capable of inciting undesirable behaviour and violence. These are unquestionably evident in the scene where Cloud surrenders the Black Materia to Sephiroth, then attacks Aerith.

Plutarch's recordings of the myth, meanwhile, offer an alternative perspective. After Ariadne goes ashore, Theseus and his ship are blown back out to sea, and he tries desperately to return to her. However, when he finally manages to land again on Naxos, his betrothed has died.

This, of course, reflects how Cloud is separated from Aerith following the events at the Temple of the Ancients. He and the others resolve to find the flower girl before it is too late, only for Sephiroth to murder her at the Water Altar. The latter detail may also be a nod to Homer's attestation that Ariadne is killed at the behest of Dionysus (by the divine huntress, Artemis).

As it happens, Theseus, the victor of the Labyrinth, is just one of many figures from Greek mythology who have likely inspired *Final Fantasy VII*. Elements of his exploits as a youth and as a king are hinted at throughout the game, but the next section of the book will examine how the tales of a more famous hero, Heracles, influenced an entire *Compilation* title in a considerably less subtle manner.

XV: THE LABYRINTH

1. The earliest traces of the Minoans date back two millennia before the Mycenaeans, who were the first distinctly Greek civilisation.

2. Typically speaking, Minos II is not to be confused with his grandfather Minos I, the inaugural king of Crete. Minos I eventually becomes one of the three judges of the underworld, as referenced in chapter VI. However, many ancient texts do consider the two to be the same individual.

3. Poseidon's strong association with bulls is established in chapter V. Archaeological evidence also indicates they were worshipped by the Minoans.

4. In an original Minoan version of the myth, it is possible that Poseidon transforms himself into the white bull rather than it being a gift from the god.

5. The Cretan Bull – as the creature becomes known – is eventually captured by Heracles during his seventh labour. Many years later, Theseus challenges and subdues it outside the city of Marathon.

6. Some accounts are less specific in their depictions. Ovid, for example, writes that the Minotaur has the lower half of a human and the upper half of a bull.

7. The difference between a maze and a labyrinth is that a maze has a non-linear route (or routes) between an entrance and exit, while a labyrinth has no exit; instead, it has a single non-linear route from the entrance to its centre.

8. Later writers such as Plutarch and Hyginus claim the tributes are only sent to Crete once every nine years.

9. In some recordings of the myth, Ariadne was already promised to Dionysus, and he is angered by her attempt to elope with Theseus. The God of the Vine's own connections to the *Compilation of Final Fantasy VII* are explored in chapter VIII.

10. This version is not Plutarch's own, but is rather credited to Paeon of Amathus.

11. *Final Fantasy VIII* is less subtle in acknowledging one of its dungeons is inspired by the Labyrinth myth. During the game, the player is sent to the Tomb of the Unknown

King to obtain an identification number. Squall and the party may then optionally explore its archaic, duplicate passages. Visiting the central room of the complex, they can battle Sacred and Minotaur (collectively known as Brothers and both resembling Asterion) to recruit them as a Guardian Force.

12. For the purposes of this chapter, reference will be made to Cloud and Aerith's journey through the Temple of the Ancients. This is because it is mandatory to have both characters in the player's party for the sequence. In the game, an optional third character is always present.

13. While it is not made explicit in *Final Fantasy VII*, evidence from the wider *Compilation* and *Remake* suggests this civilisation predates – or is at least separate to – the Cetra tribes that faced Jenova 2,000 years ago. It is perhaps also worth highlighting that there is a single instance of a female displayed on the mural – specifically on the panel where Meteor is falling. It can be presumed that the crystal she is wielding is an allusion to the White Materia, Holy, and thus parallels Aerith's role in the game.

14. The Cetra designed the puzzle so that anyone who desires to claim the Black Materia for themselves will not survive if they are inside the temple. Sephiroth's initial plan, however, is likely to have one of the black-robed clones perform the necessary tasks.

15. Cait Sith is operated by Reeve, Shinra's Head of Urban Development. Immediately prior to the Temple of the Ancients scenario, the robotic feline betrays the group by stealing the Keystone from them and delivering it to Tseng, so his sacrifice to obtain the Black Materia is also a gesture to regain their trust.

16. Most of these pyramids were built between the 1st millennium BC and 1st millennium AD.

17. Both Yaxchilan and Toniná are located in the state of Chiapas in modern-day Mexico.

18. As explained in chapter V, the *Tiny Bronco* is an airplane owned by Cid Highwind. The craft is shot down by Shinra troops and crash lands in the sea, subsequently becoming

a mode of transportation that can travel in shallow coastal waters or along rivers on the overworld map.

19. 'Doorbull' is an erroneous English localisation of the Japanese romaji '*doabūru*', which was likely intended to be a play on the word 'double'.

20. Tseng does not feature in *Final Fantasy VII* after the Temple of the Ancients scenario. Due to an ambiguous translation in the localised script, it is strongly implied that the Turk dies from the wounds inflicted by Sephiroth: In the English edition, Elena accuses the party of 'doing her boss in', which is typically a euphemism for murder. This created confusion among Western fans in 2005 when Tseng appeared again in *Advent Children*.

21. While there is no Minotaur to speak of at the Temple of the Ancients, a creature matching its mythological description is encountered elsewhere in *Final Fantasy VII*. During the Wall Market sequence early in the game, Don Corneo drops Cloud, Tifa, and Aerith into the sewer network beneath Midgar's Slums, where they are attacked by his ogrish pet Abzu (originally localised as 'Aps', although this was corrected in *Remake*). Abzu has the horns, snout, legs, and hooves of a bull but a muscular humanoid upper body. He also has metal cuffs and broken chains around his wrists, indicating he was once a prisoner in the sewers, much like Asterion is in the Labyrinth. His name, however, derives from ancient Mesopotamian lore, where Abzu (or Apsu) is the primordial freshwater sea.

22. Called the Well of Knowledge in the *Ultimania Omega*, this pool displays Sephiroth wounding Tseng in the mural room prior to the party's arrival at the temple.

23. The hands of the clock rotate above a deep pit and act as walkways between twelve stone portals. The hour hand and minute hand can be commanded by the player to create their desired path. If the seconds needle makes contact with Cloud's field model, it will cause him to fall into the pit.

24. Icarus is known as the boy who died when he flew too close to the Sun. To escape Crete, Daedalus builds wings

for himself and Icarus that are comprised of wax and feathers. When Icarus soars too high, the heat of the Sun melts the wax, causing him to plummet to his death.

25. The explanation provided in the *Dirge of Cerberus Complete Guide* is that Reeve controls Cait Sith through his inherent abilities as an 'Inspire', which allow him to breathe life into inorganic objects and animate them at will.

26. Chapter V separately details the connections between Poseidon and the Trident polearm that can be picked up for Cid at the Temple of the Ancients, as well as how the Kujata Materia may represent Poseidon's association with bulls. The latter is relevant to the origins of the Minotaur, not to mention that Poseidon was also the immortal father of Theseus.

27. The Trumpet Shell is found inside a treasure chamber that can only be accessed from the clock puzzle, thus reinforcing the link.

28. The Princess Guard is the last weapon to be obtained for Aerith before she dies. It, too, resides within a chamber accessible via the clock puzzle.

PART SIX

An Age
of Heroes

HERACLES & OTHERS

CHAPTER XVI

THE LABOURS OF VINCENT VALENTINE

Most historic cultures boast at least one myth of a heroic mortal whose destiny is divinely blessed or whose purpose it is to challenge the gods and the status quo of their era. The oldest known written account of such a figure is the *Epic of Gilgamesh*, recorded on stone tablets in Babylon around 1700 BC[1]. More recent tales, relatively speaking, might include the warrior Sigurd of the Norse *Völsunga saga* (a tradition from oral poetry that was transcribed in 13th century Iceland) or the legends of King Arthur, popularised in medieval Britain. Human societies have never been slow to place those they revere on a pedestal, often elevating them to a deific station.

Of the spectacularly grand cast of ancient Greek heroes, the greatest and most beloved among the Hellenes was Heracles[2], whom the Romans (and Walt Disney) called Hercules. Heracles is both a descendant of Perseus and himself a son of mighty Zeus[3], fated to rid the world of the monsters that plague it with his bow – gifted to him by Apollo – and poison-tipped arrows. He is a champion of the people, capable of performing superhuman feats on a whim or shaping whole dynasties to settle a grudge. As a paragon of strength and bravery, many of the Hellenic royal houses claimed Heracles as their ancestor, while later Roman emperors identified themselves with him.

Despite the myriad allusions to Greek mythology throughout the *Final Fantasy* series, neither the name 'Heracles' nor 'Hercules' has ever featured in a mainline title[4]. Chapter X of this book summarises Heracles' crucial role in the Gigantomachy (when the Giants waged war on Olympus), but this is in the context of the Titan Materia. As it happens, both the Gigantomachy and the Labours of Heracles – arguably the most recognisable story of the demigod and not to be confused with the Labours of Theseus discussed in chapter XIV – seem to be represented through *Dirge of Cerberus* in quite substantial and unexpected ways. The latter, however, will be more thoroughly explored in the next chapter.

In contrast to his effortless rejection of fear and the ease with which he amasses fame, Heracles' life is one long trial: the epitome of cause and effect; of actions and consequences. He spends many hard years atoning for fleeting moments of anger and violence, for flashes of madness over which he has little or no control. Nevertheless, Heracles generally accepts his punishments with dignity and humility, serving the sentences as best he can. In truth, the root of his suffering is not strictly his own doing but often the jealousy of the goddess Hera.

Heracles is born in the city-state of Thebes to a beautiful woman named Alcmene, who fell pregnant when Zeus lay with her in the form of her husband, Amphitryon. At birth, the baby is called Alcides (or Alcaeus, in some sources), although it is initially unclear whether he has inherited his father's divine attributes[5].

Hera, Zeus' wife, is especially infuriated by the Cloud Gatherer's infidelity in this instance and vows to make Alcides' life a misery. In a bid to placate her wrath, Alcmene and Amphitryon rename their son Heracles, meaning 'Glory of Hera'.

The boy earns a reputation in his youth for his brute power and vicious rages, but he grows to be a renowned fighter, archer, and athlete, oblivious to the Queen of Heaven's vengeful gaze. When she eventually strikes, her cruelty is absolute: Overcome by the frenzied hallucination she induces, Heracles kills his wife Megara and their children[6].

To obtain purification for this heinous blood crime, Heracles undertakes a series of twelve impossible tasks over the following decade[7]. The gruelling duties would become synonymous with the hero, known as the Labours of Heracles, and many require him to hunt monsters that have been terrorising various locations across ancient Greece and beyond.

The first labour has the son of Zeus slay the Nemean Lion, a huge leonine beast with an impenetrable hide. Heracles successfully vanquishes it through strangulation, thereafter establishing his iconic image by skinning the animal (using one of its own claws) and wearing its fur as a mantle.

In another task, he journeys to Lake Lerna to battle the Hydra, a ferocious water serpent that regrows two heads each time it is decapitated[8]. Searing the neck wounds with fire to prevent the Hydra regenerating, Heracles manages to remove its primary head and bury it in the earth, but not before dipping his arrows in the deadly venom of its blood.

Perhaps the most famous of the labours, however, is the last of the twelve: Heracles' descent into the underworld to borrow Cerberus, the multi-headed hellhound that guards its gates. Hades' pet, of course, lends his name to a title in the *Compilation of Final Fantasy VII*, but the parallels between *Dirge of Cerberus* and the life of Heracles go much, much deeper than that.

A vast amount of classical literature exists to attest the hero's many adventures and misdeeds. In addition to the Gigantomachy, these include further years of servitude in reparation for acts committed when he is seized by fits of madness, his subsequent marriages, and toppling as well as installing kings in powerful territories across ancient Greece[9]. Upon his death, Zeus grants part of Heracles' spirit immortality and welcomes him into Olympus, while the remainder of his soul joins the afterlife.

To better appreciate the context of *Dirge of Cerberus'* mythical allusions to Heracles, it is important to first acknowledge the demigod's role in the *Herakuresu no Eikō* videogame series. The initial release from 1987, *Tōjin Makyō Den: Herakuresu no Eikō* (which roughly translates as *Legend of the Fighting Demon's Lair: Glory of Heracles*), features Heracles himself as the main protagonist, and the plot loosely reflects his twelve labours[10]. He is a recurring figure in each of the other games, typically as a playable or guest party member.

A curious aspect of this is that *Tōjin Makyō Den* is the only entry in the franchise that was not scripted by Kazushige Nojima, the lead scenario writer for *Final Fantasy VII*, most of its spin-off media, and the remake project. Similarly, *Dirge of Cerberus* is the only entry in the *Compilation* that was not penned by Nojima-san. Instead, the responsibility fell to Hiroki Chiba.

Chiba-san had previously been an event planner on *Final Fantasy VII*, *Final Fantasy VIII*, and *Final Fantasy X*, all of which are based on Nojima-san's scenarios. Given that Kazushige Nojima is listed as the top name in the "Special Thanks" credits for *Dirge of Cerberus*, it is probable that

Chiba-san was familiar with his history of implementing mythology in games, dating back to his work on *Herakuresu no Eikō*. As such – in conjunction with the evidence presented in this chapter – it can be speculated that *Dirge of Cerberus* pays specific homage to Heracles.

The title's hero, Vincent Valentine, is introduced as an optional character in *Final Fantasy VII*. He is a brooding gunslinger in a crimson cloak with the capacity to morph into one of four monstrous creatures if his Limit Break is activated in battle[11]: Galian Beast, Death Gigas, Hellmasker, or Chaos[12]. Although his contribution to *Final Fantasy VII's* story is minimal, he is motived by revenge on Professor Hojo, the scientist culpable for the abominations within him[13].

In *Dirge of Cerberus*, however, Vincent takes centre stage. Released in 2006, this third-person shooter incorporates a degree of strategy with various gun models and attributes, hand-to-hand combat, and temporary transformations into an updated design of the Galian Beast.

Dirge of Cerberus is set three years after the events of *Final Fantasy VII* and its narrative focuses on the sudden emergence of a clandestine but brutal army known as Deepground SOLDIER. Vincent teams up with Reeve Tuesti, the man operating Cait Sith and now commissioner of the World Regenesis Organisation (WRO), to discover the purpose of the military group's mass kidnappings and murders.

Commanding the enemy are the Tsviets, an elite unit led by the enigmatic Weiss the Immaculate from the heart of Deepground, itself a top-secret Shinra facility located beneath Midgar. They are hunting for the Protomateria, a magical orb capable of controlling the Omega Weapon, which is the Planet's failsafe lifeform hypothesised to appear when the world is about to die.

During the adventure, Vincent learns that Deepground's plan to artificially awaken Omega is entwined with his own past, predominantly his relationship with Dr Lucrecia Crescent. Her research thesis regarding Omega's function has inspired the Tsviets, while Vincent himself carries the Protomateria. Lucrecia embedded the crystal in his chest as a means of subduing Chaos, a primeval being and the harbinger of death, which also resides within him. When Vincent is injured and robbed of the Protomateria, he struggles to contain the beast.

Deepground SOLDIER launches assaults on the WRO Headquarters and Vincent is relied upon to assist in defending the compound. The WRO responds by meeting the opposition forces in open battle around Midgar. As the conflict rages on the surface and in the skies, Vincent descends into Deepground to halt the impending apocalypse.

Despite his efforts, Omega materialises, but Vincent manages to retain his autonomy while in the form of Chaos, defeating the Weapon in an explosion of energy that causes the essence of both primordial entities to return to the

Planet. In doing so, he is finally able to find redemption for his part in Lucrecia's fate.

It would be appropriate to begin examining the parallels between Vincent and Heracles by considering their respective characterisations. Heracles is first and foremost portrayed in the myths as a hero: a strongman who can achieve the impossible. His volatile and often fatal eruptions of anger are notorious, but his persona is much more complex than that. Heracles can be violent and vengeful, yet he also has a robust moral compass; contrary to his blunt and direct approach to life, he is never cruel without good reason, and he willingly seeks penance for his transgressions.

In fact, a substantial portion of the tales regarding this son of Zeus relate to atonement of some variety. The twelve labours are Heracles' expiation for the death of his wife and children, but he had already killed a music tutor in his youth, following provocation[14], which triggered a local scandal. Even after his completion of the labours, Heracles enters into servitude once again, having hurled Prince Iphitus of Oechalia from the city walls amid one of his maddened fits.

Vincent, meanwhile, is presented in *Final Fantasy VII* as a stoic and tormented figure. He does not generally speak unless spoken to and can be frank with his observations, but there are several instances when his words are profound or poetic. Unlike Heracles, emotional reactions are not typical of Vincent, although he does express anger if he is in the player's party when Hojo is challenged atop the Sister Ray cannon. He is also selective with the truth when Lucrecia asks about Sephiroth at the waterfall grotto, protecting her from the anguish of knowing that her son is attempting to destroy the Planet. Furthermore, a gentler side to the former Turk is depicted during *Advent Children* when he grants Marlene shelter within his cloak at the Forgotten Capital.

Dirge of Cerberus explores Vincent's personality to a greater degree. His courage and self-assurance in the face of adversity, his readiness to help those around him through a sense of duty rather than desire, and his directness in handling confrontation are all reflective of Heracles.

Arguably the most significant comparison of their characters, however, might be their individual story arcs. When Vincent is first discovered in the crypt beneath Shinra Manor, he explains that he has been confined to a coffin as punishment for failing to prevent Lucrecia, the woman he loved, from offering her unborn child to the Jenova Project. His remorse over this continues into *Dirge of Cerberus*, but as the plot progresses, he begins to purge his perceived sins by overcoming the trials set out by Deepground SOLDIER. This is analogous to Heracles' purification through his labours, as detailed in the next chapter.

Norse Myths That Inspired Final Fantasy VII assesses the connections between Vincent's metamorphoses and the berserkers of Viking culture[15]. In particular, these shaman-warriors would induce rage-fuelled frenzies (the act of 'going berserk') during which they could not determine friend from foe, striking fear into the hearts of their enemies. This is not unlike the crazed and vicious trances for which Heracles was infamous, sparked by Hera or otherwise.

In *Final Fantasy VII*, Vincent's transformations occur when his Limit Breaks are utilised. The player surrenders their command over the mysterious gunman and he automatically assaults the opponent(s) on each turn until the fight ends or he is knocked out. This deals a multiplier increase of Vincent's physical attack damage at the expense of strategy, exactly as the standard Berserk status ailment does when inflicted on other characters[16].

Similar to the Viking berserkers, it could be asserted that Vincent's Limit Breaks mirror Heracles' rages, during which he loses control and creates carnage with his supernatural strength. The concept is even more prominent in *Dirge of Cerberus* after the Protomateria has been removed from the hero's chest, with Shelke – a member of the Tsviets, who has allied herself with the WRO – explicitly remarking that its absence has caused his mental state to become extremely unstable.

Vincent's inability to restrain Chaos puts the safety of those around him at risk. This is best demonstrated in a scene where he slashes through an interior wall amid a sudden and unexpected metamorphosis aboard the *Shera* airship. Moreover, when the alteration commences, Vincent is shrouded in a red mist, which likely symbolises his uncontainable rage[17].

An interesting feature in *Dirge of Cerberus* that loosely supports this conjecture is the updated Limit Break mechanic. Each time the player consumes a Limit Breaker item in the game, Vincent will temporarily shapeshift into the Galian Beast, whose speed and power are superior to his own. In addition, while the effects of the Limit Break remain in place, Vincent cannot be harmed.

Integrally linked to the ritualistic practices of Viking shaman-warriors were spirit animals, the pelts of which were typically worn by berserkers[18]. It has even been speculated that tales of berserkers becoming frenzied after 'changing form' into their wolf-skins have contributed to modern interpretations of werewolves. Applying this principle to Heracles' mantle, itself made from the impenetrable hide of the Nemean Lion, produces an explanation for why Vincent's metamorphoses in *Dirge of Cerberus* make him indestructible. The limited period of the transformation also parallels the momentary psychosis experienced by Heracles during his fits.

In the Greek myths, the demigod is commonly described as wielding a huge club (which inspired Theseus to do the same, as referenced in chapter XIV) or engaging in unarmed combat (such as his wrestling bout with the Giant Antaeus – see chapter X). Despite his celebrated strength, however, Heracles is perhaps deadliest with his bow and arrows[19], and considered to be unrivalled among mortal archers[20].

The *Compilation of Final Fantasy VII*, of course, exists in a more contemporary setting than ancient Greece, so an equivalent marksman would most likely use a pistol or a rifle, just as Vincent does. It is also plainly stated in the *10th Anniversary Ultimania* that his skill with firearms was unmatched in his days as a Turk, establishing another similarity to Heracles.

The guns available to Vincent in *Final Fantasy VII* have no noteworthy ties to mythology, whereas some of *Dirge of Cerberus'* least ambiguous allusions to Hellenic lore relate to its weapons. The foremost of these is Vincent's triple-barrelled handgun, Cerberus, which debuted in *Advent Children* (2005) but was not officially named until the 2006 game[21].

The hellhound of Hades was normally represented in antiquity as a three-headed canine. According to several sources, Cerberus is also said to have a serpent for a tail. These attributes can be found in Vincent's primary weapon, which has a snarling dog's head grafted onto each of its three barrels and a chain relief that hangs from the grip[22]. The adornment itself clearly depicts the legendary beast[23].

There are, however, other gun frames that can be obtained and equipped during *Dirge of Cerberus*. The main two are the Hydra long-range rifle and Griffon machinegun, both of which also have a trio of barrels[24]. Hydra is of particular importance as it derives from the many-headed water dragon encountered by Heracles in his second labour. More specifically, the arrows of Heracles' bow were synonymous with the Hydra because their tips had been dipped in its poisonous blood, making them fatal to anyone

330

whose skin they pierced. As such, the rifle expressly connects Vincent the gunman and Heracles the archer[25].

Griffons, meanwhile, are mythical creatures that are described in classical literature as having the head and wings of an eagle and the body of a lion[26]. These magnificent animals are not included in any Greco-Roman tales regarding Heracles, but one does appear in a montage sequence during Disney's *Hercules* (1997), an animated film based on the same character.

Intriguingly, there are a number of links to be made between the movie and *Dirge of Cerberus*. For instance, as mentioned in chapter XIII, Vincent battles against the Pegasus Riders (Deepground SOLDIERs on hoverbikes) early in the game. The winged horse Pegasus of Greek mythology is not associated with Heracles, but, just as in *Tōjin Makyō Den: Herakuresu no Eikō*, he does feature prominently in *Hercules* as the hero's steed[27]. Lucrecia's hairstyle and garb in her crystalised stasis also closely resemble those of Meg, Hercules' love interest in the film (named after Heracles' first wife, Megara). Additionally, the Hydra is a monster sent by Hades in Disney's adaptation, and its slaying propels the young champion to celebrity status.

Cerberus, too, has a couple of cameos in the movie, but an even greater – albeit indirect – hint towards Vincent's future story dwells in *Kingdom Hearts* (2002), a videogame co-written by Kazushige Nojima and jointly produced by Disney and Square[28]. During *Kingdom Hearts*, the player

331

(as the protagonist, Sora) can visit the Olympus Coliseum and participate in combat tournaments. The final opponent in one competition is Cloud Strife[29], and when the battle ends, Cerberus crashes into the arena, knocking Cloud unconscious. Hercules holds the gargantuan hellhound off while Sora temporarily retreats.

What should be emphasised here is that Cloud is wearing a frayed, high-collared, crimson cloak and has golden claws on the glove of his left arm. These are overt references to Vincent's mantle and gauntlet, which has been verified by Tetsuya Nomura[30]. It can therefore be contended that the relationship between Vincent, Cerberus, and Heracles may have originated in *Kingdom Hearts*.

This is not to suggest, however, that *Dirge of Cerberus'* plot draws primarily or even heavily from Disney's *Hercules* or the *Herakuresu no Eikō* series rather than classical lore. There is plenty of evidence to indicate Hiroki Chiba's scenario was influenced by the twelve labours, while certain elements seem to stem from the Gigantomachy.

As discussed in chapter X, Heracles is relied upon by the gods when the Gigantes lay siege to Olympus. According to Apollodorus' *Bibliotheca*, the Giants rise from beneath the earth to challenge the rule of Zeus and the Olympians[31]. They target Hera in particular because they believe that attacking her will bring disgrace to all gods.

The first Giant to attempt such an abhorrent act is Alcyoneus – the same figure who had instigated the war –

but he is shot down by Heracles' arrows, only to be rejuvenated by channelling strength from his contact with Gaia's soil. Heracles is eventually victorious in defeating Alcyoneus and his kin, returning peace to Olympus.

Neither Deepground nor its legions of unique SOLDIERs were introduced prior to *Dirge of Cerberus*[32]. To explain their absence in previous titles of the *Compilation*, it is revealed over the course of the game that the facilities below Midgar were so classified that even some directors of the Shinra Company (including Reeve) were unaware of their existence[33]. When Meteor's approach obliterates the city and its infrastructure, the men and women of Deepground are trapped, only to be freed three years later, following the restoration of the Worldwide Network[34]. The storm of death and destruction left in their wake forces the WRO into action.

A comparison can be made here between Deepground SOLDIER and the Gigantes. As noted in earlier chapters, the Giants of Greek mythology are brutes who emerge from the earth with the ambition of overthrowing the established rulers. Most of them are not portrayed as being unusually large in stature as their name might imply nowadays[35], but they are certainly strong and aggressive. Furthermore, some scholars attested that the catalyst for the Gigantomachy itself was Alcyoneus stealing the sacred cattle of the Sun god Helios.

This is reflected in Deepground SOLDIER, who are literally confined to the subterranean depths of Midgar for three years after Meteorfall. The sudden appearance of these fierce, powerful combatants finds them in direct conflict with the WRO, an organisation that has been operating as a centralised authority since the collapse of the Shinra Corporation. Where the theft of Helios' cattle heralds the Gigantes war with the Olympians, Deepground's abduction of more than a thousand people from Junon is what initially prompts the WRO to investigate.

It is perhaps also worth highlighting that Alcyoneus made Hera his prime target when he and the Giants scaled Mount Olympus. Junon is the French spelling of Juno, who is in turn the Roman counterpart of Hera. The location of the mass disappearance that precedes the events of *Dirge of Cerberus* may therefore not be a coincidence[36].

During the storyline, Deepground SOLDIER twice attacks the WRO Headquarters. This complex houses the command centre for Commissioner Reeve Tuesti, thus creating a parallel with the palaces of Olympus from which the gods govern. Just as the immortals request the support of Heracles to repel the Gigantes' invasion, Vincent is called upon to defend HQ.

Even more curiously, it is Azul the Cerulean who leads these assaults. Azul is one of the Tsviets and a colossus of a man, towering at over nine feet tall, according to official media; this makes him a giant in the contemporary sense of the word. In Apollodorus' account of the Gigantomachy, Heracles shoots Alcyoneus with a poisoned arrow, causing him to fall from Olympus, presumably to his death. Like all his brethren, however, Alcyoneus draws strength from the earth and is able to replenish his health. Similar circumstances are seen in *Dirge of Cerberus* when Vincent guns down Azul during their duel at WRO Headquarters, only for him to later rise from the dead and trigger Deepground's second offensive on the facility.

The proposed association between Azul and the children of Gaia could also be extended to his metamorphosised form, Arch Azul, which is an armoured variant of the recurring *Final Fantasy* behemoth monster types. In the Hebrew Bible, the Behemoth is the primordial beast of the land, while Hesiod's *Theogony* describes the Gigantes as being so hostile that they were born wearing armour and wielding spears.

Moreover, it can be argued that Deepground SOLDIERs in general share the attributes of Alcyoneus and his fellow Giants with respect to channelling energy from Gaia. Although it is briefly alluded to by Shelke in *Dirge of Cerberus*, the *Final Fantasy VII 10th Anniversary Ultimania* explicitly states that members of Deepground undergo rigorous experimentation to make them unnaturally strong. However, this destabilises their bodies, so they require regular mako baths and a mako current running through their unique uniforms to maintain peak condition. Given that mako is the lifeblood of the Planet, Deepground SOLDIERs, too, are sourcing power directly from Gaia[37].

It is commonly attested that Heracles' selfless and exemplary heroism in assisting the gods against the Gigantes is what finally convinces Hera to rescind her curse over him[37]. From that day on, Heracles is free of the hallucinations and fits of madness that so often drove him to seek redemption. This might be reflected in the ending sequence of *Dirge of Cerberus*, in which Vincent indicates to Lucrecia that he no longer feels the burden of his sins after the defeat of Deepground.

During the same scene, Vincent also tells her that both Chaos and Omega have returned to the Planet. This suggests he has been separated from the sentient xenoform that inhabited him for decades. While it is unclear if the cloaked marksman has retained his immortality, the split offers an interesting analogy to the death of Heracles, whose own soul may have been divided in two.

The playwrights of the Classical period and later Latin authors typically agree that Heracles does not descend to the realm of Hades when he dies, but rather that Zeus raises him up to Olympus and grants him divine status. This conflicts with Homer's *Odyssey*, which places Heracles' spirit in Asphodel when Odysseus visits the underworld. Some writers attempted to rationalise the discrepancy by explaining that Heracles' immortal soul went to Olympus, while his mortal one entered the afterlife. The Chaos aspect of Vincent's character joining the Lifestream at the climax of his story arc loosely compares to this.

Heracles will forever be remembered for his remarkable strengths and tragic flaws. Despite – or maybe because of – his many imperfections, he was considered the greatest of all Hellenes, and his adventures continue to be told through various mediums today. The goal of this chapter has been to lay the foundations of who the hero was and how his exploits likely influenced *Dirge of Cerberus*. It is the next chapter, however, that will examine the degree to which Hiroki Chiba and his colleagues were inspired by the most famous of legends, the Labours of Heracles themselves.

1. The *Epic of Gilgamesh* is a poem from ancient Mesopotamia, whose story is known to date back to at least 2100 BC. It centres around Gilgamesh, a headstrong king who befriends Enkidu, a wild man sent by the gods to end his oppressive rule. The gods later kill Enkidu, causing Gilgamesh to set off on a dangerous journey in search of the secret to eternal life. Both Gilgamesh and Enkidu are recurring characters in the *Final Fantasy* series. In 2022, the mobile-exclusive game *The First Soldier* released an outfit and weapons based on Gilgamesh, which is to date his sole inclusion in the *Final Fantasy VII* universe.

2. On a regional level, other heroes were occasionally held in higher esteem than Heracles. The most notable example of this is the Athenians' admiration for their legendary founder-king, Theseus (see chapter XIV).

3. This makes Heracles simultaneously the great grandson and half-brother of Perseus. The genealogies of classical myth can be fickle like that. Perseus' story is told in chapter XIII.

4. The name 'Hercules' appears in two spin-off games, *Final Fantasy: The 4 Heroes of Light* (2010) and *Final Fantasy Awakening* (2016).

5. In most accounts of Heracles' youth, he has a twin brother, Iphicles, who is fathered by Amphitryon. It is the demigod's unusual behaviour – such as strangling and playing with two snakes Hera sent to kill the boys – that sets him apart from his sibling.

6. Literary sources do not always agree on when Heracles kills his family. The 5th century play *Herakles* by Euripides, for example, places this event after the labours rather than before.

7. As mentioned in chapter I, the deliberate or accidental killing of a relative was considered a blood crime, the worst act one could commit according to Hellenic tradition. Only a monarch could purify an offender of such an atrocity, typically through a period of servitude.

8. The Lernaean Hydra is a child of the monstrous couple Typhon and Echidna, as noted in chapter XI. The Nemean Lion, meanwhile, is the offspring of the Chimera, which features in Bellerophon's story in chapter XX.

9. Many of the figures who Heracles places on the respective thrones are later directly involved in the Trojan War.

10. The title '*Glory of Heracles*' likely took inspiration from Heracles' own name, which means 'Glory of Hera'.

11. Limit Breaks (known by various names throughout the series) are special attacks that become available to player characters during battle, but the specific mechanics of how they are used differ from title to title. In *Final Fantasy VII,* each member of the party has a meter that increases as enemies deal damage to them, and filling the gauge allows them to unleash powerful personalised abilities.

12. There is substantial evidence to suggest Vincent's transformations were initially inspired by classic horror figures; the "Early Material File" section of the *Ultimania Omega* reveals that his original job description was horror detective. The Galian Beast resembles a werewolf, Death Gigas is a take on Frankenstein's monster, Hellmasker appears to parody Leatherface from the

Texas Chain Saw Massacre movie franchise, and Vincent himself is found sleeping in a coffin like a vampire. Chaos, meanwhile, is derived from the main antagonist of the first *Final Fantasy* title.

13. An optional flashback in *Final Fantasy VII* reveals that, prior to the game's events, Vincent was a Turk assigned by the Shinra Company to protect the scientists of the Jenova Project. Hojo shot Vincent and subsequently performed experiments on him. Further details of the circumstances can be found in the next chapter.

14. The music teacher was Linus, a brother of the divine bard Orpheus. According to Apollodorus' *Bibliotheca*, Linus strikes Heracles with a rod when the boy fails to follow instructions. Heracles' violent reaction results in the tutor's head being smashed. Linus is believed by some scholars to be the embodiment of a funerary hymn or lamentation, which is of particular interest given the title *Dirge of Cerberus* (see chapter XVIII).

15. A full explanation can be found in that book.

16. Berserk is one of several status effects found throughout the *Final Fantasy* series. A party member afflicted by Berserk typically receives a boost in physical strength and speed but can no longer be controlled by the player.

17. A 'red mist descending' is a common metaphor for a fit of extreme rage that temporarily clouds a person's judgement.

18. In the mythologies and heroic sagas of the Norsemen, the two most prominently attested spirit animals (totems) are the bear and the wolf, and the shaman-warriors associated with them were the *berserkir* ('bear-shirts') and *úlfhéðnar* ('wolf-skins').

19. Heracles is trained in archery by King Eurytus of Oechalia, said to be a grandson of Apollo himself. Eurytus is also the father of Prince Iphitus, whom Heracles later throws from the city walls of Tiryns.

20. The Olympian twins, Apollo and Artemis, are both closely affiliated with the bow and arrow, although neither ever recognises Heracles as an equal.

339

21. Like all playable characters in *Final Fantasy VII*, Vincent has several weapons that can be acquired and equipped throughout the game. Despite Cerberus featuring in *Advent Children*, there is no mention of its name or design in the *Ultimania Omega*. This would indicate that the references to Greek mythology were implemented exclusively during the production of *Dirge of Cerberus*. That said, Cerberus has been a recurring enemy type in the series since *Final Fantasy III*, including *Crisis Core*. His single outing as a summoned creature (Guardian Force) is in *Final Fantasy VIII*, also scripted by Nojima-san.

22. This applies to the default gun barrels as seen in *Advent Children* and the *Dirge of Cerberus* promotional materials. In the game, however, the barrel type can be modified.

23. An artistic adaptation of the Cerberus relief appears on the cover of this book. It should be noted that the original image also features wings, but this is not consistent with mythology.

24. Other firearms in the game include: the Shinra Handgun, which is used solely in the tutorial with Vincent wearing his Turks uniform; the Model Gun, which can be upgraded to the Ultima Weapon; and Death Penalty, which materialises when Vincent transforms into Chaos for the final chapter of the story.

25. *Dirge of Cerberus* grants the player a degree of customisation over Vincent's guns, including their barrel length. In the released version of the game, the options comprise of the Short Barrel, Medium Barrel, and Long Barrel. There is evidence to show these names were different at one stage of development, however: They were the Chimera, the Hellhound, and the Orochi, respectively. The Chimera – a fire-breathing fiend with the heads of a lion, a goat, and a serpent – was likely best paired with Griffon, the Hellhound with Cerberus, and Orochi – an eight-headed and eight-tailed dragon from Japanese legend – with Hydra. The modified gun frames also have names that include Greek letters such as β

(beta) and γ (gamma), or mythical creatures such as Gigantes.

26. Griffon-type enemies can be fought in *Final Fantasy VII* and *Crisis Core*, alternatively called griffins, hippogriffs, and tycoons. Further details are provided in chapter XX.

27. These circumstances are comparable to Pegasus appearing as Perseus' flying mount in *Clash of the Titans*.

28. The first title in the *Kingdom Hearts* franchise was developed prior to Square's merger with Enix.

29. The player can also fight against Yuffie and Sephiroth in later tournaments.

30. Nomura-san, who directed *Kingdom Hearts*, is quoted in an interview from the game's *Ultimania*, stating that he wanted to include Vincent but instead incorporated some of his costume into Cloud's design to evoke a sense of the character leaning towards a darker path.

31. Apollodorus' account differs from Hesiod's *Theogony*, in which the Gigantes are born when the blood of Uranus' castration falls upon Gaia.

32. As a caveat to this, Azul is fought by the player Turk in episode 4 of *Before Crisis*. However, the context is that he is being forcibly recruited for SOLDIER.

33. This has been altered in the continuity of *Final Fantasy VII Remake* with the appearance of Deepground SOLDIER and the Tsviets in *Episode INTERmission* (see chapter XIX).

34. It is implied in the news report shown during the opening of *Dirge of Cerberus* that Deepground was sealed off when the network went offline and required the lock to be externally released.

35. 'Gigas' or 'Giant' is more accurately translated as 'of Gaia' or 'Earthborn'.

36. Additionally, most of the mobile-exclusive companion game *Dirge of Cerberus Lost Episode* (2006) is set in and around Junon. The events of *Lost Episode* take place between chapters 4 and 5 of *Dirge of Cerberus*, during Vincent's journey to Nibelheim.

37. Special mention should be given to the DG Elite opponents Vincent encounters throughout Deepground

itself. These operatives appear to have armoured tunics and crested helmets modelled on those of ancient Greek soldiers.

38. There are some writers, however, who claim Zeus makes Hera agree to leave his son alone if he completes his twelve labours.

CHAPTER XVII

REDEMPTION

Even by Heracles' lofty standards, the legend of his twelve labours can count itself among the best loved of classical mythology. It is unclear how the details of these gruelling trials originated, but allusions to them can be found in the earliest Hellenic literature. Heracles' encounter with Cerberus in the underworld is mentioned in both the *Iliad* and the *Odyssey*, believed to have been composed by Homer around the 8th century BC, while Hesiod's *Theogony* includes stanzas dedicated to the demigod's slaying of the Hydra and Nemean Lion, for example.

Chapter XVI establishes that *Dirge of Cerberus* contains a multitude of connections to the Greek myths, with a particular focus on the life of Heracles. Some of the references in the game are fairly obvious, such as the names of Vincent's basic gun frames[1]; some are a bit subtler, like the villainous Nero the Sable transforming into Arachnero and Gorgonero during his battle with Vincent at Mako Reactor 0^2; others are open to interpretation, such as Vincent's uncontrollable rages as Chaos.

To fully appreciate the extent of the parallels between Vincent and Heracles, however, the latter's twelve labours and torment by Hera must be examined more closely. In the stories, the purpose of these impossible tasks is for Heracles to atone for his blood crimes, just as Vincent's motivation is to repent for his perceived sins. This is best expressed in *Dirge of Cerberus'* theme song, "Redemption" by Japanese musician Gackt[3].

Among the first attempts the Queen of Heaven ever makes to harm Heracles (then known as Alcides) is one that occurs when he is still an infant: She sends a pair of turquoise vipers to his crib[4], but the playful baby simply strangles the snakes. Zeus is alarmed by his wife's behaviour and hatches a plan to protect Heracles from her.

While Hera sleeps one night, the messenger god Hermes – as directed by his father – smuggles the child up to Olympus to let him suckle at her breast[5]. Heracles is unable to drain the quantity of milk that would grant him immortality, but he manages to consume enough to consolidate his supernatural strength.

As he grows, the young warrior puts his endowments to excellent use, eventually becoming celebrated as the great hero of Thebes, his home city. In time, Hera decides to rob him of his happiness and those he loves most in the world, visiting upon Heracles the fit of madness that leads him to kill his wife Megara and their children.

Distraught but determined to expiate his crimes, Heracles travels to the city of Tiryns to seek purification from his cousin King Eurystheus. Eurystheus is a wicked and jealous individual who is all too easily influenced by Hera whispering in his ear. Seated triumphantly on his throne, he decrees that his grieving kinsman is to be thoroughly punished through servitude and a series of labours over the following decade.

The oldest sources that describe these labours are neither comprehensive nor consistent, but the order provided by Apollodorus in his *Bibliotheca* is generally accepted to be the standard[6]. The labours are: (1) the slaying of the Nemean Lion; (2) the eradication of the Lernaean Hydra; (3) the capture of the Ceryneian Hind, a doe sacred to the goddess Artemis; (4) the gradual tracking and trapping of the Erymanthian Boar; (5) washing out King Augeas' stables in a single day by rerouting two rivers; (6) massacring the toxic infestation of Stymphalian Birds; (7) subduing the Cretan Bull and bringing it before Eurystheus' court[7]; (8) the theft of the four crazed Mares of Diomedes, to whom Heracles feeds their own master; (9) obtaining the girdle of Queen Hippolyta of the Amazons tribe; (10) stealing the cattle of the Giant Geryon and transporting them to Greece; (11) acquiring the golden apples from the Garden of the Hesperides by tricking Atlas (see chapter X for the Titan's story); and (12) wrestling the hellhound Cerberus, who guards the gates of Hades.

The last of the labours set by Eurystheus is a cunning and foolproof way – or so he thinks – of ensuring Heracles will not escape the realm of the dead. Accompanied by Hermes, the hero descends into the underworld, where the shades of countless souls flee before him. During the journey, he discovers and releases Theseus from the Chair of Forgetfulness, to which the Athenian king has been bound (as told in chapter XIV).

By then, it has dawned on Heracles that Hera is dictating the increasingly challenging trials. With the blessing of Hades – or his wife Persephone in some sources – the strongman earns the right to borrow Cerberus by grappling the three-headed canine into submission. Heracles returning to Eurystheus' throne room with the fearsome hound by his side signifies that his twelfth labour is complete, and that he is absolved of his blood crimes.

Set during the same ten-year period that the tasks are being carried out, there are separate myths regarding Heracles' additional exploits. His encounter with the Giant Antaeus is one of these, as referenced in chapter X, while another relates to the death of Alcestis, wife of Heracles' friend Admetus[8].

In the latter tale, Apollo convinces the Moirai (Fates[9]) to let Admetus live forever, and they agree on the condition that someone must sacrifice their life in his place. Alcestis volunteers to do so, and her spirit waits to be escorted to the underworld by Thanatos, the God of Death. Heracles simultaneously arrives at Admetus' palace and fights Thanatos when he learns what has happened, overcoming the psychopomp and taking Alcestis back to her husband.

Chapter XVI touches on a handful of elements found in *Dirge of Cerberus* that likely allude specifically to the Labours of Heracles. The Cerberus and Hydra gun frames are the most obvious instances, while the impenetrable hide of the Galian Beast may be analogous to the ferocious hero cloaking himself in the pelt of the Nemean Lion.

There is also substantial evidence to suggest it is not a coincidence that *Dirge of Cerberus'* narrative is divided into twelve chapters[10]. Although these do not generally correspond with the events of the respective labours, there are certainly several similarities that merit highlighting.

During the fifth labour, for example, Eurystheus demands that Heracles cleans out the stables of King Augeas' immortal cattle, heaped with manure that has accumulated over 30 years. Rather than tackle the dung manually, he diverts two local rivers and makes them converge at the stables, causing the flowing waters to wash away the muck. This is perhaps reflected early in chapter 5 of *Dirge of Cerberus*, in which Vincent accesses Shinra Mansion by navigating the grimy waterways of a decades-old sewer network between the Mount Nibel reactor and Nibelheim.

The Stymphalian Birds of Heracles' sixth labour might also be represented. A great flock of these huge, foul creatures has nested in the countryside around Lake Stymphalia on mainland Greece, and it is left to the famed marksman to shoot as many as he can with his arrows. Of all the fiends confronted in *Dirge of Cerberus*, the sole avian species is the epiolnis: large, flightless birds that must be gunned down by Vincent in the mountain pass leading to the WRO Headquarters. As it happens, the epiolnis monsters appear exclusively in chapter 6 of the game.

However, they are by no means the only enemies in *Dirge of Cerberus* that hint at the Labours of Heracles to some degree. Outside the various Deepground SOLDIER operative types, the most common opponents faced by Vincent are guard hounds, which could be a nod to Cerberus himself.

Another potential reference may feature in the Extra Missions mode of the game's international edition. For Heracles' tenth labour, Eurystheus instructs him to steal the entire herd of Geryon's cattle. The livestock are valuable due to their bulk and rare red hides and are protected by Orthrus, a twin-headed brother of Cerberus[11]. It is curious, then, that Tetsuya Nomura's updated design of the dual horn beasts in *Dirge of Cerberus'* extra missions should introduce attributes associated with Geryon's cattle (namely their red hide)[12], while the final mission they appear in, titled "Two-Handed", has Vincent challenge 100 of them. Furthermore, Geryon himself is a three-headed giant, which might explain why each dual horn drops a Gigas EX Medal upon defeat.

There are also some parallels to be found between characters encountered by Heracles throughout his labours and the game's primary antagonists, Deepground's elite Tsviet unit. The first of these relates to the ninth labour, in which Heracles is ordered to bring Eurystheus the girdle of Hippolyta, Queen of the Amazons[13].

The Amazons figure a number of times in ancient Greek literature and are typically described as a tribe of female warriors. They are masters of riding and archery, renowned for their military raids and strength in combat. Hippolyta herself is a daughter of Ares, the God of War, and the belt she wears previously belonged to him. Several versions of the myth depict respect (or even affection) between Heracles and Hippolyta, although Apollodorus attests that Hera sparks a brawl that ends with him slaying the queen.

In *Dirge of Cerberus*, Rosso the Crimson is a female SOLDIER who was born in Deepground. Battle is all she has ever known, and this has turned her into a bloodthirsty killer – a child of war. As a high-ranking Tsviet, she is a military commander – just as Hippolyta is for the Amazons – and leads a raid on Edge early in the game. Rosso wields a double-bladed weapon capable of firing bullets, itself shaped like a traditional longbow. This makes her proficient in both close and ranged combat, which may be an allusion to the Amazons' prowess in swordplay *and* archery.

Rosso considers herself to be a warrior whose skill is equal to Vincent Valentine's. When she loses their duel on Midgar's Plate, she takes her own life to avert the disgrace of being killed by her enemy[14], thus creating a comparison to Hippolyta's death at the hands of Heracles. It is perhaps most telling of all, however, that Rosso's outfit draws attention to the extravagant armour around her midriff, a possible tribute to Hippolyta's girdle.

Deepground itself plays a major role in *Dirge of Cerberus*, and there could well be a more significant connection between the name of the subterranean complex and Hades' legendary hound. Shinra's dark secret is repeatedly referred to as "hell" during the game, principally in terms of its geographical position beneath Midgar, the heinous practices that took place in its laboratories and military training facilities, and the confinement of individuals there after Meteorfall[15].

According to Hellenic cosmology, Tartarus is the primordial realm that exists far below Gaia. When the time comes for Zeus to allot rule over the heavens, seas, and underworld, his brother Hades establishes his kingdom in the bleak, cavernous roots of the earth. Tartarus eventually becomes an infernal prison for the spirits of the wicked and damned. It is the closest location in Greek mythology to perceptions of Hell in modern religions, and by its very cosmological definition, Tartarus is literally *deep ground*. The gloomy, crumbling city and the continuous screaming of souls resonating from Mako Reactor 0 further enhance the allegory.

To reach the halls of Hades, one must pass the underworld gates guarded by Cerberus. In his twelfth and final labour, Heracles wrestles the enormous beast in front of these gates and successfully subdues him. It is peculiar, then, that the last opponent Vincent encounters as he descends towards the immense entrance to Deepground is Arch Azul, the rampant behemoth form of Azul the Cerulean[16]. The giant Tsviet taunts Vincent during this battle and invites him to show his rage, which may imply a link to Heracles' notorious outbursts.

Among the most famous residents of Tartarus in Greek lore are Thanatos, the personification of death, and his brother Hypnos, the personification of sleep. Thanatos himself does not feature in many tales, but he is portrayed in numerous artworks and literary sources. He is often presented as being garbed in a black robe, sometimes with wings, and is said to envelop those whose spirit he has come to claim in a shadowy blue-black cloud, therein conveying them to the grimness of the netherworld. Thanatos was known to the Romans as Mors, generally imagined by them as a youth[17].

Homer and Hesiod both attested that Thanatos and Hypnos had no father: They were born to the primeval goddess Nyx (Night). Latin writers such as Hyginus, however, later stated their father was Erebus, the embodiment of darkness. The siblings regularly appear together in mythical references – Thanatos being associated with black and Hypnos with white.

There are some subtle similarities between the God of Death and Nero the Sable, one of Deepground's most senior Tsviets. Nero – whose name means 'Black' in Italian – is a young man clad in a dark leather mako suit, with mechanical wings extending from his shoulders, which mirrors the physical descriptions of Thanatos. His supernatural abilities allow him to wield 'darkness', and he does so by shrouding his victims in a black-and-purple haze, drawing them into a realm where their life force is extracted.

It is revealed towards the climax of *Dirge of Cerberus* that Nero has been commanding the Deepground SOLDIERs while his elder brother, Weiss the Immaculate, is incapacitated. This means Nero is responsible for the mass abductions at Kalm, Junon, Edge, Wutai, and other locations. Thousands of civilians have been transported to Mako Reactor 0 and added to the swell of untainted Lifestream intended to awaken the Omega Weapon. As such, his gathering of souls is analogous to Thanatos' function as a psychopomp in Hellenic beliefs.

There is also the curious connection between Nero and Chaos, the fabled harbinger of death. In her thesis, "The Planet's Pulse", Lucrecia classifies Chaos as a sentient xenoform, quoted in Cetran scripture to be produced by 'terra corrupt'[18], which is otherwise known as stagnant mako. Of the countless experiments performed in Deepground, Nero is the only child born exhibiting the properties of stagnant mako[19] – this is why he can control darkness, just as Vincent is impervious to it. In later iterations of the classical genealogy of the gods, Erebus (Darkness) is said to be the father of Thanatos, while Chaos (Nothingness) is the parent of Erebus *and* Tartarus. As such, Vincent's and Nero's relationships with darkness may derive from Chaos's and Thanatos' relationships with Erebus.

The Greek God of Death, of course, features in the story of Alcestis and Admetus, in which he is prevented by Heracles from acquiring Alcestis' spirit. There are particular resemblances between this myth and the actions of Nero during *Dirge of Cerberus*. For example, when Shelke finds him aboard the *Shera* airship, he explicitly informs her that he has come to collect more souls[20]. Vincent subsequently rescues Shelke from within Nero's darkness and returns her to the material world, just as Heracles rescues Alcestis from Thanatos. Furthermore, Shelke is liberated immediately after Vincent and Nero have duelled outside Mako Reactor 0, which compares to Heracles assaulting Thanatos.

In Apollodorus' account of the twelfth labour, Heracles traverses the underworld en route to Hades' palace. Along the way, he frees Theseus from the Chair of Forgetfulness and attempts to attack the phantom of the Gorgon Medusa. A similar scenario plays out during *Dirge of Cerberus* in a hallway adjacent to Weiss' throne room, situated at the heart of the subterranean complex. Vincent has to retrieve Yuffie from Nero's darkness[21] – which the villain refers to as "oblivion"[22] –, then battles the Tsviet in his Arachnero and Gorgonero forms, albeit the latter has no clear aesthetic link to the snake-haired Medusa.

It is perhaps also worth highlighting the relationship between Nero the Sable and Weiss the Immaculate. Like Thanatos and Hypnos, they are brothers affiliated with black and white (*'weiß'* or *'weiss'* translates as 'white' in German) who dwell in Tartarus and Deepground, respectively. Weiss is dead rather than asleep when Vincent first enters Mako Reactor 0, but his imminent reawakening with the power of Omega indicates his demise is temporary[23]. It could be contended that the allusions to Hypnos are reinforced in both the secret ending to *Dirge of Cerberus,* when Genesis cradles Weiss' body and tells him that it is not yet time for slumber, then again during Weiss' cameo in *Episode INTERmission*, in which his opening line is to ask Nero if he slept well.

Arguably the deepest parallel between *Dirge of Cerberus'* plot and the Labours of Heracles relates to the ways the protagonists' lives have been cursed. Vincent's past as a Turk and his involvement with Hojo and Lucrecia during the Jenova Project is summarised through dialogue and a brief flashback in *Final Fantasy VII*. However, *Dirge of Cerberus* substantially builds upon this and presents additional details.

30 years before the events of *Final Fantasy VII*, Vincent is assigned to protect the Shinra scientists as they carry out their research on Jenova at Shinra Manor. He is shown

affection by Lucrecia and falls in love with her, but she abandons any romantic notions when Vincent learns she was responsible for the death of his father, Grimoire[24]. Lucrecia thereafter marries Hojo and becomes pregnant with Sephiroth[25].

When the pair offer their unborn son to the Jenova Project, Vincent pleads with them to reconsider, but his concerns are dismissed. Sephiroth is taken from Lucrecia as soon as she gives birth. The psychological impact of this and the Jenova cells in her bloodstream cause her to collapse, so Vincent confronts her husband. In retaliation, Hojo shoots and experiments on the Turk, modifying his body to make it capable of hosting monstrous fiends.

Vincent believes these horrific transformations are his punishment for not stopping Hojo and Lucrecia[26], the latter of whom confines herself in crystal when she is unable to end her own life. What he is unaware of, though, as revealed in *Dirge of Cerberus*, is that a side effect of Hojo's enhancements is tissue decay. Lucrecia endeavoured to halt his deterioration with stagnant mako, unintentionally contaminating him with the so-called Chaos gene. As verified in the *Final Fantasy VII 10th Anniversary Ultimania*, it is Chaos' presence that makes Vincent immortal and thus ageless.

Early in *Dirge of Cerberus*, while Vincent and Reeve are travelling to the WRO Headquarters, there is a television broadcast from Deepground. Seated on his throne at Mako Reactor 0, Weiss declares that the time has come to cleanse the world by exterminating those tainted by Geostigma. This mission statement is what drives Deepground SOLDIER's atrocities throughout the game. Still burdened by the sins of his past, Vincent is motivated to take action.

However, when he finally reaches Deepground's reactor core and approaches Weiss, he discovers that Professor Hojo has been manipulating things all along. Fragments of the scientist's digital consciousness have recently overthrown Weiss' mind in cyberspace and seized control of the Tsviet[27]. In short, the hero has been battling against Hojo's agenda rather than Weiss'.

Vincent plays a critical role in the plot to awaken Omega because he is the keeper of the Protomateria, a special orb that allows him to suppress Chaos[28]. After Rosso – at the indirect behest of Hojo – robs Vincent of the crystal, he struggles to contain his rages. Using his proximity to Hojo-Weiss to exploit the Protomateria, however, Vincent manages to restrict the beast while unleashing its phenomenal power.

The defeat and eradication of Hojo triggers a chain of events that results in Vincent learning the truth about his survival and saving the world from the threat of Omega. By the end of *Dirge of Cerberus*, he has earned redemption and is at peace with his past.

It could be argued that the torment Vincent experiences for much of the *Compilation* is primarily attributable to Hojo and his unethical practices, just as Heracles' is rooted in Hera's determination to bring misery to the demigod's life. By equating Hojo's and Hera's functions in the stories of the respective heroes, it is possible to examine the parallels through a different lens.

In Heracles' infancy, the Queen of Heaven is responsible for both trying to murder him – by sending vipers to his cot – and for his superhuman strength, after Zeus arranges for the baby to suckle at Hera's breast. Similarly, Vincent's existence is changed forever when Hojo shoots him and genetically modifies his body, making him robust enough to become a vessel for Chaos.

Hojo's anger and retribution, of course, follow Vincent's protestations over the effects of the Jenova Project on Lucrecia. As mentioned above, the specific context here is that he is challenging Lucrecia's husband after their son has been born and immediately removed from her care. Hera herself is the Goddess of Marriage and the protector of women in childbirth, creating a unique association with Vincent's punishment for intervening.

In most accounts of the Labours of Heracles, he enters into a decade of servitude to atone for the death of his wife and children. Heracles feels solely culpable for their passing but fails to acknowledge it was Hera's delusions that caused him to attack his loved ones.

Mirroring this, when Vincent is first encountered in *Final Fantasy VII*, he has been sleeping in a coffin for around 30 years as penance for his sins. He blames his inability to

357

dissuade Lucrecia, the woman he loved, from volunteering her unborn child to the Jenova Project for the eventual tragedy that befell her. Like Heracles, Vincent assumes accountability despite the circumstances being engineered by someone else, namely Hojo, and Lucrecia being a consenting participant.

Hojo is killed and Vincent successfully helps save the Planet from Meteor during *Final Fantasy VII*, yet the former Turk remains enslaved by his sins three years later. As previously discussed, when Deepground launches its offensive, Vincent is a principal target because he has the Protomateria, and the violence is ordered by Weiss, although it is revealed in due course to be Hojo's scheme.

This, too, establishes a number of comparisons with the twelve labours. The trials themselves are willingly accepted by Heracles, who is consumed by guilt and remorse, but they are conceived by Hera. Just as the demigod is singled out by the goddess for being a son of Zeus – despite the King of Olympus fathering many children, divine or otherwise, outside of wedlock –, Vincent is singled out by Hojo and the Deepground forces due to the Protomateria.

Hera is not only responsible for the blood crimes that require Heracles to be exonerated, she also takes possession of an oracle and instructs the grieving strongman to seek expiation from Eurystheus[29], then whispers in the king's ear to suggest more and more extraordinary tasks for Heracles. As such, Hera's influence over Eurystheus and how that shapes Heracles' labours reflects Hojo's control over Weiss and how it, in turn, shapes Vincent's actions in *Dirge of Cerberus*.

Each time Eurystheus burdens Heracles with a new duty, he issues his demands from his throne in Tiryns. Weiss, on the other hand, is best known for being seated on his throne at the heart of Mako Reactor 0. Moreover, a primary catalyst for Vincent's involvement in supporting the WRO against Deepground SOLDIER throughout the game is the Tsviet leader's rogue broadcast from that very spot.

During the video stream, Weiss asserts that the time has come to cleanse the world, which may be a reference to Heracles' efforts to obtain purification. Weiss declares that the tainted will be hunted, exterminated, slashed, strangled, slaughtered, beaten, stabbed, crushed, garrotted, impaled, shot, and executed. It might not be a coincidence that these are twelve individual threats – one for each labour needed to purge the taint of Heracles' crimes[30].

According to the myths, Heracles is released from his servitude after he journeys into the underworld and brings the three-headed hellhound to Eurystheus' throne room. This has an abstract resemblance to Vincent descending into Deepground and battling his way to Weiss' throne with his triple-barrelled firearms, ultimately thwarting Hojo's plot and freeing himself of his sins. As such, in the face of impossible odds, it could be said it is Cerberus in both heroes' tales that finally delivers them redemption.

1. These frames are Cerberus, Hydra, and Griffon.
2. Reference to Arachne and the Gorgons can be found in chapters IX and XIII, respectively.
3. As well as contributing to the soundtrack of *Dirge of Cerberus*, Gackt lent his image to the character of Genesis, who appears in the game's secret ending, separate from his role in *Crisis Core*.
4. Hera releases one snake for Alcides and one for his twin brother, Iphicles, because she is not yet sure which of them is Zeus' son.
5. This is the variation presented by the Latin author Hyginus in *De Astronomica*. Other versions, such as the work of Diodorus Siculus, credit Athena with tricking Hera.
6. Apollodorus' account echoes others in that Eurystheus initially sets ten labours, then adds the final two at the end. His justification is that Heracles' received help to defeat the Hydra and requested payment from King Augeas for cleaning his stables, which broke the conditions of his servitude.
7. This is the same white bull that Poseidon sent from the sea to King Minos II of Crete and which subsequently fathered the Minotaur. The exact circumstances of this are summarised in chapter XV.
8. Differing versions of this story can be found in Apollodorus' *Bibliotheca*, Hyginus' *Fabulae*, and Euripides' play *Alcestis*, among other literature.
9. The Fates and their influence on *Final Fantasy VII* are examined in chapter XXI.
10. *Dirge of Cerberus Lost Episode* has not been included in this count.
11. As discussed in chapter XI, Orthrus (Orthros) shares a transliteration with Ultros of *Final Fantasy VI*.
12. Nomura-san's original design of the dual horns in *Final Fantasy VII* did not have the signature red armoured hide.
13. A girdle is a type of belt worn around the waist. In literature, they often have magical properties.

14. Rosso allows herself to plummet from the Plate upon a collapsing ledge.

15. How Deepground came to be isolated after Meteorfall is explained in the previous chapter.

16. While there are limited aesthetic parallels between the monstrous quadrupeds Cerberus and Arch Azul, this is by no means an isolated case in the *Compilation of Final Fantasy VII* of a behemoth marking the entrance to the metaphorical underworld, as will be addressed in the next chapter.

17. It is from the Latin '*mors*' (death) that English words such as 'mortal' and 'morgue' derive. Hypnos and his Roman cognate Somnus, meanwhile, can be found in 'hypnosis' or 'insomnia', for example. In *Final Fantasy VII*, the Hypno Crown is an accessory that improves the wearer's chances of hypnotising enemies to manipulate them. *Final Fantasy XV* fans may already be familiar with the names Somnus and Insomnia.

18. Terra is the Roman equivalent of Gaia, Mother Earth. 'Terra corrupt' can therefore be interpreted as a corruption of the Planet.

19. The circumstances of Nero's birth were briefly recounted in the discontinued online multiplayer mode of *Dirge of Cerberus*.

20. Shelke the Transparent is a member of the Tsviets, who allies herself with Vincent and the WRO during the events of the game.

21. Yuffie infiltrates Deepground at the same time as Vincent, with the mission of disabling Mako Reactor 0.

22. As a side note, Nero also calls Chaos a "daemon" in this scene. 'Daemon' is an ancient Greek term used to describe supernatural beings of a nature somewhere between gods and humans, such as nymphs or minor deities.

23. Chapter III provides a basic overview of Weiss' death. As explained in *Dirge of Cerberus*' multiplayer mode, the Tsviets' eventual victory over the Restrictors causes a fatal virus to be released into his bloodstream.

24. Lucrecia's reckless determination to uncover the mysteries of stagnant mako caused an incident in her laboratory. Grimoire, her mentor, used his body to shield her from exposure to the substance and died soon after.

25. It is confirmed in the *Ultimania Omega* and subsequent *Compilation* media that Lucrecia and Hojo were married.

26. When the player's party meets Vincent in the coffin room at Shinra Manor, they give him information about how Sephiroth became a villain. This compounds Vincent's woes because Sephiroth and his descent into insanity stem from the Jenova Project.

27. Hojo explains that he uploaded his consciousness onto the Worldwide Network before his death in *Final Fantasy VII*. When the network was restored, he hatched a plan to gain control of the Omega Weapon.

28. As highlighted in the previous chapter, the Protomateria would grant Hojo power over Omega once invoked.

29. The function of oracles is examined in more detail in chapter XXI.

30. As a callback to this scene, Weiss repeats the threats during the introduction to the player's battle against him in the Shinra Combat Simulator of *Final Fantasy VII Remake Intergrade*. However, 'hunted' and 'exterminated' have been removed from *Intergrade's* list.

CHAPTER XVIII

ENDGAME KATABASES

Myths involving the underworld, the waterways that traverse its gloomy depths, and its eclectic cast of denizens command an impressive share of Greco-Roman literature. This is hardly surprising given the natural and mysterious role death plays in the lives of all. It is curious to note, however, that while Hellenic and Latin writers were fairly consistent in their depictions of Hades' kingdom, many of the finer details differ across the myriad sources. Scholars are generally satisfied the reason for this is that authors and poets did not claim to have personally visited the nether realms – perhaps through fear of inviting the wrath of its ruler –, so their accounts are deliberately vague in places.

As this book has discussed in previous chapters, though, Hades and his domain do not appear exclusively in tales regarding those who have died. There are several stories in which mortal heroes and demigods enter the underworld and must navigate or negotiate their way out again. This type of journey is called a katabasis (meaning 'go down') and is frequently found in myth cycles or religious texts around the globe.

Examples in classical mythology include Odysseus sailing to the shores of Asphodel to obtain guidance from the dead prophet Tiresias (see chapter VI); Theseus and Pirithous' ill-fated attempt to entice Persephone to be the latter's new wife, only for them to be bound to the Chair of Forgetfulness (see chapter XIV); and Heracles' request to borrow Cerberus during his twelfth and final labour (see chapter XVII).

Katabases are typically considered to be an aspect of the hero's journey, which is itself described as a series of common events present throughout comparative mythological narratives, and a principle popularised by Joseph Campbell in his book *The Hero with a Thousand Faces* (1949). The theme of death and rebirth is a regular part of such legends, either in a literal sense or in the metaphorical reawakening of the character and their newfound wisdom or power. The *Compilation of Final Fantasy VII* repeatedly employs the template of the hero's journey, often with particular focus on the protagonist's descent into a symbolic underworld to overcome a great challenge.

It was believed in antiquity that pathways down to Hades could be reached from certain buried caves. In the works of various writers, these are normally located in or around bodies of water, such as Lake Lerna, which is said to have been in southern Greece and guarded by the serpentine Hydra, or Lake Avernus, situated within a volcanic crater in Italy. Heracles, Theseus, and Orpheus, meanwhile, access the underworld from a cave at Cape Tainaron, the southernmost point of mainland Greece.

The journey to the netherworld was not for any mere mortal, however, with most of the famed heroes of the katabases boasting divine parentage or ancestry[1]. While their motivations and their taken routes differ from tale to tale, many of their experiences do feature similarities. For instance, both Aeneas – a regal survivor of the Trojan War and the main character in Virgil's epic poem, the *Aeneid* – and Orpheus – the celebrated musician and poet after whom the Orphic Hymns are named – encounter Cerberus at the gates to the underworld and trick him into falling asleep[2]. Heracles, of course, seeks out the three-headed hellhound and subdues him with physical strength.

In addition to the shades (spirits) of people and monsters known to have died – such as Odysseus conversing with slain comrades of the Trojan War, or Heracles turning his bow on the Gorgon Medusa – there are also some unique residents of the underworld mentioned in the stories. Aeneas and Orpheus separately happen upon the court of the three judges of Hades, who determine the ultimate destination of each soul[3]. Criminals and oath breakers are condemned by the judges to the primordial pit of Tartarus; righteous and exceptional individuals are admitted to the eternal paradise of Elysium; and everyone else is sent to the ashen meadows of Asphodel.

Almost all katabasis myths provide an account of the hero(es) venturing down from the upper world, following a declining path to the entrance of Hades[4]. The descriptions often include references to infernal rivers such as the Styx, which marks the boundary of the afterlife, or Lethe, whose waters relieve souls of their memories so that they may pass into Asphodel.

Much of the underworld is comprised of bleak subterranean caverns, halls, and passages, and in its lowest realms lies Tartarus, the great abyss deep beneath the earth. It is worth highlighting, however, that the Greco-Roman figures who undertake katabases never find themselves in Tartarus, albeit Aeneas is shown the fates of the wicked[5].

The King of the Dead regularly appears in the katabasis myths, too. He is generally depicted as a stern and unwelcoming god, yet the conditions he sets when granting the heroes their wishes are usually more shrewd than unreasonable. That said, the terms of any arrangement are occasionally credited to his wife, Persephone, depending on the source.

By the 5th century BC, the Hellenes had adopted euphemisms for Hades such as Plouton, the 'Wealthy One', because they were afraid to speak his name aloud[6]. According to the philosopher Plato (in his dialogue *Cratylus*), the wealth in question was the precious minerals and gemstones that could be mined within the earth. It may also have been attributed to Hades' connection (via Persephone) to seasonal change and the revival of vegetation.

Chapter VI of this book explores the parallels between the afterlife of classical mythology and the afterlife of *Final Fantasy VII's* universe, the Lifestream. However, katabases are distinct in that they relate to a mortal hero entering a material domain where the dead reside rather than an associated spiritual plane. This might be represented through *Final Fantasy VII* as the difference between Aerith's essence joining the Lifestream upon her death and Cloud's body falling into the mako rivers when the Northern Crater collapses. As it happens, even better analogies can be found in the original game, *Crisis Core*, and *Dirge of Cerberus*, respectively: All three contain scenarios towards their climax where the hero(es) descend(s) beneath the earth to where the Lifestream is abundant[7].

The importance of life and the impact of death play an enormous role in *Final Fantasy VII*. As such, it is unlikely to be a coincidence that its endgame dungeon requires the protagonists to go deep inside the Planet, nor that they must confront Sephiroth where the world's highest concentration of spirit energy is gathered[8]. Furthermore, there are many similarities between Cloud and the others' journey into the

Great Northern Cave and tales of katabases in Greco-Roman literature.

The cavity itself can be accessed from the basin of what had been the Northern Crater. The violent eruptions and vortexes of Lifestream that were visible at the heart of the crater when the party first scaled Gaea's Cliff earlier in the story are gone at this point, having collapsed during the awakening and release of the gargantuan Weapons[9]. This produces a specific comparison to Aeneas entering the realm of Pluto – as Hades is named in Virgil's *Aeneid* – via the volcanic crater of Avernus. In addition, the lake situated at its centre was historically known to emit toxic fumes, presumably from underground vents, which mirrors mako.

A possible extension to the link with Pluto (Plouton) concerns the deity's aforementioned affiliation with the wealth of the land, including gemstones. Interestingly, four of the five biomechanical goliaths that rise from the Northern Crater are Diamond Weapon, Ruby Weapon, Emerald Weapon, and Sapphire Weapon, whose titles are based on valuable jewels commonly formed deep within the earth[10].

The Northern Cave itself is inhabited by many enemy types, some of which are synonymous with death or the underworld. For instance, dragon zombie is an undead fiend[11], while the flying, one-eyed ahriman (mistakenly called 'allemagne' in the English localisation) is a reference to the most destructive spirit in Zoroastrianism[12], often equated to the Christian Devil.

What is especially intriguing about venturing into the bowels of the Northern Cave is that the Planet's core is presented as a stormy chasm. Ferocious gales of spirit energy sweep around the floating platforms, themselves occupied by huge monsters such as the dragon zombies and iron giants[13]. This could be another allusion to Tartarus, said to be an immense gulf of swirling winds at the lowest levels of Hades, where Zeus imprisons many of the Titans.

The same imagery is used by Benny Matsuyama in the novella *Hoshi o Meguru Otome*[14], in which he describes the abyss below the final battlefield at the centre of the Planet as '*naraku*'. '*Naraku*' literally means 'unfathomable fall' (which is exactly how Tartarus is portrayed in Hesiod's *Theogony*), but it can also be translated as something akin to the 'bottomless pit of Hell' or the 'depths of Hades'.

The Banora Underground that features in *Crisis Core* is perhaps less subtle in its influence. Banora is a coastal village believed to be located on one of the islands south of Fort Condor[15], originally erected by the Shinra Corporation to conceal the abandoned mako mine beneath its rich soil[16]. The mine is rediscovered years later by Genesis, a local youth, and this is where he establishes his base after leading the mass SOLDIER desertion during the Wutai War[17].

The network of caves below Banora is *Crisis Core's* endgame dungeon, to which Genesis lures Zack in a bid to re-enact *LOVELESS* and receive the Gift of the Goddess (as explained in chapter VIII). Zack descends into the caverns from the village's ruins, by now a gorge whose river is sparkling with spirit energy. This can be compared to the underworld entrances near water sources, but Banora's proximity to the coast bears a particular (albeit abstract) likeness to Cape Tainaron, where Heracles, Theseus, and Orpheus journey down to the realm of the dead.

The first area Zack reaches is the sprawling caverns at the Depths of Judgement. Not only are the dark earthen walls and waterways there reflective of Hades' domain in general, but the zone may also symbolise the court of the three judges who determine the destination of every soul. It is additionally worth noting that this is where an unnamed Weapon can be seen behind a massive crystal formation, which mirrors the Northern Crater in creating a potential link to Pluto's wealth. As stated in the footnotes of chapter VIII, the colossus closely resembles the Emerald Weapon – arguably more so in *Crisis Core Reunion* – but the *Crisis Core Complete Guide* does not explicitly identify it as such.

Navigating the Depths of Judgement, Zack soon comes to the Lake of Oblivion, which could be a nod to the memory-sapping river Lethe. Zack can confront five makonoid abominations here: These are G-Caina, G-Antenora, G-Ptolomea, and G-Judecca – all of which are named after parts of the Ninth Circle of Hell in Dante's *Divine Comedy* –, as well as G-Lucifero. The latter is derived from Lucifer, the Devil and ruler of Hell in Christianity.

Caina represents crimes against one's kin; Antenora represents the betrayal of one's city or country; Ptolomea represents neglect of the laws of *xenia* (guest-friendship);

and Judecca represents the betrayal of one's lords and benefactors. For ancient Greeks, being guilty of any of these crimes would have resulted in the condemnation of a person's spirit to Tartarus. Tartarus, of course, is the vast prison of Hades, which itself might be referenced in an optional area of the Banora Underground that can be visited by Zack: the Cage of Binding[18].

As examined in the previous chapter, there are also parallels to be found between the classical underworld and Deepground, the covert military facility beneath Midgar. During *Dirge of Cerberus*, the Tsviets attempt to artificially activate the Omega Weapon by gathering large quantities of untainted spirit energy, thus directly associating the subterranean complex with the Lifestream. Chapter XVII proposes several similarities between Vincent's story and the katabasis of Heracles' twelfth labour, and it is speculated that Deepground's name may be yet another of the *Compilation's* allusions to the primordial depths of Tartarus.

The chapter additionally highlights that Vincent's battle with Arch Azul – the armoured behemoth form of Azul the Cerulean – immediately prior to the gunman passing through Deepground's gates could be a vague analogy to Cerberus guarding the entrance to the netherworld. Intriguingly, this theme is shared by the king behemoths of *Final Fantasy VII* and the Behemoth King of *Crisis Core*[19].

The former are exclusively encountered in a single field shortly after crossing the threshold to the Northern Cave.

This primarily echoes the katabasis of Aeneas, who meets the hellhound when he traverses the crater at Avernus. The Behemoth King, meanwhile, is an optional boss that can be challenged if Zack successfully negotiates the Cage of Binding sub-dungeon. This can be compared to Heracles' final labour, where the demigod engages Cerberus voluntarily and at the *end* of his katabasis. It should also be noted that the Behemoth King's presence prevents direct access from the area to the Portal of Severance, beyond whose gateway the showdown with Genesis takes place, just as Cerberus is posted at Hades' gates to prevent mortals from entering[20].

Of all the katabases in global mythology, among the most renowned is the tragedy of Orpheus[21]. The hero is commonly attested to be the son of Apollo[22], God of Music (and much more), and Calliope, the Muse of Epic Poetry[23]. Given his parentage, it is unsurprising that Orpheus becomes the greatest bard of the ancient world. Famed for his sweet singing and entrancing melodies, he carries his lyre everywhere he goes[24].

The tale of Orpheus in the underworld appears in literary works many centuries older than those of writers such as Virgil and Ovid (for example, in Plato's *Symposium*), but it is the later Roman versions of the legend that are best known. Orpheus eventually falls in love with and weds Eurydice, a beautiful mountain nymph. They live happily together for a time, but Eurydice is bitten by a poisonous snake and dies in her husband's arms.

Devastated by her death, Orpheus vows never to sing or strum his lyre again. Gods and mankind alike mourn the bard's silence, so Apollo descends from Olympus to comfort his son. He suggests that if anything has the power to persuade Hades and Persephone to release a soul from the afterlife, it is Orpheus and his music.

Buoyed by the possibility, Orpheus journeys into the netherworld but is halted by the canine sentinel at its main gate. As Cerberus prepares to tear the intruder limb from limb, Orpheus' song utterly tames him, causing the trio of heads to drift one by one into a gentle slumber. The ferryman of the river Styx, Charon, and the three judges of the underworld are likewise enchanted by his lyre's tunes.

When Orpheus is finally brought before Hades and Persephone in the great hall of their palace, the King of the Dead agrees to allow Eurydice's spirit to return to the upper realm should he be moved by the bard's composition. Hades is successfully charmed by the delightful music and is encouraged by Persephone, but he sets the condition that Orpheus must not look back as he leads Eurydice to freedom, lest she be confined to the gloomy depths forever.

Fearing that his wife will be lost to him again, Orpheus obeys and retraces his steps through the subterranean passages, never glancing over his shoulder. As he emerges at last into sunlight, he is so overjoyed to be reunited with Eurydice that he turns too soon – she has not yet left the shadow of the underworld. Eurydice reaches out to him in despair, but her spectre is instantly dragged back down into the darkness.

Chapters XVI and XVII explore the plethora of references to Greek mythology in *Dirge of Cerberus*, most of which focus on the Labours of Heracles. However, alternative parallels can be drawn to Orpheus and his katabasis, centring around lost love and music.

While Heracles' murder of his wife Megara commonly precipitates his labours and ultimately his own katabasis, she does not feature heavily in the standard myth. By comparison, Eurydice is a key part of Orpheus' tale, which better reflects Lucrecia's role in *Dirge of Cerberus*. The importance of Vincent's relationship with her is immediately established when the game's title is displayed: The opening scene is set at the grotto where Lucrecia remains in crystalised stasis[25].

Unlike Orpheus, Vincent's descent into Deepground is not to restore the woman he loves to the living world, but that is not to say Lucrecia is absent from his motivations. It is the Tsviets' intention to awaken Omega (as orchestrated by Hojo), based on a research thesis by Dr Crescent titled "The Planet's Pulse". Her placement of the Protomateria in Vincent's chest after she inadvertently exposes him to the Chaos gene ties him to the plot in a unique way.

Due to the concentration of Jenova cells in her body, Lucrecia is unable to die, yet neither is she truly alive. Nevertheless, she manifests before Vincent in various forms throughout *Dirge of Cerberus*, such as a holographic recording at Shinra Manor, a hallucination outside the Shinra Building while Shelke performs a Synaptic Net Dive (SND) to quote a passage from "The Planet's Pulse", or a piece of her soul from the Lifestream, which locates the Protomateria in the ethereal rivers and returns it to Vincent when he transforms into Chaos[26]. On each occasion, Lucrecia appears as a spectre, mirroring how Eurydice is presented to Orpheus in the underworld.

The third instance is worthy of special mention because it is visually depicted as Shelke's SND projection combined with a memory fragment of Lucrecia's spirit energy to deliver the Protomateria. As Vincent regains control over Chaos, he looks down to see the ghost of the woman he loves dragged back into Omega by black tendrils. This may be an allusion to Eurydice being snatched away from Orpheus and back into the netherworld when he glances around too soon.

Furthermore, during the ending sequence of the game, the story arc of Vincent and Lucrecia's relationship concludes with him making peace with his past. This is symbolised by the hero leaving the darkness of the grotto and stepping out into brilliant sunlight while Lucrecia sheds a tear inside her crystal. It could be argued that this scene is also closer in detail to Orpheus' katabasis than Heracles'.

Another abstract similarity between Vincent and Orpheus is their respective reactions to the loss of Lucrecia and Eurydice. During *Final Fantasy VII*, Vincent can be found in a coffin in the Shinra Mansion basement, where he has been sleeping for almost 30 years[27]. He believes Lucrecia is dead and has remained in seclusion to atone for his role in her tragic circumstances, only to join the player's party when the opportunity to have his revenge on Hojo arises. This is loosely analogous to Orpheus silencing his music and songs after Eurydice dies, eventually picking up his lyre again when Apollo proposes an opportunity to salvage his happiness by persuading Hades to release her soul.

While the connections to Orpheus' tale could be coincidental in isolation, *Dirge of Cerberus* also has a significant association with music. One aspect of this is that every location in the game is dotted with jukeboxes, albeit they function like vending machines for purchasing items or upgrading weapons and accessories. Nonetheless, their design is based on the jukebox that appears in 7th Heaven in *Final Fantasy VII*[28]. The devices additionally exist around Midgar's Slums and in the employee recreational area of Shinra Headquarters during *Remake*[29].

It should also be highlighted that *Dirge of Cerberus* was the first entry in the *Compilation of Final Fantasy VII* to boast a dedicated vocal theme song. Since the release of "Eyes on Me" as a single in 1999 to accompany *Final Fantasy VIII*[30], most of the series' games have included an iconic track of this nature. As mentioned in the previous chapter, *Dirge of Cerberus'* edition, "Redemption", was produced by Japanese musician Gackt, along with a second track called "Longing".

Perhaps the best evidence to illustrate a link between Vincent's story and Orpheus' katabasis, however, is that *Dirge of Cerberus* has a direct musical reference in its title. A dirge is a mournful song, piece of music, or lamentation for the dead, especially as part of a funerary rite. In the context of the game, this could be understood to mean that the sound of Vincent's triple-barrelled weapon, named Cerberus, epitomises a sorrowful wail over lost loved ones. Such an interpretation is consistent with the theme of Heracles fulfilling his labours as punishment for killing his family and of Orpheus' bid to reclaim Eurydice from Hades.

Alternatively, the 'dirge' of Cerberus may allude to the song the divine bard plays upon his lyre to placate the fearsome hellhound. His taming of the monster grants him access to the underworld, just as Vincent's mastery of his own Cerberus allows him to fight his way into Deepground.

That said, while Orpheus is considered the greatest of all musicians, it is his brother Linus who personifies funerary hymns and lamentations in classical mythology. Linus, as it happens, was a music tutor to young Heracles and the first individual to perish amid one of the demigod's uncontrollable rages.

Intentionally or otherwise, *Dirge of Cerberus'* development team did a marvellous job of tying together several loose threads of ancient Greek lore. The same is true for many elements of the *Compilation* – but not for all in this much detail. The following chapters will address some of the minor or more limited mythical inspirations embedded across the *Final Fantasy VII* saga.

1. Of all the heroes mentioned in this chapter, only Odysseus is not a demigod, although he does claim to be a descendant of Zeus via Hermes. Theseus is a son of Poseidon, Heracles and Pirithous are sons of Zeus, Orpheus is a son of Apollo, and Aeneas is a son of Aphrodite.
2. Aeneas makes Cerberus drowsy with a drugged cake; Orpheus plays a lullaby on his lyre.
3. The names of the judges are Minos, Rhadamanthus, and Aeacus.
4. Odysseus' journey in Homer's *Odyssey* is quite different: There, he sails across the great world river, Oceanus, to reach the underworld.
5. Virgil's description of Tartarus in the *Aeneid* is one of the most extensive in classical literature.
6. 'Plouton' was later Latinised as 'Pluto', after whom the dwarf planet (and Mickey Mouse's dog) is named.
7. The climax of *Advent Children* employs a curious inverse of a katabasis, whereby the undying spirit of Sephiroth is brought into the material world.
8. As referenced in chapter IV, the Planet has been redirecting spirit energy to the Northern Crater for 2,000 years in an attempt to heal the wound left by Jenova's meteorite.
9. See chapter IV for an explanation of the Weapons' emergence.
10. The fifth monster is the Ultimate Weapon, sometimes called the Ultima Weapon, although the line-up in the original Japanese release of *Final Fantasy VII* did not include Emerald or Ruby. Post-game content for *Before Crisis* continued the trend by introducing the Jade Weapon.
11. The dragon zombie's rarest attack, 'Pandora's Box', alludes to the Greek myth of the first woman (Pandora)

opening a forbidden jar and unwittingly releasing all the evils upon mankind. However, this was not the name of the spell in Japanese: It was originally '*Nantaka???*', which means 'Something???'.

12. Zoroastrianism is one of the world's oldest organised religions, originating in ancient Persia.

13. Iron giant is a recurring enemy type in the *Final Fantasy* series, but the English localisation of *Final Fantasy VII* calls him the iron man.

14. The novella is commonly known by its unofficially translated title, *The Maiden Who Travels the Planet*.

15. Neither *Crisis Core* itself nor any accompanying media have confirmed the geographical location of Banora, although the *Crisis Core Ultimania* notes it is in the same region as Mideel.

16. This information can be found in the *Crisis Core Ultimania*.

17. Chapter VIII provides more details on the circumstances of the desertion and Genesis' motivations.

18. It is heavily implied by graffiti in the Cage of Binding that the makonoids Zack fights are former inmates of the prison, presumably victims of experimentation with condensed mako on humans. The final two zones of the Banora Underground dungeon are the Portal of Severance and the Light of Doom.

19. King behemoths are also found in *Before Crisis'* endgame dungeon (the otherworldly realm of the summon Zirconiade), while a Type-0 behemoth can be battled in the underground Shinra laboratory (implied to be part of Deepground) in *Final Fantasy VII Remake*.

20. As it happens, there is a monster called Cerberus that features in *Crisis Core's* SOLDIER missions: a black guard hound akin to Rufus Shinra's pet, Dark Nation (who is identified in *Remake's* English localisation as Darkstar, although the *Ultimanias* reveal his true name is Umbra). The creature is exclusively encountered in one mission during the Great Cavern of Wonders sidequest, titled "A Lonely Journey".

21. This is not to be confused with the Orphic Mysteries, a set of cult rituals and beliefs based on hymns attributed to Orpheus. Further information about these can be found in chapter VIII, as can reference to the death of Orpheus at the hands of Dionysus' followers.
22. Some authors, such as Ovid and Hyginus, claim Orpheus' father was alternatively or additionally King Oeagrus of Thrace. Heroes and demigods often have more than one father in the myths, as elaborated on in chapter XIV.
23. The Muses are nine daughters of Zeus and the Titaness Mnemosyne, said to be the goddesses of inspiration for literature, science, and the arts.
24. A lyre is a small, stringed instrument, similar to a harp. According to legend, Orpheus' golden lyre was a gift from Apollo, who also taught him to play.
25. This follows the prologue of Vincent and Yuffie in Midgar during Meteorfall.
26. Shelke's unique ability as a Tsviet is Synaptic Net Diving. This allows her to access any network, digital or otherwise, using her mind. When the Omega Weapon materialises from the Lifestream, Shelke realises that the interweaving rivers of spirit energy also act as a network of memories and desires. She performs a dive into the Lifestream and engages with a fragment of Lucrecia's soul.
27. The details of this are explained in chapter XVII.
28. '7th Heaven' is how the name of Tifa's bar is presented in the original *Final Fantasy VII* and on the sign of the new establishment in Edge during *Advent Children* and *Dirge of Cerberus*. This was subsequently amended to 'Seventh Heaven' in the official novels and *Remake*.
29. Interestingly, the ability to select and play music tracks on the machines is not new to *Remake*. *Dirge of Cerberus'* online multiplayer mode introduced a similar feature to the jukebox of Deepground's Sector 3 training lobby in 2006.

30. The music for "Eyes on Me" was written by *Final Fantasy's* legendary composer Nobuo Uematsu, while the vocals were performed by famed Chinese singer Faye Wong.

PART SEVEN

Minor Myths
and
Mysteries

CHAPTER XIX

HUNTERS, GODS, KINGS, AND THIEVES

Most of this book has so far examined elements of Greco-Roman mythology that likely inspired some of the larger themes within the *Compilation of Final Fantasy VII* or that have required thorough analysis and discussion. However, there are also a number of tales or figures from classical literature whose influence on the metaseries is perhaps more abstract or restricted to a particular game or trivial area of interest. The following two chapters will address these minor myths, subcategorised for ease, starting with a unique perspective on one of the most iconic adversaries in videogame history.

A NARCISSISTIC VILLAIN

Narcissism can be described as a self-centred personality type. It is generally characterised by person's excessive preoccupation with themselves and their own needs, often at the expense of others. In extreme cases, it is a recognised personality disorder in which an individual may have an unreasonably high sense of self-importance.

It is common in media for villains or antagonists (or even complex protagonists) to display narcissistic traits. This is true for several figures in *Final Fantasy VII*, but none are more pronounced than Sephiroth. Key examples include the renowned SOLDIER's merciless destruction of Nibelheim, slaughtering its townspeople because he believes it is his right as the chosen one, or his summoning of Meteor to attain godhood at the cost of the Planet's wellbeing[1]. The term 'narcissism' itself is derived from the ancient Greek allegory of Narcissus, which, as it happens, shares some surprising similarities with the evolution of Sephiroth's character during *Final Fantasy VII's* development.

Ovid's account of the myth in *Metamorphoses* is arguably the best known version. It begins with the mother of Narcissus, himself the most beautiful young man in the world, taking her son to see the prophet Tiresias[2]. The seer predicts that Narcissus will live a long and happy life on the condition that he never recognises himself, although this makes little sense to them at the time.

Narcissus grows up to be a splendid huntsman, but his bad experiences with individuals of all ages and genders fawning over his unequalled looks cause him to reject love. One day, while relaxing by the side of a stream, the youth is stirred by a nymph named Echo, who has been cursed by Hera and is only able to repeat words spoken to her[3], but he chases her away.

Angered by Narcissus' spurning of Echo and others, Nemesis, the Goddess of Retribution, makes him infatuated with his own reflection in the water. Day after day, he hangs over the banks of the stream, staring longingly at the enchanting face on its mirrored surface. It is Narcissus' fate to die there; some say through exhaustion, others by drowning, yet more by his pining to be loved by the boy in the water. In any case, Tiresias' enigmatic words come true: After 'recognising' his reflection, Narcissus is ended by self-obsession.

A variant of the story was recorded by Pausanias, a Greek traveller and geographer of the 2nd century AD. In this version, Narcissus does not fall in love with himself but with his identical twin sister. When she dies, he frequents a spring so that he can see her face in his own reflection.

Most myths agree that when the young man passes away at the water's edge, his body transforms into the narcissus flower – more commonly known as the daffodil[4]. This is why the heads of daffodils are said to wilt over pools and streams, always gazing upon their exquisite bloom.

To fully appreciate how the tale of Narcissus might connect to Sephiroth in *Final Fantasy VII*, it is important to understand the changes throughout development to his relationship with Aerith. According to the "Early Material File" of the *Ultimania Omega*, one abandoned scenario concerns Aerith's unrequited love for the SOLDIER. In it, Sephiroth would have used to buy a flower from the girl whenever he saw her, sparking her feelings for him[5].

The concept of Aerith's affection not being reciprocated by Sephiroth parallels Narcissus' behaviour towards the romantic advances of others, including his rejection of Echo. Furthermore, the exact focus of their interactions is the sale of flowers, which Narcissus is inherently linked to via the mythical origins of the daffodil[6].

Another unused plot idea from *Final Fantasy VII's* production is that Aerith's mother, Ifalna, was to be captured by the Shinra Company shortly after her daughter is born. As part of Shinra's plan to create humans with abilities comparable to the Cetra's, Ifalna would have been forced to bear several children, one of whom was to be Sephiroth. Having Aerith and Sephiroth be siblings in this scenario may have been an allusion to Pausanias' account of Narcissus and his twin sister.

Chapter VII of the book explores in depth the similarities between Aerith and Persephone, an ancient Greek goddess of fertility and agriculture. In the *Homeric Hymn to Demeter*, it is specified that Persephone is plucking narcissus flowers when Hades rides forth from a cleft in the earth to carry her off to the underworld. Given the proposed association between Sephiroth and Narcissus, this could be loosely analogous to the former claiming Aerith's life at the Forgotten Capital.

Interestingly, there are fleeting moments in *Final Fantasy VII Remake* where Aerith and Sephiroth's connection to the Narcissus myth are seemingly reignited. A primary example is that Cloud hallucinates Sephiroth placing a hand on Aerith's shoulder when he first encounters her on Sector 8's Loveless Street[7]. This immediately precedes Aerith presenting Cloud with a yellow flower, then explaining that it symbolises the reunion of loved ones[8]. Later in the game, Professor Hojo is overheard pondering what it might be like to meet the offspring of Aerith and Sephiroth, his own biological son.

A final point worth highlighting is Tiresias' prophecy regarding whether Narcissus' life would be long and happy. During Cloud's flashback to the Nibelheim tragedy in *Final Fantasy VII*, Sephiroth is initially portrayed as strong and collected, capable of empathy and acknowledging the desires of others. This can be seen when he voluntarily grants Cloud permission to visit his family and friends, having learned that Nibelheim is the young man's hometown[9].

Sephiroth does not begin to exhibit narcissistic behaviour until he studies the archived tomes in the basement library of Shinra Manor. The research papers partially reveal to him the secrets of the Jenova Project and the circumstances of his birth, leading him to believe he is a descendant of the Cetra[10]. In this way, it could be contended that Sephiroth discovering certain truths of his identity is the catalyst for his death[11], just as Narcissus 'recognising' himself (in his reflection) is what ultimately results in *his* demise.

THE GIANT AND THE SCORPION

Ancient Greek mythology boasts an impressive roster of famous hunters and huntresses, both gods and mortals alike. There are many tales of individuals known for their lethal accuracy with a bow and arrow, ranging from the stalking and felling of wild beasts to their triumphs in marksmanship competitions. The divine twins Artemis and Apollo are two examples, as are the heroes Heracles and Atalanta[12].

Sharing the list with such legendary archers is Orion. While some sources depict Orion as an immensely tall and very handsome man, most refer to him as a Giant. Details of his story are recounted by a plethora of celebrated writers, including Homer, Hesiod, Virgil, Ovid, Hyginus, and Apollodorus, often with key differences.

Following the death of his wife, Side, Orion travels to the island of Chios, where he courts the princess. The king of Chios, however, blinds him and exiles him from his new home. Orion is informed by an oracle that he can recover his sight if he journeys to where Helios (the Sun) rises in the east and exposes his eyes to the solar deity's glorious rays. His guide is the god Hephaestus' servant, Cedalion, whom the Giant carries on his shoulders.

With his vision restored, Orion retires to Crete, eventually gaining the companionship of Artemis, a goddess affiliated with hunting, nature, wild animals, vegetation, and more[13]. Orion and Artemis share many great chases, with the Giant proving himself an exemplary bowman. It is on one of these outings that Orion openly brags he could track and kill anything born from the earth.

Gaia herself is deeply offended by the brash claim and takes Orion's words as a threat, for she considers all such creatures to be her children. In response, she sends an enormous scorpion to annihilate him. According to the common version of the myth, as recorded in Hesiod's *Astronomia* fragments or Hyginus' *Astronomica*[14], the scorpion is successful in fatally wounding Orion with its poisonous stinger. In an alternative account from Ovid's *Fasti*, Orion defends Artemis from the monster[15]. Admiring the courage of the hunter and Gaia's arachnid champion, Zeus raises them both into the heavens as the constellations Orion and Scorpio[16].

There is a curious comparison to be made between this tale and the character of Barret Wallace. Like some descriptions of Orion, Barret is an extremely tall, muscular figure and a hot-headed marksman, although the archaic bow and arrow are replaced by a variety of guns that can be attached to a prosthetic adaptor on his arm[17].

Arguably the least subtle analogy relates to the opening bombing mission of *Final Fantasy VII*, in which Cloud and Barret are confronted by the Guard Scorpion – called the Scorpion Sentinel in *Remake* – when they initially set the explosive to destroy Mako Reactor 1. Their activity triggers an alarm, causing the autonomous warden of Shinra's facility to respond to the threat and engage the intruders, thus initiating the game's first boss battle.

As its name suggests, the robotic sentry is a huge, mechanised scorpion that primarily attacks with its stinger in *Final Fantasy VII*, using 'Scorpion Tail' and 'Tail Laser'[18]. In this way, direct links can be drawn to Gaia summoning the giant arachnid to eliminate Orion because she perceives him to be dangerous, as well as the particular appendage with which the creature delivers its killing blow.

Interestingly, the circumstances of the Guard Scorpion's deployment at Mako Reactor 1 seem to invert the myth: Where Orion asserts that he is capable of slaying all the 'children' of Gaia, Barret's act of eco-terrorism is intended to protect the Planet (Gaia) from the Shinra Corporation consuming its spirit energy for profit. As the leader of an Avalanche cell, Barret is heavily invested in the Study of Planetary Life (called planetology in *Remake*) and the environmental wellbeing of the world. This may additionally reflect Orion's relationship with Artemis, herself devoted to nature and its flora and fauna.

While the parallels are more abstract, there are also several aspects of Barret's overall character that might allude to the broader story of Orion. For example, Barret loses his wife Myrna when Corel is burned to the ground, just as Orion's wife Side is cast into the underworld by Hera. Both giants sustain physical disabilities: Barret is expelled by Corel's survivors and requires his right arm to be amputated after he suffers a bullet wound[19]; Orion, meanwhile, is blinded by the king of Chios and exiled from the island.

A possible nod to Hephaestus' subsequent role in the huntsman's journey to restore his eyesight can also be found in *Final Fantasy VII*: The Heavy Vulcan weapon for Barret is exclusively available at Cosmo Canyon, which is itself the birthplace of Avalanche and somewhere visitors can learn about astronomy from Bugenhagen. Vulcan is the Roman cognate of Hephaestus, while the stargazing element vaguely connects to Orion as a constellation[20].

Orion is said in multiple sources to carry Cedalion, Hephaestus' young servant, on his shoulders as he travels to the east to be cured of his blindness by Helios. Intriguingly, this may have been the inspiration behind Barret's rendered character artwork for *Final Fantasy VII* and *Remake*[21], as well as one of his aesthetic changes for the latter.

The art itself depicts Barret's daughter, Marlene, perched on his shoulder – a stance that is unique to the pair – while they visit the Sector 5 Slums church. The same distinct manner of Barret holding the girl is shown, for instance, in

Final Fantasy VII at 7th Heaven when he activates the pinball machine to unveil a hidden basement, or in *Remake* when he says goodbye to Marlene at Elmyra's house.

Barret's updated design in *Remake* (produced by Tetsuya Nomura and Roberto Ferrari) includes sunglasses, which have been present since the initial gameplay reveal trailer in 2015. While there is no explicit association between Barret and blindness, the shades might symbolise him overcoming his disability and beginning a new life – the direct inverse of Orion exposing his eyes to the Sun[22].

THE ROD OF HEALING

The divinity most often affiliated with healing in classical mythology is perhaps Apollo, who could both eradicate disease and call forth plagues. Healing comes in many forms, however, which the Hellenes recognised and as can be observed in their delegation of different curative aspects to a selection of deities. Among them was Asclepius, a son of Apollo and Princess Coronis of Phlegyantis, whose specific area of expertise was medicine, veterinary, and surgery.

In Apollodorus' *Bibliotheca*, Coronis dies while Asclepius is still in the womb, but the infant is saved by his father and placed in the care of the wise centaur Chiron[23]. Asclepius is a natural and gifted healer, learning from Chiron important subjects such as anatomy or the gathering, grinding, and mixing of medicinal plants.

During his youth, Asclepius eases the suffering of a snake and is rewarded for it by the goddess Athena – to whom serpents are sacred – with a jar of Gorgon's blood, a substance that can bring the dead back to life. He eventually becomes the first physician of antiquity, embracing the image of a snake entwining a wooden rod as an emblem for his practices.

Asclepius decides to test the properties of the Gorgon's blood by reviving the corpse of a deceased patient. The temptation to conquer death grows stronger with each person he resurrects, but it incites the fury of Hades. The Lord of the Underworld implores Zeus to put an end to such blatant disregard of the natural order, so the Skyfather strikes his grandson down with a thunderbolt. In later variants of the myth, Zeus raises Asclepius to Olympus as a god.

The divine healer has influenced the *Final Fantasy* series since its inaugural title in 1987, although this is likely to have been neither obvious nor prominent for most players. White Mage and White Wizard are job classes that specialise in curative and protective spells, available to certain heroes (such as Minwu of *Final Fantasy II* and Rosa of *Final Fantasy IV*) or to all characters, depending on the game. One constant from the original *Final Fantasy* through to *Final Fantasy V* is that the weapons equipped by White Mages are rods and staves, thus maintaining the reference to Asclepius and his staff.

Final Fantasy VII does not employ a traditional job system because its alternative materia system is what allows for character customisation in battle[24]. Nevertheless, the fighting styles, equipment, and Limit Break techniques associated with each member of the playable cast generally fall into an identifiable job class. Aerith Gainsborough, for example, uses rods and staffs as weapons, while most of her Limit Breaks are curative or defensive in nature[25]. This establishes her as something akin to a White Mage and connects her function as a healer to Asclepius[26].

There are also several parallels to be found between the respective lives of Aerith and Asclepius. For instance, Asclepius is a demigod born of the Olympian Apollo and the mortal princess Coronis; Aerith is a hybrid child born of the Cetra Ifalna and the human Gast. The Cetra are a race capable of mystic feats, meaning Aerith's genealogy continues a trend from the preceding *Final Fantasy* titles: main protagonists who are the offspring of humans and supernatural or otherworldly beings[27].

Another similarity is that both Asclepius and Aerith are raised by an independent guardian following the death of their mother. Apollo rescues his son from Coronis' womb and leaves him with Chiron, while Elmyra adopts Aerith after she discovers Ifalna drawing her last breaths at the Sector 5 Slums train station[28].

Furthermore, Asclepius' propensity for healing and his interest in flora and fauna excels under the tutelage of Chiron. This is also represented in Aerith's childhood, for

396

her inherent talents as a Cetra are augmented by an upbringing surrounded by flowers[29]. In addition, the official novel *Traces of Two Pasts* confirms that the young girl paints a diverse range of flowers and creatures on her bedroom wall at Shinra Headquarters (as seen in *Remake*), then later spends hours at a time staring at trivia cards of plants and animals at Elmyra's house. The precise implication of the latter is that Aerith becomes knowledgeable about them, just as Asclepius does.

In the end, Zeus kills Asclepius for his reckless use of Gorgon's blood to save countless individuals from death. Although Aerith's actions significantly differ from this, the purpose of her invoking the ultimate protective magic, Holy, is to save the lives of everyone on the Planet from the threat of Meteor. Sephiroth's murder of the flower girl is in direct response to her endeavours.

Aerith's role in *Final Fantasy VII's* story after her demise is also analogous to the posthumous deification of Asclepius as a god of healing. She retains her consciousness in the afterlife and actively utilises her Cetran abilities to co-ordinate the Lifestream's defence of the Planet as Meteor approaches, then works to relieve the anger and spite of souls entering the Lifestream so that they can find eternal peace within the rivers of spirit energy[30]. A material extension of this is shown in *Advent Children* when Aerith produces healing rain and a spring that cures Geostigma, the plague that has afflicted much of the population since Meteorfall.

Final Fantasy VII Remake seems to reintroduce the comparison between Aerith and Asclepius on a more modest level. It is revealed that the girl mysteriously sources medicinal herbs for a doctor in Sector 5's Centre District so that he can treat his patients at the clinic near her home. After the collapse of the Sector 7 Plate, the doctor wants to aid survivors, so he asks Cloud to locate extra herbs and a mortar for crushing them. The flowers in question are discovered growing in the Sector 5 church. As such, this sidequest unambiguously links Aerith's instinct to heal people with the myth of Asclepius being a physician whose speciality is the gathering and grinding of medicinal plants.

CHARM OF THE MOON

Alongside the intrigue of Aerith's childhood, Kazushige Nojima's novel *Traces of Two Pasts* shines a light on the formative years of Tifa Lockhart, but it does so in the context of *Final Fantasy VII Remake's* continuity. The majority of details have been embellished rather than altered from previous instalments in the *Compilation*, and one in particular may be the key to joining the dots on the lore behind a certain accessory in *Remake*. The curious new detail is the name of Tifa's mother: Thea.

In ancient Greek mythology, Thea (also spelled Theia and known to the Romans as Dione) is one of the twelve Titans born of Gaia and Uranus. She is a deity of sight and brightness who is scarcely referenced in literature, yet she is mentioned as early as Hesiod's *Theogony*. Thea is arguably best recognised as the mother of Helios (Sun), Selene (Moon), and Eos (Dawn) by her brother-husband Hyperion. Selene and Eos are both feminine figures, but only the former has significant parallels to Tifa.

Selene, whom the Romans called Luna[31], features to varying degrees in a number of tales. As the personification of the Moon, she is described as a beautiful goddess whose radiance lights the heavens in the hours of darkness. She is attested in several sources to ride her winged steeds or steer a horse-drawn chariot across the night sky, and is often depicted in classical artwork as a woman riding side-saddle. Meanwhile, Nonnus' *Dionysiaca* closely associates her with cattle.

One of the most famous myths concerning Selene is her romance with Endymion, who is either said to be a shepherd prince or an astronomer[32]. According to Apollonius of Rhodes, Selene is so enchanted by the youth's looks that she asks Zeus to grant Endymion immortality and keep him in perpetual sleep, so he will never leave her[33]. The cave in which he slumbers is where Selene journeys each new moon – the sole night of the lunar month when her chariot is not seen in the sky – to consort with him.

During chapter 3 of *Final Fantasy VII Remake*, if the player completes all available sidequests, they will unlock an optional scene between Cloud and Tifa in the latter's apartment at Stargazer Heights, titled "Alone at Last". Doing so influences the game's affection mechanics and increases the probability of Tifa being the character to meet Cloud in the flower garden at the beginning of chapter 14[34]. Afterwards, the blond hero is rewarded with the Crescent Moon Charm, an earring defined as being imbued with the fervent desire to be by one's side for eternity.

Final Fantasy VII develops Cloud's complex relationship with Tifa over the course of the game. The young woman expresses her wish to stay near her childhood friend more than once and they share an intimate evening together under the *Highwind* airship before the climactic battle with Sephiroth. This is supplemented by inner monologues in *On the Way to a Smile* and *Traces of Two Pasts*, in which Tifa's love for Cloud is addressed.

It is therefore interesting that her so-called "fervent desire" is symbolised in *Remake* by a moon: This suggests a reflection of the myth regarding Selene and Endymion, whose unending sleep allows them to be together forever. Endymion's occupation as an astronomer may have contributed to the naming of Stargazer Heights, where both Cloud's and Tifa's apartments are located. However, this should not be confused with the inspiration behind Seventh Heaven (Tifa's bar) or 'Final Heaven' (Tifa's ultimate Limit Break in *Final Fantasy VII*), which more likely derive from Judeo-Christian writings.

The circumstances might seem too coincidental in isolation, but a matching Crescent Moon Charm is worn by Tifa as part of her refined indigo dress ensemble during *Remake's* Wall Market sequence[35]. This is first revealed when Cloud spots her in a chocobo-drawn carriage as the evening's events unfold. Given that the giant yellow birds are generally a replacement for horses or beasts of burden in the *Final Fantasy* series, this could be an allusion to Selene traversing the night sky in a chariot pulled by horses or cows.

The observation is further supported by Tifa's identification with another outfit. When Sephiroth and the Shinra investigation team visit Nibelheim, the girl is shown to be clothed in a tawny vest and miniskirt, complemented by a wide-brimmed hat and boots[36]. It is reminiscent of attire traditionally worn by cattle herders in North America (commonly called cowboys or cowgirls), which is heavily implied in *Traces of Two Pasts* when Tifa explicitly muses that the fashion is something an energetic chocobo rancher might wear. Not only does this hint at Nonnus' portrayal of Selene, but it also creates a vague link to one of the few canonically named chocobos in the *Compilation*: Hyperion, the black-feathered animal mentioned in *Crisis Core*, who shares a name with the moon goddess' father[37].

TRAGIC ORIGINS

Although fragments of King Oedipus's story can be found in the works of Homer, Hesiod, and later Latin authors, the most popular version comes from a trilogy of Greek tragedies (theatrical dramas) by the 5th century BC playwright Sophocles: *Oedipus Rex, Oedipus at Colonus,* and *Antigone*. The following myth is recounted in *Oedipus Rex*.

Oedipus is the son of King Laius and Queen Jocasta of Thebes. Before he is born, a prophecy is made by the oracle of Delphi that he will kill his father[38], so Laius arranges for the infant to be taken away and left on a hillside. As fate would have it, Oedipus is discovered by a farmer and eventually adopted by King Polybus and Queen Merope of Corinth. He is thereafter raised to be an intelligent and honourable young man.

Despite his parents concealing it from him, Oedipus comes to learn that he may not be a true prince of Corinth, so he consults the Delphic oracle. The priestess reaffirms that he will kill his father but adds he will also consort with his mother. Oedipus is so disgusted that he does not return to Corinth, determined to protect Polybus and Merope. Instead, he travels from town to town until he is confronted one day by a wealthy man and his guards. Defending himself and burying their corpses, Oedipus sets off in the direction of Thebes.

On a mountain pass overlooking the historic city-state, the prince encounters the Sphinx, a terrible creature with the head of a woman, the body of a lion, and the wings of a bird[39]. The Sphinx poses Oedipus a riddle, which he duly solves, causing her to throw herself off the mountainside in despair.

When he reaches Thebes, word of the monster's demise has spread. Oedipus is welcomed into the royal palace, where he finds Queen Jocasta mourning her late husband. The pair grow close over time and fall in love, marrying in due course, with the newly crowned King Oedipus adored by his subjects.

After several years, it is revealed to Oedipus and Jocasta that he is the baby who was abandoned on a hillside and the wealthy man he slew en route to Thebes was none other than King Laius. As such, the oracle's prophecy has been fulfilled. Horrified by the truth, Jocasta hangs herself. Oedipus' torment over his unintentional sins compels him to blind his own eyes as punishment and enter self-imposed exile[40].

To understand how the tragedy of Oedipus relates to the *Compilation of Final Fantasy VII*, it is best to begin with the Sphinx, whose appearances in Hellenic lore are almost exclusive to this legend. Sophocles describes the Sphinx in *Oedipus Rex* as female, with a canine body and avian wings but also a serpent's tail. Other classical sources attest it has a leonine body, while in ancient Egyptian tradition, sphinxes are predominantly male and benevolent in nature.

During *Crisis Core*, it is divulged that Angeal Hewley, Zack's SOLDIER mentor, was a child produced by the Jenova Project. Along with Genesis, he was born from a particular branch of experimentation called Project Gillian (or Project Jenova G). An important aspect of the game's plot is that both men develop the ability to copy their genetic traits onto others, although Angeal is also uniquely capable of absorbing creature attributes[41].

Before his final showdown with Zack at Modeoheim, Angeal struggles to endure the anguish over what he is. He elects to prove he is a monster to his young successor by biologically fusing with four fiends – a griffon, sahagin, ahriman, and guard hound – to become Angeal Penance. The aesthetics of this abomination include a clawed quadruped body, a single wing[42], and a trio of whiplike tails, with Angeal's human torso and head sprouting from its neck. As such, Penance bears a striking resemblance to the Sphinx in Sophocles' renowned adaptation of the myth.

Angeal's past and motivation for the metamorphosis also share interesting parallels with the origins of Oedipus. It is verified in the *Crisis Core Ultimania* that Angeal's mother, Gillian (after whom the branch of research is named), flees the Shinra Company with her infant son when he is deemed a failure of the Jenova Project[43]. They are subsequently caught and placed under surveillance at Banora, separate from Angeal's biological father, Professor Hollander, who is the lead scientist on Project Gillian. This is analogous to the baby Oedipus being discarded by King Laius of Thebes and carried off to Corinth.

Ashamed of her role in the Jenova Project, Gillian decides to keep the secret of Angeal's birth from both her son and her new husband, whom the boy believes is his natural parent. Angeal's unnamed stepfather is a sickly man, but when his adoptive son enlists to join SOLDIER, he borrows a lot of money to have the Buster Sword custom made for him. He works very hard to repay the debt and eventually dies of fatigue.

There are a few similarities to Oedipus' youth presented here. For instance, Angeal grows up in Banora under the impression he is related to his stepfather by blood, just as Oedipus is raised in Corinth by Polybus and Merope under the pretence they are his biological parents[44]. The circumstances of the boys' respective births are also hidden from them. An intriguing contrast between the pair, however, is that Angeal leaving home indirectly results in the death of his stepfather, while Oedipus leaving home results in him inadvertently killing his real father.

During the events of *Crisis Core*, Angeal learns from Genesis that he is a product of the Jenova Project and abandons SOLDIER. Gillian was a key scientist involved in those experiments, so Genesis asks her to help cure his degradation[45], but she refuses, instead committing suicide over her shame. Angeal and Gillian's actions here can be compared to Oedipus banishing himself from Thebes when the truth of his past is revealed, just as shame drives his mother Jocasta to take her own life.

However, when Hollander discloses to Angeal that he is his birth father, the SOLDIER's crisis of self reaches breaking point. This, too, echoes Oedipus' reaction when he realises he is responsible for slaying King Laius and therefore fulfilling the oracle's prophecy. Like the tragic Greek hero, Angeal perceives his own existence to be the source of his suffering and seeks to punish himself. It could be argued that this is the meaning of the name Penance[46]. Furthermore, Angeal's eyes remain shut for the duration of the battle, which may be an allusion to Oedipus blinding himself to expiate his sins.

A peculiar aspect of Angeal's transformation into a sphinx is that Penance's gender is seemingly male, thus more closely reflecting the Egyptian variants. The inherent benevolence of these creatures might be mirrored in Angeal's personal heroism and honour; even forcing Zack into the fatal duel is because he has judged himself to be a monster that should be exterminated.

There are also a couple of additional observations worth mentioning with regards to the setting of this scenario. The fight itself occurs at the hot springs bathhouse in Modeoheim, a coastal town accessed by Zack via a remote mountain pass. Bathhouses were commonplace in antiquity, and while they were not typically associated with Poseidon, certain myths do describe the Olympian forming springs with his trident. This could explain why Penance uses a trident – the symbol of the God of the Seas – as a weapon[47]. The Modeo Bathhouse being situated at the foot of a mountain ridge may also link to the tale of Oedipus and the Sphinx, which inhabited the pass that led to Thebes.

A LYRE AND A THIEF

Among the gods and immortals of Olympus, few can claim to be as fascinating as Hermes. The divine messenger is generally portrayed as the youngest of the Olympians[48], swift of foot and sharp of mind, yet his origins can be traced back to the pre-Hellenic era. He features in both the *Iliad* and the *Odyssey*, but it is the *Homeric Hymn (4) to Hermes* that first provided a substantial outline of his function in the pantheon[49].

Hermes (whom the Romans called Mercury) is the son of Zeus and the nymph Maia. Even by the Olympians' standards, he is a remarkable baby. Within hours of his birth, Hermes escapes his crib and wanders from Maia's cave, then craftily steals a herd of Apollo's oxen. From their dried intestines and the shell of a tortoise, the infant creates the lyre – an instrument later perfected by Orpheus[50] – and thus invents music. He gifts the lyre to Apollo as compensation for the theft, earning himself the adoration of the gods.

Despite his youthful appearance, Hermes is intelligent, cunning, charming, and cruel in equal measure, with a penchant for mischief. He is also lightning quick, made even faster by a pair of golden sandals (sometimes said to be winged) that are designed for him by Hephaestus[51]. These allow Hermes to zip across land, air, and sea as rapidly as the wind.

In recognition of Hermes' speed, wit, and eloquence, Zeus appoints him as his herald and bestows upon him the power to cross the boundary of life and death – to freely traverse the roads between the upper world and the underworld. The latter is crucial to facilitate Hermes performing one of his most important jobs: As psychopomp-in-chief, he personally guides the souls of priests, nobles, and extraordinary warriors to the afterlife.

By the Classical period, the messenger god was depicted as a promoter of travel and trade as well as roguishness. He became the patron of skilled thieves and conmen, of nomads and hospitality, of merchants and commerce, of shepherds and athletes, and much more. According to writers such as Hyginus and Diodorus Siculus, Hermes devises the art of fighting, and he is dependable in combat, as attested in Apollodorus' account of the Gigantomachy[52].

Contrary to his role as a trickster deity, Hermes is no stranger to helping those with whom he has a connection. He lends his divine sandals to his half-brother Perseus amid the hero's quest to slay Medusa (see chapter XIII); he chaperones another half-brother, Heracles, through the underworld during the strongman's twelfth labour (see chapter XVII); and he assists his descendant Odysseus in the Ithacan king's ten-year voyage home from Troy (a myth that will be explored in *Final Fantasy VII and the Trojan War*).

In the *Compilation of Final Fantasy VII*, no figure comes close to embodying as many of Hermes' traits as Yuffie

Kisaragi. This teenage ninja and self-styled materia hunter is devious and fleet-footed, capable of jaw-dropping heroics and the occasional betrayal to serve her own desires. Accompanying their shared characteristics, however, are several parallels to Hermes that may be found in Yuffie's personal adventures.

During *Final Fantasy VII*, the girl can be recruited to the player's party by first defeating her in a random battle, then selecting a particular sequence of dialogue options. If the wrong response is chosen, Yuffie will rob the group of gil (money) and run off, and the process must begin anew. In this scene alone, Yuffie's youthfulness, thievery, cocky attitude, and trickster behaviour are established, all of which are reminiscent of Hermes. Similarly, when she does join the company, she is a formidable ally[53].

The so-called 'Mystery Ninja' is encountered in forested areas around the overworld map (even as remote as Goblin Island or Round Island), indicating she has the fortitude for long-distance or intercontinental journeys. This is also the case in *Crisis Core*: Zack undertakes missions set by Yuffie (as a child) to locate treasure in a range of environments across the Planet, only for her to show up, too[54]. As such, Hermes' affiliation with travel is reflected in the girl.

Yuffie is an optional party member in *Final Fantasy VII*, so she enjoys less character development than most of the others. There is, however, a scenario dedicated to her at Wutai, should the player visit the town after enlisting the ninja. This subplot includes Yuffie stealing all her companions' materia, as well as luring them into a cage and trapping them there. Once again, Hermes' attributes as a talented thief and con artist can be seen throughout.

There are also a number of subtler allusions to the Olympian at various points in *Final Fantasy VII*. Yuffie's pace and acrobatics as a ninja are repeatedly displayed, while her default Limit Break is 'Greased Lightning', a term used to describe something that is very quick. When the group initially docks at Costa del Sol and pauses for a rest, the teen fills her time by working at a market stall, therefore incorporating the merchant element. Furthermore, amid the Sapphire Weapon's attack on Junon, Yuffie poses as a news reporter during a live television broadcast, which may be analogous to Hermes as a herald[55].

Dirge of Cerberus reintroduces the girl's speed, stealth, athleticism, and trickery in a cutscene where she rescues Vincent from Rosso the Crimson at Shinra Manor. Given Nibelheim's multi-layered ties to the underworld of Norse cosmology – as summarised in chapter VI –, it could be contended that Hermes' ability to pass back and forth between the land of the living and kingdom of the dead is also captured here. In a similar vein, Yuffie supporting Vincent in Deepground towards the end of the game might mirror Hermes escorting Heracles into Hades' realm, as discussed in chapter XVII.

However, the entry in the wider saga that draws the most concentrated comparisons is *Episode INTERmission*, an expansion to *Final Fantasy VII Remake* in which Yuffie is the lead protagonist. Presented as an elite special forces operative of the Wutai Government, the young ninja arrives in Midgar's undercity with the assignment of stealing the rumoured ultimate materia from Shinra Headquarters. She must first rendezvous with members of Avalanche HQ and another Wutaian agent, Sonon Kusakabe[56].

Yuffie and Sonon descend to a shipping facility beneath the Slums to assist an Avalanche contact from Shinra troopers, and he delivers them fake IDs. The pair use these to infiltrate the laboratories in the basement levels of the Shinra Building, but their movements are monitored by Director Scarlet of the Advanced Weaponry Division. Unable to stop Yuffie and Sonon herself, Scarlet activates a distress signal to summon Deepground SOLDIERs and Nero the Sable. During a haunting confrontation, Nero is overcome by the Wutaians, but he foils their attempted escape by killing Sonon and pulling him into his darkness[57].

The premise of *INTERmission's* scenario yet again portrays Yuffie as a thief — she quite literally has Steal Materia equipped at the start of the episode[58] — but also as an emissary to Avalanche HQ. In this capacity, she is specifically acting as an elite operative on behalf of her nation's ruling authority. Hermes, meanwhile, is both a master thief and a senior envoy who conveys or carries out the bidding of Zeus and his fellow Olympians, the ruling powers of the cosmos. It should additionally be noted that, besides his golden sandals, two of the god's most distinctive features in art are his traveller's hat and short cloak; these are individually reflected in Yuffie's moogle cap and poncho[59].

INTERmission includes another possible reference to Hermes that is unique to the expansion. Throughout *Final Fantasy VII*, there are six newsletters that can be read by the player which advertise the Turtle's Paradise, a bar in Wutai. There is also an online materia shop in *Crisis Core* that Zack can access via his portable terminal called the Happy Turtle. The latter name appears again in *INTERmission*, this time identifying a chain of bars with establishments in both Wutai and Midgar.

There is a sidequest available to Yuffie while she is in the Sector 7 Slums during which she can track down six promotional posters for the Happy Turtle. Each flyer is accompanied by a nearby gramophone playing a different jingle and should be returned to Old Snapper, a singing and dancing Wutaian native who is an ambassador for the Midgar bar. As it happens, Old Snapper is wearing a giant turtle shell.

The *Homeric Hymn (4) to Hermes* is unambiguous in that the infant deity is responsible for inventing music when he crafts the first lyre from the shell of a tortoise. In zoological terms, all tortoise species are land-dwelling turtles, which determines a direct link between the animals and the mythical origin of melodies. This may explain why the Happy Turtle sidequest in *INTERmission* is so heavily tied to music[60].

Like *Dirge of Cerberus, Episode INTERmission's* plot has Yuffie visit locations that are metaphorical underworlds. The two chapters of the expansion are almost exclusively set in the Sector 7 Slums, situated in the shadow of Midgar's Plate; the shipping factory and pillar maintenance complex, situated below the undercity; and the Advanced Weaponry research facility, situated in the basement levels of Shinra Headquarters. Yuffie and Sonon are able to travel between these areas using a passenger train, industrial equipment, and internal elevators, respectively, which is loosely analogous to Hermes' freedom to journey between the boundaries of the upper and lower realms.

The foremost psychopomp of classical lore is not explicitly mentioned in *INTERmission*, but this element of his character is alluded to time and again by way of comparative mythology. During chapter 1 of the DLC, the player can acquire the Chthonian Armlet, a piece of armour that is most effective when combined with either the Gozu drive or Mezu drive accessories[61]. In some Far Eastern traditions, the gates of the netherworld are said to be guarded by two demons: Ox-Head and Horse-Face. These figures are either described as the first beings encountered by a soul when it reaches the land of the dead – akin to Cerberus in the Greek myths – or the duo that escorts new spirits to the afterlife. In Japanese, Ox-Head and Horse-Face are known as Gozu and Mezu. The data drives named after the demons are both obtained from monsters in subterranean passages, while 'chthonian' is an adjective used to denote something that relates to the underworld.

413

Similarly, Yuffie can find and wield the Steel Reaper shuriken from the storage depot beneath Sector 7. It is reported to be exceptionally deadly and crafted from three scythe blades. 'Reaper' is a shortened moniker for the Grim Reaper, a fictional entity that has personified death in Western literature and pop culture since the mid-1800s. Himself a psychopomp, the Grim Reaper is typically depicted as a robed skeleton brandishing a scythe.

While navigating the Shinra research facility, Yuffie and Sonon pass a production line of aerial weapons based on the Heli Gunner of *Final Fantasy VII*. The largest of them can be observed in a maintenance hangar. This is the Valkyrie, an autonomous machine fought by Cloud, Barret, and Tifa above the ruins of Sector 7 during *Remake*. According to Old Norse beliefs, Valkyries are divine shieldmaidens who choose which warriors will be slain in battle and then carry their spirits to the heavenly domains of either Odin (at Valhalla) or the goddess Freyja (at Fólkvang). As such, Valkyries are the primary psychopomps of Viking lore[62].

A significantly more subtle continuation of this theme is found in Sonon's flashbacks to the death of his little sister Melphie. The girl is repeatedly shown with a pinwheel accessory in her hair, which is a likely nod to Yuffie's Pinwheel shuriken in *Final Fantasy VII*. The curious thing about the inclusion of the hairpiece here is that, in Japan, pinwheels symbolise the cycle of life: to become young again. They are often placed at children's graves with statues of Jizō, a Buddhist deity who is closely associated with the protection of travellers and lost souls[63]. This, too, resembles Hermes' characteristics and his role in the Olympic pantheon.

A final point to raise concerning the comparisons between Yuffie's story in *INTERmission* and Hermes the psychopomp relates to the expansion's climax. Despite her age, Yuffie is ranked more senior than Sonon as a ninja, meaning she is responsible for leading the pair into the depths of the Shinra Building. It is here that Sonon meets his end at the hands of Nero the Sable – who in chapter XVII is equated to Thanatos, the God of Death – and has his essence dragged into the Tsviet's darkness. It could therefore be contended that Yuffie herself has played the part of psychopomp in *INTERmission* by escorting her Wutaian companion to the metaphorical underworld, from which his spirit will never escape.

1. Sephiroth's goal in *Final Fantasy VII* is to absorb the Lifestream and acquire its boundless energy and knowledge, thus becoming godlike. He means to do so by smashing Meteor into the Planet, then positioning himself at the centre of the impact zone, where an immeasurable magnitude of spirit energy will be redirected to heal the wound.

2. Tiresias is a blind prophet of Apollo who lives in the city-state of Thebes. He features in several myths to varying degrees, including after his death, when Odysseus sails to the underworld to seek his advice.

3. Echo is a talkative nymph who deliberately misleads Hera with respect to Zeus' infidelity. As punishment, the Queen of Heaven turns her mute, capable only of

repeating the last thing said to her. This may be a possible inspiration behind the Echo Screen item in the *Final Fantasy* series (also known as Echo Herbs or Echo Mist among other things), which typically cures the Silence status effect.

4. As is highlighted in chapter VII, Narcissus is one of several young men in classical mythology who metamorphose into flowers at death. Hyacinthus, Crocus, and Adonis are other examples of this.

5. A remanent of this subplot still exists in how Aerith describes her history with Zack during *Final Fantasy VII*.

6. It should be acknowledged that daffodils themselves do not feature in any meaningful way in the *Compilation of Final Fantasy VII*. However, they can be seen in Aerith's flower basket during the PlayStation 3 technical demo showcased in 2005.

7. The thoroughfare is alternatively known as LOVELESS Avenue in *Crisis Core*.

8. In the English localisation of *Remake*, Aerith explicitly states the flowers symbolise lovers being reunited. However, this is not quite reflected in the Japanese script, which refers to loved ones in a broader sense (such as friends and family).

9. Sephiroth's personality is explored in more detail during *Crisis Core*, not to mention the relationship he has with his closest friends, Genesis and Angeal. This will be discussed in *Final Fantasy VII and the Trojan War*.

10. What Sephiroth learns from the basement library is incomplete because the archives predate Jenova's reclassification from a Cetra to an extraterrestrial lifeform.

11. Cloud pursues Sephiroth to the Mount Nibel Mako Reactor and kills him.

12. Atalanta is a skilled huntress renowned for bringing down the Caledonian Boar and accompanying Jason on his voyage as one of the Argonauts.

13. Some writers claim Orion becomes romantically involved with Artemis, although most are satisfied she is a chaste goddess.

14. '*Astronomia*' and '*astronomica*' mean 'astronomy' in ancient Greek and Latin, respectively.

15. Most other retellings of Orion's story have him die by one of Artemis' arrows, either by tragic accident or as punishment for his crimes.

16. In the *Odyssey*, Homer references Orion as a constellation but also notes that Odysseus observes his phantom chasing beasts in the underworld.

17. This parallels the similarities between Vincent's firearms and Heracles' divine bow that are highlighted in chapter XVI.

18. The Guard Scorpion can also deploy 'Rifle', a basic non-elemental attack that fires twin guns mounted on its arms. The 'Tail Laser' move deals far greater damage to Cloud and Barret and is infamous in the English localisation for the misleading in-battle dialogue which implies the player should strike the robot while its stinger is raised (causing it to counterattack with 'Tail Laser'). In *Remake*, the Scorpion Sentinel has a more varied arsenal and set of abilities. The Guard Scorpion is also fought in *Crisis Core* and could be encountered in the mobile-exclusives *Final Fantasy VII G-Bike* and *The First Soldier*.

19. During the construction of the Mount Corel Mako Reactor, the local townspeople are blamed for an explosion at the site. The Shinra Army razes Corel and massacres its denizens. Barret is shot while trying to flee the troops. *Before Crisis* reveals the militant wing of Avalanche is responsible for the explosion.

20. Orion's story is told by Hesiod and Hyginus in the context of how his constellation comes to exist. The footnotes of chapter IX alternatively propose that Vulcan's association with volcanoes links to the subterranean lava rivers within the canyon.

21. The character art in question was used as promotional material for *Final Fantasy VII*, but it also appears in the

PlayStation and PC editions of the game as one of the disc change prompt screens.

22. Blindness is portrayed in *Final Fantasy XV* by another main protagonist, Ignis Scientia, who dons sunglasses after he loses his sight during the events of the game.

23. Chiron was the tutor to many celebrated heroes such as Jason and Achilles.

24. The materia system is *Final Fantasy VII's* in-game mechanic for spellcasting or status manipulation.

25. Aerith's 'Seal Evil' casts the Silence and Stop status effects on all enemies, and 'Fury Brand' fills her allies' Limit Break gauge. These support the playable characters without directly attacking the opponent(s).

26. In *Final Fantasy VII Remake*, Aerith can unleash intrinsic magic attacks with her staff, suggesting her class is closer to a traditional Red Mage (proficient in both offensive and defensive magic).

27. Specifically, Terra (*Final Fantasy VI*) is the daughter of the esper Maduin; Bartz (*Final Fantasy V*) is the son of the Dawn Warrior Dorgann from Galuf's world; and Cecil (*Final Fantasy IV*) is the son of the Lunarian Kluya.

28. This event is recounted in detail in *Traces of Two Pasts*.

29. As explained in chapter VII, *Traces of Two Pasts* verifies that flowers have grown in the garden of the Gainsborough estate since before Aerith came to live there.

30. This is described in the "Lifestream: White" mini-chapters of *On the Way to a Smile*.

31. This is where the English adjective 'lunar' – relating to something determined by or resembling the Moon – comes from. The term can also be found, for example, in *Final Fantasy IV's* Lunarians – a race of people living on the moon – or *Final Fantasy XV's* Lunafreya – the oracle betrothed to Noctis (whose name means 'Night').

32. Pliny the Elder claimed Endymion is an astronomer rather than a shepherd, but either occupation explains his observations of the Moon.

33. Apollodorus attests in his *Bibliotheca* that Endymion requests this himself.

34. Much like the Gold Saucer dating mechanics of *Final Fantasy VII*, the player's gameplay choices throughout *Remake* will determine whether Cloud shares this scene with Tifa, Aerith, or Barret.

35. The refined dress is the default outfit donned by Tifa if the sidequests in chapter 3 are not all completed. Should the player access the "Alone at Last" scene, they can recommend Tifa wears the refined dress (called 'mature' prior to the *Intergrade* edition), the sporty dress, or the exotic dress. It is also worth highlighting that a crescent moon earring appears in Tetsuya Nomura's original artwork for Tifa's dress in *Final Fantasy VII*.

36. Variations of the outfit can be seen in *Final Fantasy VII*, *Before Crisis*, *Last Order*, *Crisis Core*, and *Remake*.

37. According to the *Crisis Core Complete Guide*, Hyperion and Teioh – the jet-black chocobo ridden by Joe, a celebrity jockey, at the Gold Saucer during *Final Fantasy VII* – are the same bird.

38. Chapter XXI explores the oracle of Delphi in more detail.

39. Apollodorus and Hyginus attest that the Sphinx is yet another child of Typhon and Echidna.

40. Sigmund Freud's psychoanalytic theory of the Oedipus complex is named after this myth.

41. The specifics of Genesis' and Angeal's experimental births have yielded some unusual qualities associated with Jenova. The details are described in the *Crisis Core Ultimania* and *Complete Guide*.

42. Single wings are used in the *Compilation* to signify individuals born from the Jenova Project or their copies.

43. Project Jenova is part of the wider Ancients Project, whose purpose was to produce humans with abilities comparable to the Cetra's.

44. By coincidence, in Apollodorus' summary of the Oedipus tragedy, Merope is called Periboea, which is also the name of Ajax's mother. Ajax and Angeal will be compared in *Final Fantasy VII and the Trojan War*.

45. See chapter VIII for a full explanation of Genesis' degradation.

46. Angeal Penance's attacks are also named after the seven deadly sins of Christian teachings. These are respectively 'Wings of Pride', 'Charge of Greed', 'Rage of Sloth', 'Thunder of Envy', 'Defense of Lust', 'End of Gluttony', and 'Unleashed Wrath'.

47. The polearm is an elaborate version of the one wielded by the sahagin that fuses with Angeal.

48. Chronologically, Dionysus is the last of the Olympians to be born in the ancient Greek myth cycle. Hermes' youthful appearance, however, sometimes earns him this designation.

49. The Homeric Hymns are a collection of 33 anonymously written songs that predate the Classical period and celebrate individual gods. Hermes has two separate entries dedicated to him, identified as Hymn 4 and Hymn 18.

50. See chapter XVIII for the tale of Orpheus playing his golden lyre in the underworld.

51. Hermes' Sandals, also known as Hermes' Shoes, among other things, are recurring accessories in the *Final Fantasy* series, typically associated with the Haste status effect. In the *Compilation of Final Fantasy VII*, they are instead called Sprint Shoes, although their image in the *Ultimania Omega* clearly presents them as golden sandals. The footwear is exclusively obtained at the Gold Saucer in *Final Fantasy VII* but can be purchased from the Nibel Accessories shop during *Crisis Core*. Given Nibelheim's connection with the underworld (see chapter VI), this may be a subtle allusion to Hermes' role in Greek mythology as an escort for dead spirits.

52. The Gigantomachy is the war waged on Olympus by the Giants. During this great battle, Hermes slays a Gigas named Hippolytus while wearing Hades' helmet of invisibility.

53. It is worth highlighting that the *Final Fantasy* series has conflated the thief class with the ninja class since the original 1987 title. This is because practitioners of the latter are regularly capable of ninjutsu. The franchise has adapted 'ninjutsu' to mean 'ninja magic', but it is

historically considered a collection of Japanese martial art survival techniques, including stealth, disguise, misdirection, and even freerunning. Both the traditional and magical elements are deployed by Yuffie in *Episode INTERmission.*

54. After SOLDIER's assault on Fort Tamblin early in the game, Yuffie acquires Zack's email address from 'a blond man' (which is implied to be either Lazard or Rufus). She subsequently uses it to communicate with Zack.

55. As a sidenote, chapter XIII explains how this Junon set piece compares to the Perseus myth, albeit in the context of *Clash of the Titans*. Hermes features in the classical versions.

56. Avalanche HQ is a core branch of the resistance organisation that facilitates communication and corroboration between regional splinter cells. At the time of *Remake*, Barret's cell has been disbarred for their extremist activities.

57. Nero's supernatural abilities allow him to shroud his victims in a dark haze, drawing them into a realm where their life force is extracted.

58. The materia functions as a battle command through which the player character attempts to steal an item from an opponent.

59. This outfit, in turn, is a callback to her disguise in *Dirge of Cerberus*.

60. In addition to rewarding Yuffie for finding his posters, Old Snapper is only too keen to exchange his wares for Fort Condor Coins. This could be another allusion to Hermes being the protector of merchants and trade.

61. These digital Shinra drives are described as memory modules containing the data of demons of terrible ferocity and terrifying sorcery, respectively.

62. 'The Valkyrie' is the English localised name of the weapon in *Remake*; it is still called *Heri Gannā* (Heli Gunner) in the Japanese release. Similarly, in Japanese, the Gozu and Mezu drives are *Akaoni memori* (Red Demon Memory) and *Aooni memori* (Blue Demon

Memory). Further information on the Valkyries can be found in *Norse Myths That Inspired Final Fantasy VII*.

63. Jizō is the Japanese name for the deified Buddhist monk Kṣitigarbha. In art, he is generally portrayed as carrying a staff to force open the gates of the underworld. This may be why Sonon himself wields a staff in combat.

CHAPTER XX

MISCELLANEOUS MYTHS

Continuing on from the previous chapter, what follows is a selection of myths or beliefs that have been integrated – deliberately or otherwise – into the *Compilation of Final Fantasy VII* in fun and unexpected ways. Some are relatively minor in nature, while others form part of a much grander legend. As before, the entries have been subcategorised for ease of reading.

THE CHIMERA

The winged horse Pegasus is perhaps one of ancient Greek mythology's most instantly recognisable entities. General familiarity with the stallion in the modern era is likely attributable to his appearances in *Clash of the Titans* (1981) and Disney's *Hercules* (1997), two films that recount the tales of Perseus and Heracles, respectively[1]. However, contrary to these adaptations, neither demigod gets to ride Pegasus in classical literature.

Instead, Pegasus features prominently in the story of Bellerophon, the hero who slays the Chimera (sometimes spelled Chimaera), which is referenced as far back as Homer's *Iliad* and Hesiod's *Theogony*. Bellerophon is a son of Poseidon – the sea god who originally invents horses – and has an unparalleled talent for taming steeds, including his equine half-brother, Pegasus[2].

One day, the young man is sent to vanquish the Chimera, a savage monster that has been rampaging across the countryside of Lycia (in modern-day Turkey). It is described by both Homer and Hesiod as having the head of a lion, the body of a goat (with a goat's head protruding from its back), and a venomous serpent for a tail. A terrible child of Typhon and Echidna[3], the Chimera is feared for its viciousness and capacity to breathe fire, which it uses to burn the fields and forests of Lycia in its wake.

Bellerophon hunts the beast and decides to attack it from the air, taking advantage of Pegasus' ability to fly. Diving from a high altitude, he hurls a lead-tipped spear into the maw of the goat head as it belches flames in their direction. The heat of the blaze melts the lead, causing it to boil the brute's insides, thereby fatally wounding it. Bellerophon's victory – not to mention his flying horse – earns him great fame throughout the ancient world.

Chimeras have been a recurring enemy type in the *Final Fantasy* series since the original title from 1987. An initial concept for them was produced by renowned artist Yoshitaka Amano, who was hired by director Hironobu Sakaguchi to illustrate the characters and opponents that would be encountered in the game. Amano-san's design for a chimera boasted wings and the heads of a lion, a goat, and a fire-breathing dragon, more akin to its counterpart in *Dungeons & Dragons* than Hellenic lore[4].

An evolution of this was implemented in *Final Fantasy VII* for the chimera and maximum chimera monsters. However, those who have played the international edition of the title may not be acquainted with such names. In the English localisation of *Final Fantasy VII*, the creatures are respectively dubbed 'harpy' and 'maximum kimaira'[5].

What is intriguing about this is that harpies are also found in Greek mythology, but they relate primarily to the tale of Jason and the Golden Fleece[6]. Harpies are half-human, half-bird hybrids with wings and talons, so the inclusion of avian hindquarters for *Final Fantasy VII's* chimeras likely accounts for any confusion over their identity.

Nevertheless, the game's version of the beings does enjoy some vague allusions to the legendary fiend killed by Bellerophon. Aside from the obvious aesthetic similarities in terms of animal heads and a snake at their rear, chimeras in *Final Fantasy VII* are almost exclusively battled in the Corel Desert area of the overworld map[7], accessible once the player has obtained the *Buggy* rover from Dio at the Gold Saucer. Their association with such terrain could be analogous to the Chimera scorching the land of Lycia with its flaming breath.

In previous entries of the *Final Fantasy* franchise, chimeras are sometimes aligned with the element of Fire, although this does vary. Surprisingly, in *Final Fantasy VII*, the chimeras' deadliest move is the spell 'Aqualung', which implies the exhalation of water[8]. This is the inverse of the mythical monster's fire-breathing attribute, but it might be a loose reference to Poseidon, the father of both Bellerophon and Pegasus[9]. As for the Chimera's father, Typhon (who is also the Harpies' father, according to Valerius Flaccus' Latin retelling of the *Argonautica*), the materia needed to summon his grotesque, two-headed namesake can be acquired in the Ancient Forest, located to the south of the Corel Desert.

Maximum kimairas, on the other hand, are fought towards the climax of the game. They are easy for players to miss, though, because they can only be engaged in a single field during the party's ascent of the Mako Cannon's scaffolding, immediately prior to challenging Professor Hojo. The 'maximum' variants are simply a colour palette swap of the standard chimeras, albeit they cast Ice-elemental magic.

It should be noted that the spelling used in the English localisation of *Final Fantasy VII*, 'kimaira', is in fact the Romanised spelling of the Chimera's name in ancient

Greek[10]. It may also not be a coincidence that maximum kimairas represent part of a scenario in which the heroes return to Midgar to stop Hojo firing the Mako Cannon: The group's exact means of doing so is to parachute into the city from the *Highwind* airship. As such, Cloud and the others confronting the maximum kimairas after their skydive (in Hojo's vicinity) can be compared to Bellerophon ambushing the Chimera from the air.

Even more abstractly, as proposed in chapter XIII, the *Highwind's* function in *Final Fantasy VII* equates to Pegasus' role in the *Herakuresu no Eikō* (*Glory of Heracles*) videogame series that writer Kazushige Nojima worked on before he joined Square. It could therefore be contended that the player's party accessing Midgar from the airship reflects Bellerophon soaring above Lycia on the famous winged horse[11].

TREASURES OF THE GRIFFONS

Griffons – alternatively called griffins[12] – are hybrid creatures that feature in classical literature, although their roots can be traced back to ancient Mesopotamia. They are almost universally depicted as a lion with the head and wings of an eagle, but sources are inconsistent on whether their forelegs end in paws or talons. These beasts can be found sporadically across the *Final Fantasy* series, with their sole appearance prior to *Final Fantasy VII* being in *Final Fantasy III*.

Herodotus recorded in his *Historíai* (*The Histories*, compiled in the 5ᵗʰ century BC) that griffons – known to him as *grypes* (sing. *gryps*) – are majestic animals that dwell in the mountains of northeastern Europe[13]. They guard vast quantities of gold deposits there and are hostile towards humans who try to claim it. According to Aeschylus' play *Prometheus Bound*, the gold itself comes from the underworld.

Other writers attest that griffons can be fiercely territorial but will not attack lions or tigers. The Greco-Roman biographer Philostratus provides an explanation for this in *Life of Apollonius of Tyana*: Despite their feathered wings, the creatures are not strong flyers. As such, they can take flight and strike from the air but are disadvantaged against opponents that are both large and quick.

Curiously, this point is seemingly contradicted during Nonnus' *Dionysiaca*, in which the poet states an airborne griffon circles the throne of Nemesis, Goddess of Retribution, while others draw her chariot across the sky. Nonnus explicitly calls the griffon a bird of vengeance, thus associating its character with Nemesis as well as the myths concerning its protection of gold.

In *Final Fantasy VII*, griffins are encountered on the overworld map amid the mountainous drylands that surround Cosmo Canyon[14]. Their design is reminiscent of traditions in which the front legs of the quadruped have eagle talons rather than a lion's paws, but it also incorporates the tail of a peacock.

Perhaps the most distinct aspect of battles with griffins is that they are able to flap their wings and temporarily hang in the air. Doing so increases their defensive and evasion stats but removes their capacity for physical attacks. Not only might this allude to Philostratus' description of the in-flight limitations of griffons against bigger adversaries, but the monsters of *Final Fantasy VII* being found in the Cosmo Area may not be arbitrary, either. Red XIII's leonine species is also native to the region, which could be a nod to the testimonies that lions and tigers are among the few animals that griffons will not engage. That said, the mobile-exclusive *Final Fantasy VII G-Bike* had an event challenge set in a ravine near Cosmo Canyon wherein the player faced off against a flying griffon in a high-speed motorcycle chase.

While the creature does get an honorary inclusion in *Dirge of Cerberus* as the name of one of Vincent's gun frames, its most prominent contribution to the *Compilation of Final Fantasy VII* from a mythological perspective is arguably in *Crisis Core*[15]. Having escaped Nibelheim's Shinra Manor laboratories with an incapacitated Cloud, Zack visits his hometown of Gongaga to check in on his parents. He discovers the hilltop village has been heavily damaged by an explosion at the neighbouring mako reactor, with the local graveyard indicating a substantial loss of life.

Griffons are one of the enemy types that can be fought around the outskirts of Gongaga. *Crisis Core's* incarnations more closely resemble their legendary counterparts, with the peacock tail replaced by a lion's hindquarters. In addition to random encounters, however, some of the beasts are trapped in treasure chests within the rubble of the destroyed reactor and will show aggression if these are unlocked. Others will drag Zack into combat on the mountain path that runs between the upper and lower sections of the town. It is on this hillside ridge that a minigame can be triggered in which Zack must collect treasure chests cascading down a waterfall.

Like with the Cosmo Canyon area of *Final Fantasy VII*, the griffons in *Crisis Core* are associated with mountainous terrain[16], which parallels accounts of them in Greco-Roman literature. More specifically, as early as the writings of Herodotus, griffons are said to protect the valuable gold ore that exists in their territory, with Aeschylus suggesting that the metal itself comes from the streams of Plouton. Plouton was a euphemism for Hades from the Classical period onwards and refers to the wealth – or treasures – of the earth. As such, having griffons patrolling the Gongaga hills near a treasure-loaded waterfall or actively attacking Zack when he opens certain chests is analogous to their behaviour in mythology. Furthermore, there are several examples in Roman artwork of griffons literally guarding treasure chests.

One final point to highlight is the griffons' affiliation with Nemesis. The goddess' function in the Greek pantheon is principally to punish those guilty of hubris – excessive pride in comparison to or defiance of the gods – or to deliver divine retribution to those who deserve it. There are few places in the world of *Final Fantasy VII* where the dreadful consequences of mankind's actions are more apparent than at Gongaga.

As mentioned in chapter X, the explosion at the regional mako reactor – which was draining the Planet of its lifeblood for Shinra's profit – could be speculated to be Gaia's wrath, ultimately motivating the denizens of Gongaga to abandon their consumption of mako energy. In this way, the facility itself might be said to exhibit the attributes of griffons – vengeful entities that defend natural resources from the greed of humanity.

As a side note, both *Final Fantasy VII* and *Crisis Core* also feature hippogriffs, similar to griffons, as monsters. The hippogriff was imagined by the 16th century poet Ludovico Ariosto and is described in his work as having the hindquarters of a horse rather than a lion. This is not reflected in the games, which reuse the battle model of the griffon, although *Final Fantasy VII* at least swaps the colour palette for this variant.

ARION AND THE DOLPHIN

The *Final Fantasy* series is no stranger to including weird and wonderful creatures and animal species in its titles, ranging from chocobos (giant birds typically used for riding) to moogles (furry, pompom-topped beings capable of telepathy or building their own mail network) and cactuars (animated and violent cactus-like critters). Even among

431

such an eclectic assortment, the presence of Mr Dolphin in *Final Fantasy VII* may give the player pause for thought. Incredibly, this aquatic friend of Priscilla does have a potential basis in Greek mythology via the tale of Arion[17], which was first recorded by Herodotus in *Historíai*.

Like Orpheus, who is discussed in chapter XVIII, Arion is a demigod (generally said to be the son of either Poseidon or Apollo) and famed throughout the Mediterranean for his singing and playing of the kithara (a sophisticated version of the lyre)[18]. He attends a large music festival at the prosperous port of Tarentum (now Taranto, Italy) and wins numerous competitions, earning himself a casket of riches. During his return voyage to Greece, however, the crew of the ship he sails on decides to kill Arion and seize his prize for themselves.

Praying to the gods, the young man grabs his kithara and leaps from the deck, sinking into the Ionian Sea. Before the last of the air escapes his lungs, Arion feels a powerful surge between his legs, propelling him upwards through the water. He looks down as he breaks the surface to discover he has been rescued by a dolphin. At his instruction, the cetacean carries Arion all the way to the harbour at Corinth[19].

In *Final Fantasy VII*, the player is introduced to Mr Dolphin when Cloud and the party initially arrive at Under Junon, an old fishing village that now dwells in the shadow of the fortified port city above. After Priscilla is knocked unconscious in the shallows trying to save the dolphin from a monster, Cloud resuscitates her.

The following morning, the group awakes to the blaring sound of parade music as Junon prepares to celebrate the new presidency of Rufus Shinra. Priscilla agrees to help them reach the upper city and proposes that Cloud allows Mr Dolphin to vault him from the water to the support tower overhead. The manoeuvre is successful, but the blond hero is subsequently enlisted into the military parade. If the player revisits the village's bay at any time prior to commandeering the *Highwind*, they will be given the opportunity to have Cloud ride Mr Dolphin directly to the cargo ship at Junon Harbour.

While the parallels may be relatively abstract, there are some notable connections to be made between the Under Junon scenario and the story of Arion. For example, where the demigod's marine saviour prevents him from drowning by thrusting him through the water, Cloud is rewarded with Mr Dolphin lifting him onto the tower because he rescues Priscilla from drowning[20]. Moreover, the dolphin conducts Arion to the busy harbour at Corinth at his behest, just as Mr Dolphin can be summoned to transport Cloud to the vessel moored in Junon's docks.

Perhaps the most peculiar element of the comparison, however, is the circumstances surrounding Mr Dolphin's assistance in the first place: The party is attempting to enter Junon, a vast coastal city, during a public military reception. Cloud is forced to participate in the parade and his performance can impact television ratings, resulting in him being sent a gift by the broadcast's producers[21]. This reflects Arion travelling to the affluent port town of Tarentum to compete in a regional music festival, albeit his prize winnings are the eventual cause of his need for the dolphin's intervention rather than the other way around[22].

THE HONEYBEE GODDESSES

Bees were as much an important part of antiquity as they are in the modern world. This is primarily thanks to their pollination of plants and flowers, which facilitates fertilisation and growth. A number of figures exist in ancient Greek lore to represent bees and beekeeping in a divine sense, while the food of the gods, ambrosia, is often considered to be honey[23]. In fact, it is explicitly stated to be so in the *Homeric Hymn (4) to Hermes*.

For the purposes of this book, there are a few myths worth noting with respect to bees and honey. One relates to the Thriae, a trio of virgin nymphs associated with divination and credited with helping Apollo develop his prophetic talents. These deities are each said to have the head and torso of a maiden but the lower limbs and wings of a bee. Like other bee goddesses, the Thriae symbolise purity.

There are contradictory tales regarding how ambrosia becomes the sustenance of immortals. According to the 3rd century BC poet Callimachus, when the infant Zeus is smuggled away from his murderous father, Kronos, and hidden on Crete (as summarised in chapter IV), he is cared for by the Meliae, tree nymphs that feed him honey and the milk of the goat Amalthea so he will grow rapidly. The Skyfather later introduces the sweet, fragrant delicacy to Olympus.

An alternative account can be found among the fables of Aesop, a 7th century BC storyteller. At the wedding of Zeus and Hera, a honeybee named Melissa presents the Olympians with a jar of her produce[24]. The King and Queen of Heaven love it so much that it is proclaimed the blessed food of the gods. In return, Zeus grants Melissa's wish for a stinger so that she and her descendants can defend their hives[25].

In *Final Fantasy VII*, the Honey Bee Inn is an adult establishment in Wall Market, a seedy district of Midgar's Slums. The women working there are dressed in provocative honeybee costumes, including wings, striped abdomens, and stingers. These outfits resemble the descriptions of the Thriae, which may be intentionally ironic if they are indeed based on a trio who embody chastity and purity.

Furthermore, when Cloud and Aerith first speak with the Honey Bee Inn's doorman, he informs them that it is customary for all new girls to be taken to Don Corneo's mansion. This is why Tifa is being held there. Don Corneo is the local crime lord and in the market for a bride, which could allude to Aesop's fable of Melissa and her honey at the wedding of Zeus and Hera.

The private club in *Final Fantasy VII Remake*, reinvented as the Honeybee Inn, is a very different environment. During Cloud and Aerith's quest to gain access to Don Corneo's manor, the venue's proprietor, Andrea Rhodea, takes an interest in them and challenges Cloud to a dance-off. When Andrea emerges from the giant flower cocoon at the centre of the stage, three golden holographic females begin to frolic around him[26]. This may be another subtle reference to the Thriae.

There is also a fountain sculpture in the main lobby of the club that portrays a seated humanoid female with the wings, antennae, and abdomen of a honeybee. The statue is carrying a jar on her shoulder, which is a possible nod to Melissa being the originator of ambrosia. This is additionally supported by the lack of a stinger at the sculpture's rear, as per Melissa's anatomy before Zeus grants her wish.

Intriguingly, depictions of winged bee goddesses on gold plaques have been discovered on the Greek island of Rhodes, dating back to the 7th century BC. As it happens, Andrea is a name of Hellenic origin, suggesting that 'Rhodea' might be derived from 'Rhodes'[27].

An item in *Final Fantasy VII* that finds its roots in these same myths is the Cornucopia. Cornucopias can be used to cure the Small status effect (known elsewhere in the series as Mini) and have so far appeared exclusively in the 1997 game.

In classical lore, the cornucopia (also called the horn of plenty) is a symbol of abundance and nourishment. It is most widely attested to having once been a horn of the goat Amalthea – who is sometimes thought of as a goddess herself – which was accidentally snapped off by Zeus while he was still a suckling infant among the Meliae. Given its affiliation with magical growth and endless nutrition, it is appropriate that a Cornucopia in *Final Fantasy VII* should reverse the effects of Small.

ALEXANDER THE GREAT

Unlike many entities previously featured in the book, King Alexander III of Macedon – better known by the moniker Alexander the Great – is an important figure from ancient Greek history rather than mythology. However, the legacy of his conquests was so extensive that fictitious tales of his origins and successes were told by classical writers for centuries after his death. Alexander is one probable inspiration behind his summon namesake in the *Final Fantasy* franchise, so it would be remiss to omit certain stories surrounding him, especially when the backgrounds to other summoned beings such as Hades, Titan, Typhon, and Phoenix have already been explored in earlier chapters.

Following in the footsteps of his father, Philip II of Macedon, Alexander reinforced the centralised governance of Greece when he became the region's ruler in 336 BC. He earned his reputation as one of the world's greatest-ever military commanders over the next 13 years, leading his armies without defeat against the Persians to the east and marching as far as India to establish his empire. Alexander died in 323 BC, aged 32, at his palace in Babylon, an ancient city in what is today Iraq.

Many myths exist in relation to Alexander the Great; some have historical merit, some do not. For example, in *Bíoi Parálleloi* (*Parallel Lives*), the Greek biographer Plutarch claims the young man was not the son of Philip II, but rather of Zeus himself. Even during his lifetime, Alexander is said to have believed he was descended from the gods (via the lineages of both Heracles and Achilles) and exercised his divine right as king[28].

Another common legend concerns the so-called Gates of Alexander (also known as the Caspian Gates), thought to be located in the Caucasus Mountains, a range in southeastern Europe that was traditionally considered a natural border separating Europe and Asia. According to the tale, Alexander erected a stronghold and fortified walls of iron and copper between the mountain passes to keep out the tribes beyond[29].

Among the most famous stories of Alexander the Great is his visit to Gordion (in modern-day Turkey). An ox cart had remained on display there for several generations, tied to a post by an extraordinarily complex entanglement known as the Gordian Knot[30]. It had been prophesied that whoever could loosen the knot was destined to rule Asia. Accepting the challenge, Alexander stepped forward and sliced through it with his sword, thus solving the problem by simply eliminating it[31].

In the *Final Fantasy* series, Alexander is a recurring summoned being that is typically depicted as a mechanical fortress and associated with the element of Holy. It first appeared in *Final Fantasy VI* and was designed by Tetsuya Nomura, although its aesthetics seem to have been based on Yoshitaka Amano's concept art for *Final Fantasy IV's* Giant of Babil[32]. In particular, Amano-san's illustration portrays a huge, armoured automaton with onion dome spires across its shoulders. These features are shared by Alexander, including its *Final Fantasy VII* incarnation.

The Alexander Materia is obtained by provoking and overcoming an enchantress named Snow in a cave on the Great Glacier. It is the only materia in the game imbued with Holy that can be equipped[33], and the summon's 'Judgement' attack is unique for the same reason. When Alexander is called into battle, the terrain before the opponent(s) crumbles away and the colossus rises from deep within the earth. Planting its forearm turrets, the bastion discharges twin lasers from its eyes, burning a knotted symbol on the ground that generates an explosion of fire and light.

There are numerous vague parallels here to the myths surrounding Alexander the Great. For instance, 'Judgement' itself casts Holy-elemental damage, which likely alludes to the principle of divine judgement[34]. Not only did Alexander think of himself as transcendent, but he was later also attested to be the son of Zeus, whom Hesiod describes as the

Lord of Justice in his *Theogony*. As it happens, the original name for Alexander's corresponding move in *Final Fantasy VI* was 'Justice'[35].

It additionally might not be a coincidence that the fiery, interlacing threads scorched on the ground during Alexander's attack animation in *Final Fantasy VII* form a knot. While substantially more simplistic than the Gordian Knot, its incorporation could be another reference to the life of Alexander the Great, whose divine right to rule was reinforced by the prophecy that accompanied the impossible tangle.

As for the robotic fortress' design, its main body and hulking forearms are dark silver in colour and adorned with golden bands or plating. The entity may represent the legendary fortifications in the Caucasus Mountains, said to have been constructed by King Alexander's army from iron and copper[36]. The mountains themselves are an immense range with some of the highest peaks in Europe and are known for the large amount of snowfall they experience each year[37]. As such, it is appropriate that the Alexander Materia can be acquired on the Great Glacier in the permafrost foothills of Gaea's Cliff, itself the gateway to the Northern Crater.

One of the most intriguing aspects of the summon Alexander is the onion dome spires on its shoulders. These are reminiscent of steeples and minarets found on religious buildings in Eastern Europe or the Middle East. While they likely reflect Alexander's alignment with Holy, they are also a leftover from Yoshitaka Amano's illustration of the Giant of Babil, which, in turn, almost certainly drew inspiration from the Tower of Babel allegory[38]. Religious texts generally place the tower in Babylon, the historic city where Alexander the Great died.

1. The movies' retellings are both inaccurate with regards to the source material, especially in the case of *Hercules*. Further details can be found in chapters XIII (Perseus) and XVI (Heracles).
2. Bellerophon's mother is the mortal Eurymede. Pegasus is born when Perseus cuts off Medusa's head. According to Ovid's *Metamorphoses*, Medusa is a former priestess of Athena and is turned into a Gorgon by the goddess after being impregnated by Poseidon.
3. Chapter XI contains a list of Typhon and Echidna's monstrous offspring.
4. A written description of the Chimera features in the first edition of *Dungeons & Dragons* (1974), with associated artwork appearing in the 1977 edition of the *Monster Manual* bestiary.
5. The Japanese romaji are *Kimaira* and *Makishimamu Kimaira*.
6. The story is alternatively known by the title of its retelling in the 1963 movie *Jason and the Argonauts*. During their voyage, the Argonauts chase away the harpies that have been tormenting the blind prophet Phineus.
7. A 'harpy' will occasionally appear in battle alongside a chocobo on the tracks southeast of the Gold Saucer. They can also be fought at the amusement park's Battle Square as well as in *Before Crisis* during the collapse of the Mount Corel Mako Reactor.
8. 'Aqualung' is *Final Fantasy VII's* equivalent of the 'Aqua Breath' attack used by chimeras in *Final Fantasy V* and *Final Fantasy VI*, further emphasising the contrast.

9. 'Aqualung' is also cast by Jenova LIFE during the party's confrontation with the fiend at the Forgotten Capital. Chapter V establishes a number of connections between that location and Poseidon.

10. The name in ancient Greek is written as *Χίμαιρα*. Romanisation means to transliterate letters from one alphabet into the corresponding letters of the Roman alphabet. Latinisation is the conversion of Romanised words into spellings more common to Latin.

11. As a side note, *Final Fantasy VII* and *Before Crisis* both feature separate monsters called insect chimeras (known as kimara bugs in the English localisations, including the novel *Traces of Two Pasts*). The fiends have the heads of a praying mantis, spider, and butterfly, and usage of the term 'chimera' here relates to the biological definition of an organism containing a mixture of genetically different material.

12. The spelling of the creature's name in *Final Fantasy VII* is 'griffin' rather than 'griffon', which is not incorrect. However, all other appearances in the *Compilation* use the latter variant.

13. Other sources, such the 4th century BC historian Ctesias, maintain the griffons' habitat was in India.

14. Like the harpies of the Corel Desert, griffins also appear in the Gold Saucer's battle arena.

15. This is not to be confused with the minor role played by the A-Griffon opponents, one of which fuses with Angeal and other monsters to form the sphinx-like Penance. See chapter XIX.

16. The brief for one of the SOLDIER missions confirms that griffons are indeed native to Gongaga.

17. Priscilla is a young girl who lives in Under Junon.

18. Arion the bard shares his name with the immortal black-maned steed that Poseidon fathers upon Demeter.

19. Cetaceans are marine mammals such as dolphins, whales, and porpoises. The term derives from '*cetus*' (whale) in Latin and '*kétos*' (sea monster) in ancient Greek. As referenced in chapter XIII, Cetus is the name of the colossal water serpent summoned by Poseidon to

claim Princess Andromeda as a sacrifice. This establishes a very loose connection between Mr Dolphin and how the later Junon set piece parallels the Perseus myth.

20. In addition, as explored in chapters XIV and XV, Cloud is equated with Theseus, who is another son of Poseidon.

21. Depending on the final ratings, the player will receive either a Grenade, six Potions, six Ethers, or 5,000 gil.

22. It should also be highlighted that Mr Dolphin was deemed important enough during *Final Fantasy VII's* development to merit his own character illustration by Tetsuya Nomura.

23. Ambrosia appears as a type of food that grants in-battle status buffs in *Final Fantasy XI* and *Final Fantasy XV*, respectively. It is also the name of Clive's white chocobo in *Final Fantasy XVI*.

24. The ancient Greek word for bee was '*mélissa*'.

25. The moral of the fable is to be careful what you wish for: While a bee's stinger might function as a weapon to prevent the theft of their honey, its use will kill the bee.

26. Concept art in *Remake's Material Ultimania* shows the original intention by developers was to have several nymphlike holograms dance around the lounge during this scene.

27. '*Andréas Rhódios*' (Latinised from the ancient Greek 'Άνδρέας Ῥόδιος') translates as 'Andrea of Rhodes'.

28. The divine right of kings is an ancient philosophy that suggests monarchs were appointed or approved by God or a supreme deity, generally understood to mean that their actions were above the laws of man.

29. Details of the fortifications appear in Pliny the Elder's *Naturalis Historia*, but he is clear to state that they were not built by Alexander's army when they passed through the range.

30. The knot itself was tied by Midas, son of the newly crowned King Gordias. *Final Fantasy XIV* fans may recognise these names from the Alexander raid series in *Heavensward*.

31. The Gordian Knot is nowadays used as a metaphor for how to tackle a problem by being direct and removing preconceived constraints.

32. The Giant of Babil was built to exterminate the people of *Final Fantasy IV's* world.

33. The actual Holy Materia itself, of course, is never accessible to the player (as it is first in the possession of Aerith and later lost at the Forgotten Capital). Instead, the Alexander Materia can be linked with various types of Support Materia to add the element of Holy to a character's offensive or defensive capabilities.

34. From *Final Fantasy VIII* onwards, Alexander's trademark attack has been called either 'Holy Judgment' or 'Divine Judgment'.

35. This has been renamed 'Divine Judgment' in subsequent releases of the title since 2007.

36. Interestingly, the *Final Fantasy XI* expansion *Treasures of Aht Urhgan* outright calls Alexander's shell the Iron Colossus.

37. Mount Elbrus in the western reaches of the Caucasus region is Europe's tallest.

38. The story of the Tower of Babel appears in Hebrew scriptures and other ancient sources. It relates to humanity's collective hubris in attempting to build a construct that can reach the heavens, allowing them to see God. God destroys the tower and thereafter scatters mankind. In *Final Fantasy IV*, the Giant is summoned to Earth from the Moon using the enigmatic Tower of Babil so that it can wipe out the human civilisation.

CHAPTER XXI

REMAKING DESTINY

Like many cultures in antiquity, the Greeks and Romans generally believed in the concept of a predetermined and inescapable fate. There is significant evidence to suggest that fate and its effects on individuals have been interwoven with religion for thousands of years, dating back to ancient civilisations such as those in Egypt, Mesopotamia, and India. As with other abstract principles or natural phenomena, the Hellenes told stories about deities who embody the concept, envisioning them in a very particular context.

Destiny – which will be used interchangeably with fate for the purposes of this chapter – on a personal, societal, or universal scale was perceived as a way of maintaining natural order and balance[1]. Mortals and divine beings alike are said to be bound by fate, and, according to several sources, not even Zeus is above its laws[2]. To better understand how this applied to themselves, the Greeks imagined a person's life as a length of thread that was spun from a spindle and cut at the time of death. Each thread was governed by three sisters called the Moirai (also Latinised as Moirae, loosely meaning 'Those who Allot' or 'Those who Apportion') – known more commonly nowadays as the Fates.

In Hesiod's *Theogony*, the Moirai are alternatively said to be the daughters of Nyx (Night) or of Zeus and the Titaness Themis[3], while other accounts offer an assortment of parental variations. The triad works in harmony to determine an individual's destiny: Clotho ('the Spinner') spins the thread that represents their life; Lachesis ('the Allotter') measures out the thread's length and decides how long they will live; and Atropos (the 'Unturning'[4]) chooses the manner of their demise, then shears the strand at the appointed moment[5].

The Moirai do not unnecessarily interfere in human affairs or involve themselves in trivial matters, thus allowing a person to exert a degree of influence and autonomy over their own actions. However, regarding events of significance, they are described as stern and inflexible. The Fates' remit also extends to assigning the functions and privileges of newborn gods and ensuring these deities fulfil their divine duties. For example, they decree that Athena will remain a virgin (see chapter IX), and they preside over Persephone's cyclical descent to the underworld in winter and her return in springtime (see chapter VII).

The trio additionally serve as overseers of morality. According to Aeschylus' play *Eumenides*, they are known to arrange punishment for mortals (or gods) who have broken oaths or acted in depraved ways, especially with respect to avoiding their destiny. That said, the Moirai do not typically engage directly with such offenders, but rather they dispatch the infernal Erinyes (Furies) to seek vengeance for evil deeds[6].

The name of the Three Fates derives from the Hellenic principle of *moira*, which concerns one's fair allotment or apportionment[7]. Greek tradition dictated that a person receiving more than their fair share in life would upset the natural order. In turn, this made them subject to adversity or suffering imposed by the goddess Nemesis, one of whose roles it is to balance out undeserved good fortune[8].

Depictions of the Moirai are relatively inconsistent throughout classical art and literature. Some poets, such as Ovid in *Metamorphoses*, describe them as hideous old women who encapsulate the slow, grave march of time. Other writers and sculptors portray the trio as beautiful maidens robed in white, while Plato refers to them in *Republic* as wearing crowns and singing[9]. Apollodorus even includes the sisters in his retelling of the Gigantomachy and claims that they help in defending Olympus by clubbing a pair of Giants to death.

The Moirai are the enforcers of fate and very rarely deviate from how they administer the natural laws. However, there *are* instances in the myths where they reverse an outcome or are persuaded to change an individual's destiny. One such case is their resurrection of Pelops, a young boy who is murdered by his father and whose flesh is thereafter served to the gods at a banquet[10]. Another example is how Apollo gets the triad drunk with wine and convinces them not to cut his friend Admetus' life-thread at the designated hour. They agree, but on the condition that someone volunteers to die in his place[11].

Destiny is not an alien concept to the *Compilation of Final Fantasy VII*, with allusions to its fundamentals existing since the original game. There is a running metaphor in *Final Fantasy VII* regarding a train travelling along its rails, which Cloud initially utilises to acknowledge how the denizens of the Midgar Slums can only live within the parameters of their limited means. Later in the story, though, the train comes to symbolise the party's resolve to save the Planet: There is no getting off the 'train' they are on because it makes no stops. This can be interpreted to mean the group must follow the route predetermined by the rail tracks, indicating they are destined to go where their quest takes them[12].

A less subtle example may instead be the plot of *Crisis Core*. An optional flashback in *Final Fantasy VII* reveals how Zack was gunned down by Shinra infantrymen on a bluff overlooking Midgar, so many fans played the entirety of *Crisis Core* knowing that its protagonist would not survive. This is almost the very definition of fatalism – the belief that all events are preordained and therefore inevitable[13].

The principles of destiny feature far more profoundly in *Final Fantasy VII Remake*. They are introduced to the player via the Whispers (also called the arbiters of fate), which are hooded spectral entities that observe or interfere during a number of important scenes. It is eventually disclosed that the Whispers' purpose is to ensure the flow of destiny advances as the Planet intends. By design, these arbiters will intervene in any situation that could cause a divergence from the planned course.

Cloud first gains sight of the cloaked phantoms when he encounters Aerith on Loveless Street, shortly after the bombing of Mako Reactor 1. Physical contact with the flower peddler unlocks his sensitivity to the Whispers (as confirmed in *Remake's Ultimania*), which remains for the duration of the game.

Throughout *Remake*, there are several occasions where the plot begins to stray quite substantially from the narrative of the original *Final Fantasy VII*. The Whispers materialise at these points to get things back on track, irrespective of whether it benefits the heroes or not. Examples include the ghosts orchestrating Jessie's injury so that Cloud is recruited for the mission to Mako Reactor 5, thus ensuring he falls from the facility and is reunited with Aerith; actively preventing Cloud from killing Reno at the Sector 5 church, permitting the Turk to carry out his role in the destruction of the Sector 7 support pillar; and resuscitating Barret after he has been stabbed through the chest by one of the Sephiroth clones, saving his life so he can assist in Aerith's escape from Shinra Headquarters.

In particular scenes during *Remake*, it is hinted at that Sephiroth has influence over certain Whispers, the foremost of which is identified as the 'enigmatic spectre'. As the game hurtles towards its climax, Sephiroth's power grows stronger, and the arbiters start to gather around Midgar in their thousands in a desperate bid to stop events deviating from Gaia's premeditated future so wildly that they can no longer be course-corrected.

Through her knowledge of the Whispers – which she channels to Red XIII[14] –, Aerith comes to realise that the destiny the Planet is striving to maintain does not favour humanity. It is heavily implied that the epilogue of *Final Fantasy VII* – set 500 years in the future, with Red XIII and his cubs looking down over Midgar's ruins – is, in fact, an undesirable goal.

Prepared to defy fate (which they understand may inadvertently serve Sephiroth's ambitions), the party enters the Singularity, a dimension beyond the construct of linear time[15]. They are confronted by the Whisper Harbinger, a colossal entity said to be an accumulation of arbiters. It connects to all things that shape the Planet's fate and appears when someone tries to alter destiny's flow[16]. The Harbinger summons three smaller fiends to battle the heroes, known as Rubrum, Viridi, and Croceo – verified in the *Ultimanias* to be manifestations of Kadaj, Loz, and

Yazoo from *Advent Children* –, who are fighting to preserve the future that they come from.

Having defeated the Harbinger – as well as the trio of Remnants –, the group discovers too late that their gargantuan opponent has been imprisoning the essence of Sephiroth, who was exerting his influence on the arbiters from here. Sephiroth immediately seizes control of the Whispers and absorbs them, provoking Cloud into delivering a strike so devastating that it consequently vanquishes the phantoms.

With the Whispers seemingly eradicated, the party exits the Singularity and returns to the material world. However, there is evidence to indicate that the removal of the arbiters has resulted in different outcomes for key events in the saga of *Final Fantasy VII*. The most prominent of these is Zack's survival against Shinra's military legions[17]. Nevertheless, the specific details of how these new circumstances will affect the story and characters are unlikely to be revealed before the release of *Final Fantasy VII Rebirth*.

Although the function and the aesthetics of the Whispers in *Remake* do not exactly match those of the Moirai in ancient Greek mythology[18], there is a plethora of parallels to be explored. In truth, some localisations of the game are fairly unambiguous about the comparison: in German, the Whispers are called '*die Moiren*', while in French they are '*les Fileurs*', which roughly translates as 'the Weavers' or 'the Spinners'. Spinning the threads of life, of course, is how the Hellenes imagined the Moirai determined the destiny of mortals.

In Homer's *Iliad*, there is only one Moira, and in the *Odyssey*, she is said to be assisted by an unknown number of 'spinners'. Almost all other sources of Greco-Roman literature list three Fates. This is not reflected by the Whispers in general, which can range from a handful at a time to an immeasurable quantity[19].

However, there are several instances in *Remake* where a triad of arbiters is encountered by Cloud (although it is unclear whether it is always the same trio). For example, when the blond hero has a vision of the support pillar's collapse en route to Seventh Heaven, three Whispers race off towards the Sector 7 Slums; after Biggs is wounded on the pillar, he is watched over by a trio of spectres[20]; and three shadowy entities hover outside President Shinra's office as if guiding Cloud to where the Sephiroth clone has carried the Jenova specimen, then they pursue the robed figure down the side of the tower. If it is to be presumed that this triad has special importance with regards to regulating destiny, then a distinct similarity emerges to the Moirai of Greek lore.

As an extension to this, certain scenes with the arbiters may be analogous to specific myths. When Barret is stabbed in the presidential office, for instance, the Whispers react with panic, then one quickly works to revive the gun-armed giant. Red XIII later remarks that this was not the death ordained for him by fate. It could be contended that the situation echoes the Moirai interceding when Pelops is murdered, reversing his father's abhorrent acts, and revising the course of the boy's life.

There are also occasions where the Whispers do not simply intervene to prompt an injury to a character but outright attack the protagonists[21]. The enigmatic spectre and its ghostly cohorts twice engage Cloud and Tifa in battle, while, in the Singularity, Rubrum, Viridi, and Croceo aggressively protect their own future.

Through these varying degrees of interference and hostility, loose parallels can additionally be drawn to the Moirai's part in the Gigantomachy, where they bludgeon two Giants to death. As explained in chapter X, the conflict itself is an attempt by the Gigantes to overthrow the Olympians, so the Three Fates' defence of heaven's future compares to Rubrum, Viridi, and Croceo's objective.

As for the Moirai being divinely responsible for moral behaviours and coordinating the punishment of those who have acted wickedly or dishonestly – particularly in connection with evading their destiny –, elements of this might be embodied by the Whisper Harbinger. Not only does the Harbinger seek to prevent the party from defying fate, but it also serves as a prison for Sephiroth's essence, whose existence is the greatest threat to the Planet.

Sephiroth, of course, still manages to influence the Whispers from within these confines. His will is represented in the physical world by the enigmatic spectre, which seems to impose its agenda on the arbiters around it. This reflects how Apollo is able to manipulate the Moirai with respect to the fate of his friend Admetus. Separately, Sephiroth assuming command of the Whispers in the Singularity is analogous to Zeus having sole rule over the Moirai in some classical writings.

In Greek mythology, Apollo himself is the God of Prophecy and Enlightenment, although the Moirai are sometimes considered to be the source of prophetic sight[22]. In short: How can they determine the destiny of all if they cannot see the future? The Romans called the triad the 'Parcae' (the 'Sparing Ones'), but their foresight aspect is better articulated in the alternative Latin name 'Fata', which can mean both 'Fate' and 'Prophetic Declaration'[23].

The power of prophecy played an important role in Hellenic culture – so much so that the Temple of Apollo at Delphi was said to be the centre of the world[24]. Proclamations, judgements, and instructions were delivered by special clairvoyants called oracles, themselves understood to be mediums through whom the gods spoke on matters regarding the future or the unknown. Oracles differed from prophets in that they directly channelled divine wisdom and counsel, rather than liaising with deities (through visions, prayer, or otherwise) and relaying messages on their behalf[25].

The highest authority in ancient Greece from a civil and religious perspective was the Pythia – also known as the Delphic oracle –, the seniormost priestess at Apollo's temple at Delphi. She responded to queries from peasants, kings, merchants, foreigners, philosophers, military commanders, and anyone else willing to visit the temple precinct (with the expected offerings). However, when the Pythia made assertions, she was in a trance-like state, so they were almost always cryptic, leaving them open to interpretation by the recipient or attending priests.

Exact details on how the Pythia received her prophetic visions are unclear due to inconsistent literary accounts and the inherent clandestine nature of the process. A prominent belief among scholars is that the priestess would retreat to a sacred subterranean chamber and sit above a chasm in the ground, inhaling vapours that rose from within the earth. The fumes are thought to have induced hallucinations[26], the contents of which were accepted by the people of antiquity to be messages from Apollo via the 'breath' of Gaia (Mother Earth), who was also associated with wisdom and foresight.

The title 'Pythia' itself is derived from Delphi's earlier name: Pytho. The *Homeric Hymn (3) to Apollo* explains how he came to be synonymous with Delphi and its oracle, while the background context can be found in works such as Apollodorus' *Bibliotheca* or Hyginus' *Fabulae*.

When Zeus is born, his mother Rhea secretly swaddles a large rock in blankets, which her cruel brother-husband, Kronos, gulps down instead of the infant, as intended (see chapter IV). Zeus grows to manhood on the island of Crete and returns to challenge his father, giving Kronos a potion that causes him to vomit up his children (Hestia, Demeter,

Hera, Poseidon, and Hades) as well as the swaddled stone. Zeus then takes the rock and hurls it far across Greece. It lands on Mount Parnassus at Pytho and thereafter becomes known as the Omphalos (which means 'Navel'), the spiritual centre of the Hellenic world.

Pytho is already sacred to Gaia, so she births a huge draconic serpent, Python, to protect the Omphalos and the oracle at her shrine on the mountain[27]. In time, the goddess Leto falls pregnant to Zeus with the divine twins Apollo and Artemis[28]. Affronted by her husband's infidelity, Hera instructs Python to pursue Leto and kill her, but the dragon is unsuccessful.

Shortly after Apollo is born, he journeys to Mount Parnassus and slays Python in revenge for relentlessly hunting his mother during her pregnancy. He seizes possession of the oracle from Gaia and establishes his own temple where the personified earth's cult centre existed, changing Pytho's name to Delphi.

While prophecy and fate are connected, it is necessary to clarify the difference between knowing one's destiny and glimpsing one's future. A relevant example from chapter XIX of this book is how the tragic hero Oedipus is fated to kill his father and marry his mother. When the Pythia tells King Laius of Thebes that he will die by the hand of his son, it sets in motion a chain of events that results in Oedipus growing up in Corinth. The young prince eventually visits the Delphic oracle himself and receives a similar proclamation; however, he mistakenly believes his birth parents are Polybus and Merope rather than Laius and Jocasta, and his endeavour to avoid his foretold future ultimately leads him back to Thebes as ordained by fate.

During *Final Fantasy VII Remake*, there are several occasions where Aerith comments on something that she should not yet have knowledge of, particularly with respect to events that take place in the original *Final Fantasy VII*. This is initially hinted at when Cloud first meets her and she insists that he accepts a yellow flower, said to signify loved ones being reunited. Aerith seems to be aware of her future relationship with Cloud, hence her emphasis on the symbolism.

Later, the blond swordsman regains consciousness in the Sector 5 church, and Aerith refers to him as both a SOLDIER and a mercenary. It can be assumed she is familiar with SOLDIER garb due to her history with Zack, but Cloud has not identified himself as a "jack of all trades" the way he does in *Final Fantasy VII's* corresponding scene, so this makes him suspicious of her.

A significantly less trivial example occurs after Cloud, Tifa, and Barret liberate Aerith (and Red XIII) from Professor Hojo's laboratory at Shinra Headquarters. The Cetra reveals to her new companions that there is a more serious threat to the Planet than Shinra, by which she means Sephiroth. However, this precedes the robed figures' breakout of the Jenova specimen and the group's encounter with a physical incarnation of the former war hero, so the warning must be precognition. In the original game, the party does not learn of Sephiroth's return until the murder of President Shinra.

When Aerith subsequently intimates her desire to help the others and the Planet (against Sephiroth), the Whispers manifest and begin to swarm around her, preventing her from disclosing information that could affect the flow of destiny. She tells the group that each time the arbiters touch her, she loses part of herself. It is verified in *Remake's Material Ultimania Plus* that the Whispers are removing Aerith's memories of the future[29], causing her to become less certain about what lies ahead.

According to the same guidebook, memories of the future have come into Aerith's possession during *Remake's* present by unspecified means, although their source of origin (either directly or indirectly) is likely to be the Lifestream. As explained in chapter VI, the Lifestream is a great swell of spirit energy, comprised of countless strands of memories and knowledge from all those who have ever been born, lived, and died, then returned to the Planet. Time is not measured in seconds and hours in the Lifestream, but rather by the accumulation of these memories, as described in the novella *Hoshi o Meguru Otome*.

It is important to note here that Aerith herself is not *predicting* the future by communicating with a higher power (as a prophet might) or interpreting signs (as a seer would[30]). Instead, she has received direct knowledge of the future and has the ability to also channel it to others. As such, the nature of her precognition more closely aligns with the oracles of antiquity, while the Whispers are acting to contain this spiritual knowledge.

Aerith's aptitude is depicted in *Remake*, for instance, when she transfers a memory to Barret's daughter, Marlene. This is to dispel the child's apprehension during an attempted rescue from Sector 7's imminent collapse because the flower girl is a stranger to her at this point in the story. Aerith achieves the same outcome with Red XIII in Hojo's laboratory by creating a clairvoyant connection with him. In both cases, it can be argued that the Cetra is utilising oracular gifts to settle concerns about the future or the unknown.

The visions Cloud experiences throughout the game stem from his contact with Aerith on Loveless Street, albeit there is no suggestion the transmission is intentional. The young hero glimpses moments from the original *Final Fantasy VII* out of context, such as the destruction of the Sector 7 pillar, Sephiroth clones at the Northern Crater, or the White Materia dropping from the Water Alter, all of which are set to occur in the future. What is interesting about this particular variation of Aerith imparting knowledge of the future is that it is ambiguous and difficult to decipher for Cloud, thus reflecting the oracle's cryptic messages to recipients.

Kazushige Nojima's short story *Picturing the Past* presents a different example of Aerith displaying oracular powers. During the novella, the narrator, Lonny[31], recounts how he once drew a spiral shape for Aerith, causing her to enter a frenzied trance and begin sketching visions of landscapes, faces, animals, and monsters that flooded her mind, unbidden and refusing to go away. This is the 'awakening' of her intrinsic Cetran abilities.

In the days that follow the incident, President Shinra, Professor Hojo, and other company researchers ask Aerith many questions and instruct her to draw more images of locations. They interpret the pictures to be mako hotspots that may lead them to the Promised Land of the Ancients. In this way, the tale resembles how queries were posed to oracles with the understanding that the response would come in the form of a prophetic vision[32].

It is also possible to go one step further and consider a specific parallel between Aerith and the Pythia. As a descendant of the Cetra, Aerith is inherently attuned to the Planet on a spiritual level and can commune with Gaia via the Lifestream. Mako is the liquid state of spirit energy, and the misty particles of a leaking mako pipe are exactly what the flower girl is gazing into when she first appears during the opening sequences of *Final Fantasy VII* and *Remake*, respectively. As such, it could be speculated that she receives oracle-like memories of the future through exposure to mako fumes, just as the Pythia was thought to receive prophetic wisdom by inhaling vapours floating from deep within Mount Parnassus, themselves referred to as Gaia's breath.

Curiously, *Remake* is not the first entry in the *Compilation* to infer there is a link between Aerith and oracles. In Nojima-san's novel *The Kids Are Alright*, the main character, Evan, briefly explains how his business partner at Mireille's Investigative Services, Kyrie, dresses up in a hooded black robe and deceives prospective clients into thinking she garners information from the Lifestream about missing people and lost items[33]. It is subsequently revealed that Kyrie based the scam of Lifestream readings on Aerith's unusual talents, which she witnessed when they were both children. Kyrie even proposes to Evan that they expand the business by making 'prophecies' available; however, he rejects the idea because he does not believe the Lifestream foretells things.

In addition, there is a scenario in *Final Fantasy VII* that alludes to several elements of the myth regarding the origin of the Delphic oracle: navigating the Temple of the Ancients. Immediately upon arriving at the rope bridge outside the pyramid, Aerith falls to her knees as she senses the consciousness of Cetran spirits who have remained in the temple to protect the future. This collective sentience continues to communicate with her as the party traverses the structure's interior, encountering fiends and the spectral manifestations of its long-deceased wardens, until the heroes eventually discover a mysterious shimmering pool.

This Well of Knowledge – as it is named in the *Ultimania Omega* – is described by Aerith to be filled with the consciousness of the Ancients. Again, it speaks to the girl, causing her to behave in a confused and agitated manner. As the group gathers around the pool and its rising gases, they are shown a vision of Sephiroth attacking Tseng in the mural room, prompting them to head for that chamber[34].

It could be contended that Aerith being overwhelmed by information from the shared consciousness, conveyed to her via the well and its drifting vapours, is analogous to the Pythia channelling guidance from the gods via Gaia's breath. Furthermore, the pool itself is surrounded by Corinthian columns and resides within a temple that Sephiroth attests to be a treasure house of knowledge[35] – which might, in turn, be a nod to the Temple of Apollo at Delphi.

As if to reinforce the connection, the party must defeat the Red Dragon, a monstrous drake that is battled in the mural room where the pyramid model is located[36]. The Red Dragon seems to be a sentinel of the Black Materia as it only confronts the group once they learn that the crystal can be used to summon Meteor. This may refer to Apollo slaying Python, the draconic serpent that guards the sacred Omphalos, around which the temple precinct at Delphi is constructed.

The epilogue of *Final Fantasy VII* verifies that the Planet survives Meteor's descent. It depicts Red XIII and his cubs surveying Midgar, whose ruins have long since been reclaimed by nature. As the leonine beast lets out a roar, a flock of large, white birds passes overhead and flies off into the distance. A recreation of the scene also appears in the opening to *Advent Children*.

While it is clear the Planet has made a significant recovery in the centuries since the main events of *Final Fantasy VII*, there is ambiguity with respect to the fate of humanity. The game's director, Yoshinori Kitase, was asked about this during an interview with the American magazine *Electronic Gaming Monthly* in 2005 and his response hinted that mankind was either extinct or had been critically diminished by that time[37].

In ancient Greek literature, there is no prophesied universal apocalypse comparable to, for example, Norse mythology and the foretold doom of the gods at Ragnarōk. Sources such as Hesiod's *Érga kaì Hēmérai* (*Works and Days*) predict that the current age of man will end with Zeus destroying the human race because morality and religious standards have been abandoned to the point where Nemesis – the deity responsible for divine retribution – has forsaken mankind and its excessive hubris.

The gods – including Gaia – were considered to be eternal, indicating a belief among the Hellenes and Romans that the world and its heavenly rulers will persist long after humans have perished[38]. When it comes to overseeing the fate of the gods, though, in whatever form that might take, the Moirai are not described as spinning, measuring, and cutting the threads of life; this process is reserved for mortals.

Similar to Mother Earth of classical lore, it can be deduced that Gaia of *Final Fantasy VII* also has the gift of foresight. The function of the Whispers in *Remake* is to maintain her desired destiny, which, by definition, means the Planet has knowledge of one or more possible futures and how these respectively will impact mankind.

However, contrary to her mythical counterpart, it is important to remember that Gaia of *Final Fantasy VII* is not immortal. In fact, Barret reiterates early in the story that the Planet is dying, with Bugenhagen later suggesting her demise is not far away. This is echoed by Sephiroth when he speaks to Cloud's subconscious during *Remake*.

It is for this reason that Gaia's destiny and the Whispers play such a prominent role in the latter title: By defying fate, Aerith and the party may be actively altering how and when the Planet will die. Moreover, as Sephiroth himself states: Humanity's own fate is tied to that of the Planet. In other words, if she expires, so will mankind; if she does not (as per her intended destiny), her prosperity will be directly correlated with humanity's decline, which is also something Bugenhagen contemplates when he accompanies Cloud to the Forgotten Capital during *Final Fantasy VII*.

Bugenhagen's comments are primarily a reference to the consumption of mako, a finite resource that permits humans to lead easier lives at the expense of depleting the Lifestream, and thus knowledge and wisdom from countless generations of souls. Mako energy is originally discovered and monopolised by the Shinra Corporation, whose unethical practices in the fields of war, science, politics, and more represent the scope of mankind's depravity. As such, Shinra's egotism and unfettered greed has compromised natural order and balance, making them – and humanity, by extension – guilty of hubris. Nowhere in *Final Fantasy VII* is this better embodied than in Midgar.

During their battle with the Whisper Harbinger in the Singularity, the colossus sends each member of the party an identical memory of the future: a glimpse of the epilogue from *Final Fantasy VII*. Red XIII then explains to his companions that this is what will happen should they fail to change the course of destiny. What is curious here is that the Planet's desired future in the *Compilation* parallels the fate of humanity as imagined by classical writers like Hesiod (in *Works and Days*). Specifically, in both cases, it is the hubris and immorality of mankind that ultimately results in its decimation, as symbolised in the epilogue through Midgar (the beacon of civilisation) being dominated by forests and lakes.

Furthermore, the appearance of the white birds that fly towards the ruined metropolis might not be coincidental. In Greek mythology, the goddess Nemesis delivers retribution to those exhibiting hubris. Not only is Nemesis explicitly mentioned in *Works and Days* in the context of humanity's obliteration, but the animals associated with her are the goose and the swan[39]. Having birds connected with Nemesis in the epilogue may well be a clever allegory in terms of illustrating why the Planet's chosen destiny does not feature the hubristic mankind.

Intriguingly, besides foreseeing her own future and eventual death, Gaia of *Final Fantasy VII* has prepared for the Lifestream's convergence and its transportation into the cosmos when the time comes. As revealed in *Dirge of Cerberus* (and discussed in chapter XI), the Omega Weapon exists to become a vessel that will carry the amassed spirit energy to a new planet. It should be noted that omega (Ω) is the last letter in the Greek alphabet and is often used in modern media to represent 'the end'. According to *Dirge of Cerberus*, the entity born to gather the Lifestream for Omega is Chaos[40], who shares its name with the vast nothingness from which the universe emerged in many variations of the Hellenic creation myth (see chapter IV). As such, Chaos and Omega could be said to reference the beginning and the end of life.

In *Remake*, Aerith's oracular ability to receive memories of the future helps her to recognise that the future of humanity will be bleak should either Sephiroth or Gaia get their own way[41]. If the heroes are to save mankind, they must alter destiny somehow, even though this is precisely what Sephiroth wants when he invites them to pass through the rift of time and space into the Singularity.

The eradication of the Whispers is likely to change how elements of the future are portrayed in *Final Fantasy VII Rebirth* in comparison to the original game, just as the absence of the Moirai in ancient Greek lore would no doubt have impacted the lives of all. However, there remains a question mark surrounding the degree to which deviations in the past and future will affect the overall flow of destiny.

The conundrum of the Oedipus myth is that his fate – as ordained by the Moirai – is fulfilled because both he and his birth father separately attempt to evade the future proclaimed by the Pythia. Comparing this to *Final Fantasy VII Remake* might suggest that the individual and collective fates of Cloud, Zack, and every other character – as arbitrated by the Whispers – will be inescapable despite their defiance of the future Aerith warns them of. Or perhaps the heroes have already remade destiny, and the events of *Rebirth* will pave the way to a new future for Gaia and humanity.

Only time will tell ...

1. Today, the acceptance of this natural order and the inevitable outcome of things is known as fatalism.
2. Herodotus states in *Historíai* that the gods are unable to escape the Fates; Aeschylus mentions in *Prometheus Bound* that Zeus cannot alter what has been ordained; and Ovid claims in *Metamorphoses* that the gods cannot break the Fates' iron decrees. However, in Homer's *Iliad*, Zeus has the power to weigh in on the destiny of others and can even save those on the brink of their doom; Hesiod, meanwhile, suggests in the *Theogony* that the Moirai rely on their father. The latter version is also supported in the writings of Pausanias – a geographer in the 2nd century AD –, who advises he observed multiple inscriptions in temples and sculptures around Greece that inferred Zeus alone had authority over the Fates.
3. Themis is a goddess who personifies divine law, justice, and custom.
4. 'Unturning' or 'unmoving' in this context is a euphemism for death. 'Atropos' is also where the medical term

5. In the *Iliad*, Atropos alone determines a person's fate. She is also known as Aisa in the epic.

6. The Erinyes are female entities that dwell in the underworld. They punish those who commit the worst crimes by pursuing them relentlessly and tormenting them to death.

7. There is evidence to show the concept of *moira* can be traced to the Mycenaeans of the pre-Hellenic era.

8. Some sources list Nemesis as either the daughter of Nyx or of Zeus, which would make her a sister of the Moirai.

9. The Fates are not inherently evil or cruel, but they were feared by the Hellenes, just as Hades was, due to his association with death. As such, artists and poets typically depicted the trio as attractive young women so as not to incur their wrath.

10. Pelops' father is called Tantalus and his actions are among the most despicable in all classical mythology. Tantalus causes his family to be cursed for generations, while he himself suffers eternal torment in the underworld. *Final Fantasy IX* fans may also recognise he shares his name with the group of travelling thieves that Zidane is part of.

11. Admetus' wife, Alcestis, eventually volunteers to give her life for his. The outcome of their story is discussed in chapter XVII.

12. It may not be a coincidence that a deviation in Avalanche's plans during the Midgar scenario is represented by Cloud, Tifa, and Barret literally jumping off a moving train. In addition, there is only one set piece in *Final Fantasy VII* where two separate pre-rendered cutscenes were produced, but which of them plays is dependent on the player's actions: the chase sequence where Cid has to prevent a runaway train crashing into North Corel.

13. Interestingly, *Crisis Core Reunion* (2022) was released after *Remake* (2020). Following the events in the Singularity during the latter title, an alternative history is

468

shown, in which Zack endures the onslaught and lives. This created less certainty about *Reunion's* conclusion, although it was ultimately left untouched from the original in a narrative sense.

14. When the group first encounters the fiery beast in Hojo's laboratory during *Remake*, Aerith calms him by purposefully depositing memories of their future in his mind. As a result, Red XIII receives knowledge of things to come. This is confirmed in the *Material Ultimania Plus*.

15. Aerith describes the portal between the material world and the Singularity as being destiny's crossroads, beyond which lies the boundless freedom of an uncertain future. "Destiny's Crossroads" is also the name of the final chapter in *Remake's* English localisation.

16. This is stated in the Harbinger's in-game enemy intel biography.

17. This is critical because Zack's death is the catalyst for Cloud becoming the hero that saves the world from Sephiroth in *Final Fantasy VII*.

18. *Remake's Material Ultimania* notes that the Whispers' design was inspired by the Gestalts (or Shades) of *NieR Replicant*.

19. A swarming mass of Whispers is shown to envelope the Shinra Building in *Remake*, then later to create a dome around the entire metropolis of Midgar.

20. It is uncertain what relevance, if any, this has with regards to Biggs surviving the destruction of Sector 7, as revealed once the party has exited the Singularity.

21. Examples of this include the Whispers knocking Jessie down the steps outside Seventh Heaven or later diverting the trajectory of the grenade she throws at a Shinra helicopter, resulting in her fatal wounds.

22. This is not to suggest that the Moirai typically distribute the gift of prophecy to mortals, for it is far more common in the myths that Apollo or Zeus do so. One such example is Tiresias of Thebes, who is given foresight by Zeus to compensate him after he is blinded by Hera for his perceived impiety.

23. The names of the Parcae are Nona, Decuma, and Morta.

24. The historic town of Delphi is located on Mount Parnassus, situated approximately 100 miles northwest of Athens.

25. Furthermore, oracles are not to be confused with seeresses, who interpret signs from the gods (such as studying burnt offerings or animal entrails); or shamans, who interact with the spirit world.

26. Plutarch – the 1st century AD Greek historian who became a high priest at Delphi for a period – suggested the spring waters that flow beneath the temple produced hallucinogenic vapours, while scientific research has demonstrated gases emanating from a geological fault below the mountain could have had the same effect.

27. Sources do not agree on whether Python is a dragon or a monstrous snake.

28. Little is known about Leto beyond her Titan parentage (she is the daughter of Coeus and Phoebe) and that she is the mother of Apollo and Artemis, who are respectively affiliated with the Sun and the Moon.

29. It is worth highlighting that scenario writer Kazushige Nojima's last project before joining Square in 1995 was *Herakuresu no Eikō IV: Kamigami kara no Okurimono* (*Glory of Heracles IV: Gift from the Gods*, 1994), which not only features Atropos in the opening scene but has her mention to the main character that her sisters removed his memories, just as the Whispers do to Aerith.

30. Intriguingly, Motomu Toriyama revealed in an interview with Square Enix's North American branch that there is a seer in *Remake*: Eligor. This ghastly fiend in the Train Graveyard can allegedly foresee widely fatal events by sensing an imminent mass influx of souls to the Lifestream.

31. Lonny's name does not appear in *Picturing the Past*, but rather it is confirmed in *Traces of Two Pasts*. He is a young boy who comes to play with Aerith because his mother is Ifalna's caretaker.

32. As highlighted in chapter VII, the mural on the wall in Aerith's chamber at Shinra Headquarters includes

images of the Lifestream as well as priests and priestesses.

33. Kyrie herself features in *Remake* as a loudmouth con artist from the Sector 5 Slums, as does her grandmother, Mireille, after whom the detective agency is named.

34. The circumstances of this scenario are explained in more detail in chapter XV.

35. As noted in chapter XV, the style of the pillars is specified to be Corinthian in the *Ultimania Omega*, establishing a direct link to ancient Greece.

36. The model contains a puzzle device that can be solved to shrink the temple, transforming it into the Black Materia.

37. The interview followed the release of *Advent Children*, so it is unclear if Kitase-san's comments were explicitly influenced by the events of the film. Additionally, remarks made by Kazushige Nojima during a later interview for the *Crisis Core Complete Guide* (2007) suggest *Final Fantasy VII's* epilogue may not have been intended to imply humanity's decline but simply the Planet's survival.

38. Ancient philosophers such as Anaximander (6th century BC) proposed that everything as we know it came from Chaos (the nothingness that existed before the universe) – sometimes called *apeiron* (that which is boundless or infinite) – and is destined to one day return to Chaos. In science, this is reflected in the thermodynamic laws of entropy.

39. This derives from a myth in which Nemesis falls pregnant to Zeus and becomes the mother of Helen of Sparta, over whom the Trojan War is fought. According to Apollodorus' *Bibliotheca*, Nemesis (in the form of a goose) is pursued by Zeus (as a swan) against her will; Hyginus' *Astronomica*, meanwhile, says Nemesis is the swan and Zeus is an eagle.

40. See chapter XVII for a summary of Chaos' function and its connection to Vincent Valentine.

41. In the *Compilation of Final Fantasy VII*, Sephiroth's endgame is to absorb the Lifestream and transcend to godhood, then use the Planet's husk to travel the cosmos.

GLOSSARY

A

Acheron:	(Greek) underworld river of woe
Achilles:	(Greek) demigod, hero of the Trojan War, near-invulnerable warrior, leader of the Myrmidons, son of Thetis
Admetus:	(Greek) mortal friend of Apollo, husband of Alcestis
Adonis:	(Greek) handsome youth loved by Aphrodite and Persephone; flower named after Adonis
***Advent Children*:**	(FF) movie sequel to *Final Fantasy VII*, re-released as extended edition *Advent Children Complete*
Aegean Sea:	(Greek) part of the Mediterranean Sea, located east of mainland Greece, named after King Aegeus
Aegeus:	(Greek) king of Athens, mortal father of Theseus
Aeneas:	(Roman) demigod, protagonist of the *Aeneid*, son of Venus
***Aeneid*:**	(Roman) epic poem concerning the Trojan War and Aeneas' subsequent journey, composed by Virgil
Aerith Gainsborough:	(FF) primary protagonist, half-Cetran flower girl
Aeschylus:	(Greek) 5th century BC playwright of *Prometheus Bound*, *Eumenides*, etc..
Aether:	(Greek) primordial deity of the bright upper-sky, son of Nyx; the pure, heavenly essence breathed by the gods
Aethra:	(Greek) princess of Troezen, mother of Theseus
Ages of Man:	(Greek) the five generations of humanity, culminating in the current Iron Age
Ajax:	(Greek) hero of the Trojan War, son of Telamon
***Ajax*:**	(Greek) play concerning the heroism and death of Ajax, written by Sophocles
Alcestis:	(Greek) wife of Admetus, saved from Thanatos by Heracles
Alcyoneus:	(Greek) Giant who instigates the Gigantomachy, imprisoned by Heracles
Alexander:	(FF) summoned being, associated with the element of Holy
Alexander the Great:	(Greek) historic ruler of the Greek Empire, renowned military commander and conqueror

Amano, Yoshitaka:	(FF) celebrated concept artist and illustrator associated with *Final Fantasy*
Amazons:	(Greek) tribe of female warriors, experts in horseback archery
Ambrosia:	(Greek) food of the gods, sometimes said to be honey
Ancients:	(FF) modern name for the Cetra
Ancient Egypt:	(misc.) historic civilisation dating back several millennia, situated in what is now Egypt
Ancient Greece:	(Greek) historic civilisation comprised of city-states, provinces, and islands situated in what is now Greece
Ancient Greek:	(Greek) relating to ancient Greece
Ancient Mesopotamia:	(misc.) historic civilisation dating back several millennia, encompassing the Assyrian, Sumerian, and Babylonian empires, etc., situated in what is now Iraq, Kuwait, and parts of Iran, Syria, and Turkey
Ancient Roman:	(Roman) relating to the culture of the Roman Empire
Ancients Project:	(FF) Shinra, Inc.'s venture to produce humans with abilities comparable to the Cetra's
Andrea Rhodea:	(FF) proprietor of the Honeybee Inn
Andromeda:	(Greek) Ethiopian princess, daughter of Cassiopeia; (misc.) princess of Joppa in *Clash of the Titans*
Angeal Hewley:	(FF) secondary antagonist, Zack's mentor, product of Project Jenova G, son of Gillian
Antaeus:	(Greek) Giant wrestled and killed by Heracles, son of Poseidon
Aphrodite:	(Greek) Goddess of Love, Beauty, Sexual Desire, etc., conflated with Venus, daughter of Uranus
Apollo:	(Greek) God of Prophecy, Music, Healing, etc., twin of Artemis, son of Zeus
Apollodorus:	(Greek) 1st or 2nd century AD mythographer and writer of the *Bibliotheca*
Apollonius of Rhodes:	(Greek) 3rd century BC author and composer of the *Argonautica*
Apple of Discord:	(Greek) golden apple delivered by Eris to prompt the Judgment of Paris
Arachne:	(Greek) gifted weaver, turned into a spider for her hubris
Arbiters of fate:	(FF) spectral entities whose role it is to enforce the Planet's intended destiny, also called Whispers
Archaic period:	(Greek) era predating Classical period, 750 BC – 500 BC
Ares:	(Greek) God of War, known to the Romans as Mars, son of Zeus
*Argonautica***:**	(Greek) epic poem concerning the voyage of Jason to retrieve the Golden Fleece, composed by Apollonius of Rhodes;

	(Roman) adaptation of Apollonius' epic, written by Valerius Flaccus
Argonauts:	(Greek) heroes who accompany Jason on his quest for the Golden Fleece, named after the ship *Argo*
Argos:	(Greek) ancient city-state on mainland Greece, oldest continuously inhabited city in Europe
Ariadne:	(Greek) princess of Crete, daughter of Minos II
Arion:	(Greek) demigod, mythical bard, son of either Apollo or Poseidon
Artemis:	(Greek) Goddess of Hunting, Wild Animals, Vegetation, etc., twin of Apollo, known to Romans as Diana, daughter of Zeus
Asclepius:	(Greek) demigod, gifted healer, son of Apollo
Asphodel:	(Greek) gloomy meadow within Hades where most spirits of the dead dwell
Asterion:	(Greek) real name of the Minotaur
Astronomica:	(Roman) compendium of myths regarding constellations, compiled by Hyginus
Athena:	(Greek) Goddess of Wisdom, Strategy, Handicraft, etc., conflated with Minerva, daughter of Zeus
Athens:	(Greek) ancient city-state, modern capital of Greece
Atlantis:	(Greek) fabled island nation featured in Plato's writings
Atlas:	(Greek) Titan who led his kin in the Titanomachy, punished by Zeus to hold up the sky forever, brother of Prometheus
Attica:	(Greek) historic region of Greece in which Athens is located
Avalanche:	(FF) militant organisation led by Elfe; eco-terrorist group led by Barret
Azul the Cerulean:	(FF) secondary antagonist, high-ranking Tsviet

B

Bahamut:	(FF) draconic summoned being, recurring monster
Banora:	(FF) hometown of Genesis and Angeal, affiliated with Shinra, Inc.; local plantation famed for its apples
Banora Underground:	(FF) cave network beneath Banora, base of operations for the Genesis Army
Banora Whites:	(FF) apples unique to Banora's orchards, also called dumbapples
Barret Wallace:	(FF) primary protagonist, anti-Shinra activist
Before Crisis:	(FF) mobile game prequel to *Final Fantasy VII*
Behemoth:	(FF) recurring quadrupedal monster; (misc.) primordial beast of the land in the Hebrew Bible
Bellerophon:	(Greek) demigod, kills Chimera, rides Pegasus, son of Poseidon

Berserk:	(FF) status ailment
Berserkers:	(misc.) Viking shaman-warriors
Bibliotheca:	(Greek) compendium of classical myths, allegedly compiled by Apollodorus
Bibliotheca Historica:	(Greek) compendium of myths and histories, compiled by Diodorus Siculus
Biggs:	(FF) secondary protagonist, member of Avalanche
Bíoi Parálléloi:	(Greek) anthology comparing the lives of various historical and mythical figures, written by Plutarch
Black Materia:	(FF) used to summon the ultimate destructive magic Meteor
Blood crimes:	(Greek) accidental or deliberate killing of one's kin, considered worst of all sins
Brian Lockhart:	(FF) Tifa's father
Buddhism:	(misc.) prominent religion relating to the teachings of the Buddha
Bugenhagen:	(FF) scholar and astronomer, adoptive grandfather of Nanaki
Buster Sword:	(FF) greatsword that symbolises honour and inheritance, possessed by Angeal, then Zack, then Cloud

C

Cait Sith:	(FF) primary protagonist, mechanical anthropomorphic cat, controlled by Reeve
Calamity from the Skies:	(FF) Cetra name for Jenova
Calibos:	(misc.) satyr-like antagonist in *Clash of the Titans*, son of Thetis
Cassiopeia:	(Greek) Ethiopian queen, mother of Andromeda; (misc.) queen of Joppa in *Clash of the Titans*
Centaurs:	(Greek) half-human, half-horse hybrid beings
Cerberus:	(FF) Vincent's triple-barrelled handgun; (Greek) multi-headed hound of Hades, gatekeeper of the underworld, child of Typhon
Cetra:	(FF) extinct nomadic race, proficient in magic and attuned to the Planet's needs
Cetus:	(FF) sea monster, killed by Perseus
Chair of Forgetfulness:	(Greek) bench in the underworld that inhibits the memories of those who sit on it
Chaos:	(FF) primeval entity whose function it is to end all life in preparation for the Omega Weapon's ascension, dwells inside Vincent; (Greek, Hesiod) void of nothingness that existed before all things; (Greek, Orphism) a primordial chasm and child of Chronos
Charon:	(Greek) underworld ferryman who transports the dead across the Styx

477

Chiba, Hiroki:	(FF) event planner of *Final Fantasy VII*, scenario writer of *Dirge of Cerberus*
Chimera:	(Greek) hybrid creature with the head of a lion, body and head of a goat, and a serpent for a tail, child of Typhon, killed by Bellerophon
Chiron:	(Greek) wise centaur, teacher of many heroes, learned in the ways of medicine, hunting, prophecy, etc.
Christianity:	(misc.) prominent religion relating to the teachings of Jesus Christ
Chronos:	(Greek) primordial God of Time
Cid Highwind:	(FF) primary protagonist, former Shinra, Inc. pilot
***Clash of the Titans*:**	(misc.) 1981 movie adaptation of the Perseus myth
Classical literature:	(Greek) written works attributed to ancient Greeks and Romans
Classical period:	(Greek) era predating Hellenistic period, 500 BC – 323 BC
Claudian:	(Roman) 4th century AD composer of *Phoenix*
Claudia Strife:	(FF) Cloud's mother
Cloud Strife:	(FF) primary protagonist, heroic swordsman, alleged ex-SOLDIER
Cocytus:	(Greek) underworld river of lamentation
***Compilation*, the:**	(FF) collective term for the *Final Fantasy VII* saga titles
Corel:	(FF) hometown of Barret, destroyed by the Shinra Army
Corinth:	(Greek) ancient city-state on mainland Greece
Cosmo Canyon	(FF) pilgrimage site, village where the Study of Planetary Life was founded, Nanaki's home
Cosmology:	(misc.) relating to the formation of the universe
Costa del Sol:	(FF) seaside resort town
Cretan bull:	(Greek) sacred beast sent mad by Poseidon, father of the Minotaur, killed by Theseus
Crete:	(Greek) large island in the Aegean Sea, features heavily in regional history and mythology
***Crisis Core*:**	(FF) videogame prequel to *Final Fantasy VII*, re-released as HD remaster *Crisis Core Reunion*
Cyclopes:	(Greek) monstrous, one-eyed giants, children of Gaia (Cyclops, sing.)

D

Daedalus:	(Greek) genius inventor and architect of the Labyrinth
Danaë:	(Greek) princess of Argos, mother of Perseus
Dante:	(misc.) 14th century composer of the *Divine Comedy*
Dark Ages:	(Greek) era predating Archaic period, 1100 BC – 750 BC
Deepground:	(FF) top-secret Shinra facility below Midgar

Deepground SOLDIER:	(FF) special SOLDIER branch connected to Deepground
Degradation:	(FF) phenomenon exclusive to SOLDIERs derived from Project Jenova G, in which their bodies degrade due to cellular imperfections
Delphi:	(Greek) historic town, site of Apollo's temple where Pythia was based, considered the centre of the world by Hellenes
Delphic oracle:	(Greek) high priestess and oracle at Delphi, also called Pythia
Demeter:	(Greek) Goddess of the Harvest, known to the Romans as Ceres, daughter of Kronos
Demigod:	(Greek) mortal with divine parentage
Denzel:	(FF) orphaned boy who is adopted by Cloud and Tifa after Meteorfall
Depths of Judgement:	(FF) area of the Banora Underground
Diamond Weapon:	(FF) biomechanical monster released by the Planet
Dio:	(FF) proprietor of the Gold Saucer
Diodorus Siculus:	(Greek) 1st century BC historian and writer of *Bibliotheca Historica*
Dionysia:	(Greek) Athenian festivals dedicated to Dionysus, origin of Greek drama
Dionysiaca:	(Greek) epic poem concerning the life of Dionysus, written by Nonnus
Dionysian Mysteries:	(Greek) clandestine rites dedicated to Dionysus, associated with the afterlife and harvesting of grapes to make wine
Dionysus:	(Greek) God of the Vine, Merriment, Liberty, etc., known to the Romans as Bacchus, called Twice-Born, son of Zeus
Dirge of Cerberus:	(FF) videogame sequel to *Final Fantasy VII*
Divine Comedy:	(misc.) trio of epic poems concerning the afterlife, composed by Dante
Dolphin, Mr:	(FF) dolphin that frequents the bay of Under Junon
Don Corneo:	(FF) Wall Market mafia boss
Dumbapples:	(FF) informal name for Banora Whites
Dungeons & Dragons:	(misc.) tabletop role-playing game
Dyne:	(FF) Barret's friend, biological father of Marlene

E

Echidna:	(Greek) half-woman, half-serpent monster, consort of Typhon, mother of many terrible creatures
Edge:	(FF) town built from Midgar's wreckage
Eidolons:	(FF) summoned beings of *Final Fantasy IV*
Eleusinian Mysteries:	(Greek) clandestine rites dedicated to Demeter and Persephone, associated with the afterlife and harvesting of crops

Eleusis:	(Greek) historic town where the Eleusinian Mysteries took place
Elfe:	(FF) primary antagonist, leader of Avalanche, daughter of Verdot
Elmyra Gainsborough:	(FF) Aerith's adoptive mother
Elysium:	(Greek) paradisical afterlife realm in Hades for nobility, the virtuous, and exceptional heroes, also called Elysian fields
Emerald Weapon:	(FF) biomechanical monster released by the Planet
Eos:	(FF) world of *Final Fantasy XV*; (Greek) Goddess of the Dawn, daughter of Hyperion
Erebus:	(Greek) primordial God of Darkness, son of Chaos
Erinyes:	(Greek) underworld deities of vengeance, also called Furies
Eris:	(Greek) Goddess of Strife, known to the Romans as Discordia, daughter of Nyx
Eros:	(Greek) primordial God of Love, son of Chaos; alternatively a son of Aphrodite, known to the Romans as Cupid
Espers:	(FF) summoned beings of *Final Fantasy VI*
Euripides:	(Greek) 5th century BC playwright of *Trōiades*, *Herakles*, etc.
Eurydice:	(Greek) mountain nymph, wife of Orpheus
Eurystheus:	(Greek) king of Tiryns, cousin of Heracles, instructs the Labours of Heracles
Evan Townshend:	(FF) primary protagonist, private detective, illegitimate son of President Shinra

F

Fabulae:	(Roman) compendium of classical myths, written by Hyginus
Fasti:	(Roman) epic poem concerning the Roman calendar, composed by Ovid
Fates:	(Greek) three powerful sisters who determine the destinies of all by spinning and measuring the threads of life, also known as the Moirai, daughters of Nyx or Zeus
Fatalism:	(misc.) belief that certain events are predetermined by fate and are therefore inevitable
Faz Hicks:	(FF) lab worker who helps Ifalna and Aerith escape Shinra Headquarters
Final Fantasy:	(FF) popular videogame series, originally created by Hironobu Sakaguchi and developed by Square Enix
Final Fantasy VII:	(FF) original game in the *Compilation*, released in 1997
First Soldier, The:	(FF) mobile-exclusive battle royale game, discontinued

Flaccus, Valerius:	(Roman) 1st century AD author of the Latin version of the *Argonautica*
Forgotten Capital:	(FF) ancient Cetran city, location of Aerith's death, also called the Forgotten City
Forgotten City:	(FF) ancient Cetran city, location of Aerith's death, also called the Forgotten Capital
Fort Condor:	(FF) community around a hilltop mako reactor, itself the roosting spot for a giant condor
Fort Tamblin:	(FF) stronghold in Wutai
Fuhito:	(FF) primary antagonist, leader of Avalanche

G

G-Bike:	(FF) mobile-exclusive driving game, discontinued
Gackt:	(misc.) Japanese singer, musician, and actor
Gaea's Cliff:	(FF) vast perimeter of rock encircling the Northern Crater
Gaia:	(FF) the Planet's name; the world on which most of *Final Fantasy IX* is set; (Greek) Mother Earth, primordial goddess, conflated with Terra, daughter of Chaos
Galian Beast:	(FF) beastly transformation form of Vincent
Gast Faremis:	(FF) Shinra scientist, leader of Project Jenova, Aerith's biological father
Genesis Army:	(FF) collective term for SOLDIER deserters, copies, and others who fight under Genesis' influence
Genesis copies:	(FF) individuals injected with Genesis' cells to replicate his strength and other characteristics
Genesis Rhapsodos:	(FF) primary antagonist, rogue SOLDIER, product of Project Jenova G
Geostigma:	(FF) affliction caused by the body's reaction to Jenova cells
Gift of the Goddess:	(FF) mysterious boon alluded to in *LOVELESS*, sought by Genesis to cure his degradation
Gigantes:	(Greek) Giants, children of Gaia (Gigas, sing.)
Gigantomachy:	(Greek) conflict between the Gigantes and Olympians
Gilgamesh:	(FF) recurring swordsman in the *Final Fantasy* series; (misc.) Babylonian warrior king featured in the *Epic of Gilgamesh*
Gillian Hewley:	(FF) Angeal's mother, former Shinra scientist involved in Project Jenova G
Glory of Heracles:	(misc.) also known as *Herakuresu no Eikō*, a videogame series based on Greek mythology, multiple titles were written by Kazushige Nojima
Goddess, the:	(FF) mysterious deity referenced in *LOVELESS*
Golden apples:	(misc.) Norse apples of rejuvenation;

481

	(Greek) grown in the Garden of the Hesperides, one given to Aphrodite during the Judgement of Paris
Golden Fleece:	(Greek) treasured fleece of a divine ram, sought by Jason
Gold Saucer:	(FF) giant amusement park built over the ruins of Corel
Gongaga:	(FF) hometown of Zack, site of a mako reactor explosion
Gorgons:	(Greek) trio of hideous monsters, the most famous of whom is Medusa
Greco-Roman:	(Greek, Roman) relating to shared cultural elements of ancient Greeks and Romans
Greek Empire:	(Greek) established by Alexander the Great in the 4th century BC during his conquest of Egypt, Persia, and India
Greek tragedies:	(FF) genre of theatrical drama originating from the Dionysia
Griffons:	(Greek) hybrid creatures with the body of a lion and head and wings of an eagle, associated with guarding treasure, also spelled griffins
Grim Reaper:	(misc.) personification of death in European folklore

H

Hades:	(FF) summoned being, associated with status ailments; (Greek) God of the Underworld, King of the Dead, later called Plouton (Pluto), brother of Zeus, known to the Romans as Dis Pater, son of Kronos; the underworld itself
Happy Turtle:	(FF) Wutaian bar chain; shop in Wutai
Harpies:	(Greek) half-woman, half-bird hybrid creatures
Hebrew Bible:	(misc.) primary compendium of religious literature associated with Judaism and Christianity
Hecatoncheires:	(Greek) monstrous brutes with fifty heads and a hundred arms, children of Gaia (Hecatoncheir, sing.)
Heidegger:	(FF) Shinra's Director of Public Security
Hel:	(misc.) Norse Goddess of the Underworld; the Norse underworld itself
Helen:	(Greek) queen of Sparta, alternatively known as Helen of Troy, elopes with Paris and instigates Trojan War, daughter of Zeus
Helios:	(Greek) God of the Sun, known to the Romans as Sol, son of Hyperion

Hell:	(misc.) Christian underworld, a place of torment, governed by Lucifer; generic term for the underworld
Hellas:	(Greek) historic name for ancient Greece
Hellenes:	(Greek) peoples of ancient Greece
Hellenic:	(Greek) relating to Hellenes
Hellenistic period:	(Greek) era predating the Roman occupation of Greece, 323 BC – 31 BC
Hephaestus:	(Greek) God of Fire and the Forge, etc., conflated with Vulcan, son of Zeus
Hera:	(Greek) Goddess of Marriage and Childbirth, etc., queen of Heaven, wife of Zeus, conflated with Juno, daughter of Kronos
Heracles:	(Greek) demigod, divine hero, kills Nemean Lion, Hydra, etc., conflated with Hercules, son of Zeus
Herakles:	(Greek) play concerning the life of Heracles, written by Euripides
Herakuresu no Eikō:	(misc.) also known as *Glory of Heracles*, a videogame series based on Greek mythology, multiple titles written by Kazushige Nojima
Hercules:	(Roman) demigod, divine hero, kills Nemean Lion, Hydra, etc., conflated with Heracles
Hercules:	(misc.) 1997 animated film adaptation of the Heracles myth
Hermes:	(Greek) God of Heralds, Travellers, Commerce, etc., divine messenger, trickster deity, chief psychopomp, known to the Romans as Mercury, son of Zeus
Herodotus:	(Greek) 5th century BC historian and writer of *Historíai*
Hesiod:	(Greek) 8th century BC farmer and composer of the *Theogony, Works and Days*, etc.
Hestia:	(Greek) Goddess of the Hearth, known to the Romans as Vesta, daughter of Kronos
Highwind:	(FF) flagship of the Shinra Air Force, commandeered by Avalanche
Hinduism:	(misc.) prominent religion originating in India
Hippolyta:	(Greek) queen of the Amazons, daughter of Ares
Historíai:	(Greek) compendium of histories and myths, compiled by Herodotus
Hojo:	(FF) primary antagonist, Shinra scientist involved in Project Jenova S, Sephiroth's biological father, Shinra's Director of Research & Development
Hollander:	(FF) secondary antagonist, Shinra scientist involved in Project Jenova G, Angeal's biological father
Holy:	(FF) ultimate protective magic
Homer:	(Greek) 8th century BC composer of the *Iliad* and the *Odyssey*
Homeric Hymns:	(Greek) 33 anonymous hymns dedicated to the gods, composed in the poetic style of Homer

Homeric Question:	(Greek) fields of study concerning the existence of Homer and the works attributed to him
Honeybee Inn:	(FF) adult establishment located in Wall Market, also called Honey Bee Inn
Hoshi o Meguru Otome:	(FF) short story concerning the aftermath of Aerith's death, unofficially translated as *The Maiden Who Travels the Planet*, written by Benny Matsuyama
Hubris:	(Greek) a person's excessive pride in comparison to or defiance of the gods
Hydra:	(Greek) immortal water dragon capable of regrowing its heads, child of Typhon, defeated by Heracles
Hyginus:	(Roman) 1st century AD author of *Fabulae*, *Astronomica*, etc.
Hyperion:	(FF) black chocobo
	(Greek) Titan, father of Helios, Selene, and Eos, son of Gaia
Hypnos:	(Greek) God of Sleep, known to the Romans as Somnus, son of Nyx

I

Icicle Inn:	(FF) winter town and gateway to Gaea's Cliff
Ifalna:	(FF) Aerith's biological mother, a Cetra
***Iliad*:**	(Greek) epic poem concerning the Trojan War, composed by Homer
Immortals:	(Greek) collective term to describe all gods, minor deities, and other beings that cannot die of natural causes, sometimes called the deathless ones
Indo-European:	(misc.) relating to the cultures derived from a theoretical single source in Europe and/or Asia
***INTERmission*:**	(FF) supplementary game content for *Remake*
Ionian Sea:	(Greek) part of the Mediterranean Sea, located west of mainland Greece
Ithaca:	(Greek) island in the Ionian Sea, home of Odysseus

J

Jason:	(Greek) hero of the *Argonautica*
***Jason and the Argonauts*:**	(misc.) 1963 movie adaptation of the Jason myth
Jenova:	(FF) secondary antagonist, extraterrestrial monster initially misidentified as a Cetra, capable of shapeshifting and inducing illusions
Jenova cells:	(FF) genetic material extracted from Jenova with superhuman attributes
Jessie Rasberry:	(FF) secondary protagonist, member of Avalanche
Job system:	(FF) traditional system within the *Final Fantasy* series for assigning roles and abilities

Jocasta:	(Greek) queen of Thebes, mother and wife of Oedipus
Judaism:	(misc.) prominent religion relating to the teachings of the God of Israel
Judgement of Paris:	(Greek) determination made by Paris over whom among Hera, Athena, and Aphrodite is the fairest goddess
Judges of Underworld:	(Greek) three infernal judges who preside over the final destination of one's soul, which is generally either Asphodel, Elysium, or Tartarus
Juno:	(Roman) Goddess of Marriage and Childbirth, etc., conflated with Hera
Junon:	(FF) fortified coastal city, initial location of the Sister Ray cannon
Jupiter:	(Roman) supreme deity, God of Storms, etc. conflated with Zeus, also called Jove

K

Kadaj:	(FF) primary antagonist, Remnant of Sephiroth
Kalm:	(FF) old town in close regional proximity to Midgar
Katabasis:	(FF) common type of hero journey, a mortal's descent into and return from the underworld
Kids Are Alright, The:	(FF) novel sequel to *Final Fantasy VII*, written by Kazushige Nojima
Kitase, Yoshinori:	(FF) director and co-writer of *Final Fantasy VII*, producer of *Compilation* and *Remake*
Kraken:	(misc.) sea monster of Nordic legend; replaces Cetus in *Clash of the Titans*
Kronos:	(Greek) ruler of the Titans, known to the Romans as Saturn, father of the initial six Olympians, son of Gaia
Kujata:	(FF) summoned being
Kyrie Canaan:	(FF) primary protagonist, private detective, and con artist

L

Labours of Heracles:	(Greek) twelve impossible tasks demanded of Heracles to expiate the sins of his blood crimes
Labours of Theseus:	(Greek) six tasks that Theseus undertakes during his journey from Troezen to Athens
Labyrinth, the:	(Greek) inescapable maze designed by Daedalus, built on Crete to house the Minotaur
Laius:	(Greek) king of Thebes, father of Oedipus
Last Order:	(FF) animé prequel to *Final Fantasy VII*
Lazard Deusericus:	(FF) Shinra's Director of SOLDIER, illegitimate son of President Shinra
Leaf House:	(FF) orphanage in the Sector 5 Slums

Lethe:	(Greek) underworld river associated with memory loss; Goddess of Oblivion
Lifestream:	(FF) great river of souls, the Planet's life-force, comprised of spirit energy
Limit Breaks:	(FF) unique attacks available to player characters
Lonny:	(FF) narrator of *Picturing the Past*
***Lost Episode*:**	(FF) mobile-exclusive supplementary chapter to *Dirge of Cerberus*
***LOVELESS*:**	(FF) epic poem beloved by Genesis
Loz:	(FF) secondary antagonist, Remnant of Sephiroth
Lucrecia Crescent:	(FF) Sephiroth's biological mother, Shinra scientist involved in Project Jenova S
Lyre:	(Greek) small, harp-like musical instrument, invented by Hermes and mastered by Orpheus

M

Mako:	(FF) capitalist name for spirit energy
Mako Cannon:	(FF) colossal weapon situated at Junon, later moved to Midgar, also called Sister Ray
Mako poisoning:	(FF) a collapse of the mind caused by overexposure to mako
Mako reactor:	(FF) power plants that convert mako into electricity
Marlene Wallace:	(FF) Barret's adoptive daughter
Masamune:	(FF) Sephiroth's legendary katana
Materia:	(FF) orbs of crystalised spirit energy used for casting magic
Matsuyama, Benny:	(FF) author of *Hoshi o Meguru Otome*
Medusa:	(Greek) snake-haired Gorgon, mother of Pegasus, killed by Perseus
Megara:	(Greek) wife of Heracles
***Metamorphoses*:**	(Roman) compendium of classical myths, compiled by Ovid
Meteor:	(FF) colossal asteroid, ultimate destructive magic
Meteorfall:	(FF) events surrounding Meteor's summoning and Midgar's destruction
Mideel:	(FF) village on southern archipelago, susceptible to Lifestream eruptions
Midgar:	(FF) two-tiered metropolis, base of Shinra, Inc., divided into eight sectors
Midgard:	(misc.) world of mankind in Norse cosmology
Minerva:	(FF) deified personification of the Lifestream's will; (Roman) Goddess of Wisdom, Strategy, Handicraft, etc., conflated with Athena
Minoans:	(Greek) first advanced civilisation in Europe, based on Crete and elsewhere in the Aegean
Minos II:	(Greek) king of Crete, husband of Pasiphaë, descendant of Zeus

Minotaur, the: (Greek) half-human, half-bull hybrid being, pseudonym for Asterion, dwells in the Labyrinth, son of the Cretan bull, killed by Theseus

Modeoheim: (FF) town in the permafrost region, affiliated with Shinra, Inc.

Moirai: (Greek) three powerful sisters who determine the destinies of all by spinning and measuring the threads of life, also known as the Fates, daughters of Nyx or Zeus

Mount Nibel: (FF) mountain overlooking Nibelheim, location of the world's first mako reactor, top-secret storage site for Jenova specimen

Mnemosyne: (Greek) Titaness, mother of the Muses; pool in underworld associated with knowledge and memory

Mycenae: (misc.) ancient civilisation pre-dating the Greeks

Myth cycle: (misc.) progression of myths as a story arc

Mythology: (misc.) relating to the beliefs of historic cultures

Muses: (Greek) nine goddesses responsible for inspiring art, science, music, literature, etc., daughters of Zeus

N

Nail Bat: (FF) novelty weapon for Cloud

Nanaki: (FF) real name of Red XIII

Narcissus: (Greek) handsome youth who falls in love with his own reflection; flower named after Narcissus, more commonly known as the daffodil

***Naturalis Historia*:** (Roman) compendium of work by other authors, compiled by Pliny the Elder

Nemean Lion: (Greek) monstrous lion with an impenetrable hide, child of the Chimera, killed by Heracles

Nemesis: (Greek) Goddess of Retribution, daughter of Nyx

Neptune: (Roman) God of the Seas, etc., conflated with Poseidon

Nereids: (Greek) water nymphs, daughters of Nereus

Nereus: (Greek) shapeshifting sea god, father of the Nereids

Nero the Sable: (FF) primary antagonist, high-ranking Tsviet

Netherworld: (misc.) a non-heavenly afterlife destination, synonymous with underworld, refers to the realm of Hades in Greek myths

Nibelheim: (FF) hometown of Cloud and Tifa, birthplace of Sephiroth, deeply associated with Shinra, Inc. and the Jenova Project

Nibelheim tragedy: (FF) destruction of Nibelheim and massacre of its denizens by Sephiroth, covered up by Shinra, Inc.

Niflheim: (misc.) primordial realm of mist in Norse cosmology, location of the underworld

Nojima, Kazushige:	(FF) co-writer of *Final Fantasy VII*, scenario writer and supervisor of the *Compilation* games, scenario writer of *Remake*, author of the *Compilation* novels
Nomura, Tetsuya:	(FF) art director of *Final Fantasy VII*, lead artist of the *Compilation*, director of *Remake*
Nonnus:	(Greek) 5th century AD composer of *Dionysiaca*
Norse:	(misc.) relating to the culture of the Vikings
Northern Cave:	(FF) vast cavern network beneath the Northern Crater
Northern Crater:	(FF) site where Jenova's meteorite struck 2,000 years prior to the events of *Final Fantasy VII*
Nymphs:	(Greek) minor female deities and spirits associated with nature or specific locations
Nyx:	(Greek) primordial Goddess of Night, daughter of Chaos

O

Oceanids:	(Greek) minor female deities, daughters of Oceanus
Oceanus:	(Greek) primordial world river, Titan brother of Kronos, father of the Oceanids, son of Gaia
Odin:	(FF) summoned being, associated with the Death status effect; (misc.) Norse supreme deity, God of Death, Battle, etc.
Odysseus:	(Greek) king of Ithaca, hero of the Trojan War, protagonist of the *Odyssey*, known to the Romans as Ulysses, descendant of Zeus
***Odyssey*:**	(Greek) epic poem concerning the homeward voyage of Odysseus, composed by Homer
Oedipus:	(Greek) king of Thebes, tragic hero, defeats Sphinx, son of Laius
***Oedipus Rex*:**	(Greek) play concerning Oedipus' life in Thebes, written by Sophocles
Olympians:	(Greek) pantheon of twelve ruling gods, led by Zeus, based on Mount Olympus
Olympus, Mount:	(Greek) heavenly citadel of the gods, situated on the tallest peak in Greece
Omega Weapon:	(FF) the Planet's mechanism for transporting the Lifestream to another world
Omphalos:	(Greek) stone swallowed by Kronos, located at Delphi, considered the spiritual centre of the world by the Hellenes
***On the Way to a Smile*:**	(FF) novel sequel to *Final Fantasy VII*, written by Kazushige Nojima
Oracle:	(Greek) a person through whom divine knowledge is channelled; foremost example is the Delphic oracle

Orion:	(Greek) Giant huntsman, raised to the heavens as a constellation
Orpheus:	(Greek) demigod, divine bard, tragic hero, son of Apollo
Orphic Hymns:	(Greek) collection of hymns attributed to Orpheus that recount a genealogy of the gods distinct from Hesiod's account, the basis of Orphism
Orphic Mysteries:	(Greek) clandestine rites dedicated to Dionysus and Persephone, associated with Orphism
Orphism:	(Greek) Hellenic belief system based on doctrine attributed to Orpheus
Orthrus:	(Greek) two-headed guard hound, child of Typhon, killed by Heracles
Othrys, Mount:	(Greek) original abode of the Titans, mountain in Greece
Ovid:	(Roman) 1st century AD mythographer and writer of *Metamorphoses, Fasti*, etc.

P

Palladium:	(Greek) wooden effigy sacred to Troy, carved by Athena
Paris:	(Greek) prince of Troy, chosen to judge which goddess is fairest, instigator of the Trojan War, son of Priam
Pasiphaë:	(Greek) queen of Crete, mother of the Minotaur
Pausanias:	(Greek) 2nd century AD traveller and geographer
Pegasus:	(Greek) divine winged horse, ridden by Bellerophon, child of Poseidon
Pelion, Mount:	(Greek) home of Chiron and the centaurs, mountain in Greece
Peloponnese:	(Greek) region of mainland Greece associated with entrances to the underworld
Penance:	(FF) monstrous sphinx-like form Angeal takes to battle Zack
Persephone:	(Greek) Goddess of Spring, Queen of the Underworld, known to the Romans as Proserpina, also called Cora or Kore, daughter of Demeter
Perseus:	(Greek) demigod, divine hero, kills Medusa, Cetus, etc., son of Zeus
Philip II:	(Greek) historic king of Macedonia, father of Alexander the Great
Phlegethon:	(Greek) underworld river of flames
Phoenix:	(FF) summoned being, associated with the element of Fire; (Greek) mythical firebird associated with the Sun and rebirth
Phoenix:	(Roman) poem concerning the lifecycle of the phoenix, composed by Claudian
Phthia:	(Greek) ancient city-state on mainland Greece

Picturing the Past: (FF) short story concerning the origins of the Sephiroth clones and Aerith's abilities, written by Kazushige Nojima

Pirithous: (Greek) warrior king, son of Zeus

Planet, the: (FF) the world on which *Final Fantasy VII* is set

Planetology: (FF) philosophical, spiritual, and scientific study of the Planet's workings, also called the Study of Planetary Life

Plate, the: (FF) Midgar's upper-city, divided into eight sectors

Plato: (Greek) 5th century BC philosopher and writer of *Timaeus, Republic*, etc.

Pliny the Elder: (Roman) 1st century AD historian and writer of *Naturalis Historia*

Plouton: (Greek) pseudonym for Hades after the Classical period, also written as Pluto

Plutarch: (Greek) 1st century AD historian and writer of *Bíoi Parállēloi*

Poleis: (Greek) independent city-states (*polis*, sing.)

Pontus: (Greek) primordial embodiment of the sea, son of Gaia

Poseidon: (Greek) God of the Seas, etc., brother of Zeus, conflated with Neptune, son of Kronos

President Shinra: (FF) secondary antagonist, leader of Shinra, Inc.

Project Gillian: (FF) sub-branch of Project Jenova that produces Genesis and Angeal, named after Gillian Hewley, also called Project Jenova G

Project Jenova: (FF) branch of the Ancients Project using genetic material of Jenova

Project Jenova G: (FF) sub-branch of Project Jenova that produces Genesis and Angeal, also called Project Gillian

Project Jenova S: (FF) sub-branch of Project Jenova that produces Sephiroth

Project Sephiroth Copy: (FF) experiment conducted by Hojo, implanting survivors of the Nibelheim tragedy with pure Jenova cells

Prometheus: (Greek) Titan who created mankind from clay and gave them the gift of fire and free thought, punished for it by Zeus, brother of Atlas

Prometheus Bound: (Greek) play concerning the punishment of Prometheus, written by Aeschylus

Promised Land: (FF) fabled location believed to be rich in mako; to the Cetra, it meant their return to the Lifestream at death

Protomateria: (FF) materia capable of controlling Chaos and Omega, embedded in Vincent's body

Psychopomp: (Greek) deity or spirit that escorts the souls of the dead into the afterlife

Pythia: (Greek) high priestess and oracle at Delphi

Python: (Greek) draconic serpent, guardian of Omphalos, child of Gaia, killed by Apollo

R

Ra:	(misc.) ancient Egyptian creator god, closely associated with the Sun
Ragnarök:	(misc.) foretold destruction of the universe in Norse mythology
Rebirth:	(FF) videogame re-imagining of *Final Fantasy VII*, sequel to *Remake*
Red XIII:	(FF) primary protagonist, leonine beast, pseudonym of Nanaki
Reeve Tuesti:	(FF) primary protagonist, controls Cait Sith, Shinra's Director of Urban Planning, Commissioner of the World Regenesis Organisation (WRO)
Remake:	(FF) videogame re-imagining of *Final Fantasy VII*, re-released with additional content as *Remake Intergrade*
Remnants of Sephiroth:	(FF) physical manifestations of Sephiroth's will
Reno:	(FF) secondary antagonist, member of the Turks
Reunion:	(FF) instinctual drive for the reunification of Jenova's cells
Rhea:	(Greek) Titaness, wife of Kronos, mother of Zeus, daughter of Gaia
Rhodes:	(Greek) large island in the Aegean Sea
Roman Empire:	(Roman) imperial territories governed by Rome (and later Byzantium), including the occupation of Greece (31 BC – 1453 AD)
Rosso the Crimson:	(FF) secondary antagonist, high-ranking Tsviet
Rude:	(FF) secondary antagonist, member of the Turks
Rufus Shinra:	(FF) secondary antagonist, son of President Shinra, Vice President of Shinra, Inc.

S

Sakaguchi, Hironobu:	(FF) original creator of *Final Fantasy*, producer of *Final Fantasy VII*
Sapphire Weapon:	(FF) biomechanical monster released by the Planet
Satyrs:	(Greek) humanoid nature spirits, later portrayed as goat-men
Scarlet:	(FF) Shinra's Director of Weapons Development
Sector 5 church:	(FF) church in the Slums, a flowerbed there is tended by Aerith
Sectors:	(FF) districts of Midgar, numbered 1 to 8, with Sector 0 at the city's centre
Selene:	(Greek) Goddess of the Moon, known to the Romans as Luna, daughter of Hyperion
Semele:	(Greek) princess of Thebes, mother of Dionysus
Sephiroth:	(FF) primary antagonist, former SOLDIER, hero of the Wutai War, product of Project Jenova S

Sephiroth clones:	(FF) Hojo's test subjects exposed to pure Jenova cells
Seventh Heaven:	(FF) bar owned by Tifa in the Sector 7 Slums, alternatively called 7th Heaven; re-established bar in Edge
Shades:	(Greek) spirits of the underworld, typically those who have relinquished their memories
Shakespeare, William:	(misc.) 16th century poet and playwright
Shamanism:	(misc.) relating to the interaction with the spiritual plain through an altered state of consciousness
Shelke the Transparent:	(FF) primary protagonist, high-ranking Tsviet
Shera:	(FF) rocket engineer, eventual wife of Cid; namesake for one of Cid's airships
Shinra Building:	(FF) Shinra, Inc.'s headquarters in Midgar
Shinra, Inc.:	(FF) monopolistic megacorporation controlling most political, economic, and military affairs on the Planet
Shinra Manor:	(FF) company-owned mansion in Nibelheim, secret laboratory for Project Jenova S
Shintōism:	(misc.) prominent religion in Japan
Singularity:	(FF) dimension beyond the construct of time
Sister Ray:	(FF) colossal mako cannon situated at Junon, later moved to Midgar
Sleeping Forest:	(FF) ancient forest that leads to the Forgotten Capital
Slums, the:	(FF) Midgar's lower-city, divided into eight sectors
SOLDIER:	(FF) Shinra, Inc.'s elite army of super soldiers
Sonon Kusakabe:	(FF) primary protagonist, Wutaian ninja
Sophocles:	(Greek) 5th century BC playwright of *Ajax* and *Oedipus Rex*, etc.
Sparta:	(Greek) ancient city-state on mainland Greece
Sphinx:	(Greek) hybrid creature with the head of a woman, body of a lion, and wings of a bird, child of Typhon, defeated by Oedipus
Spirit energy:	(FF) makeup of the Lifestream, equated to souls
***Spirits Within, The*:**	(FF) 2001 animated movie directed by Hironobu Sakaguchi, part of the *Final Fantasy* franchise
Square Enix:	(FF) videogame developer responsible for *Final Fantasy*, formerly Square
Study of Planetary Life:	(FF) philosophical, spiritual, and scientific study of the Planet's workings, also called planetology
Styx:	(Greek) primary underworld river upon which oaths are sworn, boundary to the afterlife; goddess of the river, daughter of Oceanus
Summoned beings:	(FF) powerful entities stored in materia that can be called into battle
Supreme god:	(misc.) head of a pantheon, the primary deity

T

Tabata, Hajime: (FF) director of *Before Crisis* and *Crisis Core*

Tartarus: (Greek) primordial god of the cavernous depths beneath the earth; a great chasm of swirling gales in the underworld where Zeus imprisons the Titans, where wicked souls are sent

Temple of the Ancients: (FF) ancient temple constructed by a Cetran civilisation

Terra: (FF) primary protagonist of *Final Fantasy VI*; a world in *Final Fantasy IX*; (Roman) Mother Earth, primordial goddess, conflated with Gaia

Tethys: (Greek) Titaness, mother of the Oceanids, daughter of Gaia

Thalassa: (Greek) primordial sea goddess

Thanatos: (Greek) God of Death, psychopomp, known to the Romans as Mors, son of Nyx

Thea Lockhart: (FF) Tifa's mother

Thebes: (Greek) ancient city-state on mainland Greece

Theia: (Greek) Titaness, mother of Helios, Selene, and Eos, known to the Romans as Dione, daughter of Gaia

***Theogony*:** (Greek) epic poem concerning the genealogy of the gods, composed by Hesiod

Theseus: (Greek) king of Athens, demigod, divine hero, kills the Minotaur, Cretan Bull, etc., son of Poseidon

Thetis: (Greek) Nereid, mother of Achilles, daughter of Nereus
(misc.) goddess and mother of Calibos in *Clash of the Titans*

Thiasus: (Greek) Dionysus' retinue of revellers and hybrid creatures

Thor: (misc.) Norse God of Storms, son of Odin

Thriae: (Greek) trio of minor deities associated with bees

Tifa Lockhart: (FF) primary protagonist, martial artist, Cloud's childhood friend

***Timaeus*:** (Greek) philosophical dialogue concerning the nature of the world, written by Plato

***Tiny Bronco*:** (FF) airplane in Cid's possession, used by Avalanche as a boat after being shot down

Tiresias: (Greek) blind prophet from Thebes, visited by Odysseus in the underworld

Tiryns: (Greek) ancient city-state on mainland Greece

Titan: (FF) summoned being, associated with the element of Earth

Titaness: (Greek) female Titan

Titanomachy: (Greek) ten-year war for supremacy between the Titans and the Olympians

Titans:	(Greek) primordial race of gods that precede the Olympians, ruled by Kronos, originally dwell on Mount Pelion
Toriyama, Motomu:	(FF) event designer of *Final Fantasy VII*, co-director of *Remake*
***Traces of Two Pasts*:**	(FF) novel prequel to *Final Fantasy VII Remake*, written by Kazushige Nojima
Triad:	(misc.) three connected or complimentary gods
Triton:	(Greek) messenger god of the seas, son of Poseidon
Troezen:	(Greek) historic city-state on mainland Greece, birthplace of Theseus
***Trōiades*:**	(Greek) play concerning events surrounding the Trojan War, written by Euripides
Trojan:	(Greek) relating to Troy
Trojan Horse:	(Greek) giant wooden horse constructed by the Greeks to smuggle soldiers into Troy
Trojan War:	(Greek) ten-year conflict fought between the Greeks and Trojans
Troy:	(Greek) fortified city-state on east coast of Aegean Sea, site of the Trojan War, also called Ilium
Tseng:	(FF) secondary antagonist, Chief of the Turks
Tsviets:	(FF) highest rank of Deepground SOLDIER
Turks:	(FF) clandestine division of Shinra, Inc. tasked with espionage, kidnappings, assassinations, etc.
Typhon:	(FF) summoned being, associated with several elements; (Greek) colossal monster born of Gaia to wage war on the Olympians, ultimately confined beneath a volcano or in Tartarus

U

***Ultimanias*:**	(FF) companion guidebooks to the *Final Fantasy* series
Under Junon:	(FF) fishing village located in the shadow of Junon
Underworld:	(misc.) a non-heavenly afterlife destination, synonymous with netherworld, refers to realm of Hades in Greek myths
Uranus:	(Greek) Father Sky, primordial god, known to the Romans as Caelus, son of Gaia

V

Valhalla:	(misc.) great hall of Odin in Norse cosmology where half of all slain warriors are welcomed so that they may prepare for Ragnarök
Venus:	(Roman) Goddess of Love, Beauty, etc., conflated with Aphrodite
Verdot:	(FF) secondary protagonist, Chief of the Turks

Vikings:	(misc.) seafaring and expansionist Norsemen
Vincent Valentine:	(FF) primary protagonist, deadly marksman, former Turk and research specimen of Hojo, vessel for Chaos
Virgil:	(Roman) 1st century BC composer of the *Aeneid*
Vulcan:	(Roman) God of Fire and the Forge, etc., conflated with Hephaestus

W

Wall Market:	(FF) seedy district in the Midgar Slums
Water Alter:	(FF) location beneath the Forgotten Capital where Aerith is killed by Sephiroth
Weapons:	(FF) colossal biomechanical monsters produced by the Planet to protect its own existence
Wedge:	(FF) secondary protagonist, member of Avalanche
Weiss the Immaculate:	(FF) primary antagonist, high-ranking Tsviet, commander of Deepground
Whirlwind Maze:	(FF) stormy vortex at the heart of the Northern Crater
Whisper Harbinger:	(FF) gargantuan entity made of Whispers that is encountered in the Singularity, connected to all threads of time and space
Whispers:	(FF) spectral entities whose role it is to enforce the Planet's intended destiny, also called arbiters of fate
White Materia:	(FF) used to summon the ultimate protective magic Holy, possessed by Aerith
***Works and Days*:**	(Greek) epic poem which includes the origins of mankind, composed by Hesiod
Worldwide Network:	(FF) comparable to the internet
WRO:	(FF) World Regenesis Organisation, authoritative body in the wake of Shinra, Inc.'s collapse, led by Reeve
Wutai:	(FF) hometown of Yuffie; nation historically in conflict with Shinra, Inc.
Wutai War:	(FF) historic war between Shinra, Inc. and Wutai

X

***Xenia*:**	(Greek) sacred laws and practices of guest-friendship

Y

Yazoo:	(FF) secondary antagonist, Remnant of Sephiroth
Yggdrasill:	(misc.) Norse cosmological tree, connecting the Nine Worlds
Yuffie Kisaragi:	(FF) primary protagonist, teenage ninja

495

Z

Zack Fair:	(FF) primary protagonist, SOLDIER First Class
Zangan, Rashard:	(FF) Tifa's martial arts master
Zagreus:	(Greek) initial incarnation of Dionysus in the Orphic beliefs
Zeus:	(Greek) supreme deity, God of Storms, etc., conflated with Jupiter, known as Skyfather and Cloud Gatherer among other things, son of Kronos
Zirconiade:	(FF) world-burning summon

BIBLIOGRAPHY

GREEK MYTHOLOGY

Campbell, Joseph, *The Hero with a Thousand Faces* (Pantheon Books, 1949)

Graves, Robert, *The Greek Myths, The Complete and Definitive Edition* (Penguin Books, 2011)

Hamilton, Edith, *Mythology: Timeless Tales of Gods and Heroes, 75th Anniversary Illustrated Edition* (Black Dog & Leventhal, 2017)

Fry, Stephen, *Mythos* (Michael Joseph, 2017)

Fry, Stephen, *Heroes* (Michael Joseph, 2018)

Fry, Stephen, *Troy* (Michael Joseph, 2020)

For everything else, the encyclopaedia at **theoi.com**

COMPILATION OF FINAL FANTASY VII

Final Fantasy VII Ultimania Omega (Square Enix, 2005)

Final Fantasy VII: Advent Children -Reunion Files- (SoftBank Creative Corp., 2006)

Dirge of Cerberus -Final Fantasy VII- Official Complete Guide (Square Enix, 2006)

Crisis Core Ultimania (Square Enix, 2007)

Crisis Core -Final Fantasy VII- The Complete Guide (Square Enix, 2007)

Final Fantasy VII 10th Anniversary Ultimania (Square Enix, 2007)

Final Fantasy VII 10th Anniversary Ultimania Revised Edition (Square Enix, 2009)

Nojima, Kazushige, *FINAL FANTASY VII On the Way to a Smile* (Square Enix, 2009. Translated by Yen Press, 2018)

Nojima, Kazushige, *FINAL FANTASY VII The Kids Are Alright: A Turks Side Story* (Square Enix, 2011. Translated by Yen Press, 2019)

Leone, Matt, *500 Years Later: An Oral History of Final Fantasy VII* (Read-Only Memory, 2018)

Final Fantasy VII Remake: World Preview (Square Enix Books, 2020. Translated by Square Enix Books, 2020)

Final Fantasy VII Remake Material Ultimania (Square Enix Books, 2020. Translated by Square Enix Books, 2021)

Nojima, Kazushige, *Final Fantasy VII Remake: Traces of Two Pasts* (Square Enix Books, 2021. Translated by Square Enix Books, 2023)

Final Fantasy VII Remake Material Ultimania Plus (Square Enix Books, 2021)

shinraarchaeology.com

thelifestream.net

finalfantasy.fandom.com

finalfantasyforums.net

Support the creators and access a range of new or exclusive content:

www.mjgallagherbooks.com

twitter.com/ffviinovels

kingcael.carrd.co

gametee.co.uk

NORSE MYTHS

THAT INSPIRED

FINAL FANTASY VII

OUT NOW

Norse Myths That Inspired Final Fantasy VII

Audiobook now available on

Read by
LIAM MULVEY

THE VOICE OF LIBERTUS OSTIUM

KINGSGLAIVE: FINAL FANTASY XV

KICKSTARTER

SPECIAL BENEFACTORS

Robyn

Toby Heagerty

Alex

Pieter-Jan Dirkx

Juelsy

Cathrine Machalski

Alex Dyer

Theodore H Chidsey

Anthony Timmons

HouseCatAlex

Chloe May

Ian Stinton

Sam Erin Scala

GamerTonberry

Jack Mayer

Liam Fenech

Taiheilus Cervidae

Daisuke Morita

Tyler Miller

Sho

Gametee, Ltd

Steven Gray

Craig Snyder

Samuel Derbyshire

John Pope

Scott Goatham

Dan Hume

Jonathon Myhre

Mike Frans

Dj Barnes

Chris Dillon

Dean Cooke

Ariana Law

Steve

Daniel Dorman

Amanda Lopez

Ryan "Dave" Davies

Bartosz Guczalski

KICKSTARTER

Many thanks to the following individuals for their support in helping me to make this project a reality

Rebecca 'Tifa' Delfin • Ian Fellows • Finley Fellows
Niki Anderson • James Wroblewski • Ben Wroblewski
Artemis Harris • Nate Muinos • Wade Shortus • Lance Shortus
Clegmir • Sunny Nagpal • Brian • Gordon

Micah Rodney • Scott Wright • Emma Taylor • Lizzie
Jennifer Spinks • Richard Bowden • Nekonym
Joshua T. Moritz • Emma Wright • Marija Pushko
Edmond Aggabao • BSauce • Gina Novelli • Keira Cullen
Joshua Albinson • Brandon S. • Gurvir Singh Deol
Kimberley Wenzlick • Sam 'Nova' McGettigan

Jo Johnston • Philip Hartshorn • Travis Lynch • Bigeaux FFXIV
Walter Koegel • Robert Molt • Ryan Culy • Ash H.
Brandy • Kasey Sargent • Tegan Gwyther • Steven "Phoenix" Kelliher
Andy Mountain • Embreane James • Jazmin Quezada
ComaliesVII • Sebastian Deken • Kevin West • Caleb Stormer
Alejandro Mery • Ben Hensey • Clara Hogan • Mike Claytor
Davide • Brent Jacobs • Chris Pelzer • Erikzy
Professional Earth Diver (PED) • Munkong Sathienthirakul
Lisa M B Easton • Ainsley Wheeler • Nicodemus Hunt
Karl Ansell • Sophie Ashburn • Antonia Mitova • Kevin
Tyke • David Dicks • Lisa Andrew • Seth Novak • Abi Johnson
Nhoj Plummer • Andrew Cleveland • Jen • Marko Burkic
Steve Miller • Luna W • Ashlee Everingham • Joseph A. Williams
Jacob Childs • Jon Thomas • Max Smith • Gary
Rebekah Jordan • Casey Putney • Rory Callaghan • Rachel Bell
Kevin Khong • Jayden Moss • Sheri Grumbling
Daniel & Laz Davey Morgenstern

Myths • Ira & Drew Creasman • Franz Galam
Noah Wine • Roberto Fregosi • Punkalyptic • StonedPanda

Kyle Aquini • EkkoHammer89 • James Baston • Andrew Duffy
Giuseppa Barresi • Jose R Gonzalez • Zach Rhodes
Kayley Henderson • Ceilidh Quinn • Frances Marnane
Kelsie Scharmann • Eden Bloze • Brody Allen • SpinDashDude
Noway • Lisa Payne • BigAle7777 • Emma Rainsford
Karina Bowater • Nick Sturniolo • Lea Emil

Rebecca Danger • April Patrick • Christine Szafranski
WardenCygnus • lesatho • Ito Chosei • Chris Aumiller
Sam Downes • LVK • Marla Hellings • Anthony Jarvis
JessicaRose • Rubén Meléndez de Toledo • Roymario • Xeno
Jett Thomas • Geoffrey A. Rosen • Robert M • Lisa Novak
Phoebe Jade Toone • Catrin Eleri • Cedar Kilcrease • Zeus's Infidelity

Shannon Morgan • Jody Hunninck • Amanda Rodgers • Mike Knight
Erika • Griffen Eastwood • Tone • Ben Kemp • Jamie L. Cruise
Lesly • Megan Francis • Pim van der Wel •Annis Saniee
Stephanie Miller • Nikki Flan-Hunter-Pike • Ben Wheare
Katie Jones • John Reaves • Krystal Bohannan • Megan Yates
Shaun Taylor-Coldwell • Rowan Beaton • Luke "Nuk3m" Williams
MissWeinryb • Pixelfox

Stephen & Laura Bell • Noel "DV8" Camacho II • Ben Leslie
Sharko • Michael Link • Robert Jones • Mareike • Elliott "Kip" Kipper
Danielle Moore • Rob Clark • Final FanTV • Crimson Sun • Cherri
Chris L. • Shakyra Dunn • Jackie Kusluch • Mercedes Lewis
GrendlsMother • Wilsonchen • Sharon S • Wade Langer (ProfNoctis)
Marek Pecho • Guy Portch • Jamie Brunton • George Ridley
Emma Holding • Bulkee • Konrad S • Liam Allen • Ryan E Feiock
Daniel Lupo • Uskaba • Shawn Sprankle • Tom Wood
Claire Rosser • Katrina Broster • Kimmymari Damacy
Jessica Raub • Lani • Kristy Bennett • Skit • Steffen Sparks
Irvin • M. Perey • King Valvados • Rosey Burgess • Gary Billson
Aisling Callaghan • sweetkala • Paul Carroll • Stephany Spencer
Matt Morgan • Sian Lloyd-Wiggins • Brandon Vipperman

Alex James • Anthony Bean, PhD (Geek Therapeutics)
Jennifer deWinter • Elora Garbutt • Kris Wall • Kellyann
Round2Gaming • JerStart • Cloudcasterv • Zack Loup
Sheena Ashby • Leonard Bartenstein • Fishfriedcat • Sonico
Grant Pidwinski • Comalie • Zeus de la Paz • khreeps • Kita
Melody Wehipeihana • Lucas Sharrett • ania • Kytetiger
Rhiannon Farrant • Russ Perry Jr • Kwarks85 • Anthony Inson
Daniel McGriskin • Joseph Terry • Aaron Dunn • Keith "Keef" Day
Mac Angco • Miranda Taylor • Tessa Hawkins • Stew Sizer

Made in the USA
Coppell, TX
24 November 2023